The Wider Worlds of Jim Henson

ALSO EDITED BY JENNIFER C. GARLEN
AND ANISSA M. GRAHAM

*Kermit Culture: Critical Perspectives
on Jim Henson's Muppets* (McFarland, 2009)

The Wider Worlds of Jim Henson

Essays on His Work and Legacy Beyond The Muppet Show *and* Sesame Street

EDITED BY JENNIFER C. GARLEN
AND ANISSA M. GRAHAM

McFarland & Company, Inc., Publishers
Jefferson, North Carolina, and London

LIBRARY OF CONGRESS CATALOGUING-IN-PUBLICATION DATA

The wider worlds of Jim Henson : essays on his work and legacy beyond The Muppet Show and Sesame Street / edited by Jennifer C. Garlen and Anissa M. Graham.
    p.   cm.
Includes bibliographical references and index.

ISBN 978-0-7864-6986-4
softcover : acid free paper ∞

1. Henson, Jim — Criticism and interpretation. I. Garlen, Jennifer C., 1972– editor of compilation. II. Graham, Anissa M., 1973– editor of compilation.
PN1982.H46W53 2013
791.5'3092—dc23   2012040985

BRITISH LIBRARY CATALOGUING DATA ARE AVAILABLE

© 2013 Jennifer C. Garlen and Anissa M. Graham. All rights reserved

No part of this book may be reproduced or transmitted in any form or by any means, electronic or mechanical, including photocopying or recording, or by any information storage and retrieval system, without permission in writing from the publisher.

On the cover: David Bowie as Jareth the Goblin King in the 1986 film *Labyrinth* (TriStar Pictures/Photofest)

Manufactured in the United States of America

McFarland & Company, Inc., Publishers
  Box 611, Jefferson, North Carolina 28640
    www.mcfarlandpub.com

Table of Contents

Introduction	1
Part One: Revisiting *Fraggle Rock*	
Fraggle Rock and the Art of World Building AARON CALBREATH-FRASIEUR	7
Outer Spaces: *Fraggle Rock* Around the Globe ANDREW LEAL	24
No Sex, Please. We're Fraggles! TAMI MEREDITH *and* MARYANNE L. FISHER	41
The Ecology of Fraggle Rock JUSTIN WERFEL	62
Part Two: Inside the Worlds of *The Dark Crystal* and *Labyrinth*	
Interpreting the Various Species in *The Dark Crystal* and *Fraggle Rock* GIDEON HABERKORN	73
"What was sundered and undone shall be whole": Union, Nature and Aughra in *The Dark Crystal* ROXANNE HARDE	88
A Natural History of *The Dark Crystal*: The Conceptual Design of Brian Froud CATRIONA MCARA	101
Finding Your Way Through *Labyrinth* TOM HOLSTE	117

Anti-Consumerism in *Labyrinth*
 DAVID R. BURNS *and* DEBORAH BURNS   131

Part Three: Storytellers and Specials

Everyone's a Storyteller: The Shifting Roles of Stories, Storytellers and Audiences in *The Jim Henson Hour*
 ANTHONY F. STRAND   143

There Is No One Story
 NATHANIEL LONG   161

Emmet Otter's Jug-Band Christmas: The Gift of the Muppets
 CATHERINE EDWARDS   173

Telling Toy Stories in *The Christmas Toy*
 JENNIFER C. GARLEN *and* ANISSA M. GRAHAM   189

Part Four: Journeys Forward and Back

The Muppetry of Nightmares: Figures of Fear, Danger and Terror in *The Cosby Show, Chappelle's Show* and *Saturday Night Live*
 MICHAEL J. BERNTSEN   199

Dinosaurs and the Evolution of the Jim Henson Company
 JENNIFER STOESSNER   213

Exploring the Alien Other on *Farscape*: Human, Puppet, Costume, Cosmetic
 SHERRY GINN   228

Muppet Memes, or Beaker Conquers YouTube
 ANISSA M. GRAHAM   241

Fandom and Nostalgia in Disney's *The Muppets*
 JENNIFER C. GARLEN   251

About the Contributors   261
Index   265

Introduction

Our first book, *Kermit Culture* (2009), focused on characters and films related to *The Muppet Show*, the television series that, along with *Sesame Street*, first made Jim Henson a household name. Film and television scholars, however, know that Henson was the creative force behind a huge catalog of television programs, films, and other productions. *The Muppet Show* gave way to *Fraggle Rock*, the Muppet movies laid the path for *The Dark Crystal* and *Labyrinth*, and Henson served as a writer and producer for dozens of other projects. Henson's legacy continued after his death in 1990 with the ongoing work of the Jim Henson Company and Jim Henson's Creature Shop, and today Henson's influence remains palpable on screens large and small.

This second book surveys the larger world of Henson's works, including projects developed during his lifetime and those that represent his legacy. Strictly speaking, these are not all Jim Henson's worlds, as some productions included here were developed after his death, but all show evidence of his influence and have strong ties to the companies he founded. It is an ambitious undertaking that looks at decades of television series, specials, movies, and new media. Included are essays on *Fraggle Rock*, *The Dark Crystal*, *Labyrinth*, *The Jim Henson Hour*, *Dinosaurs*, *Farscape*, and more. Scholars and Henson enthusiasts from around the world have contributed to this collection in an effort to convey a sense of the breadth and depth of Henson's influence on both audiences and later productions.

In understanding the scope of Henson's work, an overview of Henson projects may prove useful. Following the success of *The Muppet Show* and *Sesame Street*, Henson moved his focus to new productions that took puppetry into uncharted creative territory. While still working on *The Muppet Show*, Henson and company began production on *Emmet Otter's Jug Band Christmas* (1977), a one-hour special originally aired on HBO. This special featured Muppets that were "more naturalistic" with "rather realistic movements" (Finch

199), and this shift toward realistic puppets can also be seen in the creatures of *The Dark Crystal* and *Labyrinth*. *Emmet Otter* shares much in common with O. Henry's sentimental Christmas tale, "The Gift of the Magi," mixed with music and classic Henson playfulness. In the meantime, the original *Muppet Show* cast appeared in three films over a period of five years. *The Muppet Movie* in 1979 proved the marketability of the Muppets as big screen stars, earning praise from critics such as Vincent Canby of *The New York Times* and Roger Ebert of *The Chicago Sun-Times*. The second movie, *The Great Muppet Caper*, a tribute to crime drama/film noir with a Muppet twist, is similar to *The Muppet Movie* in that it relies on the familiarity of fans with the Muppet cast and with the popular culture it so lovingly spoofs. *The Muppet Show* cast, with some additions, returned to the big screen in *The Muppets Take Manhattan* (1984), this time a send up of the "college kids make it on Broadway" plot popular in the 1930s and 1940s; in his review of the film (written as an open letter to Kermit), Roger Ebert even calls Kermit "Mickey Rooney in a frog suit." The popularity of these films helped Henson to create other ambitious projects such as *The Dark Crystal* and *Labyrinth*.

In 1979 Henson began the first of two collaborations with artist and designer Brian Froud. With *The Dark Crystal* Henson and Froud built an entirely new world filled with flora and fauna that seem at once familiar and alien. In *Henson's Place: The Man Behind the Muppets*, narrator Julia McKenzie remarks that with *The Dark Crystal* "Jim wanted to develop and expand, to show he could do something different." In 1982, *The Dark Crystal* was released and responses to the film were mixed, perhaps because audiences were unprepared for the darker, more intense story being told. Still *The Dark Crystal* shares the themes of family and cooperation one finds in all Henson productions. Henson's second collaboration with Froud featured a more familiar mix of puppets and humans. *Labyrinth* (1986) also had a more comic twist as its screenplay was written in part by Monty Python alum Terry Jones as well as Laura Phillips, with commentary by Elaine May and a story by Jim Henson and Dennis Jones.

In between the film productions were a number of television specials and new series as well. *Fraggle Rock* began airing in 1983 and ran for five seasons on HBO. Like *Sesame Street*, the show has been lauded for its innovative attempts to teach children; in this case, the show focused on lessons of cooperation, tolerance, and peace rather than on number and letter literacy. The Muppet characters ventured into new territory in 1986 when their toddler counterparts appeared in the animated series *Muppet Babies*. The babies had appeared in *The Muppets Take Manhattan* as part of a musical dream sequence and proved tremendously popular, with the television series running an impressive nine seasons. Also in 1986 was the television special *The Tale of the Bunny Picnic*, which allowed the team to return to the storytelling of specials like the 1969 *Hey, Cinderella!* The special's protagonist, Bean Bunny, would become a part of the regular Muppet cast for later productions like *Muppets Tonight* and *The Muppet Christmas Carol*, and he would also be prominently featured in the Disney theme park attraction, Jim Henson's Muppet* Vision 3D. The ABC Christmas special *The Christmas Toy* helped to round out the Henson productions of 1986, and the one-hour story would later serve as the foundation for *The Secret Life of Toys*, a 1994 series that aired on the Disney Channel. Other series produced in the 1980s include two collaborations with singer-songwriter John Denver, *John Denver and the Muppets: A Christmas Together* (1979) and *Rocky Mountain Holiday* (1983); *The Ghost of Faffner Hall* (1989), a brief series for HBO focusing on music; and *The Jim Henson Hour* (1989), a series aired on NBC that focused on the many avenues pursued by the Jim Henson Company. *The Jim Henson Hour* would prove particularly fruitful, even though it lasted only a few months before being canceled by NBC. Episodes included serial segments of *MuppeTelevision* and *The Storyteller* as well as specials like *Monster Maker* and *Dog City*.

After his sudden death in 1990, Henson's companies continued to pursue new projects, although they also returned to the original Muppets for films and television specials. Feature films starring the core Muppet characters included *The Muppet Christmas Carol* (1992), *Muppet Treasure Island* (1996), and *Muppets from Space* (1999), along with later television specials like *Kermit's Swamp Years* (2002), *It's a Very Merry Muppet Christmas Movie* (2002), *The Muppets' Wizard of Oz* (2005), and *A Muppets Christmas: Letters to Santa* (2008). The Muppets, however, occupied only a small part of the expanding Henson universe, especially as the Jim Henson Company and Jim Henson's Creature Shop continued projects begun by Henson and developed a diverse collection of new properties for the dawn of the 21st century. The 1990s brought the production of *Dinosaurs*, a half-hour sitcom that featured full body puppets and aired on ABC from 1991 to 1994. The cult sci-fi hit *Farscape*, which ran from 1998 to 2002, took Henson puppetry into a whole new realm and became one of the best and most significant productions of the post–Henson era to date. In 2005, the Jim Henson Company collaborated with director Dave McKean and writer Neil Gaiman to produce the feature film *MirrorMask*. Other Henson Company projects have included children's programs like *Bear in the Big Blue House*, *Dinosaur Train*, and *Sid the Science Kid* as well as adult fare produced under the Henson Alternative banner. As of 2012, both the Creature Shop and the Jim Henson Company continue to be involved in the development and production of a variety of projects, although the Muppets themselves are now the property of the Walt Disney Company.

With such a tremendous number of productions to consider, it would be impossible to create a single anthology that engages every Henson project, but our collection attempts to address the most significant films and television programs and also introduce readers to some of the less familiar works. Unfortunately, some fan favorites, like *Muppet Babies* and *Muppets Tonight*, remain unavailable on DVD and therefore prove extremely difficult, if not impossible, to discuss with any authority. Fortunately, more Henson productions are becoming available all the time, and we hope that future scholars will have access to an even greater catalog of programs and films.

This collection is divided into separate but sometimes over-lapping categories that identify major groups of works. Each section addresses a specific set of programs or films, including *Fraggle Rock*, *The Dark Crystal*, *Labyrinth*, *Dinosaurs*, *Farscape*, and even the most recent Muppet film, Disney's *The Muppets*.

Part One, "Revisiting *Fraggle Rock*," engages the beloved television series, which ran from 1983 to 1987. In "*Fraggle Rock* and the Art of World Building," Aaron Calbreath-Frasieur examines the process of creating and presenting a new fantasy world peopled by a variety of creatures, each with its own cultural system. Andrew Leal explores the international aspects of the show's production in "Outer Spaces: *Fraggle Rock* Around the Globe." Tami Meredith and Maryanne L. Fisher investigate Fraggles' complex embodiments of sex and gender in "No Sex, Please. We're Fraggles!" In "The Ecology of Fraggle Rock," Justin Werfel closes the section with a uniquely imaginative consideration of Fraggle Rock as a realistic environment, echoing the tone of scientific exploration adopted by the Fraggle character, Traveling Matt.

Part Two, "Inside the Worlds of *The Dark Crystal* and *Labyrinth*," focuses on two of Henson's most important non–Muppet works, both of which have proved tremendously influential on Gen X culture. Gideon Haberkorn's essay, "Interpreting the Various Species in *The Dark Crystal* and *Fraggle Rock*," provides a bridge between the television series and the feature film and responds to various critical readings offered by other authors. In "What was sundered and undone shall be whole": Union, Nature and Aughra in *The Dark Crystal*," Roxanne Harde considers one of the film's most enigmatic characters and her relationship to the world in which she exists. Catriona McAra continues the examination of the movie's sophisticated composition in "A Natural History of *The Dark Crystal*: The Conceptual Design of Brian Froud." In "Finding Your Way Through the *Labyrinth*," Tom Holste provides a wide-ranging guide to the film's backgrounds and themes. Finally, David R. Burns and Deborah Burns address the idea of *Labyrinth* as a critique of consumer culture in "Anti-Consumerism in *Labyrinth*."

Part Three, "Storytellers and Specials," addresses a variety of projects, including the 1989 series *The Jim Henson Hour*, with its subset *Storyteller* episodes, the later mini-series of *The Storyteller: Greek Myths*, and the television specials, *Emmet Otter's Jug-Band Christmas* and *The Christmas Toy*. In "Everyone's a Storyteller: The Shifting Roles of Stories, Storytellers and Audiences in *The Jim Henson Hour*," Anthony F. Strand explores the innovative narrative strategies of the short-lived series *The Jim Henson Hour*. Nathaniel Long provides a thoughtful commentary on the paired productions of *The Storyteller* and *The Storyteller: Greek Myths* in "There Is No One Story." In "*Emmet Otter's Jug-Band Christmas*: The Gift of the Muppets," Catherine Edwards considers the ways in which the beloved Christmas special engages many of Henson's most enduring themes. Co-editors Jennifer C. Garlen and Anissa M. Graham close the section with a look at the 1986 holiday television special *The Christmas Toy*, in "Telling Toy Stories in the *The Christmas Toy*."

Part Four, "Journeys Forward and Back," ventures beyond the more familiar texts and Henson's own lifetime to look at other productions where his influence is apparent. Michael J. Berntsen travels to puppetry's dark side in "The Muppetry of Nightmares: Figures of Fear, Danger and Terror in *The Cosby Show*, *Chappelle's Show* and *Saturday Night Live*." Jennifer Stoessner offers a consideration of the themes and production history of the offbeat television series in "*Dinosaurs* and the Evolution of the Jim Henson Company." In "Exploring the Alien Other on *Farscape*: Human, Puppet, Costume, Cosmetic," Sherry Ginn examines the innovative approaches used by the Jim Henson Company and the Creature Shop to bring a diverse cast of alien characters to life. Anissa M. Graham offers a look at the ways in which Henson's most iconic characters have invaded the internet in "Muppet Memes, or Beaker Conquers YouTube." In the anthology's closing essay, Jennifer C. Garlen looks at the full circle described by the most recent Muppet film with "Fandom and Nostalgia in Disney's *The Muppets*."

The scholars and fans who have contributed to this collection hail from academic institutions around the globe and possess diverse backgrounds as writers, academics, and cultural observers. Every entry offers a unique perspective on some aspect of Henson's work and legacy. While some essays will certainly appeal to individual readers more than others, each one attempts to shed some new light on its subject and advance our collective understanding of Jim Henson's contributions to the fields of television, film, and popular culture. It's a long journey from *Fraggle Rock* to *Farscape*, but we hope readers will enjoy this guided tour of Jim Henson's many imaginative worlds.

WORKS CITED

Ebert, Roger. "The Muppets Take Manhattan." Rev. of *The Muppets Take Manhattan*, dir. Frank Oz. *Chicago Sun-Times*. 1 Jan 1984. *RogerEbert.com*. Web. 20 May 2012.
Finch, Christopher. *Jim Henson: The Works*. New York: Random House, 1993. Print.
Garlen, Jennifer C., and Anissa M. Graham, eds. *Kermit Culture: Critical Perspectives on Jim Henson's Muppets*. Jefferson, NC: McFarland, 2009. Print.
Henson's Place: The Man Behind the Muppets. Dir. David A. Goldsmith. The Jim Henson Company, 2010. DVD.

PART ONE: REVISITING FRAGGLE ROCK

Fraggle Rock and the Art of World Building

Aaron Calbreath-Frasieur

> "Every day the world begins again, sunny skies or rain, come and follow me. Every sunrise shows me more and more, so much to explore, come and follow me. While the sun goes round, I'll still be found, following the sound, something's calling me. When the world goes drifting back to bed, memories in my head, wonders follow me."
> — Matt & Gobo Fraggle

"A-ha. I am currently exploring the last uncharted section of the caves of Fraggle Rock. Soon my task will be done. (Sigh) Too bad," thinks Uncle Matt in voice-over. These are the first Fraggle words heard on *Fraggle Rock*. Uncle Matt (Dave Goelz) provides narration as he explores what he believes to be the last unmapped region of the Rock, the last place he has not been. His remark comes moments before he discovers the hole into "outer space" that leads him into our world, pushes his nephew Gobo (Jerry Nelson) into life as an explorer, and begins the story of *Fraggle Rock*. It becomes clear over the course of the series, however, that Matt Fraggle was wrong. Despite Traveling Matt's assertion that the entrance to the human world is the last "uncharted" section of the Rock, the known regions of the Rock continue to expand across the rest of the series. For the audience all the charted byways of the rock will be new discoveries, but even for the Fraggles there are new spaces to find and explore. This exploration of both the known and unknown would be a key element in the fantasy of the show.

The world of *Fraggle Rock* is a vibrant, highly detailed, yet open-ended creation. The seemingly confined spaces of the Rock always have room to grow, demonstrating what Derek Johnson, in his work on world building in franchise media, calls "persistent, self-expanding space" (176). Despite Uncle Traveling Matt's historical attempts to map the entire Rock, new caves continue to appear throughout the series, as do unexpected individuals, groups, and communities. Exploration of the world is a key theme running throughout the show's narrative, both within the Rock and in the human world. Accordingly, the world is designed to be mysterious and wondrous to suit the exploring paradigm. Moreover, the show was designed with world building in mind. As conceptual designer Michael Frith has said:

> Right from the beginning—and I think we actually discussed it, it was not one of those unspoken things—we decided that we were not going to approach this as a television series. And it was a very conscious thing, we were saying we are here to invent a world and this world is not a television world. It is one of those, we hope, kind of mythic worlds that will stand on its own in any medium, which is what the real world does. So it gave us kind of a handle on this alternate reality that you don't generally find in television production ["Michael Frith Interview," *Fraggle Rock Third Season*].

The initial creators of the show approached their task as a process of world building, before any scripts were written or characters designed.

The concept of world building is becoming critical in the production and study of media franchises. As Jeffrey Sconce, a media historian focused largely on cult and marginal media, has written concerning world building in television:

> U.S. television has devoted increased attention in the past two decades to crafting and maintaining ever more complex narrative universes, a form of "world building" that has allowed for wholly new modes of narration and that suggests new forms of audience engagement. Television, it might be said, has discovered that the cultivation of its story worlds (diegesis) is as crucial an element in its success as is storytelling. What television lacks in spectacle and narrative constraints, it makes up for in depth and duration of character relations, diegetic expansion, and audience investment [95].

The construction of enticing worlds has become a key component in the creation of successful television and media properties. While *Fraggle Rock* may not provide a full example of a "complex narrative universe" (as one might find in the *Star Trek*, *The Matrix*, *Star Wars*, and *X-Men* franchises to name a few), it does illustrate effective methods of world building and the creation of an enchanting world that successfully draws in its audience.

Academic literature characterizes world building (sometimes called "worldmaking") according to two different but compatible models. Some scholars use it to describe the detailed worlds of contemporary cinema, diegeses filled with objects and points of reference that give the world depth (Bordwell;

Thompson). Diegesis is everything that is part of the world within the story of any text. As an example, diegetic music is music the characters can hear, it happens in the world, while non-diegetic music, such as most scores, can be heard by the audience but not the characters. One of film historian David Bordwell's examples of the detailed diegesis is the densely packed mise-en-scene of *Bladerunner* (1982) wherein "the minutiae accumulate into a kind of information overload" (58). The other model of world building focuses on the spaces left open in a fictional world that allow for or promote the expansion of that story world (Jenkins; Long; Sconce). These spaces are highlighted through references to unseen characters and events. This concept has been particularly prevalent in the discourses of transmedia franchises (properties like the Muppets or *Star Wars* that appear in multiple formats: film, TV, books, and other media) and convergence (the contemporary intermingling of media formats, technology, producers and audiences; see Jenkins), as the spaces left open in one text allow for exploration in other texts and formats or in fan-produced materials. *Fraggle Rock* is a good example of both of these practices, particularly the latter. In terms of its depth and layers of detail, the show excels in the tremendous amount of extraneous activity taking place on screen. The show is even more effective at world expansion, opening up pathways of possibility through the theme of exploration and through references to unseen wonders.

The *Fraggle Rock* universe works as an excellent example of television world building and even provides some example of transmedia production through related books and comics. The creation of the world of *Fraggle Rock* involved several specific strategies that were highly effective in crafting an engaging and enticing story world. An examination of the detailed design of the world of *Fraggle Rock* reveals an expandable universe with considerable space left at the edges. This space serves as what Jeffrey Sconce has called the "diegetic fringe" that is "available for textual elaboration" (Sconce 95). To better understand the construction of this expansive world, there are a number of factors to consider. First is the issue of consistency; though coherent details of the world may not have been in place from the beginning, there was concern with continuity, and over the course of the series greater consistency developed. Further, investigating the use of detailed design for the spaces of the Rock provides insight into the depth and verisimilitude of the series. There are also several key strategies of world building used on the show, including the cultivation of a wide-open diegetic fringe, a strong reliance on viewers' "negative capability" (an audience's propensity to fill in missing information), and the ongoing theme of exploration. A final important aspect of expanding the story world and revealing that larger world to the audience concerns the visitors to the Fraggle community and encounters with other societies within the Rock. These topics are not mutually exclusive; a number of themes are significant throughout this essay, particularly exploration and the spaces of the Rock. Together these various factors illustrate the enchanting effectiveness of the world building behind *Fraggle Rock*.

Consistency of the World

While *Fraggle Rock* does demonstrate a fascinating process of world building, and the creators were actively designing a world more than a show, it should be noted that building a completely consistent world does not seem to have been a core goal. The first season in particular depicts a less consistent or coherent world than later seasons. During production *Fraggle* puppeteer Karen Prell created a guide for internal use called the *Encyclopedia Fragglia*, which contains useful information about the history of the show. In an interview, Prell described the *Encyclopedia Fragglia*:

> When I originally wrote it, it was during *Fraggle Rock* and so much was being established about the show, but not being officially recorded, so I just started writing up all the details. [...] I just wanted to get all the information written down because I enjoyed being involved in a lot of the story meetings for *Fraggle Rock* and being involved with the writers trying to come up with ideas of all the history and characters of *Fraggle Rock*. This was a way of recording all the Fraggle history that we were creating every week. Then the writers and various people appreciated having the *Encyclopedia* just to remember what characters and concepts had been created right at their fingertips to have all the information there [qtd. in Plume and Chapman].

Her comments suggest that if there was a "show bible," it must have focused on the primary characters and concepts rather than on the smaller details of the world. Until she started unofficially documenting the shows, there wasn't an organized effort to record the history being developed. The *Encyclopedia* has been used by fans to identify certain unnamed creatures (such as the Blustering Bellowpane Monster), as well as the performers for secondary characters. However, this document (at least the one available online: see Henson Staff) focuses more on production aspects than the world itself; it does not describe the world or its inhabitants in detail. It provides fairly extensive lists of the performers for puppets with dialogue and other specific puppets, but beyond these it simply lists a generic grouping:

> Various anonymous Fraggles (including Pipebangers, Firemen, Moon Greeters, and Poohbahs), Doozers, cave creatures (creepers, clingers, and crawlers) and their respective hands, paws, feet, tails, and tentacles plus assorted moving props

and flying laundry also performed by all of the aforementioned puppeteers [Henson Staff].

Thus many unnamed creatures and characters are mentioned only in a general way and not described. Notably, even the frequently appearing Inkspots are not listed by performer and fall into this generic category.

Later seasons of the show do tend towards more continuity and sometimes reference material from earlier shows. Perhaps this is because of greater investment in the world on the part of those involved in production or simply because of the amount of material already produced. Background characters also become more consistent and specific as the series goes on. The examples throughout this article tend to reflect the instances of continuity (recurring characters, locations and creatures) rather than a discussion of discontinuity. On some level, the lack of continuity or repetition is a facet of the continual expansion of the world; new additions provided more possibility than did the repetition of established material. It is, however, useful to examine briefly some issues of coherence and how even minor discrepancies do get noticed by certain audiences.

The inconsistencies that exist in the world of *Fraggle Rock* are minutiae and unlikely to be noted by all but the most dedicated fan. This is especially true of the period when the show was made; home video recording was just becoming popular, and there was not yet an expectation that audiences would be watching and re-watching shows seeking minute details. It is in the current convergent media paradigm that these kinds of discrepancies become visible, in part because of the creation of knowledge communities and repositories online, such as the MuppetWiki. Scholars have suggested that part of the audience's joy in the extensive world building of contemporary media franchises is the seeking out, collecting and collating of information concerning favorite story worlds and the participation in knowledge communities (Gwenllian-Jones 92; Jenkins).

The MuppetWiki is a perfect example of such a knowledge community. There is a great deal of information on the wiki about the Fraggle world. Episode descriptions often include "Fraggle Facts" which give "factual" information about the world. Brief moments are used to extrapolate information about the story world. Sometimes these "facts" are cross-referenced with other episodes, particularly if there is an inconsistency. For instance, the "Fraggle Fact" for the second season episode "Wembley's Egg" reads: "The Fraggles have no clue on what an egg is, despite the fact that the Storyteller Fraggle mentions a Fraggle 'hatching' in a story she told in an earlier episode, 'The Terrible Tunnel.' This also implies that Fraggles do not eat eggs" ("Episode 201"). Here fans try to piece together information to get a sense of how the

Fraggle world works, including addressing conflicting data. This particular conflict was not limited to fans, either; in an interview, *Fraggle Rock* puppeteer Terry Angus said that, "There was a lot of discussion about a lot of things background-wise that never got explained, like where do Fraggles come from, and how are they born.... One of the ideas was that they were going to have an egg with a Fraggle pop out of it, so the Fraggles were hatched, but it was never used" (qtd. in Plume). There was clearly no definitive conception of the minutiae of the *Fraggle Rock* universe in place from the beginning of the series. However, it is also clear that the creators and performers were considering these questions. The inconsistencies in the show tend to be minor: slight changes in names, dropped ideas (like Fraggles hatching), or changing character knowledge. Minimal repetition of places, creatures, and events could also be seen as detracting from a coherent story world. However, the lack of repetition in these areas, along with the constant creation of new things, demonstrates just how big the world of *Fraggle Rock* is and encourages the audience always to be imagining new vistas.

The Layered World of the Rock

In *The Way Hollywood Tells It*, David Bordwell discusses the way filmmakers are increasingly creating what he calls "layered worlds" full of minute detail that enrich the narrative and offer "a rich, fully furnished ambience for the action" (58). Film historian Kristin Thompson continues this line of thinking in her work on *Lord of the Rings*, citing the forty-eight thousand artisan-crafted items created for the films, some of which never even appeared on screen (84–96). Although *Fraggle Rock* does not implement quite the degree of detail in the worlds that Bordwell looks at and has not produced a comparable counterpart to the thousands of items crafted for *Lord of the Rings*, there is considerable depth to the Fraggle world. The drawings of Michael Frith, *Fraggle Rock*'s primary conceptual designer, were turned into physical reality by numerous puppet-builders, special effects designers, and set-designers. Key production personnel included setting designer Bill Beeton, Muppet design consultant Bonnie Erickson, Faz Fazakas in special effects and "Muppet Mechanicals," and their respective teams. Their combined efforts generated a multitude of Fraggles, creatures, Doozers, items, and locations. Beeton's concept of a modular set meant that a limited number of set pieces could be rearranged relatively simply to create dramatically differentiated spaces. Lighting, flora and other accessories further delineated these varied locations within the Rock.

In terms of material objects, the Fraggles' personal caves contain their possessions, which are sometimes recognizable objects (Gobo's lute, Boober's pans, rackets) and sometimes strange and unidentified items. The Gorgs and Doozers also have various objects that adorn their spaces. The first season is particularly filled with background objects; overdesign was critical as the creators wanted to give the audience an immediate sense of the world. In the first half of that season (before a partial redesign halfway through, most notably of the Gobo and Ma Gorg puppets) the Fraggle Five often congregate in an unnamed room (originally meant to be part of Gobo and Wembley's room) that is packed full of stuff. Indeed the original pitch brochure for the show mentions this room, "This band of five fraggles meets regularly in Gobo and Wembley's room. To them, this is the most interesting room in all of Fraggle Rock because it's crammed with junk and good stuff" ("Origins," *Fraggle Rock First Season*). The "good stuff" includes a number of paintings on the walls (including one of Gobo racing past Sprocket), cutouts of Doozers, clotheslines, paper-chains, a framed picture of Traveling Matt, postcards and other knick knacks. Objects like these extend our understanding of the material world of the Rock.

Some of these objects are only seen in the background; others are used for a specific purpose in single or multiple episodes. For instance, the Gorgs' painting of King Gorgus with Sir Hubris is only significant in the episode when it is introduced, but it appears on the show on several occasions and plays a small role in one other episode (blocking the Fraggles' escape route from the castle). Red's tug-a-tail trophy first appears in "A Cave of One's Own"; then it is used as an item to swear on in "Red-Handed and the Invisible Thief." It also appears in the background of Red's room in other episodes, as well as in a display of athletic trophies Red organizes in The Great Hall. Gobo and Wembley's room is decorated with increasing numbers of postcards, as Gobo continues to receive them from Traveling Matt. The re-use and presence of these items helps maintain continuity in the show and gives a sense of the world's verisimilitude.

It is the multi-layered activity in the show, more than the physical objects, that gives the audience a taste of the larger world of Fraggle Rock. In most episodes, numerous Fraggles, Doozers and other creatures are on screen engaging in a variety of activities. Sometimes they support the main action (singing backup, dancing, attending events), but just as often they are engaged in their own business. Because of the Henson puppeteer practice of upstaging, these moments can be dramatic and interesting performances even though they have little to do with the narrative action. Background Fraggles become increasingly recognizable as the series goes on, so that a viewer might recognize

Tosh, Rumple, Morris or others going about their lives, though they play no role in the plot of the episode and have no dialogue. These moments indicate that the plot of the show and the adventures of the Fraggle Five are only one small facet of the Fraggle world. In addition to background Fraggle activity, and in some ways overshadowing it due to sheer volume, there is in most episodes considerable Doozer performance outside the bounds of the narrative proper.

Apart from the handful of episodes that focus on Cotterpin (Kathryn Mullen) or other specific Doozers, the Doozers generally perform actions, mostly construction-related, that have little impact on the plot at hand. Behind-the-scenes material suggests that much of the Doozer activity was the product of a combination of experimentation by Faz Fazakas and the design team and excitement about new performance methods, such as radio-controlled puppetry. The producers were both testing technology and playing with it. Tom Newby, who worked as part of the electro-mechanical puppetry team, said of the Doozers that much of their activity was unscripted material, in place to "flesh that world out and create an order and meaning to it that didn't necessarily have a direct imposition on the storyline of the script but was ever-present there" ("Doozer Design," *Fraggle Rock Third Season*). The activity of the Doozers, as with that of the background Fraggles, is there to make the world more alive, more real. The first season especially has long scenes of Doozers building, with minimal purpose beyond the fleshing out of that world. The effect of this is to have a considerable amount of seemingly extraneous material, conjuring up a busy and active world that exists around the edges of the narrative.

The Diegetic Fringe and Exploration

While the activity and detail of *Fraggle Rock* furnish a vibrant story world, it is the expandable nature of the Rock that stands out as the more significant world building strategy. Sconce writes that many television shows which have developed a strong audience involvement "are those that orchestrate a strong sense of community while also leaving a certain diegetic fringe available for textual elaboration. Whatever their genre or narrative logic, they all create worlds that viewers gradually feel they inhabit along with the characters" (95). This is an apt description of *Fraggle Rock*: community is the heart of the show, and the edges of that community and world are left wide open for further exploration.

Numerous ingredients make up the story world of *Fraggle Rock*, including creatures, personalities, flora, music, and geography. The spaces and places of the Fraggle world are essential to the construction of that world, particularly because of the ongoing theme of exploration. Several key locations anchor the series. In the first season Gobo and Wembley's room, The Great Hall (including the Fraggle Pond), and the entrances to "outer space" and the Gorgs' garden, provide a stable core area for the Fraggle community. External to the Rock are the Gorgs' garden (including the Trash Heap), the Gorgs' castle and the liminal space of the first room in "outer space" (Doc's workshop in the Canada-U.S. version). In later seasons, Boober's room, Mokey and Red's shared room, and the Doozer Dome were added. Beyond these central areas numerous other caverns, holes and tunnels expanded out in all directions, potentially endlessly.

In naming these far-flung spaces, *Fraggle Rock* uses evocative descriptive naming conventions, in a manner similar to that of some children's or fantasy literature, for the various sections of the Rock. However, while much fantasy literature tends toward the ominous in place names (Mount Doom, the Swamps of Despair), *Fraggle Rock* location names tend to be less dark and foreboding. They range from the positive and cheery (Singing Caverns, Sweetwater Grotto), to the fun and silly (Messing-Around Cave, Belching Boulder), to benign descriptions (The Echo Hole, Chimney Hole Cavern), to the mildly creepy (Cave of Shadows, Great Barrens). Most locations outside the core Fraggle area surrounding The Great Hall are only referenced or seen in one episode. Across the series there are over sixty-five locations and landmarks within the Rock that are visited or mentioned. Moreover there is always the hint of further space beyond and between those named on the show: caverns, tunnels, and chasms stretching out endlessly. Those infinite pathways beyond the Fraggles' core inhabitation are potentially populated with monsters and new friends, delights and temptations, as well as adventures into the unknown. Matt Hills, who has written extensively on cult media and fan cultures, refers to this kind of extended world as a text's "*hyperdiegesis*: the creation of a vast and detailed narrative space, only a fraction of which is ever directly seen or encountered within the text, but which nevertheless appears to operate according to principles of internal logic and extension" (137). *Fraggle*'s hyperdiegesis is vast, much of it never seen on the show. One of the show's themes, however, connects this endless space with storylines. The narrative of *Fraggle Rock*, from beginning to end, is entwined with a theme of exploration. Matt's ongoing exploration of the human world punctuates each episode of the first three seasons. Gobo's role as the resident explorer in the Rock imbues all the episodes focused on him and is often mentioned in other episodes. His exploration allows the audience to see or hear about more of the rest of the Rock: the audience explores the Rock alongside Gobo. Whether the episode finds him seeking the undiscovered Cavern of Lost Dreams, mapping the Red Ridge Caves, or following Matt's map to the Hole-to-Who-Knows-Where, Gobo's need to explore constantly reminds the audience of the fringe, the literal open space at the edge of the narrative that could encompass anything imaginable. The exploration theme highlights the importance of spaces in the *Fraggle Rock* story and allows for endless expansion of the world as part of the narrative.

Exploration is not limited to Matt and Gobo; other characters engage in explorations or in the discourse of exploring. Many episodes feature discussions amongst the Fraggle Five centered on exploring. Sometimes these dialogues serve as a foil, challenging Gobo to greater exploits, but other times the characters engage more directly with the concept of exploring. In "Gobo's School for Explorers," many of the wider Fraggle community show an interest in learning how to be explorers, though after a brief session of the "school," only three of the Fraggle Five are willing to follow Gobo on an exploratory expedition. In other episodes, Red (Karen Prell) and Wembley (Steve Whitmire) either accompany Gobo on expeditions or discover new areas themselves. In the Canada-U.S. version of the show, the human living at the entrance to Fraggle Rock, Doc, is an inventor, a kind of scientific explorer (a connection which is made explicit in the final episodes of the series). Exploring the edges of the show's reality kept an ongoing engagement with the fringe.

The fringe of the show is particularly unstable since the incorporation of magic means that the parameters of the world keep changing. In some episodes magic opens up new areas of the rock, in others magic plays a role in the plot, and in some it is more incidental. The magic qualities of the Fraggle diegesis encourage experimentation with the fringe. As seasons go on, the writers are willing to incorporate a variety of magical beings whose presence is never explained. Skenfrith, Begooney, Mavis the Mirror, and the Fairy-Godmother-in-Odd-Old-Man-Disguise (all inherently-magical creatures) appear with minimal exposition and disappear again after their particular episode. The *Fraggle* fringe really could encompass anything.

That many of these magic beings are single-appearance creatures isn't indicative of a completely episodic approach to the world (though there is an element of that). Other creatures and entities appear across multiple episodes. A range of unnamed creatures are fairly consistent, moving across the background of a shot, watching the action or singing back-up. For instance, the same singing rock puppets show up in every season, and the Inkspots are frequent supporting singers in later seasons.

One of the few named creature species that appear in multiple episodes are the Poison Cacklers, mentioned in a list of horrible creatures that Boober

(Dave Goelz) fears (though no one has ever seen any of them at this point) in the first season episode, "The Beast of Blue Rock." Cacklers are then mentioned again in a second season episode, before finally appearing on screen in "The Wizard of Fraggle Rock" later that season. The monster is brought up again in season three's "Pebble Pox Blues" when Wembley hallucinates that he is being attacked by several of them. Finally, in the last season, a baby Poison Cackler hatches in "The Trial of Cotterpin Doozer." Poison Cacklers and a few similar examples enhance the possibilities of the fringe by providing continuity. The many one-shot beings, places, and monsters indicate the vastness of the Rock and all its possibilities, while those exceptions to the rule that turn up multiple times give enough of a sense of familiarity to believe that the world, though vast, is still a mostly-coherent whole. In other words, if one of the strange monsters mentioned in season one becomes manifest in later seasons, then all of them might be out there somewhere. It is in these named but unseen monsters, locations, and knowledge that we find one of *Fraggle Rock*'s most effective strategies for world-building — negative capability.

Negative Capability

A significant strategy in maintaining the diegetic fringe for *Fraggle Rock* is triggering the audience's "negative capability" through dialogue about various places and creatures in the Rock. Negative capability is a concept, originating with the poet John Keats, of how we deal with uncertainties; one facet of this is that our imagination fills in the gaps of a narrative. Geoffrey Long, a media analyst and author, has used Keats' idea of negative capability to approach film, specifically Henson's fantasy film franchises. Long writes,

> When applied to storytelling, negative capability is the art of building strategic gaps into a narrative to evoke a delicious sense of "uncertainty, Mystery, or doubt" in the audience. Simple references to people, places or events external to the current narrative provide hints to the history of the characters and the larger world in which the story takes place. This empowers audiences to fill in the gaps in their own imaginations while leaving the curious to find out more [53].

Long relates it to a similar concept of horror fiction developed by Stephen King, that the monster the audience does not see is more terrifying than the seen monster. Our imaginations fill in the details of the unknown in a way more personally terrifying than an author or filmmaker could create. Likewise our imaginations can dream up images more spectacular and wonderful than a television production team could likely devise. The evocative naming used on the show helps fuel the imagination, suggesting what the audience might imagine, but allowing them to do the work. Thus, when Fraggles reference the Singing Caverns, Screaming Ice Worms, or the time of the Third Drafting without ever explaining or showing them, the audience fills in the details in ways that appeal to their personal ideas of the fantastic.

Fraggle Rock uses this strategy regularly, dropping references into dialogue that aren't further developed. This is particularly common in naming locations within the Rock that are never seen, but also in highlighting gaps in other areas such as history and culture. Throughout the series, characters within each of the three main cultures allude to a number of stories and legends. Some are explored within an episode; others are left dangling, engaging the viewers' imagination but leaving them free to construct the story as they see fit. How we imagine these stories and legends impacts our sense of the history of the Rock. For instance, there are several episodes that utilize medieval-fantasy motifs (knights, princesses, fiery chargers) in Fraggle plays or stories. This raises questions as to whether Fraggle Rock had a medieval period or if it is simply part of their imagined world, but these references to the past and to legend are usually just hints of what might have been or might be. It is left to the audience to create the details.

It is also left largely to the audience to imagine the parameters of the Fraggle world. Just how big is Fraggle Rock? Are there other Fraggle communities? If so, what are they like? Early in the first season, in "The Preachification of Convincing John," the Fraggles swear an oath as "all the Fraggles in the world." By the end of the first season, however, we know that they are not all the Fraggles. There are in fact more Fraggles out there, though the details of those Fraggles are limited to vague hints and implied possibilities. The clues regarding those other Fraggle communities are revealed through various transient visitors to the Rock.

Expansion Through Visitors and Other Fraggles

Beyond places named and visited, the world of *Fraggle Rock* is expanded through the implied experience of various visitors to the Rock. This expansion of the world again happens primarily through negative capability; each visitor only implies and hints at what lies beyond the core Fraggle realm. These visitors include the single episode characters — the Wizard (Richard Hunt), the Old Gypsy Lady (Kathryn Mullen), Rock Hockey Hannah (Kathryn Mullen) — and the recurring visitors Cantus (Jim Henson) and the Minstrels. In the cases of the Wizard and the Old Gypsy Lady, not much information is given. It is implied that the Wizard, appearing in season two, has visited this group of Fraggles before and that he travels between communities, entertaining as he goes. Later in the second season, in "Boober's Quiet Day," Boober learns that the Old Gypsy Lady "has returned to the Rock." This statement indicates that she has been there before and that she has been traveling outside the Rock (which at this point in the series is most likely to mean she has been out in the world beyond the Gorgs' garden). These two appearances don't tell the audience much about the world beyond the core Fraggle community, except to imply that something else is out there. There is a bit more information to be gained from Cantus and Rock Hockey Hannah.

Cantus and the Minstrels are the first external visitors to the Fraggle community, appearing in the second half of season one and returning several times throughout the series. When the minstrels first appear, the Fraggles don't know who they are. Cantus explains by saying, "I am Cantus and we are The Minstrels. We wander this boundless rock of ours, finding Fraggles in distant caves. When we are near, they sing a Fraggle medley. We are near, we are here, it's your turn to sing the medley." It is unclear whether these other places they visit are Fraggle settlements or just small groups, but it does suggest that there are other communities around the rock. Only two of the five minstrels are themselves Fraggles, Cantus and Brio (Terry Angus); the others are unidentified species. In a later visit, the minstrels say that they "have traveled far and wide uniting the Rock with music." This, along with their knowledge of non–Fraggle music and their inclusion of non–Fraggle members, suggests that they visit more than just distant Fraggles. In discussing Cantus, *Fraggle Rock* co-creator and writer Jocelyn Stevenson offered perhaps the most significant insight about the actual size of Fraggle Rock. She said, "Fraggle Rock was a vast place, I mean as big as you could imagine; they went everywhere, it was all over the world. That was our conception of it" ("Cantus and the Minstrels," *Fraggle Rock First Season*). Cantus' visits imply the vastness of the Rock but tell us little about the extent of Fraggle civilization or what else might be found at the fringe of the Fraggle world.

Rock Hockey Hannah appears only in the third season episode, "Playing Till it Hurts," but the episode provides significant information about other Fraggle communities. Rock Hockey Hannah is a famous Rock Hockey player whose name is known by numerous Fraggles. Red says that Hannah was "the best Thwackaballer, the best Tug-a-Tailer, the best rock climber." In this episode, Hannah has decided to visit in order to watch Red play Rock Hockey because she has heard that Red is the best player around. The implication is that there is something of a cult of sports celebrity, as there is in the human world. It raises, but does not answer, a question of whether there is intercommunity sports competition. More direct information is contained in her letter to Red, in which she writes, "P.S. Every time I go anywhere Fraggles hold parades for me and stuff. I hate parades, so please don't tell anyone I'm coming." Unlike Cantus' more vague assertions, Hannah's letter clearly indicates that the other places she visits are Fraggle *communities*, large enough to hold parades. This episode builds on the earlier visitor episodes to suggest that the Rock is made up of numerous Fraggle settlements and that it may be much more extensive than was ever explored in the show. These visitor examples continue to utilize negative capability, hinting at other places and societies, allowing the audience to fill in the blanks in their own imaginations. However, there are two instances when the Fraggles encounter other societies within the rock.

On the sole occasion when a different Fraggle community is introduced on the show, the Fraggles themselves are surprised by its existence. All but one of the Fraggles are completely unaware of this other group. In the second season episode "Fraggle Wars," Red and Mokey stumble across a Fraggle settlement very different from their own. Mokey is captured, almost leading to a war between the two Fraggle groups. The World's Oldest Fraggle (Dave Goelz) is the only Fraggle from the core community that remembers this group which he calls "those Other Fraggles." These Fraggles are so different from the core Fraggles that it seems unlikely they are part of the network of communities suggested by Rock Hockey Hannah. They seem to have no interest in sports or any of the activities normally enjoyed by other Fraggles.

One other community appears in the final season. In "Beyond the Pond," Red follows an underwater tunnel to Merggle Lake and meets the Merggles, who are essentially mer-fraggles (with fish tails instead of legs). Red discovers that the "knobblies" in the Fraggle Pond, which she has directed the other Fraggles to poison, are in fact the roots of the Merggles' "Tree of Life." These two episodes raise the question of why *similar* Fraggle settlements are only hinted at, while the two communities actually depicted are truly *Other*, one culturally and one physically.

The two external communities that do appear on the show serve very particular narrative purposes; they aren't simply places visited for social reasons, such as seeing relatives or making new friends. The Merggles facilitate an environmental disaster episode, in which the Fraggles don't realize how they are hurting the Merggles, a society which is not highly differentiated from their own. In other environmental problem episodes, the damage tends to be coming from external sources, such as in "The River of Life," in which humans pump industrial waste into the caves. In this case it is the Fraggles causing the problem. The appearance of the "Other Fraggles" allows for a war scenario to play out within a single race. While much of the series is dedicated to different cultures learning how they are connected and moving towards intercultural harmony, this is the only time that there is conflict within the Fraggle species that goes beyond the interpersonal. The conflict between Fraggles and Gorgs borders on the war-like (certainly the Gorgs see it that way at times), but the difference in species makes it more allegorical. "Fraggle Wars" makes the war element explicit, and the correlation to humans fighting other humans is clearer. The nature of war is discussed several times, possible differences in generational approaches are touched on (with the World's Oldest and "Cave's Oldest" Fraggles leading their respective groups towards war), and the ultimate absurdity of motivations for war is parodied in that the Fraggle groups were enemies in the past largely because they didn't laugh at the same jokes. Other *Fraggle Rock* communities thus exist only as implied entities, unless they serve a particular narrative purpose. Outside these isolated instances, it is enough to know that the Rock is larger than we know.

Conclusion, Belief and Magic

So how large is Fraggle Rock? The show's answer is that, essentially, the Rock is as big as we want or need it to be. It grew when it needed to grow, and the audience was always encouraged to imagine new elements for themselves. For a fictional world to work, the audience must be able to believe in it. The audience's desire to take part in the exploration of the Rock and to allow their negative capability to take over is part of the impulse to believe in this world.

Digital media theorist Janet Murray writes:

> The pleasurable surrender of the mind to an imaginative world is often described, in Coleridge's phrase, as "the willing suspension of disbelief." But this is too passive a formulation even for traditional media. When we enter a fictional world, we do not merely "suspend" a critical faculty; we also exercise a creative faculty. We do not suspend disbelief so much as we actively *create belief*. Because of our desire to experience immersion, we focus our attention on the enveloping world and we use our intelligence to reinforce rather than to question the reality of the experience [110].

A desire to believe, to be immersed, encourages negative capability, the filling in of any blanks to make it all make sense. This desire to believe in the world was not just something the audience might feel; several of the creators and writers talk about their own experience of designing the world and writing scripts in the same terms. Michael Frith said, "It was always as if this world of the Fraggles already existed in some great encyclopedia or something, and we were turning the pages and making these discoveries as we went" ("Michael Frith Interview," *Fraggle Rock Third Season*). He was not the only Fraggle creator to voice that feeling. The story world was engaging enough that even the people crafting the show, on some level, believed in it.

Through their intentionality in crafting a world (rather than designing a television show) and their investment in that world, the creators of *Fraggle Rock* have given us a story world that is vibrant, engaging, magical and alive. The use of the explorer theme entwined the spaces of the world with the narrative action. Effective activation of negative capability expanded the onscreen world in all directions within the audience's imagination, the diegetic edge always open. The limits of the Rock were only the limits of imagination. In the final episode of the series, *Fraggle Rock* wove all these themes together: exploration, the edges of the Rock, imagination, belief, magic.

"Change of Address," the final episode, draws on the explorer theme, and once again expands the reach of the Rock. Doc (in the Canadian production) and Gobo discuss their similarities as explorers, Gobo an explorer of space, Doc an explorer of science. When they are separated, the Rock literally self-expands, through magic, as a new tunnel appears which leads to Doc and Sprocket's new abode in the desert, an airplane ride away in the human world, moments away in the Rock. Before their reunion with the Fraggles, Doc and Sprocket come to the realization that if the Fraggles can exist, then the world may contain far more than humans (or dogs) understand, that magic may exist in everything. They experience a kind of re-enchantment of the world, a renewal of wonder. The final episode brought closure to the series, while at the same time opening up the real world to new potential, to magic. As Marjory the Trash Heap says in the closing words of the series, "We cannot leave the magic!"

WORKS CITED

Bordwell, David. *The Way Hollywood Tells It: Story and Style in Modern Movies*. Ewing: University of California Press, 2006. Print.
"Episode 201: Wembley's Egg." *Muppet Wiki*. Muppet Wiki, n.d. Web. 25 July 2011.
Fraggle Rock: The Complete First Season. HIT Entertainment, 2005. DVD.
Fraggle Rock: The Complete Second Season. HIT Entertainment, 2006. DVD.
Fraggle Rock: The Complete Third Season. HIT Entertainment, 2007. DVD.
Fraggle Rock: Complete Series Collection. HIT Entertainment, 2008. DVD.
Gwenllian-Jones, Sara. "Virtual Reality and Cult Television." In *Cult Television*. Eds. Gwenllian-Jones, Sara and Roberta Pearson. Minneapolis: University of Minnesota Press, 2004. 83–97. Print.
Henson Staff. "Encyclopedia Fragglia" 4th Edition. *Muppet Wiki*. Muppet Wiki, n.d. Web. 20 Jul. 2011.
Hills, Matt. *Fan Cultures*. London: Routledge, 2002. Print.

Jenkins, Henry. *Convergence Culture: Where Old and New Media Collide*. London: New York University Press, 2006. Print.

Johnson, Derek. "Franchising Media Worlds: Content Networks and the Collaborative Production of Culture." Dissertation University of Wisconsin–Madison, 2009. Print.

Long, Geoffrey. "Transmedia Production: Business, Aesthetics and Production at the Jim Henson Company." MS Thesis. Massachusetts Institute of Technology, 2007. Print.

Murray, Janet H. *Hamlet on the Holodeck: The Future of Narrative in Cyberspace*. Cambridge: The MIT Press, 1997. Print.

Plume, Kenneth. "Reflections in Fleece: An Interview with Puppeteer Terry Angus." *Muppet Central*. Muppet Central, 1998. Web. 17 Jul. 2011.

_____, and Chapman, Phillip. "Animateer Karen Prell: An Interview with Puppeteer, Animator and Writer." *Muppet Central*. Muppet Central, 1998. Web. 17 Jul. 2011.

Sconce, Jeffrey. "What If?: Charting Television's New Textual Boundaries." In *Television After TV*. Eds. Spigel, Lynn and Jan Olsson. London: Duke University Press, 2004. 92–112. Print.

Thompson, Kristin. *The Frodo Franchise: The Lord of the Rings and Modern Hollywood*. Berkeley: University of California Press, 2007. Print.

Outer Spaces: *Fraggle Rock* Around the Globe

Andrew Leal

The origins of *Fraggle Rock*, Jim Henson's often allegorical fantasy series, have taken on some elements of legend themselves. According to the accounts of many who were there, including writer Jerry Juhl, it began when Henson made a simple pronouncement as to what would follow *The Muppet Show*, which had just ceased production in 1981: "Let's make a children's show that brings peace to the world *(World of Jim Henson)*. This statement fits with the accepted image of Jim Henson as a hippie and a dreamer. However, it also effectively underlies the essential themes of most of the episodes and the show in general and sparked an impressive and varied co-production strategy. Inspired by successful co-productions of *Sesame Street* as well as the global popularity of *The Muppet Show*, *Fraggle Rock* was an international series, conceived to address issues of global communities, better relations across cultures, and coexistence with the environment. To accomplish that, Henson and co-creator/head writer Juhl conceived the series as being adaptable to any country, "localized," by the simple expediencies of not only dubbing the main stories, but by utilizing frame scenes and filmed/videotaped inserts which could be replaced with local footage and actors, combined with the appropriate Muppet characters.

The ambitious aim ultimately resulted in only three full co-productions, for the following countries: France (broadcast on FR3), Germany (broadcast on ZDF), and the U.K. (on ITV from 1984 to 1990; this was the only series to fully adapt all 96 episodes). Yet their reception and even very existence serve as fascinating case studies which impacted not only the "home" country for each version but the general perception of the series. The approach opened up the series in a way that no previous ongoing Muppet project had, revealing the larger world (or Outer Space, as Fraggles called it) and setting a precedent for later efforts by Henson and Sesame Workshop. Through the co-productions and the postcards, the localizations in effect used the specific cultural and geographical aspects of the nations to present the show's larger theme of breaking down cultural barriers and borders. As Jim Henson said in the documentary *Down at Fraggle Rock*, "We wanted to do a show that had to do with international understanding, and a lot of the problems of the world happened because there are different kinds of people that don't understand each other, and so on Fraggle Rock we wanted to portray that and show how that happens."

Globalization Themes Within Show

The very premise of the show relied on multiculturalism and was conceived as an "international" show before it was even named; at one point Henson discussed it with his associates Jerry Juhl, Michael K. Frith, and others as "International Children's Show" (Jim Henson's Red Book). The series is discussed in greater detail elsewhere in this volume, but it's worth reiterating that the foundation lay in four interconnected cultures/races and worlds: the Fraggles, who lived for fun and pleasure and silliness, were the main protagonists (led by Gobo and his four friends). The Doozers, tiny creatures who had their own society and city, represented industry; higher above, the giant Gorgs, who considered themselves "rulers of the universe," were in essence a decaying monarchy or government.

The fourth world, which would prove crucial to the international co-production design, was "Outer Space," aka the real world (well, more or less). Uncle Traveling Matt (Fraggledom's joint answer to Jane Goodall, Charles Darwin and David Attenborough) ventured into this world and there encountered and documented the "silly creatures" (humans) in postcards (filmed inserts) sent to nephew Gobo. The postcards were the plot hinge which led Gobo into a specific portion of Outer Space, a room populated by the main silly creature (Doc, an eccentric inventor, in the North American version) and his Muppet dog Sprocket ("the hairy monster," according to Gobo). Thus Doc's workshop, although an obvious studio set, was "outer," linked to the larger world, and the various puppet fantasy realms existed parallel or below the surface.

This premise allowed for exploration of cultural conflicts and misunderstandings, unique histories and traditions belonging to each group, and negotiations of these differences and ultimately a clearer awareness of shared commonality. This was laid out in the pitch: "What the show is really about is people getting along with other people, and understanding the delicate balances of the natural world [...] These are topics that can be dealt with in a symbolic way, which is what puppets basically do all the time. These are also two of the areas that children in the next generation or so will have to deal with in very real terms" (Cheryl Henson 153). Some of this was on the micro level: Red became close friends with Cotterpin Doozer, Junior Gorg gradually came to consider the Fraggles his friends, and even Gobo befriended the "hairy monster" Sprocket. On the larger "macro" scale, the groups discovered how much they depend on each other and how symbiotic their cultures are (the shared use of radishes, the water from the Fraggle pond used by the Gorgs as a well which, in turn, comes from Doc's leaky plumbing). Doc's plumbing likewise shaped Fraggle culture: the rituals of the Pipebangers arose as a result, who when water ran dry would ceremonially bang on the metal pipes, and the clanging in turn caused Doc to work with the plumbing again. In the environmental episode "River of Life" (one of many in the series, broadcast near the end of the final season), chemicals dropped near Doc's land bring illness to all three species: Fraggles, Doozers, and Gorgs. The final two episodes even bridged the human world and that of the Fraggles, as Doc met Gobo, and discovered that somehow, wherever he was, there would be a Fraggle hole. This proof that each group or community cannot exist in isolation sets the stage well for the actual co-productions. It made sense that these "outer spaces" were where the emphasis on localization lay, through the frame scenes with the human and his dog, and through the filmed or videotaped postcards from Traveling Matt.

Co-Production Precedents

By the time *Fraggle Rock* debuted in 1983, Jim Henson had enjoyed an international career which had seen him rise from a regional puppeteer to the creator of an internationally successful comedy series and movies through *The Muppet Show*. *Fraggle Rock*, like *The Muppet Show*, was even in its English language version a co-production where national identity was shared. While *The Muppet Show* was taped in London and influenced by its British studio crew and the English music hall, the new series was produced in conjunction with Canadian Broadcasting Corporation, taped in a Toronto studio and with various real location settings utilized as the more generic "outer spaces" visited by Uncle Matt. Canadian character actor Gerard "Gerry" Parkes, with a long distinguished stage, television, and radio career behind him, played the original "Doc," setting a precedent in age for the international actors. While Henson's seasoned American Muppeteers played the principal characters, Toronto puppeteers and mimes were trained and cast as the Gorg body performers and to fill out minor roles. Thus the only truly accurate way to refer to the original *Fraggle Rock* series is as the North American version.

Fraggle Rock also expanded on a tradition established by *Sesame Street*, which by 1983 already had several thriving co-productions (including series in Germany and France). The "street" segments featured local actors and Muppet equivalents and sometimes curricular goals were altered to better suit the country's nature. The "commercials" (animated and filmed segments interspersed to teach letters or concepts) could be easily replaced by local films, and this established a precedent for the Traveling Matt segments. Even *The Muppet Show*, in the case of its German localization, went beyond dubbing. Special footage of Kermit was filmed beneath a "Die Muppet Show" logo, and other footage performed by Jim Henson to phonetic German or general vowels, to better facilitate dubbing (handled by Eberhard Storeck, who would cast, translate, and direct the German *Fraggle Rock* using some of the same voices). This fostered a greater illusion that this was a German series, although the new scenes were filmed at the usual London set. The episode with Twiggy (Season 1, episode 21) took the process even further. For a segment unique to the German broadcast, German popstar Mary Roos flew down to London, where the Muppeteers operated Rowlf and other characters (again lip-synching phonetically) for a full production number, a German translation of the song "Lean on Me." Thus Henson and company already had some experience in the localization process by 1983, but *Fraggle Rock* would mark the first time where the co-production model was part of the show's inherent design and where the content would reflect that from the outset.

From Workshops to Lighthouses

To accomplish the co-productions, producer Duncan Kenworthy was assigned the role of coordinating between Henson International Television and the individual broadcasters and local talent. Kenworthy had begun his association with Henson in 1977, as producer of *Iftah Ya Simsim*, the Kuwait co-production of *Sesame Street*, so this was a natural extension. Martin G. Baker, who had served as floor manager and production assistant on *The Muppet Show* and the first two *Muppet* films, served as production supervisor and as co-producer on the French co-production. The starting point for the co-production elements was the frame scenes, occurring outside *Fraggle Rock* and the main episode plots; even the opening titles in all versions began with this space, as the camera tracked through the human's home, through the Fraggle hole and tunnel, and into the Rock. This was referred to in Henson's initial notes as "home base," a setting that could be changed to reflect the culture.

The original concept was that of an inventor's workshop, and the sense of space or even which country it's in were left vague in North America (to suit Canadian and American audiences) with nothing that could really pin down the place, outside of eliminating arid climes (at the end of the series, neighbor and friend Ned must move to "the desert" for his health). Other suggestions for the home base included a mechanic's garage, a lighthouse (which actually was used for the United Kingdom), or a tent in an Arab market place. According to puppeteer Mike Quinn, who worked at various times on all three co-productions, a version for Saudia Arabia was planned at one point, but never materialized.

The space would reflect the host country, but the common points would be the human and a Muppet dog. The concept of Sprocket as a pantomime dog was intended to assist with the adaptation process, providing comic relief and a character whose communications and audience appeal would be unaffected by language barriers. Henson did suggest in his notes that "there may be certain Arab countries where we shouldn't use a dog," and likely another pet would have been substituted, but as events transpired, the need never arose. The sheepdog (or so the scripts alleged) was equally at home in the U.K., France, and Germany, and in reacting directly to Gobo whenever he ventured forth, he also connected the pre-produced episode bodies with the new frame stories.

The human figure (initially referred to just as an "old codger") offered greater opportunities for variation, and Henson's original notepad, as well as the more formal pitch book prepared by Henson and head writer Jerry Juhl, explore this in depth; both of the documents were reprinted as bonus booklets with the *Fraggle Rock* DVD releases. These notes said that the "recreation" of Doc could be as complete as necessary "to satisfy local audiences," but also left some freedom for character adjustment: "The role may be recast for an actress rather than an actor; and the age of the performer may alter." However, for the three actual international versions, the initial "Doc" figure remained demographically similar despite changes in demeanor, personality, and cultural markers. He was still an older male played by a character actor (all of whom were over fifty) and seemingly (or explicitly) retired from a previous occupation, thus with a background which allowed for reference to previous activities and experiences while also giving him the freedom of free time for his hobbies and to potter around with his dog. This also indicates how closely the local producers stuck to the North American template, at least in this respect. Since the show's aims were fairly lofty, perhaps there was a reluctance to experiment too far. Kindly grandfather or uncle figures in children's television had been a staple in many countries for decades. The sole exception to the "codger" would occur in the U.K. series, when actor Fulton MacKay died and was replaced by younger performers in succession.

Despite the age similarities, the performance of the character actors as Doc varied both according to script but also the very cultural and behavioral makeup of the people themselves. This is best exemplified by *Die Fraggles*, the German co-production, which is also the most difficult for an American scholar to assess. The plots were taken directly from the North American version, Doc (played by Hans-Helmut Dickow) was still an inventor, and any alterations to storyline were minimal. The decision to directly copy the Doc frame scenes, in script and general tone, rested with the producers, but Dickow refused to watch the original episodes for reference. Since his German dialogue did not always correspond as closely to the original in tone or length or even translation, it left puppeteer Steve Whitmire uncertain how to respond, as the performer recalled: "It kind of scared me to death doing this [...] our plan was to use the North American version as a model, largely because I didn't speak any German at all. And he says the first line, and Sprocket is just staring" ("Docs and Sprockets").

The relationship between Doc and Sprocket, in addition to feeling like a mere copy, was affected by this culture gap between the performers. Whitmire also recalled that Dickow "had been a Nazi soldier, actually.... Nice guy, but temperamental" (Horn 12). Born in 1927, Dickow's induction in the German army is not surprising (unavoidable without emigrating), and would have no bearing on the series for the 1980s audience. To a current scholar, however, while trying to withhold judgment, this bit of history alters how one perceives the German Doc, since with little history or unique personality traits of his own, it's harder to separate what one knows about the actor. Whitmire initially assumed that Dickow was also uncomfortable, but he found a lot of it was merely due to his performing method: "The acting style of this particular actor, some of it was very broad and bold [....] he would be more presentational than Gerry Parkes was in Toronto, and I thought, he's not enjoying this at all," and his attitude towards Sprocket as a character seemed "very stern." But the German performer at the end complimented the American puppeteer and said he'd considered the experience working with him and the Muppet dog a highlight: "It just was the difference in cultures, which is what the show was about to begin with" ("Docs and Sprockets").

For the French co-production, the setting was an old house (referred to in some references as a bakery, but not in the show itself) which the human inherited from his Uncle Georges (who had been an inventor, justifying any plots which required a mechanical device to bridge the frame and Fraggle scenes). The character is still Doc in name, but fleshed out as a personality in his own right reflecting the national culture of France. This "Doc" is a chef portrayed by Michel Robin, an actor with a round, somewhat melancholy face. This was fully expressed in storylines which had the character attempting to court Madame Pontaven, the glamorous off-screen neighbor, but typically saw him alone with his dog. In keeping with Doc's culinary bent, the dog is now named Croquette.

The relationship between the French Doc and his dog was usually warm, although the dog became more "continental," an intellectual with an interest in stamp collecting and reading high literature which is a recurring theme across episodes, often donning reading glasses. However, in one episode, where the North American Doc attempts to cure Sprocket of his fears through a "lightning deflector," the Frenchman has a different aim. He saddles his dog, who fears lightning and rain, with the device in the hopes of generating electricity and overcoming concerns over government rate hikes. The resolution has Doc realizing how valuable his pet and friend is (a theme which would be explored in other episodes of the French series), but the premise, as well as the concern, is not one which one would imagine in a North American children's show of the time.

The best example of how the co-production process could alter the feel of an episode and shape it to reflect France's own history and culture may be the second season episode "Fraggle Wars." The main story features a fairly serious examination of cultural differences and mistaken assumptions which lead to wars, and in particular the inflammatory rhetoric of civic leaders. The conflict between the Rock Fraggles and previously unknown Cave Fraggles is primarily the work of their respective elders, aged figures too set in their ways to be anything but reactionary. The North American frame scenes are a lighter counterpart, as Doc and his perennially unseen neighbor Ned Shimmelfinney conduct an escalating "war" of practical jokes. In the French series, the frame story more directly addresses actual war, including references to the Second World War, albeit in a comedic manner.

Croquette is garbed in a scarf and waving a pennant, anxious about a sporting event on the radio, but Doc enters, waving a newspaper headline indicating that France is due for invasion by foreigners and faces defeat. Doc assumes that this is yet another world war and quickly prepares bunkers with sandbags and fetches out his old resistance uniform. Finally, after a night's vigil, Croquette seeks to enlighten Doc by turning on the radio, which broadcasts a soccer match. The foreign influx was in fact the World Cup, where France's defeat seemed imminent. Sprocket waves excitedly, Doc turns forlornly and abashedly to face the camera as realization dawns, and those seemingly omnipresent horns, beeping "La Cucaracha," blare out in celebration of victory. In these frame scenes, miscommunication even within the same language is examined, as a parallel to the Fraggles' war, and the European respect for soccer and the World Cup in particular is visited (other more explicitly European sporting pastimes would often feature in the postcard segments). However, the most surprising element to an American viewer is the frankness with which a children's show acknowledges the existence of real wars, albeit in the past, and explicitly references the Blitz and the French Resistance. It's difficult to imagine the same casual treatment in an American puppet series of the time.

The longest running of the three adaptations was the U.K. version, which also was the most creative in its use of outer spaces. This time, the hole connects to the interior rooms of a lighthouse, located on a rocky point which is actually called "Fraggle Rock" by the resident Silly Creature in dialogue. The Doc counterpart, at least for the first few seasons, was the Captain, a lighthouse keeper played by Scottish character actor Fulton MacKay. Around the same time as the U.K. *Fraggle Rock* was produced, MacKay appeared in the 1983 film *Local Hero*, which itself examined international relations (American oil businessmen in Scotland to negotiate land rights), receiving third billing as an eccentric beachcombing hermit who's the chief holdout. The portrayal has clear parallels with the actor's role on *Fraggle Rock*.

The choice also acknowledges the mixed cultures and countries which make up the United Kingdom; while the setting and the postcards (often depicting Londoners) reflect England, the Captain is unmistakably Scottish, from his burr onward. In "The Minstrels," he receives a package from his niece, containing traditional regalia (including a kilt and sporran) passed down from Great Uncle Hamish. He displays visible emotion and remarks that it makes him miss the Highlands. The Captain is so overcome that he embraces his roots, not only by wearing the full attire, but practicing the bagpipes, also attached. Sprocket is indifferent to the cultural costume, and visibly dismayed by his owner's out of tune piping. As the episode closes, the Captain stands on an outside rock, rapturously absorbed by his music making; Sprocket, meanwhile. is playing a gramophone record of "Loch Lomond," with the song actually in tune. After MacKay died in 1987, the younger actors cast in turn as his nephew (P.K.) and son (B.J.) were far less explicitly Scottish (Simon O'Brien, the last actor, was in fact born in Liverpool).

The Captain, in keeping with his characterization as a retired Scots sailor, was on occasion more brusque in his conversation with his dog, treating him less as a friend at times than a menial or a ship's mate who is refusing orders. This is most obvious in the adaptation of "Boober Rock." Both North American and U.K. plotlines, which address attempts at isolation, have the human and his dog quarreling and dividing their quarters with a rope. In the U.K. version, however, the Captain is infuriated when Sprocket chews up and effectively ruins the Captain's favorite book (admittedly a greater transgression than in the original, when the dog merely leaves marks on a set of blueprints) and his anger is far more convincing. In other episodes, he seems dismissive of the dog's needs. However, most often, he appreciates the dog as someone to whom he can utter his own thoughts and reflections; compared to the original Doc, the Captain is more poetic and wistful, although less so than the French chef.

The moody attitudes and reliance on the dog reflect the close living quarters, as well as greater isolation. Duncan Kenworthy recalled that they designed and started to build the interior before choosing the exterior ("Docs and Sprockets"). They then had to find an actual lighthouse to match, which was St. Anthony's Head Lighthouse at Falmouth Harbour in Cornwall. The show's opening tracks from an overhead shot of the lighthouse, gradually moving closer and tracking inside (and into the studio representation of the Captain's home). While all of the other Docs were directly connected to the larger world, the Captain received the postcards by mail boat and communicated with friends (such as Commander Ponsonby, the Ned equivalent) through telephone. The postman and the local coast guard officer are often mentioned, and there are references to a village beyond, but in general, the Captain is closed off. In fact the outside forces are often negative, as with the landlord Mr. Bertwhistle (although why a functioning lighthouse has a landlord remains unexplained). A more realistic counterpart to Muppet Theater owner J. P. Grosse, Mr. Bertwhistle is a distant figure in London, who threatens to evict the Captain and creates a lingering off-stage menace in later episodes. He also neglects his duties, leaving man and dog in a house with poor plumbing; when water is temporarily cut off, the utility board contacts Bertwhistle rather than the Captain, and his distance prevents him from being any practical use in such a situation. The possibility of being cut off without water, food or other supplies is broached on occasion.

Despite these somewhat harsher intrusions, the U.K. frame scenes best expressed the other aim of *Fraggle Rock*, the connections not just between people and cultures, but with the environment. It offered glimpses of the natural world, as the Captain can observe a diverse avian spectrum from seagulls to puffins. The sea breezes, crashing waves, and rocky shores are regularly viewed. In "Gobo's Discovery," the Captain is enormously encouraged by and admiring of a young sailor setting out to navigate the globe. His lot was not just one of isolation. The vast expanse of ocean is a shared resource which connects more than it divides.

The Fraggleogues of Traveling Matt

The second component of the international productions was the postcard segment, a series of filmed inserts as told by the Muppet character Uncle Traveling Matt (performed by Dave Goelz). Matt was established as the resident explorer, cartographer, and by embarking on his Outer Space quest, the first Fraggle anthropologist. Uncle Matt's pompous, self-satisfied voice and even his design and attire (bushy moustache, pith helmet, and khaki shirt and shorts) fit the stereotypical image of the explorer, in particular Frank Buck of the 1932 classic *Bring 'Em Back Alive* and its sequels. In the first season, there was one postcard each episode (and they were estimated as taking up five percent of the show's running time), and while their frequency gradually decreased to leave more time for the main story, they were still a recurring element through the end of the series.

Uncle Matt's name, a pun on the film term "traveling matte," hints at the combination of elements and the panoramic aspects of the segment. The postcards mirrored the purpose of, well, actual postcards, a cultural artifact which preserves a specific place or scene and allows the recipient to respond vicariously ("Wish you were here...") while at the same time framing it in the context of the personal experience of the sender. As the primary way that the Fraggles became aware of Outer Space and its inhabitants, the postcards were also reminiscent of *National Geographic* magazine, a glimpse into the exotic shared and passed around through newsstands and doctors' waiting rooms (or in this case, Fraggle caves). Finally, as filmed inserts, the postcards are parodic travelogues which, due to the use of international locales and landmarks, serve as a sightseeing experience in their own right.

As noted, replacing filmed inserts with local content was not a new idea in itself, per the international co-productions of *Sesame Street* which frequently included local films, but these were generally produced by outside animators or studios. Here, the ambition was greater, as Henson International Television would coordinate with the local producers to send Uncle Matt (and the necessary film crew) to a wide range of locations. An individual Uncle Matt puppet was supplied to each participating country. Naturally this required multiple puppeteers, originally with the idea of using local performers, although for logistic reasons David Alan Barclay (already involved as the U.K. Sprocket) soon became the primary European Matt (performing in France and Switzerland, among others), with other British performers filling in. For postcards filmed in Australia and New Zealand, Goelz was flown over personally (and assisted by Ron Mueck, a young local sculptor and puppet maker whom Henson would later cast as Ludo in the 1987 film *Labyrinth*). These segments also had a broader global impact, since they didn't hinge on a full co-production. Through the various dubs (into Castilian Spanish, Dutch, Swedish, Hungarian, Polish, and Japanese, to name a few) and English broadcasts in places such as Australia (which also benefited from unique postcards), Uncle Matt and the rest of the Fraggles were seen and heard in over 80 countries (Falk).

According to the pitchbook, the stated goal and approach to the international cards was not to adapt but to "re-enact ... in a setting viewed as familiar by the audience, with local houses, cars, street signs and people." As Duncan Kenworthy recalled, "It allowed each co-producing country, and even some countries that weren't official full co-producing partners but were taking the show, to get their environment and their society and the look of their country into each episode, which sort of cemented the illusion if you like that the show had been created in their country" ("Traveling Matt"). The simple "recreation" goal was sometimes followed literally but often diverged, even early on. A prime example occurs in the first broadcast episode, "Beginnings," as can be seen by contrasting the North American, French, and German versions.

When Uncle Matt ventures forth for the first time, he steps into the appropriate "Outer Space" base for that country, encountering Sprocket and the human in brief glimpses. He then steps out the door and into the street (in the North American version, literally across the street from the studio) where he encounters everyday sights which alarm him: a hydrant (an unpleasant yellow fellow) and kids with baseball equipment (an army). The French equivalent is the same in narrative, but the hydrant is a different color and the "army" consists of bearded, adult tennis players. In Germany, however, Uncle Matt encounters something far more complex and fascinating. He steps into the street and, across the way, is a typical German tavern, with ornate exterior decoration. The Fraggle enters and discovers a smoke-filled world of bearded Bavarians, clad in lederhosen and Tyrolean hats: some tugging at pipes, others drinking beer, and generally participating in typical pub activities.

Muppet Wiki administrator Julian Kleibeler provided further clarification as to the main theme of the segment, which mystified this author. At a center table, two men are engaged in the traditional Bavarian, "fingerhakeln," which literally translates as finger hooking. Competitors test their strength by hooking the middle finger into a strap and then wrestling fingers. Uncle Matt presumes this is a greeting ritual and amiably extends his own hand. Naturally he's flung from the table, as the spectators cheer, and lands in a basket. A cheerful barmaid claps for him behind a tray of beer. Outside of the obvious taboos as far as North American children's television compared to the European environment (drinking is simply accepted as part of the world), the segment fully gives the episode a German sense of identity, beyond recreation, in a way that the Doc and Sprocket scenes, ironically, do not.

Duncan Kenworthy recalled that another goal was that "As we did more productions around the world, they would be shared [...] and then it turned into the most complex logistical nightmare of them all" ("Traveling Matt"). The difficulties yielded dividends, however, as the accumulated postcards were incorporated in other co-productions and even the North American version. The U.K. postcards could be inserted as they stood (although those dealing with explicitly British activities and sports, such as cricket and rugby, were omitted), but Dave Goelz redubbed the German and French voice actors. In the late 1990s, several postcards which had not been incorporated into the North American series were dubbed or edited, with a new intro and a label identifying the nation, and aired as inserts on the now defunct Odyssey Network cable channel. The new narration for the fingerhakeln segment, for example, now had Uncle Matt mistaking the men for rope testers. Twenty of the postcard segments were included as bonus featured on the second season DVD set, more as "Easter Eggs" in the third season set, and still more have appeared on Henson's official YouTube channel, as "The Adventures of Traveling Matt." So the localization process comes full circle.

Kenworthy also summarized the unique premise behind the postcards, beyond simply a way to localize the show and share neat images: "For me it encapsulated the real heart of the show, this difference of perspective: a Fraggle going out into the world and interpreting things that we and kids in their own world understood very, very easily [...] in a very, very complex and misguided way, which sometimes was sort of illuminating too" ("Traveling Matt"). While the "Doc" figure and his world are the center of the localized frames, the postcards are miniature documentaries stamped by Uncle Traveling Matt, as both chronicler and narrator/point of view figure. Comedically, many of the segments contradict Matt's knowledgeable pomposity and interpretation of his discoveries and explorations, in the same way that the voice-over in the Disney "How To" shorts with Goofy (from the 1940s and 1950s) contradicted the on-screen action.

However, there's a greater contradiction here: since the voice-over is

Matt's own, he's the classic unreliable narrator or diarist attempting to protect his own dignity and sense of self. Moreover, as the documentarian, the postcards are filtered through his own misperceptions, preconceived notions, and personal frame of reference. This is obviously played for humor, and yet the equally intended irony is that Uncle Matt is only following in the footsteps of Western anthropologists and documentarians, from 19th century photographer Edward S. Curtis and his portraits of Indians to Robert J. Flaherty's *Nanook of the North* or even Disney's *True Life Adventure* animal documentaries. These efforts, designed to create a narrative and to iconize the "exotic," were selective, often fictionalized, and ultimately misleading due to the anthropologist's perspective. Yet they shaped how native peoples, foreign lands, and wildlife were seen for decades, creating stereotypes.

Thus Traveling Matt's postcards create their own view of Outer Space, which often frightens or startles the Fraggles back home. He interprets every action and location according to his own biases and expectations of behavior, finding counterparts to Doozer towers in construction buildings, or assuming ice cream is the equivalent of the Fraggles' own "moss packs" and serves as a headache remedy. Similarly, since to the Fraggles, life is primarily composed of games, a shopping sale line is actually a race waiting for the starter's signal. For anything which does not fit into Matt's existing point of reference, he concocts an explanation, viewing most mechanical devices as living creatures. It's Uncle Matt who coins the term "silly creatures" to describe humans (although it's Gobo who refers to Sprocket as "hairy monster") and much of Gobo's trepidation towards Doc and Sprocket is based on this, mirroring real-life xenophobia and misconceptions. By the series end, Gobo and Sprocket have discovered that neither has anything to fear from the other and become friends; in the final two episodes, Gobo even speaks to Doc, and in the closing scenes, Fraggle and "silly creature" can relate to each other on a name basis.

A simple, early example shows Uncle Matt's approach to turning the familiar into something strange, and yet his logic is hard to argue with. In a first season U.K. segment ("I Captured the Moon"), Uncle Matt observes the silly creatures engaged in what, to the viewer, is the afternoon teatime tradition, something which has a certain air of ceremony and ritual in itself; to him, what could this represent other than a lip bath? He carefully notes how "special cleansing herbs" are dropped into a pot, mixed with bathwater left to cool "to the proper bathing of upper lips," then the liquid poured into individual baths (teacups). Uncle Matt even plays with national characteristics, as the teashop customers pour sugar: "I understand that by adding starch, the silly creatures are able to keep a stiff upperlip."

The ironies in the postcards are further complicated in the international co-productions and segments, since a select few were in fact reused (or redubbed when needed) in the North American version, further complicating and making exotic behaviors and spaces which range from famously familiar to mundane in their homelands. This was made so obvious however as to be ridiculous even to the youngest viewer, as when Matt concludes that Neuschwanstein castle in Germany is a Gorg home, or when he visits Buckingham Palace and interprets the traditional hats of the Grenadier guards as fuzzy pets who are chauffeured on their owner's heads in a symbiotic relationship. Uncle Traveling Matt thus proves himself a worthy naturalist as well, comparable to many human practitioners.

Other sites visited included Trafalgar Square, the Eiffel Tower, the Sydney Opera House, Sotheby's Auction House, streets near Notre Dame, and even the North American version presented its own available outer spaces, as in one episode, he mistakes the CN Tower (a Toronto landmark) for a Doozer construction. These outer spaces are explicitly those of "postcard" views, landmarks, and even when not recognized, they're clearly impressive locales. They function as a panorama. In 1985, a U.K. single based on the musical theme to the U.K. postcards, "All Around the World" summarized Uncle Matt's perspective, and an accompanying music video blended the postcard footage to compile the varied spaces. However, it's less the specific sights (and sites) that mark the postcards as originating from another country than the customs and behavior. Surprisingly, this contrast is even more marked in the U.K. than in the French and German cards. The language is shared and there's no change in voice for Uncle Matt, but he's now in a world of lip bathers, double decker buses, and automobiles stopped with colorful yellow clamps (or shoes). That's not to say that he didn't experience culture shock in other countries: in a 1984 German guest appearance on variety show *Große Show für kleine Leute*, he appears "a bit stunned from his visit to the city of Hamburg's red-light district," the Reeperbahn street in St. Pauli ("Grosse Show für kleine Leute"). Yet Uncle Matt is a true egalitarian, ignorant of national and regional distinctions, so no matter where he is, the residents are Silly Creatures and clearly their habits are all connected as part of a larger sociological pattern.

Legacy of the Fraggles

Now, over twenty years after the original series ended, one can look back at *Fraggle Rock* and its co-productions, as well as the state of the world and of critical knowledge, and wonder, did it make a difference? For that matter, did Jim Henson truly expect tangible or immediate results? Jerry Juhl assessed the matter years later: "Jim wanted to make a difference. He was brave enough to be able to say, 'I want to do a show that brings peace to the world, and I want us all to sit down and talk about it.' He knew that television shows do not bring peace to the world, but he was not so cynical as to say we can't think about it. There was a kind of idealism there that could seem naïve and childlike, but that didn't mean that it couldn't come true" (Cheryl Henson 152).

One very definite concrete result occurred within Henson's lifetime, after the series' original production ended. In 1989, the governing Soviet television body, Gostelradio, broadcast an episode of *Fraggle Rock*, dubbed using the "lektor" system (a male announcer overlapping with the original voices) which drew unprecedented ratings and letters from 3,500 viewers. As a result, the organization agreed to allow both *Fraggle Rock* and *The Muppet Show* to air the following fall, making them the first Western series to air on Soviet television. This was mere months before the fall of the Berlin Wall and the eventual end of the Soviet Union. More recently, a new dub (with multiple actors, although still overlapping) debuted in February 2011, the first new *Fraggle Rock* dub in years.

At the very least, the endeavor inspired CTW/Sesame Workshop, which beginning in the late 1980s gradually increased its international co-productions in scope, particularly evident in the Middle East, the most notable geographical area where the Fraggles made no inroads. The Israeli Sesame Street, *Rechov Sumsum*, was adapted in 1986 for the U.S. as *Shalom Sesame*, a study of Jewish culture and life in Israel combining celebrities with local Israeli actors and Muppets, and skits where the language would combine the original English and Hebrew dubbing. In 1998 *Rechov Sumsum/Shaa'ra Simsim* was launched, a particularly ambitious effort which tried to blend Israeli and Palestinian characters and cast for a show aired in both countries. This truly reflected Henson's ideals for television influencing international peace, but the project ultimately failed, with even the child audience reacting negatively towards the "other" group, while conversely the Muppet performers, working together in desert heat beneath a heavy puppet, truly bonded and overcame personal divides, according to puppeteer Gilles Ben-David (Greenberg). Most recently, and with more acceptance, a Northern Ireland production, *Sesame Tree*, was launched in 2009, again emphasizing the themes of diversity and different groups getting along with each other despite differing cultures or belief systems.

For *Fraggle Rock* itself, the series has returned to the global airwaves, currently airing on the U.S. cable channel The Hub, and the entire series can be streamed over NetFlix, bought on iTunes, and owned on DVD. Internationally, following the success of the U.S. DVDs, select surviving episodes of the

U.K. series and the bulk of the French series were released. The later discs included close emphasis on other aspects of the project, including the international merchandise and a focus on the dubbing voice actors, many of whom had distinguished backgrounds in other fields.

Beyond the availability of the original show, several attempts at reviving or continuing the series in some form have occurred with varying success. A much-hyped *Fraggle Rock* film is, at the time of writing, once again on hold, and a concept for a computer animated series starring the Doozers, although exhibited at several media fairs, never found a buyer. More successfully, a series of comic books featuring the *Fraggle Rock* characters (primarily the Fraggles but encompassing all of the groups, including Doc and Sprocket) was published by Archaia Studios Press in 2010 and collected in hardback. The company followed up by reprinting the 1986 Marvel Comics based on the series.

For a truly meaningful revival of the concept, however, one wonders if the Jim Henson Company has considered repackaging the series internationally, in those countries where it still has not aired or been dubbed. The new Russian dub certainly proves that interest is still there and works in any language. The subject matter of the episodes, from environmental concerns to the increased access of cultures (communication and distances shrunk), are surprisingly timely and relevant. With a body of existing episodes, and improved matteing and editing technology, adjustments for new frame scenes or postcards would be easier. Perhaps someday, a woman in Ireland, say, or a stalls merchant in the Middle East will find a Fraggle hole of their own, and Uncle Matt could explore and reinterpret even more cultures than before, bringing, if not peace to the world, at least a little more understanding.

WORKS CITED

"Die Fraggles." Muppet Wiki. Web. 12 Oct. 2011.
"Docs and Sprockets." Interview feature. *Fraggle Rock: Complete Second Season*. HIT Entertainment, 2006. DVD.
Falk, Karen. "The Woozle World." Liner notes for *Fraggle Rock: Complete First Season*. HIT Entertainment, 2005. DVD.
"Fraggle Rock (France)." Muppet Wiki. Web. 12 Oct. 2011.
"Fraggle Rock (UK)." Muppet Wiki. Web. 12 Oct. 2011.
Greenberg, Joel. "A Peaceful Crew Puts Muppets Where Its Mouth Is." *New York Times*. 17 June 1997. Web. 9 Feb. 2012.
"Grosse Show für kleine Leute. " Muppet Wiki. Web. 24 Feb. 2012.
Henson, Cheryl, ed. *It's Not Easy Being Green and Other Things to Consider*. New York: Hyperion, 2005.
Henson, Jim. "Jim Henson's Red Book." Web. 7 July 2011.
_____. Notepad with early outline for "The Woozle Show." Reproduction included with *Fraggle Rock: Complete First Season*. HIT Entertainment, 2005. DVD.

_____. narr. *Down at Fraggle Rock*. Jim Henson Productions, 1987. DVD.
Horn, Danny. *MuppetFest Memories!: A Fanzine of the MuppetFest Convention*. Santa Monica, California 8–9 Dec. 2001. Danny Horn, 2001. 12–13. Print.
Juhl, Jerry and Jocelyn Stevenson. *Fraggle Rock* pitch book. Reproduction included with *Fraggle Rock: Complete Second Season*. HIT Entertainment, 2006. DVD.
Kleibeler, Julian. "DAS ist gut!" Muppet Wiki message wall. 23 March 2012.
"Love Actually" production notes. Biography of Duncan Kenworthy. 2002.
Quinn, Mike. "International Fraggle 'can-o'worms.'" 18 July 2005. Muppet Central. Web. 10 Jan. 2012.
"Traveling Matt." Interview feature. *Fraggle Rock: Complete Second Season*. HIT Entertainment, 2006. DVD.
"The World of Jim Henson." *Great Performances* Dir. Judy Kinberg. PBS/Thirteen WNET, 1994. VHS.

No Sex, Please. We're Fraggles!
Tami Meredith and Maryanne L. Fisher

Dear Nephew Gobo; Today, I saw something very odd in the world of the silly creatures. It seems that, unlike in the Rock, boys and girls are expected to act and dress differently. It is all quite bizarre and not very Fraggle-like. Love, your uncle, Traveling Matt.

In the world of *Fraggle Rock*,[1] The Rock, in which the Fraggles dwell, is sandwiched between the Gorgs' garden and Doc's workshop. On either side of the Rock, we find worlds that are comfortingly familiar, although displaying a few unique quirks. "Outer-space," where Doc has his workshop, is the world in which we humans live and can be seen as generally normal, apart from an excessively anthropomorphic sheepdog named Sprocket. On the other side live the Gorgs — a King, a Queen, and the Prince, Junior. Although hairy and gigantesque, standing 22 feet (6.7 meters) tall, the Gorgs appear to be a typical family, with a father/husband, mother/wife, and their son. Similarly to the humans of Outer-space, they obey typical sex and gender stereotypes and, from this viewpoint, are quite conventional.

What lies between Outer-space and the Gorgs' garden is the predominantly genderless world of the Fraggles, which is where the majority of the action and adventures occur. The Fraggles live in a society of individuals where social institutions such as employment, government, and families are almost non-existent. Consequently, this lack of structure creates a world without gender roles; a Fraggle can express her or his personality without conforming to societal gender expectations. Fraggles still have a biological sex and can be assigned to the binary classifications of female or male, but this assignment does not automatically permit viewers to accurately predict a Fraggle's behavior using traditional gender stereotypes. *Fraggle Rock* indirectly challenges social norms by omitting them, as the Fraggles demonstrate individual expression instead of social (gender) conformity. We begin by reviewing the terminology and concepts that we use before we examine the primary[2] Fraggles in detail, and then Fraggle society in general. We conclude by examining the various contrasts woven throughout *Fraggle Rock* that are used to emphasize individual and societal differences.

Before we start, it is useful to note that we focus on the two distinct concepts of sex and gender. A third concept, sexual orientation, is frequently associated with sex and gender because of the interaction and common agreement between the three concepts. For example, men's (physical) sex is male, their behavior (i.e., gender) is predominantly masculine, and in most cases they are heterosexual and attracted to women. Indeed, the dominant (and, according to surveyed individuals, ideal) form of masculinity is "hegemonic masculinity" whereby men are aggressive, unfeminine, unemotional, and heterosexual (e.g., Peralta 742–3). However, though it is gently suggested that Boober has a crush on Tosh Fraggle (S4.E77[3]), sexual orientation as exhibited by way of romance, sexual attraction, and reproduction is almost inconsequential within *Fraggle Rock*. As the show is classified as children's television, much like *Sesame Street* and unlike *The Muppet Show*, it is possible that sexual orientation was considered an inappropriate topic for the show's intended audience. It is also possible that these concepts were omitted to remove any associated gender expectations and correspondingly allow for the expression of behavior that is not gender typical. Therefore, because sexual orientation is mostly absent in the Fraggles, it will not be discussed in this essay.

An interested reader might wonder why we are making the distinction between sex and gender. In 1979, Rhoda Unger wrote a canonical article in which she suggested that the concept of biological sex be divorced from socially constructed traits, which she termed, "gender." Previously, scholars had noticed "gender" but not examined it as a distinct concept with clear boundaries to separate it from sex. The reason Unger stressed the distinction was because much of psychology seemed to rely on the assumption that any differences between men and women were biological and overlooked the influence of environmental and socio-cultural factors. Therefore, when we use the term "sex," we are referring to the binary of male and female that is biologically determined by our genetics. To simplify our analysis of *Fraggle Rock*, we use the conventional categories of "female" and "male" and ignore any genetic variations such as "intersex" as these variations are not exhibited in *Fraggle Rock*. Thus, "in various contexts, sex can be used to describe the chromosomal composition of individuals, the reproductive apparatus and secondary characteristics that are usually associated with these chromosomal differences, the intrapsychic characteristics presumed to be possessed by males and females, and in the case of sex roles, any and all behaviors differentially expected for and appropriate to people on the basis of membership in these various sexual categories" (Unger 1085–6).

With respect to sex, determining whether a Fraggle is a female or male rests on the secondary sexual characteristic (Federman 1507) of voice[4] and, in a few cases, the presence of facial hair. In fact, the sex of the Fraggles is almost solely determined by their voices, as portrayed by their puppeteers' voice. Male Fraggles are played by male puppeteers with male-sounding voices and female Fraggles by female puppeteers with female-sounding voices. This rule applies to all major roles and is violated for only a few minor roles, such as the Cave's Oldest Fraggle (S2.E41)[5] and the Storyteller, who are both female Fraggles played by male puppeteers. There is no significant character, unless one considers Marjorie the Trash Heap (voiced by Jerry Nelson) that is played by a puppeteer of the opposite sex, unlike *The Muppet Show* where Miss Piggy was played by Frank Oz. To complement the use of voice, a couple of the male Fraggles, specifically Uncle Traveling Matt, Cantus, and the World's Oldest Fraggle, display facial hair in the form of a moustache, beard, or both, respectively.

While, of course, one would never expect to see the primary sexual characteristics (e.g., sex organs) of a character in a children's television show, it is surprising that none of the Fraggles significantly differ in shape or display any sexual dimorphism or secondary characteristics other than their voices and facial hair. Females do not have any visible physical differences from males and do not have any features that can be considered as breasts or hips. Males are not taller than females and do not display higher muscle mass, which is seen in humans (Wells 420). In fact, the tallest of the primary Fraggles is Mokey, a female. As Fraggles are "made-up" creatures, it would have been possible for the creators to develop Fraggle-specific sexual characteristics, such as making all the females pink and the males blue. However, we are not able to identify any trends with regard to coloration, tail properties, hairstyle and length, or general appearance that could be used to identify a Fraggle's sex.

Despite the lack of cues to sexual identity, the show's writers clearly identify the sex of each Fraggle through the vocabulary that they use in the scripts. That is, when speaking to each other, Fraggles use sex-specific pronouns such as "her" or "she" when speaking of another Fraggle. In this way, we are informed of each Fraggle's sex. This cue is important because, while voice is generally sufficient to make a determination, the higher pitch ranges of Gobo and Wembley make it possible that they could be females. Another reason that the pronouns are significant is because the names of the Fraggles do not convey much in the way of sex identification. Gobo is the name of a male deer in the original *Bambi*,[6] a city in Japan, a commune in Cameroon, and an instrument used in stage lighting. Mokey is the name of a 1942 U.S. film.[7] Red is a common slang name for anyone with red hair, which she has, while Wembley is a location in the greater London borough of Brent. Boober is another slang term and is potentially a derivative of "boob," which refers to one who is a stupid or foolish person.[8] Thus, their names do not signal sexual identity as do more traditional names like William or Katherine. These names are androgynous, which is noteworthy because first names signal gender more strongly than any other feature cross-culturally (Lieberson, Dumais and Baumann 1249).

As indicated, one's sex is usually in alignment with one's gender. Given that she is often heralded as one of the first to make the distinction between sex and gender, we again return to Unger. She proposed that, "The term gender may be used to describe those nonphysiological components of sex that are culturally regarded as appropriate to males or to females. Gender [...] refers to a social label [...it] may be broadened to include both attributions made by others and assumptions and suppositions about one's own properties [gender identity]" (1086). Others have extended or clarified these ideas. For example, Anderson and Hysock (46) suggest that gender is learned via socialization and that people act using gender roles, which they then define as patterns of behavior that are performed based on cultural expectations. They argue that studying gender roles does not reduce the importance of individual differences, but that it is informative to notice similarities in the socialized development of girls to women and boys to men.

Given that gender is socially constructed and culturally directed, there are many very diverse perspectives regarding what is "feminine" and what is "masculine." That is, what is considered as highly feminine in some societies and cultures, such as wearing a dress or skirt, is not necessarily seen the same way in others. Despite this socio-cultural variation, for viewers of *Fraggle Rock* we can use traditional North American perspectives, such as those catalogued by Ricciardelli and Williams (644–45). They found that femininity was composed of positive traits such as patience, sensitivity, devotion, responsibility, and appreciation, and negative traits such as timidity, weakness, need for approval, dependence, and nervousness. In contrast, masculinity was composed of positive values such as strength, confidence, firmness, forcefulness, and feeling carefree, and negative values like aggressiveness, bossiness, sarcasm, rudeness, and feeling superior.

Gender is no longer considered to be a simple dichotomy composed of masculine or feminine as scholars, such as Sandra Bem, have demonstrated that each individual displays some amount of masculinity and some amount of femininity (Bem 155). Usually, genetic males are strongly masculine/weakly feminine, with genetic females showing the opposite and being strongly feminine/weakly masculine. For example, using Bem's measure, Hoffman and Fidell (765) examined "middle-class" women aged 20 to 59 and found 47 percent were "feminine" (scoring high on feminine items and low on masculine items), 24 percent were "androgynous" (scoring high on both), 19 percent were "undifferentiated" (low on both), and 10 percent "masculine" (low on feminine items, high on masculine items). Thus, considerable variation exists, and one can be strong on both the scale for femininity and the scale for masculinity or on neither. Consequently, gender does not always fully align with one's sex.

There are many cues about someone's gender, including for example their occupational aspirations (Lippa and Connelly 1051), personality, and coping strategies (Lengua and Stormshak 787). Despite the multiple cues for gender, when asked to define femininity and masculinity, the most cited attribute about individuals' gender is their physical appearance (Myers and Gonda 514). This finding is interesting because in *Fraggle Rock*, appearance is only marginally used to indicate a character's gender.

The primary female Fraggles, Mokey and Red, have some visibly feminine characteristics, though Red is more obviously feminine in appearance than Mokey. Mokey has mixed blue and green hair, purple skin, and wears a long-sleeved green robe-like garment that could vaguely be construed as a dress. Mokey's sleeves draw attention to her hands which is important because she is the only Fraggle that can be performed with live human hands to grasp and manipulate things. She has a necklace made from a "pop tab" that was used on carbonated beverages although she is sometimes seen with a pouch around her neck (S4.E80). Her eyes have strongly pronounced eyelids that are the same purplish color as her face. Red has pale orange skin and bright orange hair. She wears a red turtleneck sweater and is the only Fraggle to style her hair. Though she tends to wear her hair in dual pigtails secured with hot pink ribbons, she is sometimes seen with it down, such as when she goes to bed (e.g., S2.E34, S3.E49).

Gobo, Wembley, and Boober, the three primary male Fraggles, wear clothing that could be considered as somewhat masculine. Gobo, who was redesigned slightly after Season 1, has purple hair and deep orange skin. He wears a brown vest and a yellow shirt with red stripes. The colorful Wembley has orange hair, bright yellowish green skin, and a white tropical style shirt with a repeating picture of crossed green palm trees in front of an orange sun—his "Banana Tree Shirt" (as it is called in S4.E79). Wembley also has the most pronounced nose of the Fraggles because of the inclusion of a hard plastic ball and a different mouth design that permits his puppeteer (Steve Whitmire) to have greater hand motion and thus display greater facial expression. Wembley is also unique in that he can roll his eyes. Boober wears a brown knit cap and has bright red hair that obscures his eyes. He has pale blue skin, a chocolate brown scarf, and is naked, except that like all Fraggles, his body is covered in thick curly fur, which is blue on Boober.

While they provide some gender cues, each character's appearance is more likely designed to permit character identification through the provision of unique (visual) signature characteristics. We suggest that Red's pigtails, Boober's hat and concealed eyes, Wembley's shirt, Mokey's height and eyelids, and Gobo's striped shirt provide rapid and effective identification. For particularly young audience members, simple and clear identifying characteristics would have likely been an important design criteria. In some cases, these characteristics can assist with contemporary gender identification, such as Red's feminine pigtails. Other signature characteristics, such as Mokey's height, hinder gender determination, although it potentially signifies that she is older than the other Fraggles. Some characteristics, such as Gobo's shirt, are gender neutral and provide no gender assignment clues.

As mentioned, sex can often be inferred from one's gender, particularly based on stereotypes associated with femininity and masculinity. A gender stereotype is a belief about the psychological characteristics of women and men, as well as the activities that are appropriate for each gender to perform; it is a belief and attitude about femininity and masculinity (e.g., Smith 75). Gender stereotypes are not taught to us formally in a classroom environment and are something we acquire through incidental learning from the moment we are born, such as when we observe the differences in behavior exhibited by mothers and fathers. For some behaviors, such as the wearing of clothing, it is considered abnormal to violate gender expectations. The sight of a man in a dress is eye-catching and notable in contemporary North American society, despite converging gender norms (e.g., Marshall 5). However, when it comes to gender, there are no rules or stereotypes in the Rock. The Fraggles both violate and adhere to gender norms by essentially disregarding them.

To satisfy others' expectations as they apply to gender stereotypes, many people use gender schemas to decide how to behave or to select their careers or leisure activities, (Helgesen 169–9). In addition, we have gender roles, which are the expectations we have for others because of their sex (Helgesen 7). While gender roles have considerable consistency (Lueptow, Garovich, and Lueptow 509), many of which are grounded in sex differences in physical ability (strength), and the physical demands of reproduction (pregnancy, lactation), they are not rigid and unchanging. Since gender itself is socially constructed, gender roles are dynamic. As the creators and writers of *Fraggle Rock* perhaps knew, television possesses the power to change how we construct and understand gender in real life (Inness 162). That is, how a female Fraggle acts has the ability to alter our perceptions on gender and women's behavior. Seeing Red Fraggle lifting weights (S3.E58), for example, has the power to change our views on women's "allowable" exercise activities.

Mokey and Red are best friends and roommates but have distinct and often conflicting personalities. Mokey is the only Fraggle with a pet, an animated plant named Lanford who is a Night-Blooming Yellow-Leaved Deathwort. She is artistic (painting; S4.E78), caring (S3.E67), nurturing (caring for her sick plant; S3.E58), and tends to display many qualities that viewers would likely consider as feminine. Mokey knits (S3.E52), writes poetry (S1.E22), performs yoga (S4.E84), and is usually the one seeking a peaceful resolution to any conflict (e.g., S2.E41, S3.E71). When something needs to be made, it is often Mokey who offers to do it (e.g., a blanket for the Trash Heap, S3.E52; a hat for Boober, S1.E4 and S3.E63). Mokey also expresses an interest in fashion, such as when she becomes a minstrel, she voices her concern, "Oh! What am I going to wear? How can I be a minstrel without the right clothes?" (S2.E31).

While Mokey is described by Jim Henson as a "den-mother,"[9] she only weakly fulfills the role. When an egg is found and the tree-creature it contains is hatched and nurtured, it is "Mama Wembley" who performs the only clear demonstration of mothering within the series (S1.E25). In contrast, Mokey also acts like the "man-of-the-house" as her job among the Fraggles is to brave danger and collect radishes from the Gorg's garden. In part, much of Mokey's compassion stems from her assumption of additional responsibility, as she is older than the other primary Fraggles. Although Mokey is seen teaching Gobo to cook (S1.E17) early in the series, the domestic roles of cooking and cleaning are more consistently performed by Boober. One would expect a mother to be protective of her children, but when Boober and Red are trapped in a cave-in (S1.E17), she fails to contribute in a meaningful way to their rescue, letting Gobo assume command of the situation.

Meanwhile, in contrast, Red is a tom-boy who is interested in athletics (training Wembley, S2.E45) and competitions (splash-a-thon, S1.E23), and who seeks attention as well as leadership roles (challenging Gobo's leadership, S1.E14). She can be seen doing many different athletic activities, such as tug-a-tail (S2.E44), rock hockey (S3.E64), swimming (S1.E3, S2.E25), climbing (S3.E51), and "pushing granite" (weight-lifting, S2.E44, S3.E58). Though she advocates peace during the Fraggle Wars (S2.E41), Red displays one of the only occurrences of physical violence (S3E60). When scared by "beluvious testing," Red picks up Wembley by the collar, throws him to the floor, and then walks across him to indicate her displeasure and to suggest that he never do it again. Rather than use reason, empathy, or explanation, Red resorts to aggressive and physical masculine acts against Wembley. During this encounter, Mokey quakes slightly when Red picks up Wembley, perhaps to provide a clear indication that Red's action is shocking from her gentler, more compassionate, and more feminine perspective.

Thus, based on her behavior and the way it breaks many traditional notions of femininity, one would not know that Red is female apart from her pigtails and voice. It is possible that Red's hairstyle is an attempt to provide her with a recognizable element of femininity and make her more palatable to audiences. As suggested by Inness (56), one way to reduce the toughness of a female character is to soften her portrayal with images that are associated with femininity. We do not believe that Red was specifically singled out to violate gender stereotypes as an "athletic tomboy," as other characters also violate stereotypes, such as Boober's domesticity from his love of cooking and laundry.

Gobo is the natural leader of the primary Fraggles as suggested in S1.E14 and is the one to take charge when there is a crisis or problem (e.g., S1.E17, S1.E20). He is always going on adventures (e.g., S1.E23) and sometimes teaching others how to adventure (S3.E59). For the first three seasons, he regularly confronts fear and danger to visit Outer-space and collect Uncle Traveling Matt's postcard from the wastebasket in Doc's workshop. Gobo is the nephew of T. Matthew Fraggle, Uncle Traveling Matt, and the great-nephew of Matt's Uncle Gobo (S3.E62). Gobo is independent, often travelling alone (e.g., S2.E33), and is sometimes skeptical, needing evidence and proof instead of trusting in belief (S3.E70).

As the leader of the primary Fraggles, Gobo demonstrates strong compliance with the social system of our world, where most leadership roles are filled by males. The predominant leader of the Doozers, the Architect, is also male as is the King of the Gorgs. Apart from the one episode appearance of The Cave's Oldest Fraggle, where the Cave Fraggles have a female leader the other leadership roles are also filled by males (e.g., Cantus of the Minstrels, Archbanger Fraggle, Felix the Fearless, Mermer Merggle). When Red (S1.E14) or Mokey (S1.E12, S1.E22) assume leadership roles, neither performs very satisfactorily. When it comes to leadership, *Fraggle Rock* depicts it as an activity best performed by males. The fact that Red is as athletic, independent, and masculine as Gobo is overlooked, and she remains unable to fulfill leadership roles to the same level of success.

Wembley is indecisive (e.g., S1.E5), usually unsure of himself (e.g., S2.E14), and generally a very agreeable Fraggle (e.g., S1.E2). He is Gobo's best friend and roommate. He is nurturing and cares for a baby tree creature he found (S1.E25) and always tries to be helpful (e.g., S1.E13). Wembley is allergic to lint (S4.E76), rock dust (S4.E86), and bonk berries (S4.E73) but is generally healthy otherwise and can defeat Gobo in athletic competitions if he puts his mind to doing so (S2.E45). Wembley is one of the more emotional characters, and in support of this role, he has a more complex facial construction that permits a greater range of expression as well as eyes that can roll. Again we see a violation of typical gender stereotypes because women generally display emotion more than men.

Compared to the others, Boober is more of a solitary Fraggle. He lives on his own, due to his love of peace and quiet, as seen when he moves to The Caves of Boredom (S2.E26). Boober is afraid of germs and of being sick (e.g., S3.E53) and, consequently, has a considerable knowledge of Fraggle medicine (e.g., "Dr. Boober Fraggle," S4.E73). Boober's true love in life is doing laundry; for instance, in S1.E24 he risks being caught by the Gorgs to get advice from the Trash Heap on how to remove grass stains. Boober also enjoys cooking and can be seen preparing food in many episodes (e.g., soup in E3.S52). What is perhaps the most interesting aspect of Boober is his alternate personality, SideBottom (who is kept inside and on the bottom, S2.E30). SideBottom is Boober's fun-loving side, which he keeps buried away until SideBottom is let out to play (S2.E30, S2.E47, S4.E73). Boober is a remarkably complex and well-developed character with a very quick wit and a sarcastic sense of humor (e.g. "Let's do lunch," when dismissing Gobo, S4.E86).

The five primary characters are thus composed of the adventurous Gobo, the artistic Mokey, the athletic Red, the agreeable and indecisive Wembley, and the neurotic, solitary Boober. We can gain additional insight into their natures from Wembley's descriptions of them to the Gorgs, "Gobo knows all the crannies in all the caves in Fraggle Rock. Red knows games. Mokey knows songs, and Boober knows special stuff that means a lot to him." With regard to the gender stereotypes of the era, we consider Gobo as predominantly masculine, Mokey as predominantly feminine, and Red as a masculine "tomboy." Wembley and Boober are somewhat effeminate males and seem more gender ambiguous than the other three primary Fraggles.

Using the adjectives of the Bem Sex Role Inventory (Bem 156), the Fraggles as a group are best described using the gender-neutral terms of happy, likable, friendly, and helpful. Specific masculine terms are best applied to Red and Gobo (independent, athletic, assertive), while Mokey and Wembley are best described using the feminine terms (sympathetic, sensitive to other's needs, compassionate, eager to soothe hurt feelings). Boober is more masculine in his independence and self-reliance. Boober and Wembley are in some ways opposite since Boober has a masculine personality but engages in feminine roles (cooking, cleaning), while Wembley has a more feminine personality but engages in masculine roles (adventuring with Gobo).

It is possible that Wembley and Boober need to maintain a modest amount of masculinity in order to avoid being considered as homosexual. In the mid 1980s, though a growing acceptance of homosexuality was present, it was still a way of life that was generally not considered acceptable. Alternatively, and in our opinion more likely, the lesson that is being taught is that males can do feminine things but not lose their masculinity. That is, according to gender ideologies as presented by Hochschild (15), the message is one of egalitarianism, where females and males can have equal power and influence in the spheres of work and home, in contrast to traditionalism, where the female's sphere is the home and the male's sphere is the workplace. The feminine activities of Boober can be considered as more controversial than the masculine activities of Red, as there may be more tolerance of women's violation of gender norms than of men's. For example, when a woman behaves assertively, someone might view it positively because she is standing up for herself, but when a man behaves compassionately, it is potentially seen as weak and un-masculine.

Figure X.1: Fraggle Sex and Gender Displays

Fraggle	*Sex*	*Gender (Personality)*	*Roles/Tasks*
Gobo	Male	Male	Male
Mokey	Female	Female	Female
Red	Female	Male	Male
Wembley	Male	Female	Male
Boober	Male	Male	Female

As Figure X.1 shows, a wide range of gender contrasts exists within *Fraggle Rock*. Gobo and Mokey are examples of a stereotypical male and female and thus provide contrast between men and women. Red and Wembley have gendered personalities that are opposite to their sex, thus showing how males or females can vary and contrast. This group of four Fraggles covers all possible combinations of sex and gender. To add further depth, gender roles and activities, such as cooking, playing sports, adventuring, are uniquely distributed and do not align with either sex or gender. Based on the diversity and breadth of the Fraggles, we believe that the Fraggles are intentionally designed to not fit any specific gender stereotypes and instead are meant to violate and explore those stereotypes. While Mokey and Gobo tend to be fairly conventional, they do so as children in a world where gender is less important because everyone plays, sings, and dances similarly.

While Fraggle society has a somewhat unorthodox 30-minute-per-week work component on a job that can provide dubious social benefit, the male dominance of the sphere is conspicuously absent. Perhaps the most important job, collecting radishes for food, is performed by Mokey, a female. One could argue that she is merely performing the traditional female role of gathering, as seen in hunter-gatherer societies, but since Fraggle society has no hunting component, the analogy is very superficial. Since Boober's job of doing the Fraggle's laundry is very domestic in nature, and traditionally performed by women, we see further erosion of the traditional male-female occupational divide. It is interesting to note that Fraggle jobs do not need to be particularly useful, as Wembley's job is to be "the siren" for the Fraggle Fire Department. The complete lack of utility associated with their jobs is reinforced by humorous elements such as nobody in the Fire Department knowing how to light a fire or Boober's love of watching socks dry even though Fraggles do not wear socks.

We note that for specific episodes a Fraggle can seem out-of-character compared to how he or she typically acts. This change may be a plot device to elevate the importance of a character for the episode. It may also be that in these episodes viewers obtain a more empathic understanding of a character by seeing things from that Fraggle's perspective. For example, Mokey seems more independent, assertive, and leader-like in the episodes in which she is the central character (e.g., S1.E22, "Mokey's Funeral"; S3.E67, "The Incredible Shrinking Mokey").

Let us now consider the gendered behavior of a single episode in more depth. Episode 52, aired in Season 3, "Blanket of Snow, Blanket of Woe," is centered on the actions and failings of Mokey. The episode begins with Mokey knitting; a feminine activity being performed by a female Fraggle. However, Mokey quickly begins to get in trouble when Red gets hurt playing hockey because Mokey has not fixed her skates as she had said she would. Playing hockey is more masculine than knitting, as is the task of doing skate/shoe repair. Thus, we have two women involved in masculine roles. We discover that Mokey has let everyone down by forgetting to satisfy her promises, such as forgetting to obtain radishes (food provision, a masculine activity) for Boober to cook soup, a feminine activity. Thus, by the time the setting for the episode is established, we have already seen as many displays of gender inappropriate behavior as we have of gender compliant behavior.

The central issue within the episode is the thawing of the frozen Trash Heap. Although all five primary Fraggles are present when Traveling Matt's postcard is read for inspiration, it is Mokey that comes up with the idea of thawing the Trash Heap with Boober's soup. We normally would expect Boober to suggest this action since, by this point in the series, it is Boober that is predominantly focused on cooking and feeding the Fraggles. When the soup is not sufficient in quantity, it is also Mokey that smells the soup of the Gorgs and comes up with the idea of using the Gorg soup. To carry out her idea, Mokey, with Gobo as her companion, comes up with the plan to get the Gorgs to throw away their soup onto the Trash Heap. Here we see Mokey "stealing" Gobo's leadership and inventiveness and becoming more decisive, action-oriented, and masculine than in other episodes. Mokey is not being motherly and protective but is rather assuming responsibility for her failings and rectifying the problems she has caused. The episode thus casts Mokey in both a feminine and a masculine light and illustrates that gender roles are very malleable within *Fraggle Rock*.

We further note that although we talked about their individual differences, there are some characteristics that all Fraggles have in common. Fraggles tend to be very helpful and come to each other's aid when needed (e.g., Mokey, Boober, Wembley, and Red trying to rescue Gobo, S1.E10). For the most part and as indicated by the lyrics of the title song, Fraggles love dancing ("Dance your cares away"), singing ("Let the music play"), and having fun ("Worry's for another day"). As indicated by the title of Episode S2.E32, "All Work and All Play," Fraggles are viewed by the Doozers, who work all the time, as doing nothing but playing all the time. Parties occur whenever a Fraggle wishes one, such as when Red celebrated her "birthday" 28 times since the Festival of the Bell to establish a new record (S4.E84). Fraggles tend to pursue goals that are enjoyable, such as solving the Riddle of Rhyming Rock (S4.E85) or building a boat (S1.E22). It is these shared characteristics that are the basis of Fraggle society where work, government, taxation, and other responsibilities are almost never seen. We propose that it is this "life of leisure" and the corresponding lack of Fraggle social institutions that creates a world free of strong gender stereotypes.

The closest thing to a leader of the Fraggles is The World's Oldest Fraggle, but his role is primarily ceremonial, as he has no real power. For example, he is the one who declares when it is "Ruler of the Rock Day" which is when the Finger-of-Light will select the Fraggle who is a temporary ruler and thus may issue three orders to the Fraggles. Mokey is selected in S1.E12. As explained by Mokey when she goes back in time and speaks to the Fraggles of the past, "We [...] have no great and wondrous leaders. We each lead ourselves, and we all lead each other" (S4.E91). Wembley repeats the latter phrase verbatim when he explains to Junior Gorg why the Fraggles have no King (S4.E94).

When Red believes her radish bars have been stolen (S3.E49), the Eminent and Venerable Council of Sages are called upon to act as judges. To settle disputes, the Fraggles go to the "Hall of Justice," as we see Boober do when Red gets paint all over his lucky blanket (S1.E15). When Red makes false accusations regarding the theft of the Fraggle Horn, it is the World's Oldest Fraggle who issues the punishment of, "No radish bars for a week" and then "Walk backwards carrying a heavy rock" (S4.E93). Apart from minor incidents like these, one would be hard-pressed to find anything else within the series that could be construed as being an element of the Fraggle Government.

When an "army" is formed in the conflict against the Cave Fraggles (S2.E41), it is primarily a volunteer organization formed to deal with a single crisis and not a formal, permanent organization. A rescue squad, with a bumbling leader named Felix the Fearless, is called upon in episode S1.E17, and to ensure water flows into the Fraggle pond, "The Pipe Bangers" exist to stimulate water flow by banging, obviously without any actual effect, on the water supply pipes (S1.E3). Almost uniformly, these groups are seen in but a single episode and exist because the plot calls for some sort of organizational presence. However, once used for plot advancement, and often in a non-serious and humorous manner, the organizations disappear and are never seen again. We thus have a society that lacks any organized government, criminal justice system, or military presence.

In Outer-space, where we as viewers exist, the social institution of marriage is used to create and continue families. We expect there to be a romantic relationship between a couple who is to be married. However, except for a few rare instances, families, marriage, and romance are lacking from the lives of the Fraggles. Traveling Matt is Gobo's Uncle, and this one relationship apart from Matt's own Uncle Gobo is the only reference to an ancestor or genetic relation. There are no notable references to mothers, fathers, children, cousins, or other family ties. The Storyteller, a female Fraggle, is obviously infatuated with Matt, as can be seen in her vision of him shirtless and posed in a Fabio-like manner (S3.E62). Mokey displays a detailed knowledge and understanding of romance when Wembley befriends Louise Fraggle, "Our little Wembley is in love" (S1.E13). SideBottom comments on Mokey's appearance, "Mokey, you look ravishing!" in a manner that is mildly flirtatious. Boober also acts as if he has a romantic interest in Tosh Fraggle in Episode S4.E77. Curiously, the most physical romantic acts to be performed by the Fraggles are all kisses between Boober and Wembley. The first act of kissing is when Boober kisses Wembley's neck, shoulders and arms when the former is under the effect of a love potion (S1.E13) and the second occurrence is when Boober chastely kisses Wembley's forehead in a rather parental manner

(S3.E60). It is highly unlikely that these kisses are intended to have any homosexual connotations and are meant only to provide an element of physical comedy. These few examples detail the majority of the Fraggles' familial and romantic activities, and, thus, illustrate how inconsequential they are within the series.

As much of our gendered behavior is associated with sex differences resulting from differing reproductive roles, it is not surprising that Fraggles lack strong gender stereotypes. Female Fraggles do not become pregnant or engage in child-care and, consequently, are not subject to all the limitations and requirements of these activities, as are women in Outer-space. Furthermore, without sexual dimorphism, there is no reason to expect any differences in the physical abilities between female and male Fraggles. Male Fraggles are not visibly larger or stronger than the females, so there are no differing gender roles based on physical ability. For example, Red's strength is demonstrated when she pulls both Gobo and Wembley out of a hole with a rope (S4.E72), and she regularly competes against Gobo in physical competitions such as rock climbing (S3.E51).

The fact that all Fraggles uniformly live a life of play, with no demonstrated sex differences in parental responsibilities, helps to create a more gender neutral society. While one could argue that the producers missed a valuable opportunity to promote more tolerance of gender and sexual difference, what we suggest is that by completely reducing the importance of gender and sex, a world was created in which there is the potential for complete equality between females and males. *Fraggle Rock* shows us a world where one's actions are not influenced by societal gender expectations. Within psychology, one's behavior is considered as a balance between genetically influenced sex differences as examined by evolutionary psychologists and between individual differences as examined by social and personality psychologists. Within *Fraggle Rock*, there are almost no sex differences, and hence there is not a strong concept of gender, thus causing Fraggle behavior to be almost totally controlled by individual and personality differences.

Now that we have examined the Fraggles and their society, let us briefly examine the other races that are an integral part of the series. We do not review Outer-space because it is our own world, albeit one that is humorously presented via postcards from Uncle Traveling Matt and the workshop of Doc and his dog Sprocket. While there are episodes devoted primarily towards the Doozers and the Gorgs, we do not consider them to be as important as the Fraggles because there are far fewer episodes centered around their societies. These supplementary groups exist to provide contrasts to the Fraggles, such as seen in the work versus play mentalities of Doozers and Fraggles (e.g.,

S2.E32). Interaction with the Gorgs and Doozers also provides a rich set of relationships (e.g., S1.E3, S1.E19) that enable the activities of the Fraggles to be influenced by, and to influence, others. As explained by the various production staff in the four DVDs of bonus features, *Fraggle Rock* was a series intended to help stop war by teaching children to understand the relationships between various societies. The Gorgs and Doozers are needed to provide the Fraggles with other societies in which their relationships can be used as an educational tool.

Doozers have a more structured society, but like the Fraggles, females and males have equal opportunities. Families exist, as do children, occupations, and other roles, but both female and male Doozers are equally likely to be found as workers on construction teams or as architects, who serve as construction supervisors and are the de facto leaders. The primary role of a Doozer is to build, even though the building is unnecessary and serves no purpose. It is performed in the hope that the construction will be destroyed (i.e., eaten by a Fraggle) to make space for more building. When the Fraggles cease to eat and destroy the Doozer constructions, the Doozers prepare to leave the Rock when they run out of building space (S1.E6).

As Doozers have jobs and families, viewers will likely consider their society to be more familiar than Fraggle society because of its similarities. However, the unifying social desire to build seems to replace gender roles with employment-based ones. As the rebellion of Cotterpin Doozer (S2.E32) and her refusal to "take the helmet" demonstrates, Doozers identify more strongly with being a worker than with being female or male. Both female and male Doozers can participate on construction teams, be architects, or select new flavors for construction materials, such as mustard by the female Doozer Modem or tomato by the male Doozer Flange (S2.E36). Their society thus seems more familiar but in reality displays a level of sexual equality that is far different from our own.

Shifting to the world outside the Rock, the focus is on two settings: Outer-space and the Gorg's garden. When they need to seek advice from their oracle, the Trash Heap, or they need to collect radishes to eat, the Fraggles venture forth into the land known as the Gorg's Garden. Gorgs, though unique to *Fraggle Rock*, are somewhat similar to the Muppet character Sweetums in their appearance and demeanor. However, as aptly put by the Gorg Queen, "Gorgs hate Fraggles" (S2.E34).

As the following examples demonstrate, the Gorgs are very traditional in gender ideology. The female fully adheres to the role of being a mother, and even uses lines such as, "I must do something about these tears, I'm a mother" when she hears the caged Gobo crying (S2.E34). She screams quite dramatically when shown a Fraggle, much like women are popularly portrayed in their reaction to mice (S3.E65), cooks (e.g., S3.E52, S4.E83), cleans (S3.E55), sews (S2.E26), diets (S2.E26), and has a romantic interest in her husband (S4.E88). The male Gorg is very chauvinistic and expects his wife to cook and clean their home, as well as forbidding her to do masculine tasks such as using tools to make repairs. In Episode S3.E56, he makes his beliefs clear, "What? Fix it yourself? A Queen fixing a roof, climbing ladders, using tools? No, no, no, nooooo! Your place, my dear, is in the kitchen baking things, not fixing leaks." He hides his fears, such as of heights (S3.E63), displays interest in historical and military matters (S2.E33), uses weapons (e.g., carries a sword, S4.E92; builds a bomb, S4.E94), and has a romantic interest in his wife (S4.E88). When all of these features are considered, they are very similar, in gender ideology terms, to a conservative human couple. Their son, Junior, displays an interest in one day marrying a Princess (S2.E40) and uses his father as a role model. He assists his father with repairs (S3.E63), gardens (S3.E61), performs chores (S2.E27), and is generally a hard working teenage son. He tends to be respectful of his parents, but he is independent and rebels slightly at times, such as making garlic popcorn against his mother's wishes (S3.E68) or disregarding his father's orders to exterminate the Fraggles, with whom he enjoys playing (S3.E65). He has a sense of morality, such as can be seen when to honor tradition and determine his greatness as a ruler, he risks banishment and attempts to play the Royal Kazoo (S4.E75).

There are clear but tasteful displays of heterosexual attraction between the King and Queen of the Gorgs (e.g., S3.E68). It is obvious that they love each other, such as through the use of pet names such as "Duckykins" (e.g., S4.E83), and that they engaged once in a reproductive activity, as the presence of their son indicates. In Episode S4.E92 they renew their wedding vows, as required every 513 years, with a wedding ceremony that includes a ring, cake, and afterwards, a honeymoon. They sometimes use the terms "husband" and "wife," providing additional evidence that they adhere to the social convention of marriage. The Gorgs can be seen as providing a way to express human behavior and social conventions without using humans. This simple change may allow viewers to examine Gorg behavior more objectively because they are a different species, and in turn, see parallels with human behavior.

The characters, societies, and places we have just described are generally consistent throughout the series. Although a few new places are found, such as the land of the Merggles (S4.E89) or the T. Matthew Fraggle Room (S3.E74), they are few and far between. We know that the Gorg's Garden was not always accessible to the Fraggles and was discovered after Traveling Matt caused a cave-in as a youth (S3.E62). As well as new places being found, other changes occur across the four-year duration of *Fraggle Rock*. Food preparation, which is traditionally viewed as a feminine task, is originally performed by the female Fraggles: Red (S1.E17), and Mokey (S1.E24, soup). In Season 2, Boober makes a soufflé (S2.E25) and performs most of the food preparation for the remainder of the series (e.g., S2.E43, radish gumbo; S3.E52, soup; S3.E65, radish dip; S4.E90, peach and pepper potage; S4.E92, radish ratatouille). Other changes include Mokey and Red moving in together in Season 2 (Episode 44) and Gobo beginning to wear his vest in Season 2 (Episode 25). Relations between the Doozers and the Fraggles begin to develop in Season 2 (S2.E32), mostly involving the Architect's apprentice, Cotterpin Doozer (e.g., S2.E37, S3.E66). As the series concludes, Junior Gorg becomes the King (S4.E94), but as his first royal decree, he abolishes the kingship. Doc finally sees Gobo in the penultimate episode (S4.E95), after which Sprocket and he move to the desert only to find that a new Fraggle tunnel has come into existence with an exit into his new home (S4.E96).

For specific episodes, temporary changes can occur, such as Boober believing he is a Gorg (S4.E83) or Mokey shrinking in size (S4.E67). Within Episode S2.E27, "The Trash Heap Doesn't Live Here Anymore," a significant level of sex fluidity is demonstrated when Marjorie the Trash Heap is moved to a new location. This move causes her to spontaneously become male, with a male voice, and to be addressed using the male-oriented salutation, "Sir." A second sex-change occurs when the trash-heap is moved back to her original location. In the same episode, Wembley is referred to by the male trash heap, as "Fragglette," and Uncle Traveling Matt's postcard is about "odd little rooms that transform people" (actually he sees an elevator). He observes "two of the male creatures walk into this room. The doors closed, and a moment later when they opened again they had turned to ladies." The theme of the episode is that of change, but it is unclear as to whether such changes are perceived as more shocking and memorable by the audience, or whether there is a subtle message that viewers should learn that sex and gender are more fluid than we sometimes believe.

We propose that the use of gender contrasts is a common theme of Jim Henson. For example, in *Kermit Culture* Fisher and Cox discuss how Miss Piggy of *The Muppet Show* provides a rich set of contrasting masculine and feminine attributes. Within *Fraggle Rock*, gender contrasts exist on both a social level between the Fraggles and the Gorgs and on an individual level, such as between Gobo and Wembley, or Red and Mokey. The fifth main character, Boober, exhibits a duality of personality, as evidenced by his second persona of SideBottom (S2.E30, S2.E47, and S4.E73). We do not see strong gender contrasts between Boober and SideBottom as the two differ more in personality, but some difference exists as Boober displays some feminine attributes (e.g., risk-aversion) and SideBottom displays some masculine ones (e.g., risk-taking).

The reason that these issues matter is because what we see on television influences our attitudes and beliefs. There have been many studies on how media shapes us, and how it depicts gender and sex. For example, in a review of 83 "notable children's books" that were considered outstanding by the American Library Association, female characters were more likely to be shown interacting with children and performing domestic activities, while male characters were shown in more diverse roles (Gooden and Gooden 89). In coloring books, almost half (44 percent) of the male characters were shown in traditionally masculine activities, such as driving a racing car, while over half (58 percent) of female characters were depicted in traditionally feminine activities, such as cooking or childcare (Fitzpatrick and McPherson 132). Television advertising directed at children reinforces these gender stereotypes, as boys are often shown as active and dominant, while girls are shy, passive and giggling (Browne 94). Media, in particular television, has the power to change how we understand and construct gender in our daily life (Inness 162).

Red and Mokey, although both are female, exhibit many differences. These differences are intentional, since Gobo comments, when Red and Mokey decide to become roommates in Episode S2.E44, "Why, you two are so different, why, you couldn't even agree which cave to live in." Red's often masculine behavior (competitiveness, athleticism) matches, and possibly further encourages, women's increased endorsement of masculine-stereotyped traits (Twenge 305), while Mokey's stereotypical feminine behavior provides a contrasting view of womanhood for the girls who watched the show.

Gobo and Wembley, like Mokey and Red, are also best friends and roommates. They also exhibit differences, but the nature of those differences seems to lie more within what viewers would consider masculine behavior. Gobo is decisive where Wembley is indecisive to the extent that "wembling" is a Fraggle verb for being indecisive (S2.E38). Gobo is a natural leader, whereas Wembley gets overwhelmed when he is submissive and agrees to assist each of the other Fraggles in a different task (S1.E13). Though he lacks many of the strongly masculine characteristics of Gobo, and he does display some feminine characteristics, such as hatching an egg and nurturing a baby tree-creature (S2.E25), his behavior is more androgynous than feminine. As suggested by Jean Twenge, changes over time have resulted in "women's increased endorsement of masculine-stereotyped traits and men's continued nonendorsement of feminine-stereotyped traits" (305). Thus, to appeal to male viewers, it is likely that Wembley must maintain elements of masculinity, such as assisting

Gobo to confront the Beast of Bluerock (S1.E23) or beating Gobo in the Great Race (S2.E45).

Community level contrasts exist between the Fraggles and the Doozers, as shown in the episode "All Work and All Play" (S2.E32) where Cotterpin Doozer rejects the work-oriented Doozer lifestyle to pursue a play-oriented Fraggle one. Doozers are similar to Fraggles in that they show a high level of sexual equality, but they differ in that they have clear family units with mothers, fathers, and babies. It is curious that in his original notes, before the name of "Fraggle" was selected and they were called "Woozles" that Jim Henson anticipated the show to be about a family of Woozles. As described in his original notes, "We concentrate on one particular family of Ma and Pa Woozle, a couple of kid Woozles, one of which is probably our main character. Then there's Grandma Woozle and a few baby Woozles that are ever so cute and adorable." Somehow, it seems that a few of these ideas are realized by the Doozers while the Fraggles became a cohort of five friends living and playing within a society that lacks almost any significant social institutions.

The world of the Fraggles exhibits utopian qualities in that Fraggles can simply express themselves freely and without any required compliance to socially constructed gender roles. Females can be competitive athletes as easily as they can be poets and artists, while males can cook and clean without fear of being classified as overly feminine. Fraggles are not constrained by the social institutions of family and employment, thus allowing them to live more spontaneously and to do the things that they enjoy. Although we cannot free ourselves from our gender roles to the same extent as do the Fraggles, the series through its depiction of happy, fun-loving Fraggles shows us that a world where one is less concerned with gender image is not necessarily a bad place. Women can explore caves, and men can enjoy watching their socks dry if that is what their hearts desire. In a Rock without gender, where life is all play, we see that love, friendship, and happiness are a product of being true to ourselves and our values.

Notes

1. There were 96 episodes of *Fraggle Rock* that aired over a four-year span from 1983 to 1987. Although there were several international production variants (e.g., France, Germany) with alternative characters, all references in this essay will be with respect to the North American release that was predominantly filmed in Toronto, Canada. This release starred the inventor Doc played by Gerard Parkes and his sheepdog, Sprocket, played by puppeteer Steve Whitmire. In part, this limitation is to permit us to interpret gender with respect to the audience for which it was primarily intended and of which both authors, as Canadians, are intimately familiar.

2. The *primary Fraggles* are those that are in almost every episode and consist of Gobo, Wembley, Mokey, Boober, and Red. Though he is in almost all episodes, prior to Season

4 Uncle Traveling Matt's contribution was to provide amusing anecdotes rather than advance the plot, and thus we do not consider him a primary Fraggle.

3. We will reference a specific episode using the notation S4.E77 to refer, for example, to the 77th episode (of the 96 total) that was produced and aired as part of Season 4. Episode numbers are taken from the 20 DVD *Complete Series Collection* distributed by Maple Pictures.

4. The deepening of the male voice at puberty is a secondary characteristic, but variation in male and female voices is also a consequence of men having larger voice boxes and is not fully due to hormonal effects.

5. The Cave's Oldest Fraggle appears in one episode only as the spokes-Fraggle of a rival group of Fraggles, cave Fraggles, and should not be confused with the recurring character of the World's Oldest Fraggle.

6. Salten, Felix. *Bambi: A Life in the Woods*. 1946, Grosset — English. Originally in German, 1926, *Bambi: eine Lebensgeschichte aus dem Walde*.

7. Mokey, 1942. Metro-Goldwyn-Mayer. Wells Root, Director. Black & White. http://www.imdb.com/title/tt0035074.

8. While more modern meanings of "boob" can be used, we base our derivation from personal experience. A comprehensive listing of definitions can be found at http://www.urbandictionary.com/define.php?term=boob.

9. Behind the Scenes, Bonus feature found on Disk 5, Season 1, 20 DVD *Fraggle Rock Complete Series Collection* distributed by Maple Pictures.

WORKS CITED

Andersen, Margaret, and Dana Hysock. *Thinking about Women: Sociological Perspectives on Sex and Gender* (8th edition). New York: Pearson, 2009. Print.

Bem, Sandra. "The Measurement of Psychological Androgyny." *Journal of Consulting and Clinical Psychology* 42 (1974): 155–62. Print.

Browne, Beverly. "Gender Stereotypes in Advertising on Children's Television in the 1990s: A Cross-National Analysis." *Journal of Advertising* 27 (1998): 83–96. Print.

Federman, Daniel. "The Biology of Human Sex Differences." *New England Journal of Medicine* 354 (2006): 1507–14. Print.

Fisher, Maryanne, and Anthony Cox. "The Uniquely Strong but Feminine Miss Piggy." *Kermit Culture: Critical Perspectives on Jim Henson's Muppets*. Eds. Jennifer Garlen and Anissa Graham. Jefferson, NC: McFarland, 2009. Print.

Fitzpatrick, Maureen, and Barbara McPherson. "Coloring within the Lines: Gender Stereotypes in Contemporary Coloring Books." *Sex Roles* 62 (2010): 127–37. Print.

Gooden, Angela, and Mark Gooden. "Gender Representation in Notable Children's Picture Books: 1995–1999." *Sex Roles* 45 (2001): 89–101. Print.

Helgesen, Vicki. *The Psychology of Gender* (4th edition). New York: Pearson. 2012. Print.

Henson, Jim. "The Woozle World." Notebook replica included in *Jim Henson's Fraggle Rock: Complete First Season*, HIT Entertainment, 2005. DVD.

Hochschild, Arlie. *The Second Shift*. New York: Avon Books, 1989. Print.

Hoffman, Donnie, and Linda Fidell. "Characteristics of Androgynous, Undifferentiated, Masculine and Feminine Middle-Class Women." *Sex Roles* 5 (1979): 765–781. Print.

Inness, Sherrie. *Tough Girls: Women Warriors and Wonder Women in Popular Culture*. Philadelphia, PA: University of Pennsylvania Press, 1999. Print.

Lengua, Liliana, and Elizabeth Stormshak. "Gender, Gender roles, and Personality: Gender Differences in the Prediction of Coping and Psychological Symptoms." *Sex Roles* 43 (2000), 787–820. Print.

Lieberson, Stanley, Susan Dumais and Shyon Baumann. "The Instability of Androgynous Names: The Symbolic Maintenance of Gender Boundaries." *American Journal of Sociology* 105 (2000): 1249–87. Print.

Lippa, Richard and Sharon Connelly. "Gender Diagnosticity: A New Bayesian Approach to Gender-Related Individual Differences." *Journal of Personality and Social Psychology* 59 (1990): 1051–1065. Print.

Lueptow, Lloyd, Lori Garovich, and Margaret Leuptow. "The Persistence of Gender Stereotypes in the Face of Changing Sex Roles: Evidence Contrary to the Sociocultural Model." *Ethology and Sociobiology* 16 (1995): 509–30. Print.

Marshall, Katherine. "Converging Gender Roles." *Perspectives*, Statistics Canada, July 2006. Web. 1 Sept. 2011.

Myers, Anita, and Gail Gonda. "Utility of the Masculinity-Femininity Construct: Comparison of Traditional and Androgyny Approaches." *Journal of Personality and Social Psychology* 43 (1982): 514–23. Print.

Peralta, Robert. "College Alcohol Use and the Embodiment of Hegemonic Masculinity among European American Men." *Sex Roles* 56 (2007): 741–56. Print.

Ricciardelli, Lina, and Robert Williams. "Desirable and Undesirable Gender Traits in Three Behavioral Domains." *Sex Roles* 33 (1995): 637–55. Print.

Smith, Barbara. *The Psychology of Sex and Gender*. New York: Allyn & Bacon, 2007. Print.

Terman, Lewis, and Catherine Cox-Miles. *Sex and Personality: Studies in Masculinity and Femininity*. New York: McGraw Hill. 1936. Print.

Twenge, Jean. "Changes in Masculine and Feminine Traits over Time: A Meta-Analysis." *Sex Roles* 36 (1997): 305–25. Print.

Unger, Rhoda. "Towards a Redefinition of Sex and Gender." *American Psychologist* 34 (1979): 1085–94. Print.

Wells, Jonathan. "Sexual Dimorphism of Body Composition." *Best Practice & Research in Clinical Endocrinology & Metabolism* 21 (2007): 415–430. Print.

The Ecology of Fraggle Rock
Justin Werfel

The documentary series *Fraggle Rock* gives us a rare window into an exotic underground ecosystem. We're granted glimpses of rich networks of interacting species and their life cycles, but only glimpses; the environment is nearly inaccessible and no field biologist has yet made it the subject of his or her studies. Drawing rigorous conclusions about these organisms and their interactions is therefore difficult, due to the lack of opportunity for direct studies. Nevertheless, a number of inferences are possible based on the observations that are available to us.

In this essay, I explore several issues regarding the ecology of the Rock environment, compare it to other natural communities, and highlight ways in which the Rock is rare or unique among cave ecosystems.[1] Numbers in parentheses below refer to episode numbers of the eponymous documentary series, based on the Lionsgate/HIT Entertainment series release of 2008.

Key Species and Their Behavior (or: Doozer Is as Doozer Does)

Dozens of species populate the tunnels of Fraggle Rock. This diversity is rare among caves; only 36 known caves worldwide have as many as 20 distinct species, and only 6 caves have 40 or more (Culver and Pipan 168). Despite this richness, only two underground species have received more than passing attention.

The first, of course, are the Fraggles for which the Rock is named. While they live primarily underground, they are not obligate cave-dwellers ("troglobionts"). Rather, like bats, they leave the cave to forage. Their foraging is communal rather than individual, with a limited subset of animals recovering food for the population. Some individuals as a result may be enabled to spend their entire lives underground, yet all retain the adaptations that allow them to function on the surface; the specialization is behavioral rather than morphological. Foragers recover vegetable matter to feed the colony, as well as collecting other items with no obvious direct purpose, as animals like packrats and magpies do. These items have been observed to include examples such as postcards, radios (39), bottles (57), colorful rocks (77), and various processed foods that they evidently do not recognize as edible (96).

The second species are the Doozers, whose characteristic behavioral trait is their construction activity. This habit of collecting material from the environment and using it to build structures that transform their living conditions is one that they share with animals from multiple phyla. Many animals (e.g., most nesting birds) that build do so as a solitary endeavor, or one shared with a mate; Doozers are part of a more exclusive class of social builders, where each member of a larger group contributes to building a communal structure and shares in the benefits. A well-known example of such builders among the mammals is the beaver, which constructs lodges to live in and transforms landscapes with the dams it builds; typical group size for a colony of beavers is on the order of ten. At the other extreme of group size among builders are certain social insects; social wasps can live thousands of individuals to a nest, honeybee colonies typically include tens of thousands of workers in the hive, and mound-building termites can have millions of individuals contributing to construction, foraging, and maintenance. In between are animals like the sociable weaver birds, whose communal nests may house dozens to a few hundreds of individuals. Doozers are probably closest to these last in terms of community size, with at least several dozen distinct individuals identified (though no careful census has yet been taken).

Other species are less thoroughly characterized but are notable here for certain behavioral traits that make them unique. Ditzies (42), for instance, produce light. While bioluminescence is observed in numerous other organisms (notably certain arthropods, fungi, and deep-sea fishes and invertebrates), Ditzies are extremely atypical among troglobionts. Luminescence in general is very rare in cave environments, the chief example being glowworms living in only a few caves in Australia and New Zealand; and in no other instance is enough light produced to see and function by (Culver and Pipan 1), as is the case with the Ditzies. Another notable feature of Fraggle Rock is the apparent prevalence of motility in organisms characterized as plants. Examples showing a substantial range of sustained rapid motion include Clinging Creepers (59), Night-Blooming Yellow-Leaved Deathwort (44, 59, 80), and Singing

Cactus (80). In other environments, of course, plant motion is limited to very slow, protracted movements (tracking the sun's direction in heliotropes, or blossoms opening and closing), or quick single movements based on the slow accumulation of stored energy (a Venus flytrap snapping shut).

Diet and Trophic Relationships (or: The Great Radish Caper)

Again, while many hours of recorded observations about the behavior of Rock dwellers are available to the scholar, and dozens of named species are known, relatively little is known about basic trophic interactions. This lack of information about trophic structure is a widespread problem in cave ecology (Romero 211).

Like other cave environments, the ecosystem critically relies on food brought in from the surface (Culver and Pipan 3). Radishes in particular are the critical resource for both Fraggles and Doozers, the two populations most thoroughly documented; in an event where the supply of radishes was temporarily disrupted, the results were catastrophic for both populations (19). This heavy reliance on a low variety of resources, compared to surface communities, is a typical feature of subterranean ecosystems (Culver and Pipan 23).

Fraggles are at least primarily herbivorous. Their main food source is radishes (and radish derivatives like Doozer constructions made from that vegetable), but they have been observed to eat a number of other vegetables as well (e.g., mushrooms (63), peaches (90), peppers (90), turnips (90), tomatoes (36), mustard (36), grapes (52), rutabagas (43), skunk cabbage (43)).

Doozers' feeding habits have not been directly observed, but indirect accounts have them eating "food pellets" filled with jelly or custard, typically the latter (58). The derivation of these pellets is unknown. The animal protein in custard (eggs and milk) raises the possibility that Doozers may be omnivorous, although some animals classified as herbivores are known to eat both eggs and milk.

Predatory animals in the Rock are rare and include Gridgen Spiders that presumably prey on the numerous insect species (23). Doozers are the largest species with an observed predator, in the form of a large purple Glob seen to prey on them on one occasion (51). The rarity of this predator is evident not only from the single occasion on which it is observed but from the evident unfamiliarity of the other species with it, in particular the Doozers' lack of fear or avoidance behavior. The latter suggests that it is not a usual predator in this environment. In fact there is insufficient evidence to conclude it is a cave dweller at all; as Fraggles live underground and forage outside, so the Glob may live outside and occasionally enter the cave to hunt. Such behavior has been observed, as in the case of giant Amazonian centipedes that enter caves to prey on bats (Molinari et al. 340).

A number of named species pose hazards to Fraggles (e.g., Invisible Garboil (21), Poison Cackler (35), and Avalanche Monster (80)), but evidence for their eating them for food is absent. The evident rarity of large predators suggests that any such animals have very large foraging ranges, or else that the set of caverns we see in the series is protected from incursions by such invaders.

A few possible examples of carnivorous plants are worth noting. These are described as "possible" because direct observational evidence of their consuming animals is lacking; however, circumstantial evidence suggests that the possibility is worth investigating further. A species of large purple-flowering plants has been observed to entrap Fraggles in immobilizing creepers (26). The Snareblossom Flower captures insects that land on it with a sticky secretion, as a sundew does (79). The Night-Blooming Yellow-Leafed Deathwort resembles a Venus flytrap, with a large "mouth" and prominent sharp teeth (44, 59, 80); it has been observed to ingest material through this "mouth" (80), though the material was identified only as "plant food" and its composition remains unclear. If these or other plants are truly carnivorous, their presence is another factor in the Rock's uniqueness, as carnivorous plants have never been observed in other subterranean environments. The nearest thing to an exception occurs in one genus of surface plants that capture and digest microscopic worms with sticky leaves that grow under the surface of the soil (Pereira et al. 1154).

Dispersal and Migration (or: Born to Wander)

Fraggles are primarily a highly social species, colonizing a given region and rarely venturing from it for the most part. Individuals may display a characteristic propensity for roaming behavior, some living away from the colony for extended periods with only occasional returns (18, 29, 35, 65). Even more sedentary individuals are observed to travel away from the colony on occasion (12, 17), although there is an innate tendency not to travel if it can be avoided (24). The overall tendency for social living does not imply uniformly shared space within the colony. While some communal areas exist, individuals are usually territorial and inhabit a characteristic space for sleeping and other activities. Forcing two Fraggles to coinhabit the same den can lead to conflict (44).

There is some indication of potential for mass migrations of Fraggle populations (39), as animals like lemmings will sometimes do in times of overpopulation. There are also known cases of small colonizing parties attempting to settle new areas (26, 44); these colonizing attempts frequently meet with failure (26), which is typical for such attempts, and to be expected in that easily habitable areas are typically already inhabited. The lack of large predators around the main caverns populated by Fraggles, and the relative frequency of dangers encountered during travel beyond that area, illustrates this point.

Less is known about the dispersal habits of Doozers. However, on one occasion in which they ran out of space to build, they began exhibiting behavior indicating preparation for large-scale departure from the Rock (6). This incident suggests that Doozers likewise undergo mass migrations in times of need.

Mutualisms and Ecosystem Stability (or: A Friend in Need)

Another way that Fraggle Rock is unique among subterranean environments is the degree to which mutualistic relationships (those of benefit to both parties) among different species occur. Symbiosis in underground ecosystems at the microscale is known and widespread (Wolfe, ch. 4–5): the well-known ability of legume plants to fix atmospheric nitrogen derives from a mutualistic relationship with bacteria, and mycorrhizae (symbioses between fungi and plants) are perhaps the most common mutualisms in the world. However, mutualistic relationships among larger fauna in caves are essentially unknown (Culver and Pipan 93).

By contrast, Fraggle Rock has numerous examples of mutualisms between macroscopic animal species. The best-known is between Fraggles and Doozers: the former eat the latter's constructions, providing the former with nourishment and the latter with building space (6). Another connects Fraggles and Ditzies: the former produce sound that sustains the Ditzies, while the latter produce light without which Fraggles and other fauna become comatose (42). These tightly coupled interrelationships contribute to a markedly fragile ecosystem. Such fragility is characteristic of subterranean ecosystems, which are generally much less robust than surface ones (Culver and Pipan 195). Several occasions, even in the limited set of observations available to us, have demonstrated how disruptions to the biotic communities can occur and put the continued survival of certain populations at risk.

Interference with a keystone species or its normal behavior has far-reaching, potentially catastrophic effects on the Rock ecology. The loss of radishes deprives Fraggles of their primary food source and Doozers of their primary building material (19). Whether those populations could adapt to use other resources is not clear; Fraggles have relied on other food sources (notably mushrooms) before cultivated radishes became part of their regular diet (63), and Doozers sometimes incorporate other vegetables into their building material (36). When Fraggle depredations on Doozer constructions cease, Doozers quickly run out of a necessary resource (empty space) and cannot continue to live in that environment (6). In a sense, Fraggles play the role of decomposers in the food cycle, breaking down a waste product of Doozer metabolism and renewing their environment to make it livable on an ongoing basis. When Fraggles stop vocalizing, Ditzies weaken and die (the sounds produced by other fauna are evidently insufficient in quantity or quality to sustain the Ditzies alone); when Ditzy light fails, other Rock dwellers fall comatose (42). Disruption of this last cycle has clear potential to lead to extinctions of local communities (though the existence of isolated populations in other caves (41) implies that local extinctions need not mean loss of entire species). Subterranean ecosystems are also vulnerable as a rule to outside disturbances, in particular to pollution or other contamination of groundwater supplies (Culver and Pipan 203, Romero 189), and Fraggle Rock is no exception (88).

Anomalies of Environment and Morphology (or: The Finger of Light)

Several respects noted above in which Fraggle Rock is highly atypical or unique among subterranean ecosystems may lead us to ask the question: is the Rock in fact a true cave environment? Indeed, the physical environment has at least one key feature distinguishing it from all other known caves, and this difference is reflected in the morphological adaptations (or lack thereof) of its inhabitants. The defining feature of a subterranean habitat is the total lack of light (Culver and Pipan 1). In contrast, Fraggle Rock is well illuminated throughout, with even the darkest tunnels lit enough to see by, thanks to the anomalously bioluminescent Ditzies (42). Perhaps as a result, Rock dwellers have not broadly evolved the adaptations otherwise widespread among obligate cave-dwellers: lack of pigment, eyelessness, and elongated appendages (Culver and Pipan 45). We consider each of these features in turn.

Depigmentation is clearly not a typical feature of organisms in this ecosystem; on the contrary, bright colors are the norm. The Fraggles in particular have the interesting additional characteristic of significant variability in coloration between individuals. This variation is not merely the sexual dimorphism common in aboveground animals; rather, a wide spectrum of hues exists across the population, without clear correlation with traits such as sex or age. The mechanism behind coloration is not known — whether it derives from pigments produced by the animals themselves, from some element or elements of their diet (as flamingos famously derive their pink color from the shellfish they eat), and/or from the microscopic structure of their coat producing refractive effects (as with the mechanism responsible for blue feathers in birds, for instance). Nor is the population structure well characterized, in terms of relatedness, making it difficult to estimate what component of coloration (if any) may be heritable. This unusual color variability is an interesting potential area for future study.

Eyelessness does not appear to be widespread among Rock dwellers; rather, one of the notable features of many of the animals we see is pronounced, bulging eyes. Such a characteristic is not surprising in an environment with low but not zero light levels (Romero 134). A few organisms are eyeless. These include several of the organisms characterized as plants that exhibit animal-like motility, noted earlier (e.g., 44, 80); if closer study of these organisms revealed them to be true plants, their eyelessness would of course be unsurprising, but the possibility should not be ruled out a priori of their actually being animals that have lost the morphological feature of visible eyes through adaptation to the cave environment. Occasional individuals (particular Fraggles) also lack visible eyes, although this seems more likely to be a limitation in our ability to observe them rather than an actual lack of the physical feature. However, if closer examination were to reveal this phenomenon to be true eyelessness, existing as a common variation but not a species-wide adaptation, such a case would call for further investigation. Either the lack of eyes would represent a neutral feature, with no selective pressure acting either to increase the prevalence of the trait in the population or to eliminate it, or else we would happen to have stumbled onto a population early in the evolutionary history of the appearance of a new trait. In either case it would represent a fascinating system to observe further in a long-term study.

The last typical feature of obligate troglobionts, elongated appendages, is defined relative to surface-dwelling near relatives. A rigorous evaluation of this feature would require clear knowledge of relatedness to aboveground species, based, e.g., on comparative genomic studies, currently lacking. However, judging relatives based on superficial appearance, the residents of Fraggle

Rock do not appear to have particularly elongated appendages compared to otherwise phenotypically similar organisms.

The conclusion is that the inhabitants of the Rock are, in general, not troglomorphic. There are at least three possible contributing factors: (1) The habitat lacks key typical features of subterranean environments, in particular widespread darkness. (2) Some inhabitants are not obligate troglobionts but rather trogloxenes (organisms that spend significant time in caves but show no modifications in the usual features), as in the case of the Fraggles. (3) Not all subterranean species are troglomorphic (Culver and Pipan 46, Romero 136), nor are the "typical" patterns of feature reduction or enlargement always consistent (Romero 133); accordingly, some Rock dwellers may simply be exceptions to the general rule.

Evolutionary History (or: Mokey, Then and Now)

Evolution is notoriously difficult to reconstruct, even when much more information is available than in the present case. In the absence of genomic studies or at least a partial survey of intermediate forms in the fossil record, the best we can do is speculate based on indirect observations and comparisons to known cases. The lack of availability of information is exacerbated by several features of the cave environment, including its inaccessibility, the fragility of the ecosystem (making extinctions of near relatives to surviving species more frequent), and the rarity of representatives of many species. This rarity is typical of underground environments, with most species known based on only a few specimens (Culver and Pipan 131, 177). In Fraggle Rock most named species are observed on only a single or at most a few occasions; their rarity is often highlighted by the reactions exhibited to them by more common fauna (51, 90). It is likely that other extant species that might shed light on the evolutionary history of the Rock have yet to be discovered, due to sampling limitations (new species are still being identified even in the longest-studied caves (Culver and Pipan 156)) and to geographic circumscription of where observations have taken place: endemism, the limitation in distribution to a very restricted range, is very pronounced for subterranean fauna (Culver and Pipan 197), with almost half of all known species having been found only in a single cave (Culver and Pipan 148). Because of these factors, sampling of existing species, and identification of near relatives, can easily be very sparse and incomplete. We are fortunate in the case of Fraggles to have two evidently near relatives available for comparison.

A physically separated population termed Cave Fraggles (41) has been observed inhabiting a region isolated from the primary Fraggle population documented in the series. Cave Fraggles are distinguished by their coloration and behavior: they are generally duller in appearance than Fraggles of the primary population, and less energetic, engaging in qualitatively different activities. Whether they represent a truly distinct species, or whether the two groups belong to the same species with the observed differences due to purely environmental influences, cannot be unambiguously determined without closer study, ideally including a genomic analysis. The latter scenario might occur for instance if Fraggle pigmentation is indeed obtained from diet: due to their isolation, it is not clear that Cave Fraggles have access to the same food sources as the others, and conceivably they are restricted to lower-nutrition resources that both fail to provide pigments and limit their metabolic energy.

However, evidence suggests that Cave Fraggles may well constitute a distinct species. Even if full speciation has not yet occurred, the situation matches the classic theoretical scenario for the emergence of a new species from a parent lineage (Townsend, Begon, and Harper 52). The physical separation of the two populations opens the door for genetic divergence between the two, through adaptation to their specific local environments or simply through neutral drift. Reproductive isolation is increased through prezygotic mechanisms, such as behavioral differences that reduce the probability of two individuals interbreeding even if they do encounter one another. The hostile reactions observed when members of the two populations do come into contact (41) indicate such behavioral obstacles to interbreeding at work.

This separation by physical isolation is the most unambiguous scenario for the origin of new species, termed "allopatric speciation." The separation is especially complete, and the process correspondingly clear, in island populations, as most famously with Darwin's finches (Townsend, Begon, and Harper 54). The analogy to be drawn between caves and islands is pronounced (Culver and Pipan 162). To truly evaluate whether these two Fraggle populations have become distinct species would require observing their reproductive habits in the wild, a process yet to be observed even in the primary population about which the most information is available. The lack of data on this topic is less surprising considering the relatively low reproduction rates of subterranean fauna (Culver and Pipan 195).

No difficulties of interpretation arise when we consider Merggles (89), which are clearly a distinct species morphologically as well as behaviorally. The evolutionary history of the two species is necessarily a matter of speculation—for instance, was the most recent common ancestor terrestrial or aquatic? The ability of both species to operate in the other's environment—the amount of time Fraggles spend swimming, and Merggles spend basking out of the water — suggests that whichever was the case, the ancestor's presumed competence in the alternate environment may have served as a preadaptation facilitating its success in that environment and the eventual emergence of a new species specialized for that niche. It should be noted, however, that the notion of preadaptation can be controversial, particularly in biospeleology (Romero 145).

Directions for Further Study (or: The Challenge)

Two recurring themes emerge from the preceding discussion. The first is that in many different respects, Fraggle Rock represents an ecosystem so unusual among cave environments as to be unprecedented. The second is that very little detailed information about the organisms dwelling there is currently available. Taken together, these two points emphasize the pressing need for a thorough new study.

In some ways, it is not surprising that the Rock has received so little scientific attention to date. Like most subterranean habitats (Culver and Pipan 179), it is largely inaccessible to human visitors (no human has ever entered it in person) and correspondingly difficult to sample from. The one scientist (Dr. Jerome Crystal) who has devoted attention to the Rock, performing limited tests in a small area very close to one entrance, encountered inconclusive results during the brief period of his study (95). No observations have occurred since 1987, and a tentative new expedition that would allow for renewed study, first announced in 2005, has repeatedly encountered obstacles and delays.

One possible way to collect data from within the Rock, considering its relative inaccessibility, might be the use of cameras mounted on animals, sent to explore the environment and recovered at a later time. Such an approach has been very fruitful, for instance, in studies of underwater environments using various aquatic animals, including mammals, reptiles, birds, fish, and crustaceans (Moll et al. 660). If no native species can be obtained for this purpose — a strong possibility, considering the rarity of encountering Rock dwellers and the difficulty of observing them even when they do venture into human-accessible environments (95) — then one could potentially use a small terrestrial animal, as has been known to enter the Rock and travel extensively within it (71). Another possibility is to attempt to recover living samples for closer study in a controlled laboratory environment. However, it is doubtful whether a laboratory population could be maintained, especially in the long term; very few cave organisms have successfully been maintained in captivity (Culver and Pipan 74).

No matter the approach to gathering data, it is critical that any future studies take precautions to minimize disruption to the ecosystem. The proposed upcoming large-scale expedition in particular, if it does ultimately take place, will need to take extreme care to avoid contamination of a place of such importance; it would be all too easy for such an incursion to transform its target unrecognizably. The fragility of the Rock ecology, and the rarity of most of its species, has already been noted. The consequences of even minor perturbations can be catastrophic for such cases. Small populations in particular are unusually vulnerable, due to factors such as lack of genetic diversity through inbreeding and random variations in demographics or environmental conditions; these elements together combine into what conservation biologists call the "extinction vortex" (Culver and Pipan 199). The loss of any of these fascinating organisms as a result of careless human intervention would be a grave disservice to the children of tomorrow.

Notes

1. Note that the scope of this discussion is limited to the Rock proper, and does not extend to consider familiar surface-dwelling organisms like dogs and Gorgs seen frequently throughout the series.

Works Cited

Culver, David C., and Tanja Pipan. *The Biology of Caves and Other Subterranean Habitats.* Oxford, U.K.: Oxford University Press, 2009. Print.
Molinari, Jesús, Eliécer E. Gutiérrez, Antonio A. De Ascenção, Jafet M. Nassar, Alexis Arends, and Robert J. Márquez. "Predation by Giant Centipedes, *Scolopendra gigantea,* on Three Species of Bats in a Venezuelan Cave." *Caribbean Journal of Science* 41.2 (2005): 340–346. Print.
Moll, Remington J., Joshua J. Millspaugh, Jeff Beringer, Joel Sartwell, and Zhihai He. "A New 'View' of Ecology and Conservation through Animal-Borne Video Systems." *Trends in Ecology & Evolution* 22.12 (2007): 660–668. Print.
Pereira, Caio G., Daniela P. Almenara, Carlos E. Winter, Peter W. Fritsch, Hans Lambers, and Rafael S. Oliveira. "Underground Leaves of *Philcoxia* Trap and Digest Nematodes." *Proceedings of the National Academy of Sciences of the United States of America* 109.4 (2012): 1154–1158. Print.
Romero, Aldemaro. *Cave Biology: Life in Darkness.* New York: Cambridge University Press, 2009. Print.
Townsend, Colin R., Michael Begon, and John L. Harper. *Essentials of Ecology.* 3rd ed. Wiley-Blackwell, 2008. Print.
Wolfe, David W. *Tales from the Underground: A Natural History of Subterranean Life.* Cambridge, MA: Perseus Publishing, 2001. Print.

PART TWO: INSIDE *THE DARK CRYSTAL* AND *LABYRINTH*

Interpreting the Various Species in *The Dark Crystal* and *Fraggle Rock*

Gideon Haberkorn

In 1982, Universal Studios released *The Dark Crystal*, an ambitious fantasy film peopled completely by puppets. Set in "the age of wonder," the story takes place on the planet Thra, which is home to a large collection of mostly sentient beings. The two most dominant among these, at least in the context of *The Dark Crystal*, are the Skeksis and the urRu — two species which used to be one, but split when they cracked the Crystal of Truth. The film deals with the quest of the last two surviving Gelflings, small elf-like creatures, to restore the crystal, make whole the urSkeksis, and heal the land.

One year after the release of *The Dark Crystal*, the Canadian Broadcasting Corporation began running *Fraggle Rock* (January 1983 to March 1987), a television show peopled mostly by puppets. The eponymous Fraggles are a carefree people spending most of their time enjoying themselves. They live in a network of caves which they call Fraggle Rock and which is home to a variety of mostly sentient beings. Perhaps most prominent among these — in terms of number and narrative focus — are the diminutive Doozers. The caves of Fraggle Rock connect on one end to the world of humans, often referred to as 'outer space,' and on another end to the world of the Gorgs. This giant species seems to consist only of a family of three, who refer to themselves as the rulers of the universe: Pa, the king, Ma, the queen, and Junior.

Both *The Dark Crystal* and *Fraggle Rock* present ecosystems of interacting sentient creatures of various species. These can be interpreted in several ways, four of which will be covered in this article: Taking the settings, characters, and events presented pretty much at face value, we can work from the premise that they can be related to ecological questions in the real world. If we do not take them at face value, we can instead relate them to racial and ethnic questions, taking the different species to represent different ethnic divisions of humanity. Working from the premise that the settings, characters and events presented can be related to questions of class and economy in the real world, we could adopt some version of Marxist criticism. Finally, taking into account the specific characteristics of the fantasy genre, both *The Dark Crystal* and *Fraggle Rock* can be read as a special kind of metafiction, narratives about the making of narratives.

It's Not Easy Thinking Green: Eco-Criticism

Interaction between species in nature is a lot more complex than most people would assume. Biologists have documented, among other things, different frog species forming a coordinated mixed-species chorus (cf. Phelps, Rand, Ryan); the ability of the yellow-bellied marmot and the golden-mantled ground squirrel to recognize and respond to each other's alarm calls (cf. Shriner); the ability of red-breasted nuthatches to understand and react to at least some of the "complex information about the size and risk of potential predators" encoded in the alarm calls of black-capped chickadees (Templeton, Greene 5479 et al.); the ability of Verreaux's sifaka and redfronted lemurs to understand each other's alarm calls (cf. Fichtel); the fact that bonnet macaques apparently understand the alarm calls of Nilgiri langurs, hanuman langurs, as well as sambar deer (cf. Ramakrishnan, Coss); or the yellow-casqued hornbill's understanding of the difference between the different alarm calls Diana monkeys utter for leopards and eagles (Templeton, Greene 5479). Nevertheless, however sophisticated the interactions between species may be in the real natural world, they are qualitatively different from those portrayed in either *The Dark Crystal* or *Fraggle Rock*.

An extensive ecocentric interpretation of the fictional ecosystems of Thra and Fraggle Rock would seem to depend on a reading of the creatures and their interactions as representing real creatures and their interactions. However, the ecosystems depicted cannot, I believe, be interpreted usefully as realistic ecologies.

On the one hand, such an interpretation would have to leave out a large amount of complex information: The fictional ecosystems are dominated by sentient beings of various species willing and able to communicate with each other at a significant level of complexity. In the cases where such communication succeeds, individuals do not only comprehend the approximate meaning of a call, they comprehend one another's approximate mental state. None of this has — as far as we know — a reasonable parallel in real ecosystems.

On the other hand, such an interpretation would have to deal with significant gaps and simplifications in both *The Dark Crystal* and *Fraggle Rock*: Neither ecosystem is plausible enough to stand up to even superficial scrutiny. To pose just three questions, for the sake of illustration: How can so many species share such a complex language? How come the ecosystem of Fraggle Rock contains no serious predators? How can we understand the split between the Skeksis and the urRu in any way that is not clearly metaphorical?

The fictional ecosystems of *The Dark Crystal* and *Fraggle Rock* cannot be interpreted usefully as reflecting the natural world. Nevertheless, some of the concepts dear to ecocentric critics — such as balance and imbalance, symbiosis and mutuality, sustainable or unsustainable uses of resources, and collective ethical responsibility, especially to the world beyond ourselves — may very well prove useful at a later stage in the discussion.

The Empire Has a Beak: Postcolonial Criticism

Faced with the story of Thra's two last surviving Gelflings, a Biblical scholar might see a connection to either Adam and Eve or the creatures on Noah's Ark, two of every kind. A biologist might remark that two individuals represent far too shallow a gene pool to start — or restart — a population. A cultural critic, especially a postcolonial one, would probably note that we do not see any proper Gelflings in *The Dark Crystal* at all: Both Jen and Kira have been raised in other cultures — Jen among the urRu and Kira among the Podlings. The only true Gelfling culture we see takes the form of ruins, and thus is truly dead and decaying. In a way, Kira and Jen are examples of cultural *hybridity*, with its horticultural roots — "the cross-breeding of two species by grafting or cross-pollination to form a third" (Ashcroft, Griffith, Tiffin "Hybritity" 118). However, they are not simply caught between cultures, belonging neither to one nor the other. If the concept of race lacks objective reality,[1] or rather, only gains it "through the behaviour of people" (Ashcroft, Griffith, Tiffin "Race" 205), then these Gelflings are caught between the ethnic and racial context they have grown up in, and the image of Gelfling identity transmitted to them by their environment — urRu and Podling society respectively. Jen and Kira will not only have to re-start the Gelfling species biologically, they will also have to redefine their identity independent of that forced upon them by others.

While the racial identity of the Gelflings might be problematic because of its lack of focus, other such identities are problematic precisely because of their clarity or even starkness. All Skeksis are decadent, devious, and evil. All Garthim and Crystal Bats are mindless servants to the Skeksis. All urRu are wise, peaceful, and contemplative. All Podlings are cheerful, kind, and harmless.

The urRu and the Skeksis seem to embody a black and white dichotomy between rational and magical, mechanic and organic: The urRu can be seen shaping mystical spiral symbols in the sand, while the Skeksis use laboratory devices to extract a youth serum from Gelflings and Podlings — effectively performing experiments on higher animals. Thus the Skeksis combine soulless science with sinful decadence; the seven deadly sins are well represented in the Castle of the Crystal. The urRu, on the other hand, are noble and mystical friends of the earth. Thus, they are one part of *The Dark Crystal*'s idealized noble savage imagery, expressing "nostalgia for a simple, pure, idyllic state of the natural," whereas (presumably ignoble) civilization embodies "industrialism and the notion of overcomplications and sophistications" (Ashcroft, Griffith, Tiffin "Savage/Civilized" 210). Such noble savages often serve to embody what civilized humanity has ostensibly lost: "natural innocence, freedom and equality" (210) — and it is indeed hard to argue that the Skeksis and the urRu are presented as two equal halves of their former selves. Rather, the urRu are idealized noble savages while the Skeksis seem intended to represent all that is bad about civilization. What if the story were told using human actors instead of puppets; what if the racial differences were indicated by skin color, possibly with added mystical paint marks or tattoos? Surely, we would be dealing with crude racial stereotyping.

There is a second part to *The Dark Crystal*'s idealized noble savage imagery, the peasant-like Podling society. We see the little creatures celebrate, eat, drink, and dance. We see them being abducted, tortured, and generally maltreated by their feudal overlords, the Skeksis. We never see them farm or hunt or gather any of their food or manufacture anything. One cannot help but wonder how such utterly hapless and helpless creatures fare in the everyday ecology of Thra, unable to defend themselves against anything that considers them a protein rich food source. Again, an image of idealized simplicity is constructed to contrast with the society of the Skeksis. Again, the result is a sharp dichotomy.

A post-colonial reading should ask to what end different species are presented in such noticeably different lights. What ideological content colors the way these dichotomies of nice and nasty are constructed? What ideology is contained in the fact that each species — despite having a mind surely capable of much more complexity — has so simple a character that one of two adjectives suffices to describe it? What does it mean that nurture and free will are almost irrelevant, while birth and blood and genes determine so much? After all, the Gelflings are chosen people because of their species, not their culture. How can Aughra be dealt with — a character who seems to constitute a species of her own? Not to belabor a point, but in the context of postcolonial criticism, it is deeply worrying that the species of Thra are so clearly marked as good and bad, with all kinds of easy tags and labels, and that one species — the Gelflings — is especially special, a kind of chosen people, since a Gelfling is destined to save the world. Only the fantasy setting saves these racial and ethnic identities from the accusation of cardboard caricature and racism.

Of course, this is only problematic if we insist on reading the fantastic creatures in *The Dark Crystal* as making some kind of statement about the different human races. If we view any ecosystem filled with fantasy species as completely detached from our own world, it does not mean anything. So if reading it in post-colonial context proves less than useful, what else can we take the various species to mean?

Gulliver's Fraggles: Marxist Criticism

If the fantastical species peopling an invented world cannot usefully be related to ethnic or racial identities, maybe they can be related to social identities, to classes. In fact, two of Fraggle Rock's three major species, the Doozers and the Gorgs, seem to correspond quite clearly to, respectively, a working proletariat and a kind of feudal upper class. Can *Fraggle Rock* be usefully read as social commentary?

There is another fantastical social commentary with at least some superficial similarities to Fraggle Rock: Jonathan Swift's *Gulliver's Travels*. Just as Lemuel Gulliver occupies a middle ground between the diminutive inhabitants of Liliput and the giants of Brobdingnag, so the Fraggles, at about 18 inches, occupy a middle ground between the diminutive Doozers, at 6 inches, and the giant Gorgs at 22 feet. Just as Gulliver serves as the normal point of comparison against which all the abnormal people and societies he encounters are measured, so the Fraggles are obviously established as the norm: The scale most clearly established as normal sized is that of the Fraggles — Gorgs and humans are larger than normal, Doozers are smaller than normal. Just as in Gulliver's case, of course, the biggest hint is in the title: Fraggle Rock is after all referred to as *Fraggle* Rock. Working on the hypothesis, then, that *Fraggle Rock* explores questions of social roles and classes, and that it established one such group, that of the Fraggles, as a point of reference, what readings does that suggest?

Classes are primarily economic groupings and usually divide society into those who have more power and those who have less (cf. Edgar, "Class" 64). A lower class will be "active economic producers," though "not [in] control [of] the production process," and not "able to retain the full value of what they produce," and the dominant class, in turn, will "control the society's stock of economic resources," thereby controlling "the fate of whatever is produced with these resources" (Edgar, "Class" 65). The relationship between these two classes will usually "be one of exploitation, although the precise nature of exploitation will depend upon the particular historical stage, or mode of production, in which it occurs" (65). Questions we need to ask of *Fraggle Rock* are therefore: Can the various fantasy species be read as references to social classes? What are their economic characteristics? Who owns the means of production? Who does the actual work? What are the economic relationships between the groups?

The Doozers, to begin at the bottom, live to work: As they announce in the show's opening song, they "work [their] cares away." Doozers do things. With ant-like patience, they industriously construct extensive translucent scaffolding, assembled from 'Doozer sticks,' which consist of a candy-like substance made from ground-up radishes. The purpose of Doozer architecture remains unclear.

Doozer society values cooperation and good work, and the common good is put before individual interests. Therefore, no single Doozer is expected to take personal credit for her or his work. Competition is seen as a vice and is strongly discouraged. The proletariat of Fraggle Rock seems to exist in a simplistic version of communism.

Only one Doozer is shown to actively reject this lifestyle: In episode 208, "All Work and All Play," Cotterpin Doozer runs away to be a Fraggle. In the end, however, she is forced to realize that Doozers have to be Doozers, even though she is given the chance to be an architect rather than a builder. The Doozers, it is quite clear, are born to be workers, and there is little (if any) chance of them ever leaving their class. In fact, the idea that fantasy species represent classes establishes a metaphor which clearly precludes any social mobility: No member of one species can ever join another—although the Doozers apparently have a story which parents tell their children as a warning, "The Legend of the Doozer Who Didn't," which claims that Doozers who don't do become Fraggles.

Fraggles, in contrast to the Doozers, "dance [their] cares away." They sing and eat and travel and explore. They value individualism and independence. They enjoy races, games, and competitions. While the life of a Doozer seems to consist mainly of work, the life of a Fraggle seems to consist entirely of spare time. Their diet consists largely of two things: Doozer sticks and radishes stolen from the garden of the Gorgs. In episode 106, "The Preachification of Convincing John," Mokey tries to convince all her fellow Fraggles to stop eating Doozer sticks, but the plan backfires: The Doozers run out of space and have to leave Fraggle Rock, since to stop building is to stop being a Doozer. Mokey realizes her mistake only at the last minute. Another episode makes it quite clear that the Doozers not only do not mind the Fraggles eating their architecture, they actively encourage it: In episode 212, "The Doozer Contest," a rather uncharacteristic argument breaks out over which is the better added flavor — tomato extract or mustard powder.

Here, then, is a species of workers who live to work, and who labor with the express intention of having their work taken away and consumed. The Doozers are clearly being exploited by the Fraggles, who value their architecture only insofar as it provides them with a snack. In fact, the major food sources of the Fraggles are obtained only by stealing from the Doozers and the Gorgs. The full extent of the interdependence of Fraggles, Doozers, and Gorgs — all connected through the humble radish — becomes apparent only in episode 119, "The Great Radish Famine." It turns out that, while Doozers cannot do without radishes, and Fraggles cannot eat, Gorgs cannot be visible: Without their radish-based 'youth and beauty cream,' the Gorgs slowly become invisible. While the Gorgs farm the radishes and the Doozers turn them into Doozer sticks, the only service the Fraggles provide to the community is apparently to consume.

The Gorgs appear to be a family of three hairy giants, who consider themselves to be the rulers of the universe. Ma and Pa are king and queen; they wear crowns. Their house looks somewhat castle-like, but it is rather small and somewhat dilapidated. Their grounds consist of a garden patch — one of which is infested with Fraggles. In a certain light, this royal family looks more than a little like peasant farmers. In fact, when Junior is tricked into selling their home and grounds to Wander McMooch in exchange for a handful of fake Peas of Power in episode 216, that episode is titled, "Junior Sells the Farm." Incidentally, McMooch is in the end discouraged from turning the Gorgs' land into a housing development because he finds it infested with Fraggles.[2]

What the Gorgs do to get rid of their cares is never really established, as they alone of the three major species in Fraggle Rock do not get to sing in the theme song. This makes them the least understood social group right from the start.

How can all of this be read as a commentary on social classes? What are we to make of a class of workers who are made and meant to work, and who do not feel exploited if all their hard work is simply consumed, without compensation, by another class; of a class of stupid, lumbering farmers, whose produce is stolen, without compensation, by the two other classes — one of whom at least uses the loot to manufacture something, while the other just consumes. The Fraggles, who seem to be in it just for fun, and do not seem to contribute anything worthwhile to society, are clearly a kind of parasite class. They can only live by exploiting the stupid farmers and the industrious workers. And yet, since the Doozers need to have someone who consumes their architecture, and since the Gorgs can spare a few radishes for the comparatively small Fraggles and positively tiny Doozers, everything seems to be as it should be. *Fraggle Rock*, read as a commentary on social classes, seems to be a crude justification of the exploitation of the lower classes by a leisure class. The species of Fraggle Rock form a natural caste system.

But is the lesson of Mokey's failed attempt to preserve Doozer architecture really that we should not stand up for the working classes? And which aspect of the Gorgs is more relevant: The bloated useless rulers who just get in your way, or the peasants whose produce you can steal? Is there a comment about the value of education — after all, what the Fraggles consider a wise oracle is in fact the Gorgs' trash heap; or vice versa? If we were to explore the economic angle further, we would quickly have to concede that the class system of Fraggle Rock does not seem even remotely viable: How do the Gorgs feed, and who produces that food? Do they buy it? Surely they cannot live only on a handful of radishes. Where do the Doozers get their machines? Who manufactures them? It seems that reading *Fraggle Rock* as a narrative about social classes yields results which are contradictory, muddled, or highly unlikely.

Generic Criticism: How Fantasy Species Mean

Interpreting the interactions between the various fantasy creatures of *Fraggle Rock* and *The Dark Crystal* as references to interactions between actual species, in search of ideological content pertinent to eco-criticism, yields no useful readings. Interpreting them as references to interactions between groups of various ethnic backgrounds, in search of ideological content pertinent to post-colonial criticism, proves little more successful. Finally, interpreting them as references to interactions between various social castes or classes, in search of ideological content pertinent to some version of Marxist criticism, seems equally fruitless. Yet, if species are not species, or even races, and classes are not classes, how else can such things be interpreted, without producing some kind of *anything-goes* reading, in which anything can mean anything? After all, there need to be some reasonable guidelines for what can mean what, otherwise communication breaks down completely. Interpretation must somehow remain distinguishable from over-interpretation. The answer, I believe, is to interpret the interactions between the various fantasy creatures of *Fraggle Rock* and *The Dark Crystal* in the context of a certain kind of narrative: They are part of fantasy narratives, and to interpret them, we must turn to genre criticism.

A central premise of genre criticism is that there are distinct groups of texts or artifacts, that the members of these groups have certain typical characteristics, and that the way an artifact can usefully be taken to mean something is influenced by what genre it belongs to. You can insist on reading a Dali painting as an example of realism, or on reading the Bible as a noir thriller, and you may even succeed in producing a semi-coherent interpretation, but a more reasonable reading usually takes into account an artifact's genre. What, then, can we say about the fantasy genre? How do we know if *The Dark Crystal* and *Fraggle Rock* belong to that genre? Finally, how should our interpretation of the various species of Thra and Fraggle Rock be influenced by the fact that they appear in fantasy narratives?

Modern fantasy was born as a literary genre.[3] As a distinct field, it is a surprisingly young phenomenon, younger than, for instance, the detective narrative: the genre crystallized in the mid–20th century, when two separate traditions came together. The two unwitting founding fathers were J.R.R. Tolkien and Robert E. Howard (cf. Schweitzer, "Conan" 977, and "Heroic" 379), and we can thus pinpoint the birth of modern fantasy to the unauthorized publication of Tolkien's *The Lord of the Rings* in the United States by Ace in 1965, and the publication of the paperback edition of Howard's *Conan* stories in 1966 (cf. Pesch 36–37).[4]

On Howard's side, fantasy is a child of *pulp* fiction with its cursory characterization and formulaic plots (cf. Pesch 36; Attebery, "Magazine Era" 34), and because of its emphasis on "physical conflict between heroes and supernatural creatures like gods and goddesses, demons, witches, or wizards," it is hence most commonly labeled *sword and sorcery* (Gramlich, "Sword" 779). One aspect typical of this tradition is the *sense of wonder*. Some have argued for this concept as a feature that distinguishes *science fiction* from all other forms of fiction, "including most fantasy," and describe it as "a sudden opening of a closed door in the reader's mind"— a moment in which readers "can glimpse for themselves [...] a scheme of things where mankind is seen in a new perspective"

(Nicholls and Robu, "Sense of Wonder" 1084). It has the power to make readers conscious of their world, to transform acceptance into amazement, and to make the mundane appear spectacular (cf. Senior, "Oliphaunts" 117–118 et al.). Such a sense of wonder is an important aspect of modern fantasy.

The second tradition which spawned modern fantasy is the one which culminated, in the first half of the 20th century, in Tolkien's *Lord of the Rings*, and which Schweitzer refers to as the "literary stream" ("Heroic" 379). This stream "grew out of and has been greatly influenced by fairy tales, the body of narratives derived from the oral folktales of magic" (Eilers 319). It can be argued that the main reason fantasy does not simply form a continuous tradition with most if not all fiction that went before is simply the profound shift in the horizon of expectation affected, at least in Europe and Anglo-America, by the rise of the novel (see Eilers 335 et al.; Clute, "Taproot" 921). Clute suggests that texts on which modern fantasy clearly draws but which were written before this shift be labeled taproot texts (Clute, "Taproot" 921). Through its taproot texts, the literary tradition of fantasy links back to a largely oral tradition of storytelling; however, it could not begin to congeal as a genre before the conventions of literary realism had fully developed. Clute emphasizes the changes the realist novel brought to readerly expectations, while Eilers insists that fantasy "originated when writers began applying the techniques of literary realism in stories in which the extranatural played a fundamental role" (Eilers 335). Thus, the literary stream brings to fantasy a fusion of conventional realism with the subject matter of non-realistic fiction. Its writers "manifested a modern emphasis on the individual by developing original plots, particular characters, and particular settings," and employed "a largely descriptive, referential prose instead of the refined, condensed style that had been traditionally employed" (335). In essence, the tradition of literary fantasy carries at its heart the depiction of extranatural events in a way which creates an "illusion of reality" (318).

A narrative belonging to the genre of modern fantasy can thus be expected to create a sense of wonder through the realistic representation of counterfactual events, settings, and characters. Since they cannot create realism through accuracy, they must compensate through adequacy — i.e., the deficit in historical plausibility is made up for in narrative plausibility.

Are *The Dark Crystal* and *Fraggle Rock* fantasy narratives? They do depict counterfactual events, settings, and characters. They arguably create a sense of wonder. But surely using puppets as protagonists can hardly count as 'realistic representation'? In fact, it can be argued that puppets are very suitably employed in fantasy narratives: A puppet without a puppeteer is dead matter, and the audience knows this. In a puppet performance, inanimate objects are endowed with design, movement, and speech in a way that suggests that they are alive. The magic of the puppet as performed material is closely related to the magic of fantasy as realistic counterfactual utterance.[5] As fantasy turns from oral or written narrative to performance, the use of puppets can be argued to be very much in keeping with the genre.

What does it mean for a reading of *The Dark Crystal* and *Fraggle Rock* if they can be considered fantasy narratives? Specifically, what does it mean for a reading of the fantasy species inhabiting these narratives? Most importantly, modern fantasy has the potential to become what Currie calls *theoretical fiction*, i.e. self-reflexive fiction, fiction about fiction (52)—the more usual term is *metafiction*, which Waugh defines as works that "create a fiction and [...] make a statement about the creation of that fiction" (6). By presenting counterfactual events, settings, and characters in a realistic manner, fantasy has the potential of opening a space in which to question the construction of consensus reality. It is capable of foregrounding its discourse and narrativity, simply by being the most explicitly fictional of all genres. It does not bend or fudge the rules; it breaks them.

Usually, the more metafictional a narrative becomes, the more effectively any verisimilitude is deconstructed (cf Waugh 53). At the extreme, experimental fiction turns the tools of creating a narrative into the subject; it focuses on the how instead of the what. As a result, the illusion of realism is broken (cf. Wolf 35). By contrast, because fantasy can place "questions of cause and effect, identity, point of view, and fictionality at the level of story," the actual level of discourse need not be violated (Attebery, "Re construction" 97). Modern fantasy combines experimental potential with a high level of readability. It can become quite experimental without breaking the suspension of disbelief. Not all works of modern fantasy realize this potential; in fact, the majority do not, at least not fully. The potential, nevertheless, exists.

Reading the Main Species of Thra and Fraggle Rock as Aspects of Fantasy Narratives

By describing counterfactual events, settings and characters, fantasy narratives make it quite clear that they are not to be taken literally, at least not necessarily. Species are not necessarily species or even races. Classes are not necessarily classes. In that way, modern fantasy can be compared to an extended metaphor. The characters of fantasy narratives should in some way be readable as metaphorical statements on the way we tell stories about identities, about belonging to groups, about interacting with other groups. In this way, the fictional ecosystems do not have to refer to actual ecosystems but can provide a tool for thinking, talking, and telling stories about our socially constructed reality: They are reifications of internal landscapes — what Zerubavel refers to as mindscapes.

Doozers are the people who do things, who work their cares away, who patiently, selflessly, and in cooperation construct complex edifices for the pleasure of others. Fraggles are independent and individualistic people, who sing, eat, travel, explore, and dance their cares away. Once the idea that Doozers who stop working die or become Fraggles is separated from notions of species, race or class, it becomes much more reasonable: If you change your personality, you stop being the type of person you were, and you become a different type of person. In a way, your worker personality dies, and you are reborn as another, different person. In that sense, both stories about Doozers who stop doing could be true at the same time.

Every other high school novel or film has a scene in which the various 'clans' of students are introduced — the nerds, the jocks, the cheerleaders, and so on — but only a fantasy narrative can express just how different such groups often feel from one another by turning them not only into real clans, but physically different species. If the emphasis was on otherness and alienation, the various species could well be shown to speak different languages and seem strange and alien to one another. Instead, *Fraggle Rock* emphasizes the ways in which we can interact successfully, even though we may sometimes feel as if we are dealing with members of another species: Learn the culture, accept that they are different and that your culture is not necessarily superior, and be aware that they may have a worldview radically different from yours.

Narratives about counterfactual ecosystems peopled by nonexistent species can still communicate concepts near and dear to the hearts of ecocentric critics — such as balance and imbalance, symbiosis and mutuality, sustainable or unsustainable uses of resources, and collective ethical responsibility, especially to the world beyond ourselves. After all, many of the species of Fraggle Rock live in various combinations of symbiosis and mutuality, most clearly perhaps the Doozers and the Fraggles: They depend on each other to manufacture part of their diet and to clear space for new constructions, respectively. Both Fraggles and Doozers depend on the Gorgs to grow radishes, and when their home is about to be taken from them by Wander McMooch, the Gorgs benefit from the Fraggle infestation. The radishes also serve quite nicely to illustrate the theme of sustainable or unsustainable use of resources, as do, at one remove, the Doozer sticks. In both cases, we are dealing with renewable resources. Repeatedly, various characters learn that they need to take collective ethical responsibility for the world beyond themselves — not least when "The

Great Radish Famine" breaks out. This also touches upon the theme of balance and imbalance. Since Fraggle Rock is a fantasy narrative, it can treat these themes metaphorically. Rather than dealing only with literal symbiosis, for example, a fantasy narrative can deal with the abstract concepts involved: What can it mean to have a relationship based on mutual benefit, which is so finely tuned that neither individual could survive without the other? What does it say about the builders and architects that they depend on those who 'consume' their constructions just as much as those people depend on them?[6] Rather than any real ecosystems, Fraggle Rock can be related to the socially constructed systems of our mental landscape. The characters are turned inside out: they look like who they really are.

Once *The Dark Crystal* is read metaphorically, the fact that Aughra seems to be the only member of her species, rarer even than the Gelflings and surely doomed to go extinct, is no longer a biological fact. It is a reification of her role as an outsider, an eccentric, a mind unlike any other on Thra. And the split between the urRu and the Skeksis, associated with the cracked crystal, can refer, for example, to the notion of splitting personalities into an idealized, sanitized part that contains all that is deemed good and noble, and another part that functions as a dump for all that is deemed evil and detestable. It makes sense, then, that the Skeksis are associated with sin. It is also noteworthy that whenever a Skeksis dies, an urRu dies also, and vice versa: We may be able to split ourselves into such artificial and unnatural half-beings, but we cannot get rid of one half without destroying the other. The good and the bad belong together and form a whole. Indeed, a bringing together of both halves, an acknowledging of both sides is necessary to heal the land. Thus, what seemed at first like a rather simplistic black and white moral landscape can actually be read as a warning against such lazy thinking: You cannot have dark without light, Skeksis without urRu.[7] If fantasy species are read metaphorically, they can be understood as reifications of mental characteristics, personality traits, and cultural allegiances. The inner landscape, or mindscape, is externalized. Thus, fantasy species — sometimes incorrectly labeled fantasy races — embody a kind of inverted racism: Instead of suggesting that all people of a certain ethnicity have common characteristics, fantasy depicts people with certain characteristics as having the same, albeit freely invented, ethnicity. They can offer a space for exploring the ways in which people sort themselves into tribes with cultures of their own, how such mental tribes, such species of mind, can often give a truer map of belonging than a description of actual physical characteristics. Fantasy species, by embodying and performing mental events, like the rift between Skeksis and urRu, can also point out truths about such mental events precisely because nothing they depict is true. Despite being counterfactual — possibly *by* being counterfactual — they can get the facts straight. This is a potential inherent in the fantasy genre, and one that is realized by many narratives featuring fantastic species. Such an interpretation of fantasy species offers, in many cases, a much more complex and rewarding reading.

Notes

1. As Pinker notes, "human divisions such as race and ethnicity" are based on "differences [which] are minor at most and scientifically uninteresting" (340).
2. Thus, we learn two things: There must be creatures called Fraggles elsewhere, or he would not know them; and Ma and Pa are not alone in considering them pests.
3. For a somewhat more extended version of what follows, with a specific focus on the fantasy hero, see Haberkorn, "Cultural Palimpsests" 323–327.
4. The emphasis is here on publication in the United States, and in book form. The first volume of the *Lord of the Rings* had been published in Great Britain in 1954, its precursor, *The Hobbit*, in 1937. Conan the Cimmerian had first appeared in the short story "The Phoenix and the Sword" published in *Weird Tales* in 1932 (cf. Tiner 221).
5. A slightly more elaborate version of this argument can be found in Haberkorn, "Muppets" 30–31.
6. Arguably, houses only fulfill their potential if they are used, i.e. lived in; otherwise they are merely rather dull exercises in cluttering up the landscape.
7. The exploration of various aspects of the human psyche in fantastic form — usually as literal manifestation — extends from various mythological tales through Stevenson's *Jekyll and Hyde* to the angels and demons on the shoulders of various cartoon characters. Under headings such as double, shadow, and doppelgänger, such literal manifestations are usually interpreted as "repressed secret selves" which are 'left out' when we construct our "civilized 'social selves'" (Stableford 285) — with Stevenson's story as one of the best known examples. In fantasy, such a "separation of the self into discordant elements" is usually a "tragic circumstance that must somehow be transcended" (Clute, *Fantasy* 855). Some further thoughts on the human self can be found in my essay "Muppets as a Metaphor for the Self."

Works Cited

Ashcroft, Bill, Gareth Griffith, Helen Tiffin. "Hybridity." In *Post-Colonial Studies: The Key Concepts*. 1998. London: Routledge, 2000. 118–121. Print.
_____. "Race." In *Post-Colonial Studies: The Key Concepts*. 1998. London: Routledge, 2000. 198–206. Print.
_____. "Savage/Civilized." In *Post-Colonial Studies: The Key Concepts*. 1998. London: Routledge, 2000. 209–210. Print.
Attebery, Brian. "Fantasy's Reconstruction of Narrative Conventions." *Journal of the Fantastic in the Arts* 1 (1988) 85–98. Print.
_____. "The Magazine Era: 1926–1960." *The Cambridge Companion to Science Fiction*. Ed. Edward James and Farah Mendlesohn. Cambridge: Cambridge University Press, 2003. 32–47. Print.
Clute, John. *The Encyclopedia of Fantasy*. Ed. John Clute & John Grant. London: Orbit, 1999. 855–856, 921–922. Print.
_____. "Taproot Texts" *The Encyclopedia of Fantasy*. Ed. John Clute & John Grant. London: Orbit, 1999. 921–922. Print.
Currie, Mark. *Postmodern Narrative Theory*. Basinstoke: Palgrave, 1998. Print.

Edgar, Andrew. "Class." In *Post-Colonial Studies: The Key Concepts*. Ed. Andrew Edgar and Peter Sedgwick. 1999. London: Routledge, 2002. 64–68. Print.
Eilers, Michelle L. "On the Origins of Modern Fantasy." *Extrapolation* 41 (2000): 317–337. Print.
Fichtel, Claudia. "Reciprocal Recognition of Sifaka (Propithecus verreauxi verreauxi) and Redfronted Lemur (Eulemur fulvus rufus) Alarm Calls" *Animal Cognition* 7 (2004): 45–52. Print.
Gramlich, Charles. "Sword and Sorcery." *The Greenwood Encyclopedia of Science Fiction and Fantasy: Themes, Works, and Wonders*. Ed. Gary Westfahl. Westport: Greenwood Press, 2005. 779–781. Print.
Haberkorn, Gideon. "Cultural Palimpsests: Terry Pratchett's New Fantasy Heroes." *Journal of the Fantastic in the Arts*. 18.3 (2008): 319–339. Print.
_____. "The Muppets as a Metaphor for the Self." In *Kermit Culture: Critical Perspectives on Jim Henson's Muppets*. Ed. Jennifer C. Garlen and Anissa M. Graham. Jefferson, NC: McFarland, 2009. 25–39. Print.
Nicholls, Peter, and Carnel Robu. "Sense of Wonder" *The Encyclopedia of Science Fiction*. Ed. John Clute and Peter Nicholls. London: Orbit, 1999. 1083–1085. Print.
Pesch, Helmut W. *Fantasy: Theorie und Geschichte*. Diss. U Köln, 1982. Passau: Erster Deutscher Fantasy Club, 2001. Print.
Phelps, Steven M., A. Stanley Rand, Michael J. Ryan. "The Mixed-Species Chorus as Public Information: Túngara Frogs Eavesdrop on a Heterospecific." *Behavioral Ecology* 18 (2007): 108–114. Print.
Pinker, Steven. *The Blank Slate*. London: Penguin, 2002. Print.
Ramakrishnan, Uma, Richard G. Coss "Recognition of Heterospecific Alarm Vocalizations by Bonnet Macaques (Macaca radiata)." *Journal of Comparative Psychology* Vol 114 No 1 (2000): 3–12. Print.
Schweitzer, Darell. "Conan the Conqueror by Robert E. Howard (1959)" *The Greenwood Encyclopedia of Science Fiction and Fantasy: Themes, Works, and Wonders*. Ed. Gary Westfahl. Westport: Greenwood Press, 2005. 975–977. Print.
_____. "Heroic Fantasy" *The Greenwood Encyclopedia of Science Fiction and Fantasy: Themes, Works, and Wonders*. Ed. Gary Westfahl. Westport: Greenwood Press, 2005. 379–381. Print.
Senior, William A. "Oliphaunts in the Perilous Realm: The Function of Internal Wonder in Fantasy" *Functions of the Fantastic*. Ed. Joe Sanders. Westport: Greenwood, 1995. 115–124. Print.
Shriner, Walter McKee. "Yellow-Bellied Marmot and Golden-Mantled Ground Squirrel Responses to Heterospecific Alarm Calls" *Animal Behaviour* 55. 3 (1998) 529–536. Print.
Stableford, Brian. "Doubles" *The Encyclopedia of Fantasy*. Ed. John Clute and John Grant. London: Orbit, 1999. 285–286.
Templeton, Christopher N., and Erick Greene. "Nuthatches Eavesdrop on Variations in Heterospecific Chickadee Mobbing Alarm Calls." *Proceedings of the National Academy of Sciences*. 104.13 (2007): 5479–5482. Print.
Tiner, Ron. "Conan." *The Encyclopedia of Fantasy*. Ed. John Clute and John Grant. London: Orbit, 1999. 221. Print.
Waugh, Patricia. *Metafiction: The Theory and Practice of Self-Conscious Fiction*. London: Routledge, 1984. Print.
Wolf, Werner. "Radikalität und Mässigung: Tendenzen experimentellen Erzählens" *Radikalität und Mässigung: Der Englische Roman seit 1960*. Ed. Annegret Maack and Rüdiger Imhof. Darmstadt: Wissenschaftliche Buchgesellschaft, 1993. 34–53. Print.
Zerubavel, Eviatar. *Social Mindscapes: An Invitation to Cognitive Sociology*. Cambridge: Harvard University Press, 1997. Print.

"What was sundered and undone shall be whole": Union, Nature and Aughra in *The Dark Crystal*

Roxanne Harde

The ending of Jim Henson's 1982 film, *The Dark Crystal*, offers a study in reunification and rejuvenation. At the moment that the three suns of the planet Thra line up in the "Great Conjunction," the Gelfling Jen reunites the Dark Crystal with its shard, and the urRu and the Skeksis are reunited into the urSkeks. The Gelfling Kira, murdered by the High Priest skekZok, is restored to life by the leader of the urSkeks, and the enslaved Podlings have their "essence of life" returned; they are again lively and colorful. As the castle sheds its dark encasement and again shines as pure crystal, the barren landscape becomes richly verdant. With the alignment of the suns and the reunification of the crystal, the balance of good and evil is restored in the urSkeks, and a destroyed world and its devastated species are rejuvenated into vibrant life. Like so much of Henson's work, *The Dark Crystal* carries clear political and environmental themes and messages; to paraphrase ecocritic Sidney Dobrin, the film sees through green eyes ("Through" 276). Its ending suggests that Henson's focal species, the Gelflings and the Podlings, rooted as they are in the natural world, will continue to support and enrich the ecosystems of Thra, a planet that honors, as Muppeteer Jane Gootnick explains, "the emotional qualities of all living things, including minerals and vegetables" ("World").[1]

However, amidst the pure joys of union at the film's close (Kira and Jen staring into each other's eyes, preparing to be the Gelfling Eve and Adam; the Podlings dancing their way home to their villages; the urSkeks returning to their home world in a unified blaze of light), Aughra stands alone. The only one of her species, Aughra seems by her very nature destined to be alone. However, "born from the need for rocks and trees for an eye to see the World," Aughra is also intrinsically connected to all the biosystems and species on Thra (Froud 13). In keeping with Michel Foucault's argument that "power is that which represses nature, instincts, a class, or individuals" (*Society* 15), Aughra witnesses many repressions as power circulates through the film. Born of rocks and trees, she shares joy with the Gelflings, folklore with the Pod People, and learning with the urSkeks and then the urRu, even as she shuns the Skeksis' abuse of power. While each featured species offers messages about care of and connection to the natural world, Aughra functions as the earthy matrix of the film's environmentalist politics. Amidst the connectedness with nature in and the workings of power on the various species in *The Dark Crystal*, Aughra functions as an ethical force who is both eye and voice for the natural world.

"Of course not; you're a boy":
The Gelflings and the Pod People

The Jim Henson Company celebrated the 25th Anniversary of *The Dark Crystal* with a high-definition DVD of the film that included "The World of the Dark Crystal." This bonus disc consists of documentary footage filmed alongside the movie, deleted scenes, and new footage filmed for the anniversary edition that includes interviews with key players in the movie, among them Jim Henson and his co-director Frank Oz, his co-writer, David Odell, artistic director Brian Froud, and puppeteers Jane Gootnick and David Goelz. In the documentary, Jim Henson states that from the earliest stages of planning, he meant that "not a single human being will appear on the screen." His goal was to "create the world first, plants, trees, rocks, and then have the story grow" ("World"). From the world of Thra grew its two native bipedal hominoid species, the Gelflings and the Podlings, also called Pod People, although puppeteer Jane Gootnick points out that in *The Dark Crystal*, puppetry provided "an opportunity to anthropomorphize *all* living things," so everything seems sentient, from the plants that walk to the mushrooms that need to be caught to the flowers that decide for whom they will bloom ("World"). Henson notes that he intended the Gelflings as "bridge characters through which the audience enters this world," and he recalls that being the most human, they were the hardest to create and operate ("World"). Aside from Jen's rather disturbing similarity to Aerosmith frontman Steven Tyler, lately a judge on *Amer-*

ican Idol, the Gelflings are as much a mix of animal — fox, deer, chimpanzee — as human. Henson's Conceptual Designer, artist Brian Froud, emphasizes that "the Gelfling are the ones *we* identify with," "we" being the human audience ("World").

If we do indeed identify with the Gelflings, then we do as a colonized people, one whose population has been decimated and whose land has been devastated by a dominant and foreign race or species. Aughra describes the Gelflings before the First Conjunction, as a race who "were earth and spirit, masters of song and shaping. They carved wood and stone to set free the shapes that lay hidden in them; they molded metal to exult in its new form" (Froud 39). The First Age of Aughra, as she terms the period after her creation by the world, "was of innocence, and it was long. Then it was Aughra and the race of Gelfling who shared the world. The Gelfling sang and danced for the joy of their lives, and I was part of that joy" (Froud 13). Aughra makes clear in *The World of the Dark Crystal*, which purports to be a translation of the found "Book of Aughra," that she was created and lived in a time of harmony before the First Conjunction. She describes the Crystal as hidden in its mountain, but all the creatures of the world knew it was there, and when "a Sun shone down the shaft of the Crystal, all would touch rock and feel the trembling from the Crystal" (Froud 15). The light of the First Conjunction destroyed one of her eyes when she insisted on watching the Three Suns stand together — the Dying Sun a dark pupil in the center, surrounded by the pale Rose Sun, in turn encircled by the white light of the Great Sun — to form a magnificent eye staring down the shaft at the Crystal. In that moment, Aughra's eye was destroyed, and the urSkeks entered their world. Afterwards, "The Gelfling taught me to dreamfast by the touch of hands," Aughra notes, "then I could see into their minds and they into mine. I showed them the beauty of the Crystal when the light of Suns in conjunction shone upon it" (Froud 15).

The Gelfling and Aughra faced the coming of the urSkeks together and found it a time of joy as the shining newcomers "hollowed out the mountain around the Crystal and built a castle of lesser crystals" (Froud 16). The castle, of course, appears as dark rock until the end, when it again becomes glistening quartz. The urSkeks shared their knowledge with Aughra and created her Observatory, which held an Orrery that modeled Thra in its universe, and "from them the Gelfling learned to sing new songs" (Froud 16). However, if the thousand trine between the first two Conjunctions was as shining as the strangers, the Second Conjunction showed the reason the urSkeks came, and Aughra notes that "the joy I had in the urSkeks [is] bitter, sour, poisoned rock to me now" (Froud 16). In so doing, she traces Thra's history in the terms of the rocks that birthed her as she comments on the suffering she sees throughout Thra, on the power wielded by the colonizers, on forms of domination that must be challenged and changed. With Aughra's view of power relations, the film offers a discourse animated by freedom and resistance, much like the one Foucault offers in *Society Must Be Defended*. The environmental devastation in the film shows that power relations, the practices of domination and subjugation, are not exclusive to totalitarian states; they function just as well in enlightened societies motivated by learning and progress.

In *The Dark Crystal*, the creatures who paid the highest price for the advanced knowledge and imperial power of the urSkeks — and the urRu and Skeksis into which they divided with the force of the Second Conjunction — were the Gelflings, who became just another natural resource to be harvested by the Skeksis. That race was in no small part motivated by the Gelfling prophecy that said an orphan from among them would heal the Crystal and end the rule of the Skeksis. With "ice in their blood and a thirst for blood and darkness," the Skeksis lured the Gelflings to the Castle with flattery and then harvested their essence, or life force, to make an elixir that would prolong Skeksis life (*Dark*). When luring no longer worked, the Skeksis created their Garthim, giant black monsters reminiscent of lobsters and cockroaches that helped the Skeksis destroy every Gelfling but two, Jen and Kira, who are orphaned then rescued, one by the urRu, the other by the Podlings.

When Jen, sent on his quest to "find the shard and heal the Crystal" by his dying urRu master, finally meets Kira, it seems as though Henson and his creative team have divided them along an oppositional and hierarchical binary (*Dark*). As Kira points out to her pet, Fizzgig, a furball with front legs, a giant mouth, and rows of razor-sharp teeth who grazes on flowers and grass, "He's like me, only different" (*Dark*). Jen is quickly aligned with the urRu (also called the Mystics) and their knowledge. He is literate and understands their runes; he has the arts of numbers and of music, although his two-pronged pan flute is nothing like the lutes and lyres they play with their four arms and two feet. Kira, raised by the Pod People, can speak to all the living beings on Thra, makes most of her decisions by instinct, and has the kind of earthy good sense equated with "earth mother" figures. She is heart, and he is head; she seems to equal nature, and he culture. However, Henson and his team are neither reductive nor simplistic. Brian Froud describes the world of *The Dark Crystal* as one "where everything was linked and everything has to come back together" ("World"). The shooting script for the film describes their bonding in this way:

> Jen and Kira are floating down the river at sunset in the shell of a great dead whirligig beetle. The landscape along the river is alive with humming Spanish

moss, whistling trees, and resonant bubbles that surface from the mud, creating a musical landscape. Kira sings a wordless ancient melody, and the landscape comes alive with sweeping colors and movement as well as sound. Jen takes out his old hand-carved flute and accompanies her. It is a moment of achingly perfect union between them, and harmony with the environment [unp].

This brief scene offers the audience both a sensual feast of sound and sight and an interlude of calmness before the action heats up. The "perfect union" between the Gelfling boy and girl and their surroundings emphasizes what their world has lost and what is at stake in their quest.

Moreover, the links between the Gelflings run deeper than overlapping food chains and biospheres, dreamfasting and romance. Jen operates on instinct as much or more than Kira, and his connections to the natural world are as deep as hers. When he has to choose between the right shard and those that the Skeksis have manufactured as decoys, he plays his flute and the shard responds and identifies itself by blushing a rich pink. He is as comfortable as Kira with non–Gelfling creatures, once he meets them. He plays music with members of her Podling village and rides a Landstrider with purpose. Those Landstriders, rabbit-eared, furry, long-legged, might look cuddly, but they hate the Garthim and fight them valiantly, offering one of the most poignant moments of the film when two of them save the Gelflings and the kidnapped Podlings but die fighting the Garthim. At that moment, Kira both enhances and belies her strong connections to the earth when she and Jen need to jump off a cliff to escape the Garthim soldiers. As her wings unfurl and she lands them on safe ground, Jen exclaims over her ability to fly. When he points out that he does not have wings, she explains, "Of course not, you're a boy" (*Dark*). They may have a gendered division of labor, abilities, and secondary sexual characteristics, but both show courage and a willingness to sacrifice for the good of their world. As the Gelfling Adam and Eve, Jen and Kira are charged with fulfilling a prophecy and then restoring and repopulating a devastated planet. Their syncretic methods, learned from the conquering urSkeks and the colonized native peoples, point towards the success of the narrative's happy ending and successes beyond.

The planet's other native hominoids, the Pod People, were designed by Brian Froud; he based their appearance on potatoes, because he wanted them to appear as "part of the earth itself" ("World"). The Podlings are so named because they make their homes and villages in giant seed pods that are native to their lush forest; the Book of Aughra notes that their name for their race translates at "master gardeners who live in bulging plants" (Froud 42). Aughra describes this short, tuber-like race as peaceful and innocent: "They felt only the joy of abundance of their plants and the herding of the Nebrie grubs.

They tended all things that grew, above all the great Pod plants in whose vast seed-pods they made their villages; there they thought only of laughter, food, and music" (Froud 42). They are also kind; they adopted the orphaned Kira and taught her the ways and speech of the natural world. The Podlings are seen first as slaves to the Skeksis, all in shades of beige and grey, their eyes milky opaque orbs, their hair colorless and straw-like. When Kira brings Jen to meet her adoptive family, the audience meets the real Podlings, colorful and vibrantly alive little people who live in symbiosis with the natural world, who love to make music and dance. While the movie leaves it tacit, there are interesting undertones to the way that the Skeksis' life-draining machine leaves the Pod People alive, if without their souls or life force, when it kills the Gelfling. One analogy that might be drawn is to the differences between indigenous first nations; the Gelflings are a threat to the Skeksis because of the prophecy, but Jen and Kira's determination suggests that these are a people who might have tried to take back their world. Therefore Gelflings must be exterminated. The Podlings are peace-loving farmers, easily trapped and converted into slaves. Their rejuvenation at the end of the film — color restored to their hair, skin, and clothing, vitality to their eyes as the Crystal is healed — gestures towards both the meaning of an intrinsic connection with nature (a life-giving force) and the transitory nature of power.

"Prophets don't know everything": The Skeksis, urRu, and urSkeks

Power and its workings are explicit when *The Dark Crystal* focuses on the Skeksis and far more tacit when the urRu and urSkeks are onscreen. As the ostensible villains, the Skeksis are front and center through much of the film. They are discussed at length in "The World of the Dark Crystal": Henson notes that they are modeled on the Seven Deadly Sins; David Odell says they are "an uncomfortable mixture" of male and female; Frank Oz says the Skeksis "were designed to look untrustworthy"; and Froud describes them as "evil, part reptile, part predatory bird, part dragon." They are hideous, but dressed with a shabby opulence that looks like a Renaissance court fallen on hard times. Their layers of rich fabrics display detailed needlework and elaborate collars, cuffs, capes, and accessories, but everything seems somewhat worn and unkempt. When the Emperor dies and the Chamberlain loses his quest for the throne to the General, the hierarchical nature of their society is made evident in their clothing as the Chamberlain is stripped down to his undershirt as punishment. Like the Mystics, they are six-limbed, but their second pair of arms has atrophied from disuse and is seldom seen. In short, the film suggests that the Skeksis display their greed and corruption through the appearance of their bodies and clothing.

While the predatory and greedy nature of the Skeksis shows in the devastated landscape around the castle and in their colorless, near-lifeless Podling slaves, their incessant hunger seems to be about power as much as greed. They accumulate wealth, but their enjoyment comes from the suffering they cause more than the goods they possess. They clearly enjoy abusing their slaves, the native species they keep caged, and each other. The banquet scene offers key insights into the Skeksis as the film moves from the scene where Kira's Nebrie friend rescues Jen from quicksand to the banquet. As Kira and Jen walk off, hand in hand, the giant Nebrie is joined by her two babies, who nuzzle up to her. As the film cuts to the banquet hall in the Crystal Castle, slaves carry in a roasted baby Nebrie. The Skeksis greedily rip shreds of meat from the still steaming carcass. "At its core, the split of the Urskeks into the Mystics and the Skeksis is not simply a split of good and evil but a split couched in terms of environmental harmony and environmental destruction," Sidney Dobrin argues: "It is particularly telling that Henson and Froud developed the ecology of the world of the Dark Crystal so that the conflict between its ruling beings is based in the political (and magical) agenda of how the world's resources should be used. Use and depletion of resources, control and abuse of animals are in the world of the Dark Crystal simply bad. Environmental harmony is good" ("It's" 245). It seems more than a matter of a greedy and unsustainable harvest of resources, though.

The Skeksis, as much as they enjoy the roast Nebrie, are far more excited about dessert, a basket of small animals who skitter across the table while the Skeksis use whatever tools are at hand to spear them and get them into their mouths so they can chew and swallow the still-squirming little creatures. Michel Foucault differs from Marxist theories of power which locate political power as centered in the economy in that he looks for other ways to theorize the "indissociability of the economy and politics" and asserts, in part, "that power is not primarily the perpetuation and renewal of economic relations, but that it is primarily, in itself, a relation of force" (*Society* 14–15). Foucault explores that premise in *Society Must Be Defended* (2003), in which he sees power as "the implementation and deployment of a relationship of force" and suggests it should be analyzed "in terms of surrender, contract, alienation" (15). The Skeksis revel in the force they use; the banquet suggests they take as much pleasure from the violent acquisition of Thra's resources as from the resources themselves.

The Chamberlain's political intrigues—his quest for power, saving the

Gelfling, trying to persuade them of his good intentions so he can use them to regain his lost power — demonstrate the Skeksis' enjoyment of political maneuvering for power. Having created the "Garthim soldiers" to do their bidding, the Skeksis clearly embrace imperial military power; their colonial enterprise might begin with the quest for the natural resources on Thra from the Crystal to the Nebrie and beyond, but their enjoyment of the suffering of every being they exploit and every part of the blasted landscape they leave behind them suggests that power, its acquisition and deployment, are at the core of their quest. As Aughra points out, on the day the urSkeks used the Crystal to achieve their ends, "The Skeksis woke from the shock of division, and they woke full of violence and anger. They stormed into the Crystal Chamber, staggering with the strain of their new bodies, grasping each other in order to stand yet hating each other's touch"; in their anger they hit the Crystal, a shard flew out, and "the light left the Crystal" (*World* 26).

If the one half of the urSkeks emerges violent, angry, and sociopathic, what about the other half? This discussion of the Skeksis and power begs the question, are the urRu any different? Froud describes them as "gentle old wizards, strange animals," and the film seems to set them up as the purely good opposite to the purely evil Skeksis ("World"). They are four-armed, benevolent-looking, ungendered in the main, with long tails, elongated necks and heads; they are similar to the Skeksis in body shape but wise and calm, not ugly or frightening like their counterparts. After all, the UrSkeks intended to use the Second Conjunction to conquer evil for once and all. When they split the crystal, turning it dark, they split themselves into separate beings, like multiple and longer-lasting Jekylls and Hydes. Where the Skeksis took control of the planet and used the darkened Crystal to harness the force of the suns and draw the life force from the planet and its inhabitants, the urRu passively retired to their valley to play music, chant, and meditate, to draw their symbols, read the runes, and prophesy. However, passivity does not necessarily mean good. Dobrin reads Henson's "explicit agenda of ecological literacy promotion" as a binary: "Couched in this ecological masterpiece is the issue of environmental ethics, of seeing environmental harmony and protection as good and the environmental pillaging and oppression as bad" (234, 247). I suggest it might not be that simple.

Aughra explicitly links the Mystics to their own quest for power; in their valley, "the urRu made stone circles of power, the framework of the valley, everlasting protection" (*World* 28). Moreover, for each Skeksis there is a counterpoint Mystic; when one dies or is injured, the same thing happens to the other half; for example, when Jen wounds SkekSil the Chamberlain, urSol, the Chanter, magically has the same wound. The urRu are as intrinsically passive as the Skeksis are violent. In their passivity, they are as culpable for the destruction of Thra and its native species as their enterprising other halves. Their culpability is evident in the film: the first shot of Jen shows him in a lush setting which turns out to be a verdant oasis in the desert valley in which the urRu live. They have chosen to inhabit an area that looks like the one surrounding the Castle, which suggests a deeper connection between these two. If the urRu were not, at the very least, complicit, the Skeksis could not have harvested and destroyed to the extent they did. Their ties and joint culpability are also evident through the Crystal. In its darkness, the Crystal resists the Gelfling prophecy and light and summons the Skeksis for updates on the Gelflings, but it also summons the Mystics to the castle as the Conjunction approaches. Thus, the urRu might be read, in part, as those who might not be actively abusing and oppressing the natural world but are passively allowing that devastation to happen. The urRu seem aware of their own failures, failures so enormous they might be seen as a type of evil, when they explain to Aughra that when the urSkeks used the Crystal, "instead of perfection they had achieved division, dark from light, force from virtue, Skeksis from urRu" (*World* 29). Secure in their own protective power, they send the young Gelfling on his mission to prevent the Skeksis and their Garthim from destroying "all things old and good," by which they might mean themselves as much as any part of Thra (*Dark*).

The urRu might also include the urSkeks in their concern for the "old and good," but Aughra reports that those first colonizers of Thra were as concerned with power as any. She describes power at the center of the teachings they shared with her: "There is power in the Universe that is there to be used by those who dare to control and shape their destiny. There are many levels of power; only the fully initiate can wield the fullest power. To gain this strength takes many trine and a great will" (*World* 18). The urSkeks came to Thra specifically to claim the power of its Crystal. They "had left their former world to follow a great design that their fellow urSkeks thought a dangerous folly," Aughra explains, "They could not use the Crystal that was the heart of the urSkeks' world, so they came to ours" (*World* 20). The urSkeks came during one Great Conjunction to use the next to purify themselves, to burn away all that was imperfect; their Skeksis parts planned to use the Third Conjunction to attain immortality. Of the first, Aughra points out that the urSkeks "had not understood the balance of their souls; they had thought there could be light without darkness, stillness without motion" (*World* 20); of the latter, she notes that where she had once moved freely between the Skeksis in the castle and the urRu in the valley, she stopped going to both because "the Skeksis fell into worse evils, I visited the castle no more. And in the valley the urRu lived their gentle lives and died their quiet deaths" (42). In considering the folly of the urSkeks, Audra concludes, "and yet they knew so much of triangles, of numbers that combine and do not oppose" (*World* 18). The urSkeks, the Skeksis, and the urRu, whether separate or joined, are set up as bastions of knowledge and civilization. Their will to power is also a will to perfection, a will that positions them as superior to the humble Podlings, intuitive Gelflings, and the walking trees, meat-eating rocks, and sentient flowers of Thra. However, when Jen and Kira find the ancient Gelfling carvings that prophesy the fall of the Skeksis at the hands of a Gelfling, and when they mount the Landstriders for their ride to the Castle, Jen points out that their actions were not in the prophecy. Kira responds, "Prophets don't know everything" (*Dark*). In so doing, she calls into question all the knowledge that came with the light of the urSkeks, not just their portents and prognostications, not just the science of the colonizing, planet-destroying Skeksis, but also the benign and visually beautiful wisdom of the Mystics.

"Could be anywhere then": Aughra

The film works very hard to tie Aughra to knowledge and to mysticism but also to the planet and its various environments. It suggests that while she has been beguiled by both the enlightened urSkeks and the creatures they became, she is part of Thra, as Thra is part of her. She might explain her origin and eyes, but she leaves the stone in the center of her forehead tacit; it is both birthright and reminder of her purpose. Henson notes that his creative team strived for "the edges of things, parts of life — a depth that you don't know about," so they created an entire natural history for this world, with rooted animals and plants that move about, because "we have to know it in order to get this entire world working as a reality" ("World"). Froud explains that in this "world with an ancient history; a world where everything was linked and everything has to come back together again," Aughra exists as "a product of the landscape" ("World"). Created by the rocks and roots to be the eye for their world, "The wind blew and the blind trees sand and roots twisted in the dark rocks and the roots sang and the rocks cracked and I was Aughra," she is, like most colonized peoples, both damaged and expanded by the coming of the urSkeks. (*World* 13).

She is the paradox of the film and Henson's messages about understanding of, respect for, and union with all living creatures ("World"). On the one hand, Aughra embraces the enlightened urSkeks, the knowledge they bring and their alien worldview. She even picks up on the attributes of the creatures they become: she understands and incorporates the many symbols used by the urRu; she wears a tatty red satin dress that would look fitting on one of the Skeksis. The urSkeks build her an observatory that defies gravity and includes an amazing Orrery, but she communes with the plants, rocks, and creatures of Thra with an offhand fluency that matches or outpaces Kira's. Her awareness of and communion with everything that lives on Thra, including the Crystal, extend to everything that has died on Thra. She speaks of the ways in which she finds shelter for the bodies of dead, often murdered, Gelfling, but implies that their spirits are still around. In the film, she asks Jen the whereabouts of his master, the wisest of the urRu. He explains that urSu has died; "Dead. Could be anywhere, then," she comments (*Dark*). In *The World of the Dark Crystal*, however, she elaborates, "Of the dead I will not speak; their presence may be felt anywhere, learn from them yourself" (44). In sum, Aughra functions as an ongoing conjunction of the planet and everything it holds and the entire universe that holds it. Her Skeksis-like garment hides little of her body; her large, pendulous breasts with their prominent nipples, her rounded belly, are clearly outlined. One suspects that at the end of the film, after she has recited the now-fulfilled prophecy and waddled offstage, she loses the garment imposed on her by colonial powers, returning to nudity and displaying a body that must look like fertility goddesses from any number of original peoples. This impression is enhanced by the many scenes in which Aughra squats. Every time she pauses to explain something that is relevant for the fulfillment of the Gelfling prophecy, Aughra squats as if giving birth. She seems a primeval force birthing the ideas and actions that will rebirth the planet and all its inhabitants. From the center of Thra to the suns that sustain its life, Aughra functions as a connective force, tying together all life in a place where everything is understood to be alive.

On the other hand, Aughra is profoundly singular, separate, and alone. She explains, "Of the race of Aughra, I, Aughra, am alone, the first and last" (*World* 13). An accompanying translator's note elaborates that "race" also means "destiny," "alone" suggests both "perfect" and "incomplete," and "first and last" means both "in my end is my beginning" and "in my beginning is my end" (*World* 15). Physically, the film gestures towards Aughra's function as the catalyst that moves events towards the fulfillment of the prophecy. Psychically, she seems to be the matrix of life on Thra, born from its primeval forces, circling among and through all its relations. When Froud explains that "you never really know which side she's on," he gestures towards her singular ambivalence about the events and beings swirling around her. When the Garthim capture her in their failed attempt to kill Jen, she berates the Skeksis for sending their "stupid Garthim" to ruin her observatory when they could have asked her where the Gelfling was hiding (*Dark*). Aughra leaves tacit whether or not she would have handed over Jen to the Garthim, and she might simply be emphasizing the breadth and depth of her knowledge. She clearly admires the learning of the urSkeks who found her after the First Conjunction: "they healed my burns; but I was now gnarled root and weathered rock; the heat of the Suns had burnt my first growth away. When I was healed, the urSkeks taught me knowledge; they built for me the great Observatory that I might see all the paths of the World" (*World* 16). However, she also notes that in the newly colonized Thra, "the shining strangers changed our World and our lives forever. I lived all my time in my Observatory, no longer walking and wandering, no longer speaking with Gelfling" (*World* 16). If Aughra was isolated after the first alignment of the suns, she was even more so after the second; unable to stand the evil of the Skeksis and the passivity of the urRu, she concludes, "I am of rock; I stand firm," and retires to her Orrery "to watch the stars and Suns, in hope they would reveal some better change" (*World* 42).

As the film moves towards the nexus of the Third Conjunction, Aughra's aloneness becomes increasingly stark as the Gelflings find each other, the suns move into alignment, the urRu move towards reunification with Skeksis, and the entire planet yearns for the healing of the Crystal. There is "a purity to [puppetry]," Henson says, "a puppet is a symbol of whatever you're trying to portray" ("World"). As the only one of her race, Aughra's destiny, her symbolic value, seems to be the representation of the planet that birthed her. Eternally alone, she is both incomplete but perfectly connected to all life around her. Having been born of Thra, she has seen it through the three Great Conjunctions that have returned it to the state of her birth; her beginning is her end, which is in turn her beginning. She concludes: "I have seen great glory perish, I have seen strength decay and color dim, I have seen freedom lost and wisdom perverted, I have seen the Crystal darken. And at the end of the suffering I saw the Crystal healed and the World restored. Now I can return to the embrace of rock and root, for I have seen the light rekindled" (*World* 15). Loving both light and darkness, Aughra sidesteps simple binaries like good and evil, and looks for the more circular nature of harmony.

Immediately after Jen replaces the shard and heals the Crystal, the urRu and Skekis reunite into the urSkeks, and Aughra recites the Gelfling prophecy:

> When single shines the triple sun,
> What was sundered and undone
> Shall be whole, the two made one [*Dark*].

The chain of events that follow — the Podlings are restored, Kira resurrected, the urSkeks return to their home in a blaze of light — iterate the chains of connections that reverberate through the film. Christopher Finch notes the repeated connections between all things; for example, the matching symbols "on Jen's robe, the Weaver's loom, the Emperor's scepter, the masonry of the Crystal Chamber" (3). He suggests that this "cosmos has been fragmented into different and conflicting cultures, but each has grown from the same root" (3), and as Henson's symbolic center and coming from rocks and roots, Aughra is that root. Theodore Geisel argued that "in *The Lorax* I was out to attack what I think are evil things," and *The Dark Crystal* uses Aughra to attack evil, not the urSkeks or even the Skeksis, but the quest for power that sees peoples conquered and environments devastated (qtd. in Cott 118). "Of all the projects that I've worked on," Henson affirms, "it's the one that I'm most proud of" ("World"). While the film closes with the injunction to "make your world in its light" as the Crystal transforms the blasted area outside the castle into a lush green landscape, Henson's joining of lightness and darkness in Aughra, her combinations of instinct and intellect, earth and sky, rock and root, make her, as screenwriter David Odell suggests, "a more perfect expression of his philosophy or his spiritual insights," the eye and the voice for a world ("World").

Notes

1. My primary sources share names, so for the sake of clarity the film *The Dark Crystal* will be identified by that name in italics or in the citation (*Dark*). I refer to the shooting script from the film as "The Dark Crystal" or ("Dark"). The book, *The World of the Dark Crystal*, by Brian Froud and J. J. Llewellyn will be designated by that title or (Froud), while the documentary appended to the 25th Anniversary Edition of the film will be "The World of the Dark Crystal," or ("World").

Works Cited

Cott, Jonathan. "The Good Dr. Seuss." In *Of Sneetches and Whos and the Good: Essays on the Writings and Life of Theodore Geisel*. Ed. Thomas Fensch. Jefferson, NC: McFarland, 2005. 99–124. Print.
The Dark Crystal. 1982. 25th Anniversary Edition. The Jim Henson Co. 2007. DVD.
"The Dark Crystal." 3rd rev. shooting script. Rev. 22 March 1981. *Muppet Danny*. Web. 27 September 2011.
Dobrin, Sidney I. "'It's Not Easy Being Green': Jim Henson, the Muppets, and Ecological Literacy." In *Wild Things: Children's Culture and Ecocriticism*. Ed. Sidney I. Dobrin and Kenneth B. Kidd. Detroit: Wayne State University Press, 2004. 232–53. Print.
_____. "Through Green Eyes: Complex Visual Culture and Post-Literacy." *Environmental Education Research* 16.3–4 (2010): 265–78.
Finch, Christopher. *The Making of the Dark Crystal: Creating a Unique Film*. New York: Holt, Rinehart, and Winston, 1983. Print.
Foucault Michel. *"Society Must Be Defended": Lectures at the College de France 1975–1976*. Trans. David Macey. New York: Picador, 2003. Print.
Froud, Brian. *The World of the Dark Crystal*. Text J. J. Llewellyn. London: Henson Org. / Mitchell Beazley, 1982. Print.

A Natural History of *The Dark Crystal*: The Conceptual Design of Brian Froud

Catriona McAra

Three decades have passed since Jim Henson and Frank Oz's cult fantasy film *The Dark Crystal* was first released in 1982 after over five years of production. Reflecting on the film, the conceptual designer Brian Froud recently likened the production to an archaeological excavation:

> [A]s I drew and designed, I seemed to discover creatures and places from a civilization that had been long lost. It was more like archaeology than art, yet art it was [...] There had to be a feeling of a layered, half-forgotten history [...] There was flora and fauna diverse and exotic, all permeated with symbol and metaphor to give a depth of meaning to the myth-like story. When we finished the film we knew that we had only seen a fragment of this other world... [2011].

The film is indeed set in an otherworldly, fairy tale terrain called Thra which moves between desert wastelands and bucolic landscapes, loaded with traces of history and mythology. The story follows the trials and tribulations of its protagonist, Jen the Gelfling, a small, handsome, elfin orphan raised by the Mystics or urRu, a race of gentle wizards who are now dying. Jen is tasked with returning the Shard to the Crystal, in order to restore balance to the universe, and embarks on his journey. Along the way he meets a series of friends and foes: a winged female Gelfling companion called Kira, her dog-like pet, Fizzgig, a magical astronomer called Aughra, the child-like race of Pod People, and the shifty-looking Chamberlain, an ostracized member of the evil Skeksis who have spread a reign of terror. The quest narrative is fairly straightforward and the characterization is often stock, but what is most striking about this 89-minute feature is the imaginative investment and level of craft and detail devoted to the background and landscaping of this magical world. Such research-based design arguably enabled the realistic creation of this fantastical domain, and the boundaries between two worlds are blurred as we begin to investigate the intersection between the inner workings of *The Dark Crystal* and the production world of Jim Henson.

Landscaping the World of the Dark Crystal

The conceptual roots of *The Dark Crystal* can be found in the volcanic, prehistoric scenery which was used for Henson's "Land of Gorch," an experimental slot on *Saturday Night Live* which ran from October 1975 until April 1976 (Harris 28; Jones 34–5). Though this feature folded after 15 episodes due to an unworkable script, the "Land of Gorch" interestingly transplanted the puppets within their own fantastic sphere. As with *The Muppet Show*, the puppeteers did not appear on camera, and the only humans who ever interacted with the inhabitants of Gorch were guests with such contact taking place off set in the liminal world of the studio offices. The "Land of Gorch" is represented as a distant and far-removed place with its own culture, traditions, and idiosyncrasies — much like *The World of the Dark Crystal* would become. The idea of a feature-length, self-sustaining puppetry world devoid of human presence began to grow in Henson's mind. He was adamant that the characters in his new fantasy project should sit somewhere between his earlier puppets and Muppets franchise as "creatures" (Horsting and Stein 53). Key details from the "Land of Gorch" that helped provoke a more realistic vision, such as the innovative use of taxidermist eyes, were conceptually preserved for this future project, in its early stages simply referred to as *The Crystal*. According to one of two insightful articles on the making of *The Dark Crystal* by Alan Jones, Henson was also influenced by Leonard B. Lubin's nonsense illustrations of crocodiles for a 1975 edition of Lewis Carroll's poetry (35). One can easily see how Henson would have been drawn to Carrollian representations of the fantastic which have endured the test of time, no doubt due to their sensitive appreciation of a child's understanding of the world. Around this time Henson's licenser Jerry Juhl discovered *The Land of Froud* (1977) at a book fair in San Francisco (Zimmerman 34) which would prove to be a very significant moment in the making of *The Dark Crystal*. Henson soon met with the picture book's author, the English illustrator and fantasy artist Brian Froud, who would help the nascent project grow to fruition.

Jim Henson's Creature Shop in London was established in the build up to this film, although preproduction mainly took place in New York followed by filming in EMI Elstree Studios outside of London. Much of the film's resulting production materials and artwork are now housed in the Jim Henson Company Archive, maintained by Karen Falk in Long Island City but currently inaccessible to the public.[1] This essay will, therefore, draw on the more publicly available book illustrations and conceptual designs of Froud which can be found in the accompanying guidebook, *The World of the Dark Crystal* (1983), as well as the documentary film of the same title (first aired on January 9, 1983, and later included on the digitally re-mastered version of *The Dark Crystal* in 2005) and the behind-the-scenes book, *The Making of the Dark Crystal* by Christopher Finch (1983). Reference to the related science fiction fanzine ephemera of the era (including *Cinefantastique, Fantastic Films, Starburst*, and *Starlog*) facilitates a more complete representation of this "natural history." In the accompanying documentary, Henson reveals that the overall color-wash (a light flex with color tint) was conjured by cinematographer Oswald Morris in response to the conceptual designs of Froud which were inspired by the English countryside and dramatic landscapes of Froud's home in Dartmoor, Devon. The film's highly tactile aesthetic and materiality were arguably enhanced by pre-CGI technologies and vintage effects, including glass-matte painting for the backdrops by Michael Pangrazio and Chris Evans at ILM (Industrial Light and Magic, San Francisco), and miniature models for some of the more monumental, architectural aspects. Harry Lange was tasked with translating Froud's designs into practical life-size sets where every object had to be researched, constructed, and artificially aged (Jones 46–48). Henson further explains the lengths to which his production company went in order to achieve a believable world, including the collection of flora and fauna samples, worthy of a naturalist or explorer. As with Froud, Henson's description is worth quoting at length:

> There is a wonderful texture and depth to this world [...] in creating the world we had to [...] create all of that depth from the beginning, and so we went into a great deal more work than we probably needed to in order to have thought out the history [...] We had to work out all kinds of the background behind things, behind the visuals, we knew the landscape, we had maps of the landscape [...], the color schemes of all these different areas and the different kinds of animals and plants that lived there. Very little of this ends up on the finished film but we have to know it in order to believe this whole world, to get the entire thing working as a reality. Then, even if we only show a small portion of it as part of this film, we are dealing with something that has substance [*WDC*].

What emerges from such "depth" and "background" is a film of epic proportions, offering a layered archaeology of materiality to excavate and detailed cartographies to survey. A thousand years are said to have passed since the legendary Cracking of the Crystal as evidenced by the weathered

Gelfling art and ruins, the Murals of Commemoration, the Wall of Destiny, scrolls, and engravings or "words that stay," which are catalogued and deciphered in *The World of the Dark Crystal* (9, 24, 118). This lavishly illustrated companion book augments the expanse of histories, mythologies, typologies, and symbols, the surfaces of which can only be skimmed over in the film. It fills in the gaps and emphasizes the meticulous role that Froud's conceptual design played in effectively imag(in)ing the world which *The Dark Crystal* is set in for Henson. Following Juhl's discovery of *The Land of Froud*, Henson claims that he first saw three or four illustrations by Froud in Dark Larkin's edited collection *Once Upon a Time* (1976) (Horsting and Stein 52; Jones 35). One can think about this collaboration in terms of Froud visualizing Henson's ideas, and Froud's designs, in turn, translated into three-dimensional form by the puppet-makers. This arrangement resulted in a situation where, unlike most films, the story followed the creation of the fantasy world (Jones 35). For Froud, the role of conceptual designer and the medium of film offered new possibilities and challenges compared to small-scale visual narratives for books.

Born in England in 1947, Froud graduated from Maidstone College of Art in 1971 and has since been involved in a variety of projects, most notably the illustrated taxonomy with Alan Lee, *Faeries* (1978). One is tempted to compare their commitments to craft- and research-based conceptual design; Froud for Henson's *The Dark Crystal*, *Labyrinth* (1986), and *The Storyteller* (1988), and Lee and John Howe for Peter Jackson's more recent film trilogy of J.R.R. Tolkien's *Lord of the Rings* (1998–2003), the accompanying documentary which is comparable to *The World of the Dark Crystal* in its attention to detail. Both Froud and Lee use a mixture of watercolor and pencil, and the work of both appears stylistically reminiscent of the English art historical tradition, including the early twentieth century "goblin-master" illustrations of Arthur Rackham and the mid- to late nineteenth-century paintings of the Pre-Raphaelite Brotherhood, such as John Everett Millais and Dante Gabriel Rossetti, who dedicated themselves to detailed study of the natural world while depicting scenes from Shakespearean literature and Arthurian legend. Building on Tolkien's epic imagination, the conceptual design for *Lord of the Rings* perhaps finds its conceptual precursors in both *Faeries* and in Froud's designs for *The Dark Crystal*. Indeed Jones aptly describes *The Dark Crystal* as "a standard quest saga in the richly landscaped Tolkeinian [sic] tradition" (23). One might comfortably compare the dark and light aesthetics of the Orcs and Elves of *Lord of the Rings* with the Skeksis and urRu in *The Dark Crystal*, and compare the Hobbits with the Gelflings. Where Tolkien's characters Bilbo and Frodo Baggins are the custodians of the ring, Jen's magical object is the Crystal Shard. Moreover, the landscapes are marked by conflicting moral standpoints; where the goodness of the Shire is represented as green and leafy, evil Mordor is mountainous and jagged. This is true too of the contrasts between Kira's Swamp and the Skeksis' Castle of the Crystal, the political implications of which can be explored further with reference to another, more contemporaneous fantasy trilogy. Visually and ideologically, *The Dark Crystal* lends itself to further comparison with the contemporaneous sci-fi trilogy *Star Wars*, particularly the third film, *Return of the Jedi* (1983), which features the tree-dwelling Ewok tribe. As with the heroes of *The Dark Crystal*, the Ewoks conceptually play on the aesthetics of the cute, cuddly, and furry as a kind of plush taxidermy that is highly marketable. There were, however, some small distinctions in their performances. On the one hand, the characters of *The Dark Crystal* predominantly involved sophisticated puppetry techniques while the Ewoks were portrayed by dwarf actors, including Warwick Davis, in costumes. Jones tells us that Henson was hesitant to use actors due to his "commitment to the puppet medium" (49, 54), though children and little people were employed for the full-length shots in *The Dark Crystal* and puppetry techniques and expertise were deployed for *Star Wars*. In fact, *The Empire Strikes Back* (1980), the second film in the initial *Star Wars* trilogy, utilized a cross-fertilization of conceptual design between the two production teams. The producer of *The Dark Crystal*, Gary Kurtz, helped George Lucas co-produce the first two films in the early *Star Wars* trilogy. However, Kurtz and Lucas did not work together on the third film, *Return of the Jedi*, supposedly after a disagreement over the mythological aspects of the films. Jones claims it was because Kurtz wanted to pursue his own project and had already committed to co-producing *The Dark Crystal* in return for Frank Oz and Wendy Midener's assistance with Master Yoda's conception (36–7). There are certainly similarities in the respective conceptualizations of fantasy landscapes. In Marcia S. Calkowski's persuasive article on Ewokese linguistics and semantics, she argues that a political message can be perceived through their Tibetan-inspired culture and use of guerrilla warfare tactics as well as the rural setting of the forest moon of Endor versus the technologically-advanced evil Empire in their encroaching space station (58). *Return of the Jedi* offers clear-cut, binary representations of the 'goodness' and 'wholesomeness' of craft-based nature versus 'the dark side' of the Empire; what the cultural theorist Walter Benjamin would describe as the politicization of art versus the aestheticization of politics (235).

In *The Dark Crystal*, the political situation is similarly mirrored in the landscapes: Kira's sun-lit Swamp is lush and fertile while the evil Skeksis live in a dry, barren desert with a lightning storm brewing above. We can observe this dichotomy further in the Castle of the Skeksis versus Valley of the Mystics, again a corrupt, violent civilization versus gentle, moral nature. Jones explains that the black/white morality was supposedly the result of a conversation Henson had with his twenty-two-year-old daughter Lisa during the initial stages of the project (22; 35). However, Froud insists that: "We didn't want this to be just *black and white*. We didn't want 'evil' against 'good.' We wanted to show that both have their qualities and their drawbacks" (Zimmerman 64). It is now necessary to consider the surface and depth of the world of *The Dark Crystal*, arranged taxonomically by character units as species or fantasy races.

Aughra: The Astronomer

Of the race of Aughra, I, Aughra, am alone, the first and last [WDC, 13].

Aughra, a Keeper of Secrets, is perhaps the strangest character encountered in *The Dark Crystal*. As the book explains, she is an ancient and unique being, close to the race of Gelflings but forged from the landscape of roots and rocks that puts her in touch with nature (13). As Gideon Haberkorn points out in his essay in this volume, Aughra, the last of her race, faces inevitable extinction which lends her an extra-ordinary wisdom and poignancy (85). Froud appears to have conceived of her as a wrinkled, matriarchal creature, swamped in the natural history which she embodies. Like the witches from Shakespeare's *Macbeth,* she is a prophetess with a detachable eye; a visionary Sibyl or sorceress with powers of foresight. Much of *The World of the Dark Crystal* is thus narrated through her as the *Book of Aughra*, a fictional, translated version of her "manuscript," serving as a pseudo-encyclopedia to the strange world she exists within. She inhabits the Observatory that appears like an over-stuffed curiosity cabinet or sixteenth-century laboratory, a Galilean site of knowledge augmented by the giant Orrery, a mechanical, planetary device which models the universe in a heliocentric configuration. According to the book, such "astronomical calculations" are beyond "Newtonian or Einsteinian" physics (22), which highlights the physical difference between our real world and the imaginary world of *The Dark Crystal*. Aughra serves an epistemological role within the film; where the Mystics are wise, she is the key "researcher" or scholar who has been assigned as the custodian of the Crystal Shard until the prophecy can be fulfilled. Aughra, or more accurately Froud, has charted the universe by drawing up a detailed mathematical astrology of the Dying Sun and its immanent triple convergence with the other two suns (the Great Sun and the Rose Sun) known as The Great Conjunction. The copious diagrams and ciphers often appear as hieroglyphic, rune-like pentagrams suggesting that Aughra has pagan leanings. Her post-menopausal, disheveled representation of femininity marks her in the tradition of the archetypal crone while her ram-like horns add a note of astrological association and gender-bending enfreakment like sideshow representations of the bearded lady. Her swollen bosom and enormous cranium seem disproportionate for her size, and when she kneels the weight of body forces the expiration of an arthritic groan. Like Master Yoda of the *Star Wars* films, there is a lot of Frank Oz's personality in her character (Jones 34, 37). Oz embroidered a complex transvestitism into her conception, though it is the female actor, Billie Whitelaw, who is credited with Aughra's voice. Aughra is the unrivaled, favorite character of both Froud and Oz. The puppet itself was realized from Froud's design by a team which included Lyle Conway and Tom McLaughlin, who made fourteen skins for Aughra from an innovative latex mixture, though only three such pelts were accepted (Jones 45).

The Gelflings

> "I thought I was the only one!"–Jen
> "I thought I was!"–Kira

According to Froud, the Gelflings are the heroes and protagonists of the film, the ones that we feel the most empathy with, and, in Henson's view, the "bridge characters [...] through which the audience enters this world" (*WDC*). Elsewhere, Henson further explains the need for their "clichéd appearance": as stock characters or blank canvases, the heroes act as the "audience's stand in," guiding us through the narrative (Horsting and Stein 55; Jones 49). This is not to suggest that the Gelflings are entirely vacant. There is evidence of post-traumatic stress and survival instincts built into their characters' portrayal as well as the more common heroic traits of love and courage. But the world of *The Dark Crystal* is a complex place, so the story had to be relatively simple and the characters readily identifiable in order to create a legible fantasy.

The Gelflings are the most distinct in gendered terms. At first believed to be an orphan and the last of his kind, Jen's discovery of Kira is important because her existence implicitly means that reproduction of their endangered species is still a possibility. Both are capable of sharing their memories through touch, known as dreamfasting. Through this act, they learn that they had similar infancies, rescued from extinction after attacks by the evil Garthim. Jen was adopted by the Mystics, while Kira joined the Podlings, divergent cultural upbringings which are reflected in their choices of dress (Finch 22). The Gelflings are equipped with different skills and survival tactics. Kira can speak many languages while Jen can read. Later in the film, we learn that female Gelflings have wings that distinguish them from males, reminding one of a stereotypically feminine fairy.² Though the Gelflings are both 'feminine' in their elfin appearance, Kira is pinker, perkier and blonder in her coloring with rosy cheeks, whereas Jen is darker and earthier with blue streaks in his hair. Traditional notions of gender representation, typical of many fairy tales, are therefore sustained where they had been transgressed against the older body of Aughra. The Gelflings were mainly designed by Wendy Froud (*née* Midener) who talks through their conception in the documentary. She wanted them to be humanoid but found it challenging to make the female "pretty enough" (*WDC*). Jen was initially designed with blue skin that would have aligned him with the Hindu deity Rama, though he was later modified to a warm-blooded, human color (Jones 32). At first sight it is tempting to compare Kira and Jen with popular gendered children's toys of the 1980s such as Barbie and Ken, or the colorful, cute aesthetics of the Cabbage Patch Kids or My Little Pony, though, on closer inspection, the dolls and puppets which Wendy Froud sculpts are specialized, hand-crafted art objects which are far more intertextually complex than commercial playthings, drawing on her interests in the Pre-Raphaelites, Greek mythology, and fairy tales including those by Carroll and Adrienne Segur (see *The Art of Wendy Froud*, 10–12).³

The Mystics Versus the Skeksis

The Mystics (urRu) and the Skeksis are the "goodies" and "baddies" of the film. We learn that they were once the same race, the ethereal Urskeks, but upon the previous conjunction of the three suns, were correlatively divided in their beings into diametric opposites; one group being the reverse of the other. Froud has continued an awareness of fantasy dichotomies in his topsy-turvy book, *Good Faeries, Bad Faeries* (1998), where he accepts the existence of creatures with malicious purpose as the antithesis of their more morally upright counterparts (11).

Both species appear in some way primal as if they had evolved from dinosaurs. The Skeksis are reptilian and vulture-like, while the Mystics seem more reminiscent of a weighty and ponderous, long-necked dinosaur. The Mystics are stylistically closest to the giants Froud had been illustrating prior to his design work for *The Dark Crystal*, especially if one considers Froud's front cover illustration for Larkin's *Once Upon a Time* and, as Howard Zimmerman suggests, the Troll Witch from *The Land of Froud* (36). In the case of the Skeksis, Froud claims that they are "part reptile, part predatory bird, part dragon," and he insists he always began their designs with the focus on the "penetrating" eye of each character (*WDC*; Finch 21). Angler fish were also researched as possible visual sources (Zimmerman 34, 36). *The World of the Dark Crystal* book further charts the evolution of Froud's designs, hinting at a "mutation" which the Skeksis have declined to document themselves (102). Commenting on their construction, Conway explains how the Skeksis puppets became more realistically revolting in appearance as production went on: "rotting rubber, permeated with cold KY jelly and putrefying noodles" (43). The Skeksis are, indeed, a rotten civilization predicated on greed, jousting, and lack of table manners. The spiral tattooed, long-haired Mystics are far wiser, slower, and more restrained in their actions, like aging hippies. While the Skeksis are grotesque, carnivalesque monsters (Haberkorn "Muppets" 27–8), the Mystics comport themselves with more dignity. When the emaciated Emperor of the Skeksis dies, his face crumbles and implodes while the wisest of the Mystics evaporates more gracefully in a puff of twinkling stars. While the disheveled Skeksis parade their torn rags and garish bling designed by Kathryn Kubrick, the Mystics wear subtle, decorated coats and amulets with a pseudo–Celtic symbolism (*WDC*, 52, 54, 59). Elsewhere, Finch notes the motifs from Neolithic and Mesopotamian archaeology that have been borrowed for Froud's "cosmography" (28). As Froud admits: "I steal from everywhere. I trace out of the best books!" (qtd. in Jones 47). Tracing paper is included in *The World of the Dark Crystal*, creating an overlay between the symbolic geometries and the conceptual sketches. Again Henson credits Froud, who: "developed a whole symbolic structure that permeates the 'reality' of *The Dark Crystal*" (Horsting and Stein 52). Furthermore, the English writer and linguist Alan Garner was credited for his assistance with the ancient Egyptian-derived language which was initially devised for the Skeksis, though it was later decided that they should speak English for the sake of audience accessibility (Hutchison 19; Jones 53).

Like the Gelflings, both groups have stock character types within them. The Mystics include: the Ritual-Guardian, the Healer, the Chanter, the Alchemist, the Cook, the Herbalist (credited as the Hunter), the Scribe, the Numerologist, and the Weaver, while the Skeksis (or Masters of the Dark Crystal) are cast as: the High-Priest (Ritual-Master), the General (Garthim-Master), the Chamberlain, the Scientist, the Gourmand, the Slave-Master, the Treasurer, the Historian (Scroll-Keeper), and the Ornamentalist. Again, the evolutionary precursors can be found in the Land of Gorch where the characters were more obviously a family kingdom: King Ploobis, Queen Peutra, their son Wisss, the servant girl Vazh, the servant boy Scred, and a stone oracle called the Mighty Favog. Henson explained that the Skeksis were loosely based on the seven deadly sins, even though they ended up with nine different characters (*WDC*). Furthermore, the banquet scene appears oddly reminiscent of the Biblical *Last Supper* imagery in its composition, which may be a deliberate parody.

In terms of gender, the Garthim-Master Skeksis seems the most traditionally "macho" in strength, aggression, and leadership, though some of the Skeksis are more ambiguous in their conception, possibly an amalgamation of both male and female, including the camp Gourmand, the effeminate Ornamentalist, and the weak and sleazy Chamberlain. On the whole, gender and sexuality are more difficult to discern among the Skeksis and the Mystics than with the two Gelflings.

The Garthim Versus the Landstriders

The varying landscapes and clear-cut representations of female and male, light and dark, good and evil, seems to have been more visibly absorbed by the supporting cast of working creatures. The Garthim are dark, crustacean-like masses, while the Landstriders offer their visual antonym as light, tall, and elegant creatures. The Garthim are the armored bouncers or warriors created by the Skeksis to guard their castle and capture the Pod People. The Garthim are clumsy and accidentally incarcerate Aughra after breaking into her observatory, ruthlessly vandalizing her property, and mistaking her for a Gelfling. The oaf-like characteristics of the Garthim remind one of troops that kill ruthlessly in the pack mentality but are incapable of thinking for themselves as individuals. According to Jones, Froud based the Garthim on insects, particularly beetles, for their hard shells, large claws, and scuttling movements (46). The insect world is an alien place that entomologists are still exploring, and thus a useful source of inspiration for Froud. In *The World of the Dark Crystal* book, the Garthim are suspected to be a mere "thought projection" of the Skeksis because they disappear at the moment of defeat (116, 126).

The Landstriders are the tamable, long-limbed, "beasts of swift passage" for the Gelflings in their quest to The Castle of the Crystal (116). According to Finch, the meat of a fallen Landstrider is the Skeksis' favorite meal (13). Froud reveals that the Landstriders evolved from "land spiders" as his designs moved off the page and into three-dimensional action (Zimmerman 37). One aspect that the documentary makes clear is the physical investment of the puppeteers in Froud's designs. The Landstriders were played by costumed performers on stilts while the Garthim wore heavy costumes that required the performer to crouch uncomfortably for short periods of time. Henson claims he always put emphasis on the performer rather than mechanics or technologies that could only enhance the performance. Many of the movements were choreographed by a Swiss mime, Jean Pierre Amiel, for consistency (Harris 31; Jones 48).

Other Species/Miscellaneous Designs

The Podlings, Pod People or "master gardeners" (*WDC* 43) are perhaps the most reminiscent of the Muppets and the most literally "down to earth" of all the species within Henson's fantasy world. In the documentary, Froud explains how their closeness to the earth meant their visual conception was very much based on the shapes of potatoes (*WDC*). Historically, potatoes are the food of the working classes as seen in well-known representations like Vincent van Gogh's painting *The Potato Eaters* (1885). Spud-like, the Pod People are kind, generous, wholesome, musically gifted, and communal in their activities. They are also the most defenseless and the most easily captured and corrupted. They are perhaps not the brightest of creatures — a potato having connotations of thickness and simplicity.

Another curious creature is Kira's pet Fizzgig, credited as "A Friendly Monster," who at first seems to consist of little more than an angry mouth, like a distant relative of the Muppet character, Animal. Fizzgig is well-named, often fizzing up and flying off the handle before cowering and whimpering apologetically. In the book, his species is described as "quadruped" (43), and in the film we later see that his body includes feet and a tail. Jones explains the hybrid combination of lion, fox, raccoon, lamb, and opossum gleaned from old fur coats (39, 41), and the amount of effort and characterization that sculptor Rollie Krewson and performer Dave Goelz put into "what is essentially a ball of fur" (41). Fizzgig is perhaps best likened to a small Shih Tzu who is both a loyal, canine companion and badly tempered, spoilt familiar reminiscent of Miss Piggy's lapdog Foo-Foo on *The Muppet Show*.

The Crystal Bats are part-mammal, part-mineral, a discreet, closed-circuit surveillance system sent by the Skeksis as literal spy glasses. As mentioned earlier, it is significant that Froud tends to begin his characters by drawing their eyes. Like any crystal ball, they offer a view of what is happening elsewhere in their world and have adapted to a wide variety of conditions in order to map diverse terrains. They are an enemy of the Gelflings and a guide to the Garthim, who also have Crystal eyes (*WDC* 116). Surveillance in the fantasy genre often strikes a sinister tone. Compare the Crystal Bats with monumental burning Eye of Sauron from *Lord of the Rings* or the red and green glowing crystal ball of the Wicked Witch of the West in Victor Fleming's

1939 film adaptation of *The Wizard of Oz*. Where Aughra's single eye is a symbol of knowledge and foresight, the Crystal Bats are mindlessly fishing for information.

The remainder of flora and fauna in the film, book and world of Thra are said to have the triadic structure which reflects the "dominant patterns of thought" and the prevailing shapes of the universe as observed and catalogued by Aughra (10, 61). As Haberkorn suggests: "The fictional ecosystems of *The Dark Crystal* [...] cannot be interpreted usefully as reflecting the natural world," for one must remember that this is a fantasy space however lifelike the environment appears (75). Indeed one might question the limits of the conceptual designer's ability to play naturalist. Working in the fantasy genre, Froud's project is always more natural fiction than natural history. On the other hand, the sheer extent to which he and the production team went allows a greater suspension of disbelief. Among the profusion of "environmental creatures" designed by Froud (see Finch, 73), many "strange beasts" are said to have appeared since the "darkening of the world," as listed in *The World of the Dark Crystal* (34). One thinks of the organic aberrations that emerge after a nuclear disaster. Some of the vegetation in the Swamp of the Black River is carnivorous, like a Venus Flytrap, while the mosses offer more healing properties. Considering the extreme attention to detail and the commitment to believability so far, it comes as no surprise to learn that John Coppinger, an expert in scientific sculpture from the Natural History Museum, was recruited to advise on the Swamp's set design (Finch 71).

Mineral Treasures: The Crystal and Its Shard

> "What was sundered and undone shall be whole — the two made one."
> — Aughra and Ancient Prophecy

While the Crystal and its Shard lie at the heart of the narrative as coveted, fairy tale objects, they are easy to overlook within the aestheticized paraphernalia of surrounding genus and species, myth and legend. The breaking of the Harmony or the Darkening of the Crystal was the symbolic event which heralded the split between good and evil. The book explains that the cracking of the Crystal and the loss of the Shard occurred after the violent Skeksis first emerged and fought. The film's narrator presents a slightly different version of events: that the cracking of the crystal was the cause of the splitting of the UrSkeks. Perhaps the legend is so old that no one can really remember the chain of events of this chicken or egg scenario. Either way, the darkness of the film's title suggests that the moral balance has tipped over into evil and that goodness and light require restoration. This is part of the prophecy that has been foreseen. The Crystal is suspended above a pit of fire and ice at the center of the Castle of the Crystal and is amethyst in color and texture, illuminated by the rays of the Dying Sun. It is much coveted and a great source of power for the Skeksis. They have exploited its powers by placing a reflector underneath to hypnotize more innocent species, like the Podlings, and suck out their "essence." This essence reverses the aging process, like cosmetic Botox or collagen implants, and provides long life for the Skeksis. Such essence-drinking is arguably the darkest part of the film as it involves one species forcing another in a form of ritual sacrifice and animal cruelty. The emaciated, hollowed out appearance of the Podlings, post-essence extraction, may also be an intentional visual reference to concentration camp victims, again reminding us of the horrors of the dark empire.

Meanwhile, the Shard is the missing piece in the puzzle. As its temporary custodian, Aughra produces a selection of crystal shards for Jen to choose between upon his arrival to fulfill his destiny. Like a handful of keys, Aughra has forgotten which one is the true Shard, but Jen quickly whittles down his selection to a short-list of three and identifies the correct piece by blowing his pipes and enchanting a glowing amethyst color from it. The Shard is a synecdoche of the larger Crystal, a part that stands for the whole. Like Jen, it represents a microcosm of the larger universe. Once the Shard is restored to its rightful place within the Dark Crystal, the world is reunified, and evil is conquered. The purple-tinged Dark Crystal becomes the gleaming white Crystal of Truth.

Another mineral documented in the film and book is the *Haakskeekah* Stone, an imitation of the Dark Crystal, suspected to be made of basalt or a variant, which is much less powerful and less valuable than crystal. The Skeksis use it within their ritual jousting, "trial by stone," to determine who will emerge triumphant as the next emperor (*WDC* 112). The Dark Crystal and the *Haakskeekah* Stone both mirror Froud's architectural designs for the Castle of the Skeksis. Like the recurrent motif of the astronomical triangle, the twisted crystal shapes seem to be a metaphor for foreboding time and space.

The Production Team and Audience

At this point it is worth returning to the background of the production team as their own invisible species in order to more fully appreciate their motivations and dynamics. Often the production team appears to have mimicked the otherworldly taxonomies and behaviors of the characters in *The*

Dark Crystal. In the film's credits, Creative Fabrication is listed in units: Gelfling Unit, Skeksis Unit, Mystic Unit, the Garthim Unit, Aughra and the Urskeks Unit, Landstriders Unit, and Podling Unit. In the documentary, the various puppet-making groups are said to have developed tribal instincts:

> The various groups of people did become very attached to their creatures and there was a little bit of rivalry sometimes between the groups, not only over the creatures themselves but sometimes over how much time they had to finish. Occasionally there was jealousy because one group was needed before another group [*WDC*; Conway, 44].

This suggests that the production team had become so immersed in this fantasy world that they had started to mimic the characters on set as well as off.

Moreover, the innate *darkness* of *The Dark Crystal* leads one to question its audience which was interestingly a mixture of both adult and children. This is true too of Froud's *œuvre* which on a surface level may appear like children's book illustrations, but on closer inspection can be demanding in its complex taxonomies and intertextual sources. Today Froud's work is arguably as coveted by an adult collector's market as its childhood readership. By extension, *The World of the Dark Crystal* is not to be confused with conventional children's illustration but is more of an *objet d'art* or *Livre d'Artiste* (artist's book). However, one might argue that children are far more capable of dealing with the darker side of this world than many would care to accept and that Froud is highly empathic and shrewd in this regard.

Conclusion

The Dark Crystal is now being re-interpreted by a twenty-first century audience as a cult classic. By moving between the inner fantasy world of the film and book and its real-world fabrication, we have been able to trace the archaeology of Froud's illustrations and think about him as a "naturalist" of the world he has designed. In many ways the illustrations speak for themselves; playing on familiar dichotomies found in fairy tales, the denotations of light and dark are easy to interpret. Representations of gender and class are more variable between species but are often binary, with a small number of exceptions in between. Masculinity and femininity are stereotypically represented in the case of the Gelflings but more creatively reinterpreted in the cases of Aughra and some of the Skeksis. Class distinctions are denoted through the architecture: the Mystics and Pod People inhabit the earthy valley while the ruling Skeksis live in the Castle. The most extreme dichotomy is the schizophrenic split that has occurred between the Skeksis and the Mystics as good versus evil, dark versus light. While this seems to have been the initial idea on Henson's part, Froud's conceptual designs have elaborated the dark/light fantasy split into a multilayered natural history.

The emergence of *The Dark Crystal* in the early 1980s provoked a wealth of texts, graphics, and fanzine-ephemera to excavate. More recently, Froud's graphic novels, *The Dark Crystal Creation Myths*, are beginning to help fill in the gaps in the narrative and natural history that were left open or unexplained in the film. It seems important to preserve and acknowledge the documentary material surrounding this cult classic in the lead up to the sequel, *The Power of the Dark Crystal*, which is currently in production by the Jim Henson Company and Omnilab Media in Australia. This film will feature new technologies of 3D live action that may enhance, revolutionize, or even damage both the complicated stratigraphy so carefully represented in *The World of the Dark Crystal* and the craft and skill of the potentially obsolete puppet film industry. While one may be skeptical of the lack of materiality endorsed by new technologies, Brian Froud's involvement in the conceptual design of this forthcoming film surely inspires a great deal of confidence and anticipation.

NOTES

1. Grateful thanks to Karen Falk for her suggestions for alternative research materials and to the editors for their helpful comments which helped shape this paper.
2. However, the recent *Creation Myths* explain that the female Gelflings' wings have more empowering origins, a coping strategy representing the strength of the maternal body (Holguin 2011 unpaginated).
3. Work by Wendy Froud was included in *The Doll as Art* exhibitions curated by Neil Zukerman's whose CFM Gallery in New York also deals the Surrealist art of Leonor Fini whose paintings, in turn, have a similar doll-like aesthetic. Surrealism's commitment to alternative realities also offers a possible precursor for 1980s fantasy realms.

WORKS CITED

Benjamin, Walter. "The Work of Art in the Age of Mechanical Reproduction." *Illuminations*. Ed. Hannah Arendt. Trans. Harry Zorn, London: Pimlico, 1999. 219–253. Print.
Calkowski, Marcia S. "Is There an Authoritative Voice in Ewok Talk?: On Postmodernism, Fieldwork, and the Recovery of Unintended Meanings." *Culture: From Method to Modesty: Essays on Thinking and Making Ethnography Now*. 11.1–2 (1991): 53–63. Print.
Carroll, Lewis. "The Pig-Tale." Illus. Leonard B. Lubin. New York: Little Brown and Co. 1975. Print.
Conway, Lyle. "Confessions of a Creature Craftsman." *Cinefantastique* 13:4 (April–May, 1983): 42–44. Print.
Finch, Christopher. *The Making of the Dark Crystal: Creating a Unique Film*. New York: Henson Organization Publishing, Holt, Rinehart and Winston, 1983. Print.
Froud, Brian. *Good Faeries, Bad Faeries*. Ed. Terri Windling. New York: Simon and Schuster, 1998. Print.
_____, and B. Holguin. *The Dark Crystal Creation Myths*. Volume One. Los Angeles: Archaia and the Jim Henson Company, 2011. Print.

Froud, Brian, J.J. Llewellyn, and R. Brown. *The World of the Dark Crystal.* London: Henson Organization Publishing Inc. and Micheal Beazley London Ltd. 1982. Print.
Froud, Wendy. *The Art of Wendy Froud.* Los Angeles: Imaginosis, 2006. Print.
Haberkorn, Gideon. "Interpreting Various Species in *The Dark Crystal* and *Fraggle Rock.*" *The Wider Worlds of Jim Henson: Essays on His Work and Legacy Beyond the Muppet Show and Sesame Street.* Ed. Jennifer C. Garlen and Anissa M. Graham, Jefferson, NC: McFarland, 2012. 73–87. Print.
_____. "Muppets as a Metaphor for the Self." *Kermit Culture: Critical Perspectives on Jim Henson's Muppets.* Ed. Jennifer C. Garlen and Anissa M. Graham, Jefferson, NC: McFarland and Co. Inc. 2009. 25–39. Print.
Harris, Judith P. "Of Precocious Pigs, Singing Cabbages, and a Little Green Frog Named Kermit: The Story of Jim Henson and the Muppets." *Cinefantastique* 13:4 (April–May, 1983): 25–31. Print.
Horsting, Jessie and Michael Stein. "Interview with Jim Henson and Gary Kurtz." *Fantastic Films: The Magazine of Imaginative Media.* 32 (February 1983): 51–55. Print.
Hutchison, David. "Producing the World of *The Dark Crystal*: A Candid Conversation with Gary Kurtz." *Starlog: The Magazine of the Future.* 66 (January 1983): 16–20. Print.
Jones, Alan. "The Making of *The Dark Crystal.*" *Starburst: The Magazine of Cinema and Television Fantasy.* 55 (March 1983): 22–27. Print.
_____. "The Dark Crystal: The Behind-the-Scenes Story of One of the Most Complex and Imaginative Fantasy Films of All Time." *Cinefantastique* 13:4 (April–May, 1983): 32–41; 45–55. Print.
Larkin, David ed. *Faeries: Described and Illustrated by Brian Froud and Alan Lee.* New York, Harry N. Abrams, 1978. Print.
_____. *Once Upon a Time: Some Contemporary Illustrators of Fantasy.* New York: Peacock Press, 1976. Print.
Schneider, Lynne D. "Stuffed Suits and Hog-Wild Desire." In *Kermit Culture: Critical Perspectives on Jim Henson's Muppets.* Eds. Jennifer C. Garlen and Anissa M. Graham, Jefferson, North Carolina: McFarland, 2009. 40–53. Print.
"The World of the Dark Crystal." *The Dark Crystal 25th Anniversary Edition DVD*, Prod. Anthony Goldsmith. Sony, 2007. DVD.
Zimmerman, Howard. "Inside the Dark Crystal." *Starlog: The Magazine of the Future.* 66 (January 1983): 34–37, 64–65. Print.

Finding Your Way Through *Labyrinth*

Tom Holste

Audiences often have a difficult time navigating their way through Jim Henson's *Labyrinth*—that is, understanding what the film is about, and why it was made the way it was. Initial reactions to the movie were largely negative. Roger Ebert gave the film only two stars out of four, noting, "I have a problem with almost all nightmare movies: they aren't as suspenseful as they should be because they don't have to follow any logic. Anything can happen, nothing needs to happen, nothing is as it seems and the rules keep changing." His fellow reviewer, Gene Siskel, was even less enthusiastic about the film. He gave it only one star and said, "What an enormous waste of talent and money is *Labyrinth*." Leonard Maltin was a bit more favorable. He assigned three stars to the movie— the same rating he gave the first three Muppet movies and *The Dark Crystal*— noting, "I couldn't ask for a more imaginative film." Indeed, since Maltin's review was one of the few favorable, it adorned the cover of the VHS release of the film. Inexplicably, the 2007 DVD cover carries a quote from Ebert about "a real inspiration," somehow missing the point of the rest of the review.

Perhaps due to the overall negative reviews, audiences stayed away from the movie. According to the report "1986 Domestic Grosses, #1–100" on BoxOfficeMojo.com, the film earned a paltry $12,729,917, placing at #66 on the list of films of 1986. For comparison purposes, George Lucas' ill-fated *Howard the Duck*, which also came out that year and quickly became the poster child for box office turkeys, placed at #53 and earned over $16 million. Another reason for the film's poor performance may have been parents' bad experience a few years earlier with Henson's similar-looking film, *The Dark Crystal*, which frightened many children. Considering how successful and acclaimed Jim Henson's work was with light-hearted fare such as *Sesame Street* and *The Mup-*

pet Show, it must have been baffling to audiences of the time as to why Henson would want to make another dark and scary film.

Of course, society tends to hold a double standard when it comes to artists and entertainers. Artists can go from subversive work to something intended for children, but not the other way around. Thus, Ringo Starr and George Carlin both spent time as hosts of PBS's *Shining Time Station*, but once Henson had been branded as a provider of children's or family entertainment, anything darker was seen by the viewing public as a betrayal of what they should expect from him. In fact, if the public had longer memories (or if they had seen some of Henson's other lesser-known works), they might have realized that *Labyrinth* is the result of everything that Henson had done prior to it, from his 1950s TV series *Sam and Friends* up to and including his more mainstream work. The film is the synthesis of all of Henson's creative work, and the movie deserves more consideration than it often gets.

Comparisons and Contrasts to The Dark Crystal

Jim Henson's first foray into a darker fantasy world — at least, darker than his mainstream audiences were used to — was the 1982 film, *The Dark Crystal*. That movie boasted sumptuous visual design and a fully realized fantasy world created by Brian Froud, a haunting and majestic symphonic score by Trevor Jones, and astonishingly complex puppetry by the Henson team. However, critics did not respond kindly to that film either, perhaps even less kindly than to *Labyrinth*. Vincent Canby of *The New York Times* wrote at the time of *The Dark Crystal*'s release:

> The screenplay ... is without any narrative drive whatever. It's without charm as well as interest. A further problem is that the animated "characters," with the exception of the Gelfling boy and girl, are so unexceptional that, most of the time, they could be part of the very busy background.... Most surprising is the lack of either humor or wit.

Steven D. Greydanus of DecentFilmGuide.com echoed similar sentiments of the time when he called *Crystal* "a distant, uninvolving experience ... [C]haracters and emotions, even by the standards of high fantasy, never come to life, and the overarching mythology seems too self-consciously contrived." Perhaps stung by criticism of this nature, Henson took an entirely different strategy with *Labyrinth*. He kept all of the things that worked about his previous film — the design by Brian Froud, the score from Trevor Jones, and the amazingly complex puppetry by his own team — and then, to that, he added the elements that made *Sesame Street* and *The Muppet Show* work so well.

A Sense of Humor

Henson wisely realized that his previous successes connected with their audiences in part because they were so funny. Characters like Cookie Monster, the Swedish Chef, Ernie and Bert, and Fozzie Bear immediately bring a smile to viewers' faces because of the amusing things these characters have done over the years. When these characters are mentioned, people immediately start thinking of their favorite sketches. To aid him in adding humor to *Labyrinth*, Henson sought out former Monty Python member Terry Jones. The addition of humor makes *Labyrinth* a much more palatable movie than *The Dark Crystal* and puts it more in line with the spirit of *The Muppet Show* and *Sesame Street*. However, it's not just any style of humor; it's a "sick" sense of humor.

The aforementioned *Sam and Friends* frequently featured macabre humor, with the characters exploding or being eaten by other characters. In one sketch, an Alfred Hitchcock-like character brags that his armchair is "made out of real arms." Another example of this vein of "sick humor" (as Muppet writer Jerry Juhl would call it in the 1994 PBS documentary *The Worlds of Jim Henson*) was a popular sketch that Henson frequently did on variety shows around the same period, called "Inchworm." In the sketch, a pre–*Sesame Street*, pre–*Muppet Show* Kermit sits on a brick wall and hums to himself while an inchworm crawls up to him and taps him on his side, trying to get past him. Kermit inquisitively sniffs the creature, then after a moment's thought, swoops down and eats him up. Shortly thereafter, another inchworm comes along the same path. Kermit laughs a wicked laugh, then swoops down and eats the second inchworm. After a few more seconds, yet another inchworm attempts to make its way across Kermit's path. At this point, Kermit starts to get annoyed. He swoops down to eat the third inchworm, but to his surprise, he cannot eat this worm as easily as the others. The more he pulls on it, the more that the inchworm seems to come out from behind the stage. A baffled Kermit keeps pulling and pulling. Finally, the truth is revealed: This "worm" is actually the long snout of a very angry monster. The monster eats Kermit and then disappears behind the stage.

In light of these previous works, some of the things that happen in *Labyrinth* no longer seem so surprising. Early in her journey, Sarah encounters sweet-looking fairies, but the dwarf Hoggle shoots the fairies with insect repellent. When an alarmed Sarah sympathetically picks up one of the wounded fairies, the fairy bites her. Dropping the fairy, Sarah expresses her surprise, saying that she thought fairies did nice things like grant wishes. Hoggle replies, "Shows what you know." Later, when Sarah encounters the giant creature

Ludo, the poor animal is being tortured by a group of goblin soldiers who have pinchers on the ends of sticks. The pinchers are living creatures, hideous-looking vermin with bulging eyes. Soon, thanks to Sarah's resourcefulness, the soldiers start accidentally hitting one another's helmets. The pinchers swing around wildly and bite the other soldiers in the posterior region. Eventually the soldiers retreat, but since all of them have been blinded by having their helmets knocked sideways, they wind up running into each other and collapsing unconscious on the ground. At another point, Sarah encounters creatures known as Fierys. These creatures can remove any of their body parts. Their heads can fly, using their large ears as wings. One Fiery takes off his leg and uses it as a croquet mallet on another Fiery's head. Still another Fiery pulls out his eyeballs and rolls them on the ground like dice. When they stop rolling, all of the Fierys cheerfully exclaim, "Snake eyes!" Soon, the Fierys attempt to remove Sarah's body parts, insisting, "You don't need *two* ears." To audiences who were most familiar with "Bein' Green" and "Rainbow Connection," the choice to include such scenes must have seemed bizarre. Taking a larger view of Henson's work, however, these scenes are all very much in the spirit of humor that ran through the works he created.

Interaction with Humans

Henson had made the mistake once before of not including humans in one of his productions. He had produced a pilot for *The Muppet Show* for ABC in 1975; cheekily titled "Sex & Violence," the program was essentially harmless, but Henson was making a bold statement that this special wasn't just a *Sesame Street* rehash. The show was chock full of zany monsters and creatures, with a character named Nigel as the host, but not a single human appeared onscreen during the program. While the special is quite funny and holds up very well over time (it can be seen as a special feature on *The Muppet Show* Season 1 DVD), the program didn't do well in the ratings. Almost immediately after the show had completed filming, Henson realized that he had made a mistake by not allowing his characters to interact with humans, thus providing a source of stability and identity for the people watching at home. By the time *The Muppet Show* finally premiered in first-run syndication in 1976, the characters always had a weekly guest star with whom to interact. In *The Dark Crystal*, Henson once again experimented with having a cast completely devoid of humans and drew much criticism as a result. Henson avoided this problem by placing Jennifer Connelly and David Bowie at the center of the story in *Labyrinth*.

Musical Numbers

Music had been a fundamental part of Henson's work since his earliest professional efforts. Henson's first success was on a nightly local TV show in Washington, D.C., called *Sam and Friends* (1955–61). In that series, which ran daily at five minutes per episode, his characters would often pantomime to records. With the advent of *Sesame Street* came original songs like "C is for Cookie" and "Rubber Duckie." The Muppet theatrical movies were also loaded with wonderful original tunes like "Rainbow Connection." While *The Muppet Show* rarely had original music, the Muppets covered everything from old standards to then-current favorites. *The Dark Crystal* had no musical numbers, but for *Labyrinth*, David Bowie wrote all of the songs and performed many of them in the film as well, from the romp "Magic Dance" to the ballad "Within You." These songs enhance the film greatly and contribute to its lasting charm.

A Fractured View of Time

Throughout the 1960s, Jim Henson experimented with a number of unusual films, many of them featuring no puppets at all. In 1965, for instance, he released a surreal short film called *Timepiece*. By design, the film has no plot; it is mainly a series of strange images and scenes juxtaposed against each other. A man paints an elephant pink, a person in a gorilla suit jumps on a pogo stick, a cowboy walks out into the street and has a shoot-out with a Mona Lisa painting, and so forth, but everything is set to a constant rhythm, like the ticking of a clock or metronome. Clocks and watches of all sorts appear frequently throughout the film. A theme that can be drawn from the film is the idea of humanity futilely trying to run from time—in essence, from one's own mortality. Henson himself plays a man seen running throughout the film. Finally, this man winds up on a deathbed. After the cover is pulled over the man's face, the camera pulls back to reveal that the doctor is exactly the same man as the corpse.

Time is a common symbol in *Labyrinth* as well. Time is splintered and (as Shakespeare would say) out of joint in the film. Jareth gives Sarah thirteen hours to rescue her brother, on a special clock of Jareth's that actually has thirteen hours on it. When Sarah refuses to cower before Jareth midway through the movie, he speeds the clock up, thus further splintering time. At the climax, when he attempts to show Sarah how generous he is in his eyes, at least, he pushes time back again, creating another splinter. When Sarah breaks Jareth's spell, she's returned to her own world, where the clock strikes twelve on a normal grandfather clock. The natural order of time has been restored. However, time in this film does not seem to be representative of mortality so much as it highlights the "unreality" of the events. When Jareth's spell is broken, all real elements are restored, such as the regular progression of time.

The Theme of Being Trapped

Timepiece was not Henson's only foray into surreal, non-puppetry filmmaking. He also created a short teleplay called *The Cube*. In that special, the protagonist (an unnamed man) is trapped in a cube, a room with no windows or doors, like a prison. Inexplicably, others can come into the room and even exit when they wish. The protagonist, who has no name, cannot remember how he got into this room, does not know the purpose of his being there (is it a punishment, or did he choose to be there for some reason?), and does not know how to leave the premises. Some characters who visit him try in vain to be helpful; others ridicule him for not being able to leave. The story ends much as it began, with one bizarre situation following another for the beleaguered man, who never escapes. Samuel Beckett, the author of the absurdist play *Waiting for Godot*, would have been impressed.

While many interpretations of *The Cube* are possible, one idea is that the man is trapped in a prison of his own making. The people represent aspects of the man's own psyche as he tries to figure out how to make his way through the world. The man can't leave the world of his mind for the same reason that none of us can leave our own minds. Each of us is trapped in a world of our imperfect thoughts and irrational emotions, a world of our own making.

It can be argued that Sarah, too, is in a world of her own making. At the beginning of the film, Sarah complains about having to take care of her brother. She throws a tantrum and says that she doesn't want anyone to talk to her. When her father takes her at her word, she paradoxically gets angry at him for not trying harder to reason with her. Sarah is also cruel to her stepmother, unintentionally misinterpreting everything that the stepmother says as a personal attack on Sarah herself. In a clever twist on traditional fairy tales, the stepmother is the nice one, and the "princess" is insufferable. Sarah's life is fraught with difficulties, but she doesn't realize that she herself has made it so. Only by journeying through a labyrinth from which there seems to be no escape can Sarah finally break free from the things that hold her back.

Indeed, Henson himself suggested that the entire story may take place only in Sarah's imagination. Speaking once about the events of the film, Henson rhetorically asked, "Is it all a dream, like *Alice's Adventures in Wonderland* or *The Wizard of Oz*? In my mind it is. But it's all rather ambiguous — dream or reality? Fantasy or fact? It's whatever you like to make it" (qtd. in Finch 183). In that sense, the movie is similar to the film version of *The Wizard of Oz*, which ends with Dorothy waking up in bed and being insistent that all of the events really happened, even though the others laugh and doubt her. The viewer is left to make up his or her own mind as to what has happened to Dorothy. Indeed, one of the books lying around Sarah's room is *The Wizard of Oz*, so we can be pretty sure that the reference was intentional.

A Massive Metatext

The prefix "meta" indicates a work that refers back to itself. Thus, when Homer Simpson once mentioned that comedienne Tracy Ullman used to have a sketch-comedy show with "crudely animated filler material" (that material, of course, being the early *Simpsons* shorts), the show is making a meta-textual reference. In Henson's works, characters also often comment on the artificiality of the construct in which they appear.

For instance, *The Muppet Movie* starts with all of the characters gathering in a theater to watch the same movie that the audience itself is about to see. When Kermit's nephew, Robin, asks if this film represents the true story of how the Muppets came together, Kermit responds that it's "sort of approximately how it happened." Halfway through the story, the film reel breaks, and the characters all enjoy an intermission while the projectionist (the Swedish Chef) repairs the film. After the big finale with all the characters singing a reprise of "Rainbow Connection," the human-sized monster Sweetums accidentally bursts through the screen. Then as the end credits roll, all of the characters stick around in the theater and talk about how much they enjoyed the movie. At the end of the credits, Animal looks directly at the audience and tells us, "GO HOME!" before saying, "Buh-bye," and passing out from exhaustion. Worth noting is that the movie proper makes perfect sense without any of these additional scenes. Why include them, then? My theory is that Henson never wanted his audience to become too attached to the images on the screen. As much as he wanted the audience to enjoy the film, he never wanted them to forget that they were still just watching a film.

The next Muppet movie, *The Great Muppet Caper*, opens with Kermit,

Fozzie, and Gonzo in a hot-air balloon. As the opening credits start to roll, the characters decide to read them. When a cinematographer's credit comes up, Fozzie asks, "What does A.S.C. stand for?" Finally, the balloon lands in the middle of the street, and the characters, along with supposedly random strangers on the street, burst into the opening song, complete with perfectly choreographed dancing. The song is called "Hey, a Movie!" Again, it's a reminder that we're watching a fictional story. During an interlude in the song, Kermit explains the basic setup of the plot to the audience, ending with, "Boy, I wish I were you people, seeing this for the first time!" Finally, as the end credits roll, Gonzo, playing a photographer in this movie, turns his camera on the audience and says, "Smile!" As the bulb flashes, the screen goes to black, and the audience hears Gonzo's absurd promise: "I'll send each of you a copy!" Again, at every turn the audience is being reminded that this movie is just a fictional construct. Even as the movie dazzles the audience's imaginations with many impressive sights, including all of the characters riding bikes and Miss Piggy doing a flawless tap-dance routine, Henson never allows the audience to get sucked into the proceedings so much that it loses its grip on reality.

Labyrinth, of course, is also a metatextual work. For instance, the audience gets many references to earlier fantasy works that have inspired this one. In addition to *The Wizard of Oz*, Sarah has a copy of *Alice in Wonderland*, another story that informs the proceedings here. Also, characters and figures in Sarah's room resemble those she meets later. A bookend is in the form of a dwarf that looks quite a lot like Hoggle. A picture of Disney's animated version of *Robin Hood* is also visible; when Sir Didymus appears, the similarity of his outfit to Robin Hood's is astonishing. Most notably, a maze by M.C. Escher hangs on Sarah's wall; at the climax of the movie, Sarah must rescue her brother from an Escher-like maze inside Jareth's castle. Many fantasy films reference earlier ones; few others, if any, actually indicate which of those works are being referenced within the body of the story itself. One can hardly imagine a scene with Harry Potter sitting down to read *Lord of the Rings*. Each moment in the film reminds the audience that it's watching an artificial construct, just like the stories that came before it.

Another clever conceit of *Labyrinth* is to give us a story within a story. In the first scene of the film, Sarah is reciting lines from a book, possibly a play, although the film itself does not make this point clear. She attempts to confront the Goblin King of that story with the lines she recites. When she can no longer remember the lines, she pulls the book out and re-reads them: "[...] You have no power over me." However, the Goblin King does indeed seem to have power over Sarah, as well as the rest of the fantasy world that

Sarah reads about. According to Sarah's stepmother, Sarah never hangs out with friends or goes on any dates; she seems to spend all of her time obsessed with this story and with the other stories in the books in her room. While the reasons for her behavior are never fully explained in the film, photos of Sarah's biological mother adorn Sarah's mirror. One might deduce that the loss of her mother, whether through death or divorce, drove Sarah to try to escape from the harshness of reality.

Sarah retells the story of *The Labyrinth* (the story within the story) to her brother Toby while he's crying, engaging in wishful thinking about the Goblin King taking Toby away from her so that she won't have to take care of a crying baby anymore. Unbeknownst to Sarah, a group of goblins wake up and take notice of the activity in Sarah's house. Thus, a story (Sarah's book *The Labyrinth*) which is fictional within the confines of Sarah's "real world" turns out to be true after all. Alternatively, one could say that Sarah's real life and the world of the Goblin Kingdom exist on exact same level. In other words, neither world is actually real.

The point is further driven home during the latter half of the movie, when Sarah runs into an old Junk Lady who convinces Sarah that her adventure up to this point has simply been a dream. The Junk Lady leads Sarah back to her bedroom with her toys, but when Sarah attempts to go downstairs to see her mom and dad, she finds that her room only exists within the Junk Lady's junkyard. Sarah has not really woken up from a dream at all; her room is an illusion that can only be maintained if she stays in that one place with her toys and her books. The Junk Lady tries to convince Sarah that having all of these "things" is enough for a satisfactory life. Finally, Sarah finds one of the items that she cherishes so deeply: her copy of *The Labyrinth*. Reading the lines of the play, Sarah is reminded of what she needs to do: "...take back the child that you have stolen." Quickly, Sarah begins destroying the "room," which collapses, filling with the dirt of the junkyard, and Sarah is reunited with her comrades from the Labyrinth who want to help her save her brother.

The layers of symbolism in this scene are astounding. Sarah enters her room, a place that looks more like our definition of "real life" than a goblin kingdom, but "real life" in this sense is simply another illusion. Sarah has only her superficial possessions to keep her happy in this false version of reality. The words of a book bring her back to her senses. However, the book itself is a false construct within the movie; no such book exists outside the fiction of the film. Look at the layers of reality or, if you prefer, the layers of illusion. Sarah is taken from her normal, everyday life into a world where the words of a fictional book turn out to be true. When Sarah first thinks that she has returned home, she is actually just living in an illusion. The "real world" is just a trap to keep her from moving forward in her goals in the Goblin Kingdom, which actually is real. Nonetheless, even when Sarah gets back to the regular, everyday world, even *that* is just an illusion, another fictional story being told to an audience. Sarah's story ends happily in her bedroom, the "real" one to her, but just another fiction for us.

The theme is revisited in the climax. Sarah confronts Jareth and begins reciting the lines of the book to him. Jareth knows that since the book is all based on the reality of his world, all will be lost for him if she finishes reciting the words. Jareth yells, "Stop!" and begins tempting Sarah with everything she wants if she surrenders what she truly needs (Toby) to him. "Let me rule you," he tells her, "and I will be your master." Finally, a look of clarity comes into Sarah's eyes. She remembers the line and says it: "You have no power over me." The reason she can finally remember the line is because she finally means it. Thus, Jareth's world disappears, and Sarah is returned to the real world, or at least, as real a world in which Sarah, a fictional character, can ever live.

However, Henson gives the audience a postscript. The heroic characters from Sarah's fantasy reappear in her mirror, but when she turns around to see them in her room, the characters are not there. Looking back in the mirror, the characters tell her that "should you need us, for any reason ..." Sarah tells these characters, "I do need you. I don't know why, but every so often, for no reason at all ... I need you." With that invitation, the characters can magically break through the barrier between the worlds. Sarah is reunited with her friends, while Jareth, now trapped in the form of an owl, is left outside. In the language of cinema, a mirror is a symbol of a person's identity. In the labyrinth, the mirror in Sarah's fake room needed to be destroyed because it represented the false trappings of her personality. By the end of the film, the mirror represents the healthy side of her imagination. All of Sarah's friends can return, so long as Jareth (i.e. the controlling, obsessive part of fantasy) remains outside.

The Theme of the Projection of Sexuality

The costume designers for the film (Brian Froud and Ellis Flyte) gave David Bowie an extremely well-endowed pair of tight pants. Many people joke about Bowie's pants in the film; men tend to dislike the look, while women generally are in favor of it. However, according to the 1986 documentary *Inside the Labyrinth*, the filmmakers reveal that all of the above elements were quite deliberate in the crafting of the character of Jareth, from his costuming to his casting. If Jareth is indeed a projection from young teenage Sarah's imagination, of course he would be a rock star. Naturally, for a girl just entering puberty, her fantasy man would be hyper-sexualized. Of course he would have a sexy British accent, and for that matter, in 1986, a male rock star would inevitably have long hair and wear makeup. Even if we choose the interpretation that Jareth is real, we know that Jareth is a shapeshifter: he transforms into an owl and back again. Although the movie never spells the concept out, one can deduce that Jareth might have taken different forms for other people that he tries to draw into his world. If the story had been about the temptation of a young boy, perhaps Debbie Harry would have played the role.

The ballroom scene is particularly significant. Bowie/Jareth sings the lovely romantic ballad "Within You" while Sarah, in the same type of dress found on her doll in the glass container, dances with him. The scene is almost romantic, until one considers that David Bowie was 38 when the film was being made, and Connelly was 15. Suddenly, the scene takes on creepy connotations. However, once again, as the documentary makes clear, the creepy sensation that the audience gets was an intentional reaction that Henson was trying to draw out. The other dancers in the masquerade ball wear grotesque masks that underscore the creepiness of the scene. Eventually, Sarah herself chooses to pull away. She gets to the end of the room and sees her own distorted reflection (another mirror). She takes a chair and breaks the mirror, destroying another illusion and bringing her out of the crystal ball in which she had been trapped and back into the labyrinth. Henson noted that Sarah is of the age where she's no longer a girl but she's not quite a woman. She's trying on the "grown-up girl" clothes in her fantasies, the way it's natural for a teenage girl to do. But she must pull away, because there are some rites of passage that a fifteen-year-old is not quite ready for yet.

An Attack on Superficiality

The discussion now needs to go back to the scene in Sarah's "room" in the junkyard one more time. Sarah takes her favorite possession, a beautiful princess doll in a glass container, and smashes her mirror with it to escape. As previously mentioned, mirrors are symbols of identity in film. Therefore, by this act, Sarah smashes her false version of herself, an identity based on what she owns.

At the beginning of the movie, Sarah flies into a rage when she realizes that Lancelot, her teddy bear, has been taken from her and given to her infant brother Toby. Her rage may come from her sense of identity being violated by the loss of the teddy bear. When one's identity is wrapped up in possessions, such reactions are the natural result. At the end of the movie, having reclaimed what was really important (Toby), Sarah gladly gives Lancelot back to Toby to help him sleep.

Similarly, when Sarah smashes the mirror with the ballerina, she shouts, "It's all junk!" Indeed, one could say that all of our possessions are "junk" in comparison to family (i.e. Toby). But taking the illustration a step further, all of our possessions are indeed "junk." Ultimately, no person can take his or her possessions into the afterlife, and most of our possessions will likely end up in the junk pile of future generations. In contrast, the connections that we as a species make with others are the truly imperishable things of life.

The Healing Power of Art

Even though Henson used this film to warn against the dangers of falling too far into a fantasy world, he nonetheless understood the importance of art as a healing tool. Yes, Sarah obsesses a little too much over her favorite play but keep in mind that the same play holds the words necessary for her to triumph over Jareth: "You have no power over me." Since, in Henson's interpretation, Sarah likely imagines the whole experience anyway, one can see the movie as a story about a girl who reads through her favorite fictional work until she finally understands the meaning behind it all. The story helps Sarah move on with her life. Art can powerfully heal and instruct, and Henson shows a keen awareness of this concept.

The Hero's Journey

Labyrinth fits quite well into the theory of story structure known as the Hero's Journey. The Hero's Journey was first defined by Joseph Campbell when studying myths and folklore though he did not use that term to describe it. He explained the similarities in all myths in his book *The Hero with a Thousand Faces*. Christopher Vogler in *The Writer's Journey* then picked up on Campbell's theories and applied them to screenplay structure, coining the term "The Hero's Journey." The rules can be applied to many movies. To name just a few, there's *The Wizard of Oz*, the original *Star Wars* movies, *The Muppet Movie*, the *Indiana Jones* films, *Back to the Future*, Disney's *Beauty and the Beast*, the *Toy Story* films, *Lord of the Rings*, *Shrek*, *Groundhog Day*, and (perhaps most surprisingly) *Pulp Fiction*.

In summation, the Hero's Journey contains multiple steps, including the Ordinary World where the story begins (such as Sarah's life at home); the Call to Adventure (such as Jareth sending Sarah out into the labyrinth); the tests, allies, and enemies (such as the trials Sarah faces along the way, with the help of her friends Hoggle, Ludo, and Sir Didymus); a new Approach (when Sarah's selfishness no longer works for her, she learns to be kinder and more resourceful); the biggest Ordeal (the confrontation with Jareth); and the Return with the Elixir, or the reward (Sarah's return home with Toby). It's perhaps no surprise that George Lucas was an executive producer and story consultant on this film, since Lucas was a long-time student of Campbell.

A Redemption Story

A redemption story is quite a different type of tale from a hero's journey, but *Labyrinth* manages to be both. As previously mentioned, Sarah is insufferable at the beginning of the film. While the audience receives hints about the tragedy that has informed her life, none of her "suffering" seems quite so bad. She gets wet in the rain when she forgets to come home on time; her dog has to go to the garage so he doesn't track mud in the house; she has to stay home and babysit her little brother. These are all petty annoyances, not the types of things that should cause a wrathful reaction. Nonetheless, Sarah has nothing but wrath for anyone in her vicinity. Based on the comments of the stepmother, it seems that Sarah has no friends or romantic interests, either. Thus, Sarah's loneliness is a result of having the happiness of her real world shattered, drawing her into a fantasy world as an escape from harsh realities, and the movie is a story of drawing Sarah out of her self-centeredness and into a life where she can be productive and happy again.

Sarah is far from the first character to be the center of a redemption story, of course. Perhaps the most famous story of a protagonist who gets redeemed is Charles Dickens's *A Christmas Carol*. Conventional wisdom suggests that because Bob Cratchit is likeable and Ebenezer Scrooge is not, the audience should want to follow Bob Cratchit through the story, but that isn't the case. Cratchit is indeed likeable, but Scrooge is *compelling*. He's fascinating to read about or watch, depending on which medium the audience is experiencing the story through, and the audience finds itself curiously rooting for his redemption, perhaps because of that part of Scrooge that lives within us, too. Many modern TV shows, such as *House, Firefly, Battlestar Galactica, The Office*, and *Torchwood*, all owe something to works of fiction that have come before wherein the protagonist was not likeable at the beginning of the story. *Labyrinth* is also one such story where the character ends in a much different place than she began.

In Conclusion

Although misunderstood by audiences and critics of the time, *Labyrinth* is the zenith of Jim Henson's creative efforts. It contains everything that worked about his previous fantasy project, *The Dark Crystal*, while adding in the elements of humor, music and human interaction that worked so well on *Sesame Street* and *The Muppet Show*. The story also shows a surprising complexity of theme that even pulls from Henson's lesser-known, more avant-garde works.

Over the years, audiences have come to appreciate this masterpiece more and more. At the time of this writing, the voters at The Internet Movie Database rate it at an average of 7.3 out of 10, a very respectable rating. The film has been released multiple times on DVD due to its continued strong sales. The success of *Labyrinth* and of *Dark Crystal* on home video prompted Sony Home Entertainment to ask the Jim Henson Company to create another fantasy film called *MirrorMask*, a direct-to-video project in 2005, and on Roger Ebert's own website, next to his 2-star review, the average rating of visitors to the site for the film is 3½ stars. Such signs are encouraging. Although the film confused and alienated audiences at the time of its release, the movie is finding new audiences who appreciate Henson's achievement and want to go one more time into the Labyrinth.

WORKS CITED

Canby, Vincent. "Henson's 'Crystal.'" Rev. of *The Dark Crystal,* dir. Jim Henson and Frank Oz. *The New York Times.* 17 Dec. 1982. *The New York Times.* Web. 6 Apr. 2012.
Ebert, Roger. "*Labyrinth.*" Rev. of *Labyrinth,* dir. Jim Henson. RogerEbert.com, 27 June 1986. *Chicago Sun-Times.* Web. 6 Apr. 2012.
Finch, Christopher. *Jim Henson: The Works.* New York, Random House, 1993. Print.
The Great Muppet Caper. Dir. Jim Henson. Perf. Frank Oz, Dave Goelz, Jerry Nelson, and Jim Henson. ITC, 1981. DVD.
Greydanus, Steven D. Rev. of *The Dark Crystal,* dir. Jim Henson and Frank Oz. *Decent-Films.com* Web. 6 Apr. 2012.
Labyrinth. Dir. Jim Henson. Perf. David Bowie, Jennifer Connelly, Toby Froud, Brian Henson, and David Goelz. Henson Associates, 1986. DVD.
The Muppet Movie. Dir. James Frawley. Perf. Frank Oz, Dave Goelz, Jerry Nelson, and Jim Henson. ITC, 1979. DVD.
"1986 Domestic Grosses, #1–100." *BoxOfficeMojo.com* Web. 6 Apr. 2012.
Siskel, Gene. Rev. of *Labyrinth,* dir. Jim Henson. *Metacritic.com,* 30 June 1986. *Chicago Tribune.* Web. 6 Apr. 2012.

Anti-Consumerism in *Labyrinth*

David R. Burns and Deborah Burns

"Don't tell me the truth hurts, little girl
Cause it hurts like hell"

—*Labyrinth*

The fairy tale nature and impressive special effects draw viewers into the visual fable that is Jim Henson's *Labyrinth*. In *Labyrinth*, Henson educates viewers about the illusive qualities of overconsumption and encourages viewers to resist the mass media and contemporary culture's messages of overconsumption. Through Sarah's education in this bildungsroman film, Henson reveals the uncomfortable truth that consumer goods fail to provide the fulfillment of genuine human relationships and have a deleterious effect on planetary ecology. Henson encourages viewers to resist mass media and contemporary culture's messages of overconsumption, reduce their consumption of consumer goods, and embrace the fulfillment of human relationships.

Henson skillfully integrates his criticism of overconsumption into *Labyrinth*'s traditional bildungsroman format. In *Labyrinth*, the protagonist Sarah, a teenager who is on the cusp of becoming a young woman, navigates the difficult life transition from childhood to adulthood. Henson describes Sarah as "'at the point of changing from being a child to being a woman'" and experiencing a time "'of transition'" (Finch 183). Sarah's education about the illusive qualities of overconsumption is part of her broader growth and development as young woman in the bildungsroman film (Buckley 13). Through Sarah's journey in the labyrinth, the challenges she faces in her quest, and her interactions with the other characters in the film including, Jareth, the Goblin king, Hoggle, Sir Didymus, and the Junk Lady, Sarah embraces opportunities to learn and mature into an adult (Arendt 42). This process enables Sarah to boldly declare her independence when she twice exclaims "You have no power over me" to Jareth, an overpowering adult character, after her steady move closer to coming of age in the film. By the conclusion of the film, Sarah has transformed from a girl into a young woman.

Labyrinth joins the strong opposition to overconsumption that has been growing for decades. There is strong criticism of overconsumption in other 1980s films including *Blade Runner* and *Repo Man* (Beliveau and Lewis; Bruno 64). Like *Labyrinth*, these films expose the excess amount of waste and grim realities that result from overconsumption. In the years following the release of these films, scores of films and books including the famed *Affluenza, Shop 'til You Drop*, and *The Overspent American: Why We Want What We Don't Need* criticize the common practice of overconsumption in the West. Broadly defined, overconsumption is understood as the consumption of a greater number of goods and services than is necessary for a sensible lifestyle and level of material comfort (Humphery 22). The anti-consumerist movement has criticized overconsumption as causing the erosion of family and community connections and contributing to environmental challenges including pollution, waste, and dwindling natural resources (Humphery 23). Through its use of a visual fable to illustrate these negative implications of overconsumption, *Labyrinth* adds to existing visual and textual anti-consumerist narratives.

Overconsumption and Erosion of Family Connections

In *Labyrinth*, the persistent difficulties that Sarah has connecting with other people and forming meaningful human relationships are associated the overconsumption of consumer goods. Sarah's family exemplifies the middle class U.S. family's "work and spend" cyclical ideology that "undermines the daily life conditions" required for "reciprocal bonds" and meaningful relationships (Holt 8). This "work and spend" cycle is pervasive among U.S. workers who toil long hours in the labor market because they feel the pressure to keep up with rising consumption norms (Holt 8). These norms include the customary social behaviors and mounting pressure related to purchasing larger and larger homes and acquiring increasing amounts of consumer goods. U.S. workers spend extended hours at their jobs in order to meet these norms, and this leaves them with diminished free time and opportunities to connect with each other (Holt 8). As with many U.S. families, Sarah's family's large home and overconsumption of consumer goods erodes the relationships in Sarah's household.

Sarah's family's house is grand with a long staircase, lush carpeting and furnishings, and a decorative chandelier. Sarah's bedroom door is the entry point to many of the consumer goods that separate her from her family members and are associated with the erosion of her connection with her family and community. During and following her interactions with her parents, Sarah isolates herself in her lavish, richly appointed and wallpapered bedroom that contains massive piles of consumer items including jewelry boxes, a globe, and a music box with a dancer resembling Sarah. Sarah's bedroom has collections of costly books, fancy furnishings, and toys. Her bedroom features an overflowing library of books including *The Wizard of Oz* and *Grimm's Fairy Tales* as well as ornate wood furniture. Some of the toys that are heaped throughout Sarah's room include representations of characters from the film including Hoggle, Jareth, Sir Didymus, Ludo, and a Fiery.

This overconsumption of consumer goods exacts a social price on Sarah and her relationship with her family. In her rush to retreat to and isolate herself in her bedroom filled with consumer items, Sarah fails to meaningfully connect with her immediate family members. Likewise, in their rush to leave Sarah with Toby, Sarah's parents are unsuccessful in meaningfully connecting with Sarah. *Labyrinth* draws on the traditional fairy-tale trope of the evil stepmother when Sarah arrives home an hour late and argues with her stepmother about how often Sarah's father and stepmother have the opportunity to go out together (Arendt 41). While Sarah believes that her parents go out every weekend, Sarah's stepmother disagrees and believes that they go out "very rarely" (*Labyrinth*). Sarah longs for her parents to include her in their plans and spend more time considering her interests. Sarah expresses her belief that her stepmother lacks the time and concern to understand her interests when she says, "You don't even ask what my plans are" (*Labyrinth*). After Sarah repeatedly raises her voice to her stepmother, her stepmother says that Sarah treats her like "a wicked stepmother" (*Labyrinth*). These limited exchanges between Sarah and her stepmother illustrate how long working hours and pressures to keep up with social norms erode family relationships.

Henson also reveals this erosion of family relationships when Sarah and her father fail to bond with each other. Although the family's large house allows it to meet prevailing middle-class consumption norms and keep up with the proverbial Joneses, Henson disabuses viewers of the myth that these middle-class consumption norms have solely beneficial effects on family relationships. With *Labyrinth*, Henson illustrates how large homes extend the distance between family members and negatively impact familial relationships. Sarah and her father converse in raised voices along the extended staircase that separates the house's entryway from its bedrooms. In response to her father's query about talking with her, Sarah speaks to her father through her bedroom door and says, "There's nothing to talk about!" (*Labyrinth*). Sarah tells her father that he should hurry for fear of being late for his date with her stepmother and then criticizes him for leaving before he can thoughtfully speak with her. Sarah says, "You really wanted to talk to me" and "practically broke down the door" (*Labyrinth*). The family's large house and its increased physical distance between family members work to erode instead of strengthen relationships within the family. Moreover, the "work and spend cycle" ideology that pervades Sarah's family and other middle-class families weakens familial bonds and reduces opportunities for building strong relationships (Holt 8).

The exchange between Sarah and her father also illustrates how people use consumer items as a replacement for social connections (Rindfleisch, Burroughs, and Wong 4). Instead of engaging in meaningful relationships with her family, Sarah gazes at her reflection in the large mirror that is prominently featured in her bedroom and converses with her multiple and overflowing toys. The large mirror in *Labyrinth* references the mirror sequence in Disney's *Snow White and the Seven Dwarfs* when the queen talks to the mirror instead of the other characters in the film. Like the queen who converses with the mirror, an inanimate object, Sarah appears more than content sitting amongst her consumer goods and conversing with herself and her stuffed animals; she declines to open her bedroom door to reach out to her father. With Sarah talking to a mirror and her stuffed animals instead of her family members, Sarah's relationship with her family exemplifies the ways that people use consumer items as a replacement for social connections.

It is in her parents' simple, clean, and uncluttered room, a room with few consumer goods and the room that Toby, Sarah's infant brother, shares with them that Sarah begins to realize the importance of human relationships. The piles of toys and consumer items in Sarah's bedroom that isolate Sarah from connecting with her family stand in stark contrast to the dearth of consumer goods in the bedroom Toby and her parents share. In their bedroom, the sparse furnishings are far less fancy than those in Sarah's room, and there are few consumer items other than a rocking horse and rocking chair. The shared bedroom is relatively devoid of consumer items, and this lack of consumer items allows Sarah to think clearly about the importance of human relationships. After Sarah overcomes her anger about her stuffed teddy bear Lancelot's disappearance and realizes the implications of her wish to have the goblins take Toby away, Sarah engages with Jareth, the goblin king, in an extended conversation about the importance of her relationship with her brother.

Jareth urges Sarah to "forget about the baby" and return to her room and "play" with her consumer goods, her "toys" and "costumes" (*Labyrinth*). Jareth offers her a crystal, a consumer good, which holds the promise of revealing her dreams. However, in Sarah's parents and Toby's bedroom, a room that is relatively devoid of consumer items, Sarah begins to see the uncomfortable truth that consumer goods such as toys, costumes, and crystals fail to provide the fulfillment of genuine human communication and connection. Sarah rejects the crystal and Jareth's recommendation that she return to her bedroom. She empathizes with Toby's plight and grows concerned that he is scared in the goblin kingdom. Although she may not yet fully understand the import of her quest, Sarah is embarking on her journey of understanding the uncomfortable truth that consumer goods serve as barriers to forming meaningful human relationships and fail to provide the fulfillment of genuine human relationships. After expressing her desire to reunite with Toby and unsuccessfully pleading with Jareth to return him, Sarah is determined to solve the labyrinth and reunite with her brother.

Overconsumption and Erosion of Community Connections

In *Labyrinth*, the frequent difficulties that Sarah has connecting with other people in the community and forming meaningful human relationships is associated the overconsumption of consumer goods. When she alludes to Sarah's inactive dating life, Sarah's stepmother reveals Sarah's challenges with connecting with community members beyond her family. Sarah spends her time alone in her room with her consumer items and outside with her pet, Merlin. She uses her imagination to entertain herself and does not reach out to others in her age group to form meaningful relationships. Instead, she uses consumer items as a replacement for social connections. Sarah's challenges connecting with other people in the community are associated with the overconsumption of consumer goods in both the ballroom and junk world sequences in the film.

In the ballroom sequence, a dreamlike reverie that she falls into after she ingests the poisoned peach, Sarah continues her educational journey about overconsumption in her conscious and subconscious mind. The ballroom revelers, who are dressed up in fancy consumer items and costumes for the masquerade party, stare at Sarah and shake their heads at her without connecting with her. Like the revelers, Sarah is dressed in a fancy masquerade ball dress and wears elaborate jewelry. Although Sarah dances with Jareth, the goblin king, she does not communicate with him. Even the revelers have difficulty communicating with one another; they have masks, consumer goods, which physically prevent them from viewing their fellow revelers, and they scarcely communicate with one another. In fact, the masquerade party revelers, with their overflowing consumer items, work in a concerted effort to keep Sarah from connecting with her brother, Toby. Dressed in fine costumes and silken gloves, they physically block her and hold her back, preventing her from leaving the ballroom and connecting with Toby. The overflowing and exquisite consumer items in the ballroom sequence hinder human companionship between Sarah and the revelers, the revelers themselves, and Sarah and her brother.

With the ballroom sequence in *Labyrinth*, Henson reveals the illusive qualities of overconsumption. The ballroom and its fancy consumer items showcase the competitive consumption that pervades Western society and the common practice of "the lifestyles of the top 20 percent" becoming "an emulative target for the whole society" (Holt 12). Luxury goods, such as those in the ballroom sequence, are mass-produced, and even economically disadvantaged members of society aspire to buy small pieces of an upper class, luxury lifestyle. Jean Baudrillard discusses this mass production of mechanically reproduced consumer goods and how it permeates Western society and culture (11). He suggests that these models of reality, endless replicas of consumer goods, become more real and valuable to people than the models' original forms (Baudrillard 12). However, despite these consumer items' purported and growing value, consumer items such as those that fill the ballroom, the fancy dresses, linens, hanging jewels, and lavish serving items, serve as barriers to forming meaningful human relationships. These items prevent Sarah and the other masquerade participants from connecting with each other.

As the clock strikes, Sarah recalls her purpose and views the mass-produced consumer items in the mirrored reflection of the ballroom. She sees that the beneficial qualities of these items are illusive because they serve as barriers to human relationships. Sarah learns the uncomfortable truth that consumer goods contribute to the erosion of human connection and she determines that she needs to exit the overconsumptive ballroom environment. Using a powerful, symbolic action, Sarah grasps one of the many ballroom chairs, a consumer item, to destroy the overconsumptive ballroom and shatter the mirror to pieces. With this action, Sarah practices resistance to overconsumption and uses a consumer item to destroy an overconsumptive environment. Sarah's understanding that consumer goods contribute to the erosion of human connection motivates her to act on her understanding with this anti-consumerist action. She escapes the consumer goods in the ballroom that isolate her and distract her from her human relationship with Toby and resumes her quest to find her brother.

Sarah also encounters the uncomfortable truth that consumer goods contribute to the erosion of human connection when she meets the Junk Lady in the rubbish-filled environment of the film. When Sarah reaches out to connect with the Junk Lady and touches her back, the Junk Lady agitatedly responds, "Get off my back!" (*Labyrinth*). The Junk Lady shirks away from human connection because she has too many discarded consumer items collected on her back. These items are literally weighing on her and preventing her from standing upright. The Junk Lady is burdened by the collection of rejected consumer goods on her back, including a chair, hat, drum, cage, stuffed animal, and cooking pot. In *Labyrinth*'s junk world, there are multiple junk people who are all weighed down by the discarded consumer items on their backs. These junk people do not communicate with one another, but rather wade through the piles of discarded consumer items. They do not even look at one another, and the Junk Lady rarely, if ever, maintains eye contact with Sarah.

Like the ballroom revelers, the junk people in *Labyrinth* represent the growing influence of consumerism and its resultant overconsumption on industrialized societies. Consumerism can be viewed as an ideology that plays a prominent role on "identity and social life" in Western society (Holt 5). During the 1980s, the time period when *Labyrinth* was first released, people in industrialized nations began an "intensified competitive consumption" with people spending more time working to consume material possessions and less time socializing with one another (Holt 12). The masses, including middle-class families such as Sarah's family, replaced interpersonal communications with the ideology of consumerism. Juliet Schor explains that because of the dominance of consumerism over people's time, there was an "erosion of the social fabric" (Holt 6). The junk people exemplify this erosion of social fabric with their rejection of human connection. They favor collecting consumer goods over forming meaningful relationships and are representations of how consumer goods can both literally and figuratively weigh upon people and separate them from others. Similar to the ballroom revelers, the junk people illustrate how consumer goods physically prevent people from forming social bonds.

The Junk Lady and the commercials and consumer culture she represents act like a recurring interactive commercial that repeatedly advertises consumer wares to Sarah in an attempt to distract her from her relationship with her family. When she displays Sarah's stuffed teddy bear, Lancelot, the same toy Sarah searched for in Toby's room before being transported to the goblin kingdom, the Junk Lady attempts to convince Sarah that she is looking for material possessions instead of her human relationship with her brother. When Sarah appears somewhat unconvinced that Lancelot is the goal of her search, the Junk Lady continues her endeavor to convince Sarah that she is looking for material possessions instead of human relationships by drawing Sarah towards a junk world recreation of Sarah's bedroom. Within her recreated bedroom, Sarah suspects that she is dreaming, and the Junk Lady tries to distract her from her human relationship with Toby by urging her to stay in her recreated room with all of her material possessions. Similarly, when Sarah sees the *Labyrinth* book and remarks, "There was something I was looking for," and begins to connect the book with her relationship with Toby, the Junk Lady responds "Ah, don't talk nonsense" (*Labyrinth*). Like a commercial, the Junk Lady even attempts to distract Sarah from the *Labyrinth* book by showing her a candy shop toy and says "Everything in the world you've ever cared about is all right here" (*Labyrinth*). Indeed, the Junk Lady and the commercials and consumer culture she represents attempt to persuade Sarah that material items can serve as distractions from and impediments to social connections.

The Junk Lady and all her companions in the junk world are dark doubles of Sarah and the revelers in the ballroom sequence. Just like the excess of consumer goods stifle communication between Sarah with the revelers in the ballroom, the piles of discarded consumer goods work as obstacles to the junk people's connections with one another and with Sarah. These discarded consumer goods are what are left after the fancy ballroom party, our consumer driven lifestyle, has concluded. Even when the festivities have come to an end, the consumer goods associated with these festivities are left behind to stymie human communication and connection.

More specifically, the Junk Lady can be viewed as Sarah's dark double. When Sarah looks in the mirror, she sees the Junk Lady and the viewer is drawn to the similarities between the two characters. Just like the Junk Lady, Sarah has heaps of discarded consumer items including stuffed animals, pencils, slippers, and a printing game on her back. The Junk Lady piles these consumer items on Sarah in her attempt to distract Sarah from reuniting with her family and finding the fulfillment of genuine human communication and connection. Sarah, similar to the Junk Lady, is unable to sit upright under the weight of these goods. Like the Junk Lady in her environment of discarded consumer goods, Sarah sits in her re-created bedroom environment of consumer goods.

Indeed, the Junk Lady's reflection in the mirror foreshadows what will befall Sarah if she fails to change her consumerist perspective and attitude towards life and continues to prioritize the collection of consumer goods over the importance of human relationships. The Junk Lady foreshadows a future version of Sarah if Sarah continues to isolate herself with her material possessions. However, Sarah begins to resist this possible Junk Lady destiny when she reads the *Labyrinth* book and views the mass-produced consumer items and the Junk Lady's reflection in the mirror. Sarah says, "It's all junk" when she looks at her toys (*Labyrinth*). Sarah's conclusion that these items are junk reinforces her understanding from the overconsumptive ballroom environment that the beneficial qualities of consumer items are illusive because they serve as barriers to human relationships. When she looks in the mirror, Sarah begins to face the truth about the emptiness of consumerism reflected in her real room with all its consumer goods. In the junk world sequence, Sarah gains more evidence to support the uncomfortable truth that consumer goods contribute to the erosion of human connection.

Similar to her realization that she needs to escape the ballroom environment earlier in the film, Sarah determines that she needs to exit the overconsumptive junk world environment. Sarah destroys her music box, a material representation of herself, and throws off the junk piled high upon her back. When Sarah performs this act, she is no longer a reflection or double of the Junk Lady. She mentally and physically frees herself from the burden and weight of her consumer goods. In fact, in an action strikingly similar to her destruction of the mirror in the ballroom sequence, Sarah breaks through the mirror of her material existence to destroy the overconsumptive environment that surrounds her; the walls of her junk world bedroom disintegrate revealing the junk world outside. With her destruction of the mirror, Sarah again practices resistance to overconsumption and uses consumer items to destroy an overconsumptive environment. Sarah's deeper understanding that consumer goods contribute to the erosion of human connection motivate Sarah to act on her understanding with another anti-consumerist action. Sarah escapes the overconsumptive environment that isolates and distracts her from her human relationship with Toby and resumes her quest to find her brother.

Overconsumption and Its Deleterious Effect on Planetary Ecology

Sarah's experiences in the junk world environment enable her to understand the deleterious effect of overconsumption on the planet. The junk world environment in *Labyrinth* provides a compelling visualization of the negative impact that overconsumption has on planetary ecology. According to Schor, one of the most serious problems facing the world today stems from the destructive effects of "consumer activity on the planetary ecology" (Holt 6). This excess of consumer activity and its resultant waste, a North American phenomenon that is rapidly spreading worldwide, is polluting the planet and destroying its wildlife (Holt 6). In fact, Kim Humphery warns that when overconsumption is left unchecked, nature will be subject to its "final, irrevocable destruction" (5). Sarah encounters a window into this destruction when she explores the junk world in *Labyrinth*.

Labyrinth's junk world is filled with discarded consumer items commonly found in industrialized nations. The items that fill the screen in the junk world suggest the unending and overwhelming amount of waste that results from discarded consumer goods. For example, the Junk Lady is physically burdened by the collection of rejected consumer goods on her back, including a chair, hat, drum, cage, stuffed animal, and cooking pot. One junk person's back is piled high with discarded consumer items that include a cage, cooking pot, chair, rake, and wrench. Although gently used, all of these items are not junk and would be valuable to people who are not caught in the "work and spend" cyclical ideology (Holt 8). The junk world reveals what happens when people with overconsumptive lifestyles discard consumer items that could have been retained or used by others who need these goods.

In the junk world sequence, Sarah learns the dark side of overconsumption and how it is connected with the growing problem of pollution and waste. Even the colors of the junk world are dark; the gray, ashen, and muted wasteland of the junk world stands in stark contrast to the bright, verdant park in the opening of the film. The junk world represents the degradation of the environment because of the poor choices as overconsumptive consumers and the way they carelessly discard consumer items. The mountains of junk in the junk world result from society's excessive consumer waste and the poisoning of the planetary ecosystem. In her ongoing education during her quest to finish the labyrinth, Sarah rejects and abandons the overconsumerist junk world to reunite with her brother and embrace the fulfillment of genuine human relationships.

Conclusion

In *Labyrinth*, Henson uses film as a site of resistance against the dominant media's support of consumerism and overconsumption. With the rising prevalence and importance of advertising and television viewing in the 1980s, media played a major role in the rise of consumerism and contributed to the "important shift in the decline of the social" (Holt 14). Advertising and television viewing greatly influenced the mass consumption in the 1980s and the weakening of social relationships (Holt 13–14). Henson's release of *Labyrinth* in 1986 supported an "ethos of ethical and responsible consumption" and worked as a site of resistance to the dominant media's messages of consumerism and overconsumption (Humphery 6–7). Sites of resistance such as Henson's *Labyrinth*, Scott's *Blade Runner*, and Cox's *Repo Man* are liminal places that offer the potential to challenge the current power structure in society (de Certeau 117). They are films that provide an alternative narrative to consumerism and overconsumption.

Through Sarah's education in *Labyrinth*'s bildungsroman format, Henson challenges the dominant media by bringing anti-consumerist messages to viewers in a visual fable. Viewers accompany Sarah as she gains the understanding that consumer goods contribute to the erosion of human connection and have a deleterious effect on planetary ecology. They watch when she acts on this understanding and embraces the fulfillment of human relationships. In the film's final moments, Sarah embraces her relationship with Toby and continues her genuine concern for his wellbeing. She reaches out to her family by openly communicating with her father. In a final anti-consumerist action, Sarah puts away many of her consumer goods. Through Sarah's journey of understanding about the truth behind the illusive qualities of overconsumption, Henson delivers strong anti-consumerist messages to both young and mature audiences. Throughout the film and especially when Sarah looks in the mirror in both the ballroom and junk world sequences, Henson is reminding viewers to look into the mirror themselves. Using film as a site of resistance, Henson encourages viewers to reflect on their consumerist lifestyles, resist mass media and contemporary culture's messages of overconsumption, reduce their consumption of consumer goods, and embrace the fulfillment of human relationships.

Works Cited

Affluenza. Dir. John de Graaf. Bulldog Films, 2005. DVD.
Arendt, Elicia. "The Feminine Spectatorship of Jim Henson's *Labyrinth*." In *Braveheart and Broomsticks: Essays on Movies, Myths, and Magic*. Ed. Elicia Arendt. Haverford, PA: Infinity, 2002. 38–53. Print.
Baudrillard, Jean. *Simulacra and Simulation*. Trans. Shiela Faria Glaser. Ann Arbor, University of Michigan Press, 1994. Print.
Beliveau, Ralph, and Lewis, Randolph. "Alex Cox." *Senses of Cinema* 48 (2008). Web. March 2012.
Berger, Arthur Asa. *Shop 'til You Drop: Consumer Behavior and American Culture*. Lanham, MD: Rowman & Littlefield, 2005. Print.
Bruno, Giuliana. "Ramble City: Postmodernism and 'Blade Runner.'" *October* 41 (1997): 61–74. Print.
Buckley, Jerome Hamilton. *Season of Youth: The Bildungsroman from Dickens to Golding*. Cambridge: Harvard University Press, 1974. 1–27. Print.
de Certeau, M. *The Practice of Everyday Life*. Trans. Steven Rendall. Berkeley, University of California Press, 1984. Print.

Finch, Christopher. "The Fantasy Realms of *The Dark Crystal* and Labyrinth." *Jim Henson: The Works*. New York: Random House, 1993. 164–195. Print.
Holt, Douglas B. "An Interview with Juliet Schor." *Journal of Consumer Culture* 5.1 (2005): 5–21. Print.
Humphery, Kim. *Excess: Anti-Consumerism in the West*. Cambridge, U.K.: Polity, 2010. Print.
Labyrinth. Dir. Jim Henson. Perf. David Bowie, Jennifer Connelly, Toby Froud. Columbia TriStar Home Video, 1999. DVD.
Rindfleisch, Aric, Burroughs, James E., and Nancy Wong. "The Safety of Objects: Materialism, Existential Insecurity, and Brand Connection." *Journal of Consumer Research*, 36.1 (2009), 1–16. Print.
Snow White & the Seven Dwarfs. Dir. William Cottrell et al. Walt Disney Enterprises, 2001. DVD.

PART THREE: STORYTELLERS AND SPECIALS

Everyone's a Storyteller: The Shifting Roles of Stories, Storytellers and Audiences in *The Jim Henson Hour*

Anthony F. Strand

Introduction

Throughout his career, Jim Henson displayed an interest in tearing down the barriers between performers and audience. This is evident in productions ranging from the 1968 public television special, *The Muppets on Puppets*, which demonstrates the versatility of "Anything Muppets" by changing their features onscreen, to *The Great Muppet Caper*, with its repeated reminders that it's just a movie. Of all Henson's projects, *The Jim Henson Hour* carries this tendency the furthest, blending the roles of performers, audience, and even the story itself.

The Jim Henson Hour debuted on NBC on April 14, 1989. The show was presented as an anthology, with Henson himself serving as the program's host. Most installments were split in two, with a "MuppeTelevision" segment starring Kermit and a mix of new and familiar characters followed by an independent half-hour story. Four of the show's twelve episodes devoted the full hour to a single piece. On *The Jim Henson Hour*, the audience at home is given plenty of attention. Some of that is in the *Muppets on Puppets* vein, as the show reveals its magic on a regular basis. During the closing tag of each episode, Henson shows the audience how they achieved one particular puppet trick or special effect. One whole episode, entitled "Secrets of the Muppets," is devoted to showing just that. But even when maintaining its internal reality,

The Jim Henson Hour has a hard time presenting it with a straight face. In nearly every segment, the show calls attention to the relationship between the storytellers, the characters, the audience, and even the story itself. That relationship is so fluid that boundaries between the four groups often cease to exist.

"I'm the narrator. You're the everyman main character!": Characters as Storytellers

On some level, all fictional characters are storytellers since they help to move along the narrative in which they're appearing. The characters on *The Jim Henson Hour* are more directly involved than that. Some consciously decide to influence the show's direction, while others grab control of their own images by modifying others' perceptions of them. Whatever the method they use, many of the show's cast members are aware that they're on television and hope to use that fact to meet their own goals.

As to be expected, the lead storyteller within the MuppeTelevision segments is Kermit the Frog. Since much the show's content is said to be "beamed in" from other sources, he doesn't shape the stories on *The Jim Henson Hour* as directly as he had on *The Muppet Show*. Instead, he almost seems to control reality itself. When Jim Henson reveals that he's going to show "The Secrets of the Muppets," in the episode of the same name, Kermit is the only character who isn't worried. He already knows the secrets. Revealing them won't take away his powers. Additionally, that power has a wide range of applications. When Kermit takes a vacation and the rest of the gang doesn't know how to make a closing number, he comes to their rescue. "It's simple," he says. "Cue the opening number!" And with that, he wills a song into being. When Bean Bunny bounces out of his monitor, Kermit wards off chaos with a helpful reminder that "Bean, that's cute, but you're breaking our reality there." When the band is making noise in the control room, Kermit influences their set list just by reacting. "Don't you know you're driving me crazy?!" he shouts, and they launch into a song called "You're Driving Me Crazy." That last one is clearly intended as a joke, but it's a perfect example of the way that Kermit works as the glue that keeps the show together. The rest of the characters on MuppeTelevision bend to his will. At one point Gonzo wonders out loud about who put Kermit in charge. The show never provides a definitive answer to that question. It doesn't need to. Kermit is in charge because it's the only way this world makes any sense.

Other than Kermit, no character takes more advantage of MuppeTelevision's storytelling opportunities than Bean Bunny (performed by Steve Whitmire). Bean was introduced in a 1986 TV special entitled *Tale of the Bunny Picnic*. In that program, he is portrayed as adorable, nervous, and somewhat cowardly. When he is brought back three years later as a regular on *The Jim Henson Hour*, that cuteness is presented instead as a deliberate choice — his inclusion a self-conscious decision to ensure that the show appeals to audience members who enjoy cute things. Throughout the series, Bean uses his inherent adorability to put himself in control of situations and of his own image. When Kermit's aforementioned vacation leaves the other characters scrambling to fill air time, Bean smoothly declares that it's story-time, and he's going to be the storyteller. After a false start, he does tell a story — about a land where the king starts acting like a commoner. That story is only tangentially about Bean himself, but it reflects his role in the show — it's about doing what you want and being happy with yourself even when others try to put you down.

Bean's other turns as storyteller more directly comment on that role. In the episode guest-starring Smokey Robinson, he appears as the host of an exercise show. Typical fitness show hosts are in great shape: muscular and toned. The floppy-eared, squishable Bean has a look that's the opposite, but in his mind, it doesn't matter at all. He's in better shape than anyone. He stretches that conceit to its breaking point in a pair of movie trailers he introduces in the "Dog City" episode. The first, *Bean Bunny and the Cuteness Thief*, positively engulfs the audience in Bean's expected image. (Robotic programmer Digit even complains that his circuits are corroding from the sweetness). But Bean promises that the second one "goes against my image." Indeed, the movie is a *Rambo* parody entitled *Beanbo*. Bean carries machine guns and shoots defenseless animals while a narrator menacingly intones, "Anger has a new name, rage has a voice, and revenge has a new face. *Beanbo*. Now Cute.... Has Learned to Kill." Bean can be whoever he decides to be because he has the power of filmmaking at his disposal.

The power of filmmaking is also used by the title character in *Miss Piggy's Hollywood*. Billed as "Miss Piggy Presents a Miss Piggy production starring Miss Piggy," the show proudly announces that its star is also its key storyteller. For a half-hour, we see Piggy's failed attempts to present herself as a member of the "Big Happy Hollywood Family" that ties all movie stars together. Time and again, though, the show pulls the rug out from under Piggy's version of reality. She tries to show off her star on the Walk of Fame, but it's portable. She brags about shopping on Rodeo Drive, but when the opportunity to actually spend money presents itself, she makes excuses not to because she doesn't have any. She claims to be on a first-name basis with the stars, but she squeals with delight at the first sight of one (TV star George Wendt). When she urges Wendt to support her tales of the hobnobbing they've done together, he insists he's just a regular guy who doesn't socialize much. Miss Piggy is telling us that she's a superstar, but the evidence says she's just a pig. In the end, Piggy breaks down and cries, admitting that she isn't Hollywood royalty and this isn't the show she envisioned. Once that happens, one celebrity (Dudley Moore) shows up who truly does view her as the greatest star in the universe. He takes her on a tour of his house, which is full of her image, and they sing a joyous duet together. Once Miss Piggy the storyteller comes to terms with reality, reality turns around and tells us that she was right all along, at least in the eyes of Dudley Moore.

A further example of a character creating a new perception of reality occurs in the environmental fable, "Song of the Cloud Forest," where the jungle animals live in fear of the terrifying "Uprights" (humans). The key sequence displaying the roots of this fear comes from a song sung by Ralph Robin (performed by Jerry Nelson), who claims to have seen the world of the Uprights. He sings of living metal machines devouring animals and destroying everything in their paths. He paints the Uprights as a race of savages who don't know the concept of kindness or mercy. They live only to kill, he says. This is, of course, misinformation being spread through the words of an unreliable narrator. The effectiveness of this scene depends entirely on this disconnect between Ralph's immediate audience (the jungle animals) and his secondary audience (the viewer). The viewer knows that he's spinning wild exaggerations based on half-truths. But within the program's world, the storyteller is all-powerful. His word is truth, and the animals believe him absolutely.

Another prominent on-screen storyteller is the unnamed little girl who controls MuppeTelevision's "Bootsie and Brad" segment. The title characters here are played by humans in plastic Ken-and-Barbie makeup (he even has plastic hair). In each sketch, a little girl and her (Muppet) dog look down into the playhouse, where we see the adult actors. They are completely alive, and we see how their adventures appear in her mind. In one sketch, Bootsie and Brad pretend to be married, and their dialogue clearly comes from the mind of a little girl imagining what marriage is like. "You just came home from the end of a long day," Bootsie tells Brad to set the scene. "Go out and come in again," she adds, since that's all the girl knows about adult relationships. They discuss the difference between boys and girls, which consists mostly of the presence or lack of bumps on a person's top half. In another, President Bootsie gets applause simply for the act of standing at a podium, since that's what presidents do. Occasionally the girl will even reach into the scene and affect it directly while it's in progress. Sometimes she'll give the pair a new friend (a disgruntled talking teddy in one episode, a G.I. Joe parody called Sgt. Killer Death Machine in another) or a prop (such as a rocket ship or a small cup of water) to interact with. One sketch even comes to an abrupt end when the girl's dog grabs Bootsie out of the playhouse and runs away. At all times, they are at the mercy of the girl's whims.

A number of other characters fulfill the role of storyteller (including the title character of *The Storyteller*, but we'll get to him later), but I want to specifically mention Clifford's role as narrator of the closing number in the MuppeTelevision episode guest-starring Ted Danson. Clifford (performed by Kevin Clash) is the shades-wearing bass player in the show's house band, and his narration here almost threatens to break open the viewing audience's TV sets. In "A Fish Story," Clifford tells the tale of Ted, an aquatic life form who crawls onto the surface and slowly forgets about his family back home. Eventually, Ted wastes most of the resources on Earth, endangering the lives of his family on land and at sea. Danson, a passionate environmentalist, stars (first voicing a Muppet, then as a human after some steps up the evolutionary ladder.) The sketch is designed to urge the audience to act, and Clifford makes sure that we know he's talking directly to each and every one of us watching at home. When Ted asks him early on if he could keep his voice down, Clifford responds, "Hold it down? I'm telling your story. I'm the narrator. You're the everyman main character." Ted isn't just one guy — he's every man. He later solemnly intones that "the Earth became uninhabitable, and that was the end." When Ted complains that it's not a happy ending, Clifford says that it could be if he'd change it, closing, "Maybe they even lived happily ever after. It's all up to Ted," and by extension the viewer. This isn't just a story, he (and the show) says. Every single person watching at home needs to join him in shaping that story.

"Just rewind me a little. I'm on tape deck 4.": Characters as Stories

With so much storytelling occurring on MuppeTelevision, it was perhaps inevitable that the characters sometimes morph into stories themselves. They do this by taking advantage of the show's fascination with technology. They harness it to make duplicate versions of themselves, create a permanent record of their activities, or step into stories which were recorded long before they arrived on the scene. Several times on MuppeTelevision, characters are transformed into living stories, playing out before the eyes of their cast mates.

As mentioned, one of the conceits of MuppeTelevision is that the programming isn't produced in the studio, but is instead beamed in from all over the universe. This extends even to the program's special guest stars. Unlike on *The Muppet Show*, where the guests spend a lot of time hanging out backstage with the Muppets, the guest stars on MuppeTelevision are never seen in the control room. Instead, they reside on monitors and interact with Kermit and the others through that barrier. This has the odd effect of reducing the guest star from a "Special Guest" to simply another channel among the thousands from which Kermit can choose. The first episode stresses this feeling with guest star Louie Anderson. When robotic programmer Digit (performed by Dave Goelz) discovers some alien programming, Anderson worries out loud that his spot on the show will be canceled to make room for it. Kermit assures him that he'll just cancel "some of the boring parts of the show" instead, which makes the point clear — the guest star might not be boring, but he also isn't an invaluable individual. He's just one potential story for the show to mess around with.

In that same scene, Digit is also transformed into a story. When he picks up a feed of alien sitcoms through his antenna, Digit can't figure out how to hook it up to the control room in Muppet Central. Instead, he watches the shows inside his head and talks about what he's seeing. At first he's simply an audience, of course, but then he decides to go ahead and plug himself into the master feed. Soon, the programming takes over his brain completely. He becomes increasingly manic, spouting one TV catchphrase after another—"'Lucy, I'm home. And here's bachelor number two! One of these days Alice — Pow! Right in the kisser! Dr. Welby, will he be all right? Nanu Nanu!" Finally, he passes out, unable to deal with a brain taken over by the voices of fiction.

The episode starring Buster Poindexter contains the other two most notable examples of characters becoming stories, both dealing with the recording process. First, Gonzo has two commitments at once, a problem he solves by leaving a pre-recorded version of himself behind. This recording looks just like Gonzo and interacts with the other characters naturally. Kermit thinks it's a lie, but Digit (and Gonzo, in unison) insists that Taped Gonzo can interact naturally because he's "very good at predicting what you're going to say next, Kermit!" "Gonzo, that is absolutely the most preposterous thing I have ever heard in my whole life!" replies an exasperated Kermit, with Gonzo matching his intonation to the syllable. Gonzo finally convinces Kermit by asking Digit to rewind him. Kermit turns this around and eventually gets rid of him by fast-forwarding him. Gonzo isn't pleased by this development, but he isn't surprised either — he'd predicted it, so he continues begging Kermit to stop. Kermit does, but not until Gonzo reaches the end of the tape and turns into a set of color bars. Kermit's assistant Vicki — the show's youngest character, and therefore the most aware of technology — takes it all in stride, muttering, "That's the worst tape of Gonzo I've ever seen," as she passes him.

Gonzo has turned himself into something very much like any episode of a TV show. Within the show's reality, he is now a pre-recorded artifact that can be watched infinite times. Outside of the show's reality, this moment can be seen as a comment not only on TV but on puppetry. Gonzo and Digit were both performed by Muppeteer Dave Goelz. If such moments were handled the same way here as on *The Muppet Show*, we can assume that one of the characters was performed by someone else and dubbed later (Finch, *Of Muppets & Men* 40). On set, one was a copy who wasn't quite the actual character. He only truly came to life through post-production.

Later, when Kermit picks up a satellite feed of Poindexter performing the closing number as "a remote from a nightclub across town," Kermit is surprised to see the band in the show, noting that they were just in the control room. Digit supposes that it might be a satellite feed, or they might have recorded it earlier, or it might be a special effect. With that, Digit inserts himself and Kermit into the nightclub location and they join in the song. As this number shows, *The Jim Henson Hour* doesn't believe in the reality of its various locations. It's all pre-recorded, and there's no reason to worry about real-world logistics. The show proudly announces that it's going to use every trick at its disposal to move its characters from place to place, with the end goal always being entertainment. The characters behave like stories because that's all they are — pawns to be moved around by the storytellers.

"Something That Would Appeal to the Average Consumer": Audience as Storytellers

As Christopher Finch notes in *Jim Henson: The Works*, part of the inspiration behind *The Jim Henson Hour* was "Jim's interest in the way people were beginning to watch TV — jumping from channel to channel with their remote controls, rarely watching one show in its entirety" (*The Works* 218). Among the MuppeTelevision characters, this is reflected in an obsession with appealing to multiple demographics. Over and over, the show stresses that the audience is an important part of the storytelling process. If the audience doesn't like what they're doing, they don't see much point in trying.

Waldo C. Graphic — the show's resident morphing, CGI clown — is officially employed as a demographic tracker, and most of his appearances deal with bringing up possible audiences they could appeal to. After a number, Waldo will often rush into the control complaining that "we need something that would appeal to the average consumer" or "Preteen females are having a negative reaction to all of the jokes about trash!" (The living trash bags that have been hanging out in the control room add that they should have their own demographic, since they have "plenty of disposable income" — this is yet another sign of the show's fascination with demos.) Those two moments act as set-ups for a) a sketch about a super-powerful grocery store stockboy, and b) a joke about showing "Spot that Blemish" on Channel 7. Most of Waldo's material appears to be strictly for laughs, at least on the surface. Another example occurs when Waldo complains that "we're not addressing the Danish cowboy crowd at all." This isn't an idea for a real sketch — it's just an excuse for Waldo to transform himself into Sheriff Hamlet.

The Muppets had joked about this sort of thing before. On *The Muppet Show*, Kermit sometimes speaks of empty theaters and even emptier cashboxes. But here the obsession with demographics extends well past simple jokes, and it's not difficult to theorize why. For all of his success, Jim Henson had never had a series on prime-time network TV before. *Sesame Street* was an icon of public television; *The Muppet Show* had thrived in syndication; and *Fraggle Rock* aired safely in the pay-cable nest of HBO. *The Jim Henson Hour* really was new territory in Henson's career, so it's no wonder that he and the writers spent a lot of time worrying about just who would be watching it.

Early in one episode, entitled "The Ratings Game," Vicki rolls out a machine that visually divides the show's demographics into increasingly narrow categories, including "Men, women, youth, retirees, black, brown, white, yellow, green, graduates, and Mr. Harry Stapleton." After this conversation causes the ratings to dip ("Viewers hate watching people talk about charts," says Vicki), they suddenly spike with the appearance of the show's most adorable character. In a play on Bean Bunny's previously-established massive cute appeal, the ratings show that every single demographic goes up in droves whenever he's on screen. Excited that people are watching, Kermit throws integrity out the window. "We'll be back with some great songs, and sketches, and maybe a little sex. But it's all gonna star Bean Bunny!" In real life, the creators intended Bean Bunny to be the show's breakout character, and the story of this episode — shot as the pilot, aired as the fifth installment — is dedicated to willing his popularity into existence. Not content to show the audience why they should love Bean Bunny, they look the audience in the eye and tell them they already do.

In the episode's closing sequence, we get the most literal interpretation of Jim's idea that the show would be like flipping channels. Waldo creates the "Response-O-Matic"—a new ratings system that allows the program to change in response to the audience's preferences. Over the course of the sketch, Gonzo and Link Hogthrob are forced to adapt to their changing surroundings—soap opera, game show, police drama, *Star Trek* parody. Henson and the other creators are practically begging the audience at home, "Tell us what you want to see. We're trying to please you!" The end of the sketch, however, reveals that they don't intend to follow focus groups or market research. Kermit shuts the machine down, saying that a machine can't create the show for them. Instead, he says, they need "a warm musical number with the whole Muppet family!" Mr. Harry Stapleton, the lone man with his own demographic, speaks for the first time to agree. The message is clear—the audience just wants to see the Muppets act like Muppets, or at least the creators hope they do.

One element of the episode that really stands out is Mr. Harry Stapleton himself, the show's first example of an "audience member" getting involved as a performer within the show itself. Mr. Stapleton is just one man, but he's a stand-in for every single audience member. The Muppets are trying hard to appeal to Mr. Stapleton, but they're going to try just as hard to appeal to everyone else watching. Unlike the rest of the audience, Mr. Stapleton appears on screen. He is a part of the show's content. But like the real-life audience, he doesn't actually do much of anything. He just stands there and stares out at the Muppets. They could have recorded any real viewer and gotten much the same effect. Audiences are by definition passive, and Mr. Stapleton is an accurate on-screen representation of an audience member.

Later, the show portrays another set of audience members as active and passionate. In two episodes, a (Muppet) group named "Gorilla Television" breaks into the feed. Their stated mission is to bring down Jim Henson and bring you "things the network doesn't want you to see." They are, of course, portrayed by the show's regular puppeteers, and the material they present was approved by both the network and Jim Henson. The sketches, however, are presented as being outside of the show's regular parameters, which allows them to take a point of view that the Muppets normally wouldn't. In the group's second appearance, leader Zondra rails against advertising, exclaiming, "You people will eat anything if you see it on television!" To prove her point, she reaches farther into the show's viewing audience, producing a housewife named Mrs. Vivian Eggloff. They show her commercials, and she immediately wants the products. But so does Zondra's sidekick Ubu, so Zondra is unable to make her point fully. Even when the audience hacks directly into the show's content, they can't overwhelm the power of commercial broadcasting.

"Welcome to Family Programming, Folks!": Characters as Audience

When *The Jim Henson Hour*'s audience doesn't appear on screen, its characters spend a lot of time acting as an audience for one another. Sometimes this means watching each other perform, other times it means commenting on programs they aren't directly involved in, and sometimes it means referring back to other parts of the Jim Henson Company's rich history. In all cases, the show's characters function as a stand-in for at least part of the audience at home.

Since MuppeTelevision's content is said to be beamed in from channels originating outside of the control room, the core cast is presented as not having been involved in the creation of most of the sketches. This means Kermit is not just the host. He's the first level of the show's audience — he screens all of the sketches so that he can filter out the bad ones before they reach the screen. This means not only that there's no spontaneity to the sketches, there's also no risk of going without programming. When something goes wrong — for instance, when Kermit, Waldo, and handyman Lindbergh are zapped inside Digit's brain — Kermit simply tells Digit (and the audience at home), "Hey, listen, if you can't get us out, watch the fashion doll sketch on monitor 8." On *The Muppet Show*, problems backstage affect the sketches. On *The Jim Henson Hour*, the sketches are all pre-loaded and safely transported to the air, since The Muppets are only an intermediate audience, not entertainers in their own right. This removal from the material reaches its breaking point at the end of the episode starring Louie Anderson, when Digit receives a feed featuring a variety show from outer space. It stars "The Teppums," photo-negative versions of the Muppets with backwards names like "Timrek the Gorf" and "Oznog." In this case, the Muppets are literally watching themselves on a screen. It seems like the show's creators know that the audience would rather watch the Muppets put on a show than import one, but the only way to achieve that is to have the Muppets import themselves from a foreign planet.

However, the characters don't only watch the program itself. On several occasions, they show familiarity with past Muppet programming. In one episode, Kermit declares that they're going to show "a cute children's program." A chicken squawks in protest, screaming, "What ELSE is on?!" She might not mention *Sesame Street* by name, but the chicken clearly has no interest in revisiting it or any of its peers. In other instances, some trash bags tell Kermit they recognize him "from TV and movies," and Vicki reminisces about watching *The Muppet Show* at her preschool. These moments serve two functions. They make Kermit feel old, of course, but more importantly, they tell us that within the show's continuity, the illusion that *The Muppet Show* was just a stage show isn't allowed to stand. It was a TV show, and it had a home viewing audience just like *The Jim Henson Hour* does.

Outside of MuppeTelevision, *Muppet Show* mainstay Rowlf serves as the narrator (and connection to the audience) for the hour-long gangster spoof *Dog City*. Many of his lines are in the vein of "In dog terms, this is what we call chasing a schtick" or (upon the revelation of the villain's name) "Bugsy Them — that's right, folks, yet another cheap joke name." His function is to point out that the show's writers (like the audience) recognize that all of these dog jokes are silly. Rowlf talks directly to the camera, but his audience is represented on-screen by the dogs that populate the show's primary bar setting. They all laugh uproariously at his jokes, much like a studio audience at a sit-com taping. They also function as something of a Greek Chorus, howling in unison when Ace says the word "How" or yelping with glee when Ace's girlfriend Colleen sings a torch song. Later, a dog sweeping up claims, "I know a guy who knows the writers," and proceeds to tell Rowlf a series of false spoilers for the rest of the special. He's completely wrong, of course. This is partially to set up Rowlf's punny response ("My mother always told me to let sweeping dogs lie"), but it also sends a message that the audience can't predict what's coming, so they should just relax and enjoy the show. In all of these cases, the actions of the dogs indicate how the storytellers want the audience to react — express your enjoyment loudly, and don't spend too much time worrying about what's going to happen next because it's all just silly fun anyway.

Another dog who spends a lot of time worrying is the nameless Dog owned by The Storyteller in the recurring segment of the same name. Like Rowlf, The Storyteller looks directly into the camera because he's really speaking to the people watching on TV, but ostensibly, he's telling all of the stories to his dog, the only other being in the room. The Dog makes for a very enthusiastic audience indeed, as he frequently comments on and sometimes even changes the flow of the story. Occasionally that means interacting with the stories themselves, but usually it just means saying what the audience is thinking. When the personification of Death from the episode, "The Soldier and Death," appears in the Storyteller's glass, the Dog gets frightened and jumps. By doing so, he's telling children at home that it's okay to be afraid. In "The

True Bride," the Dog laughs when the villainous troll falls into an empty lake and apparently dies. The Storyteller admonishes him, "You may laugh, but it had repercussions." Keep watching, he's telling those of us who had the same reaction. This is serious business. Later, when a trollop (female troll) appears and the Storyteller says, "It must be — it can't be — but it must be *his daughter*!," the Dog joins him in exclaiming the last two words. Similarly, much of the audience will undoubtedly recognize the episode titled "Sapsorrow" as being an earlier version of the Cinderella fable. The Dog voices that familiarity, saying, "The Prince will marry the girl who fits the golden slipper! Bleh!" The audience is going to make these connections, too, and the creators know it.

"Chauncey didn't make me! You did! In your dreams!": Stories as Characters

The Jim Henson Hour was so focused on the act of storytelling that it was inevitable some of those stories would take on lives of their own. In many instances, fictional characters move up one level of reality to interact with their creators. This allows the series to explore the mindset of those creators. It shows how the fictional worlds they create are inspired by what they think, feel, and experience. It demonstrates how the characters — and the process of creation — help the storytellers work through other issues in their lives. Further, it shows how stories benefit the rest of the world that they enter.

MuppeTelevision only features a few minor examples of this, such as graffiti drawings jumping off of a wall to dance with Bobby McFerrin, but the best example doesn't involve any Muppets at all; it's guest star Buster Poindexter. Poindexter, best known for his hit song, "Hot, Hot, Hot," is as much a fictional character as any of the Muppets. He's a creation of David Johansen, former lead singer of the New York Dolls. He's treated the same way as any other guest star, making this appearance just one more segment of the elaborate joke staged by Johansen over the course of several years. Years earlier, Peter Sellers had refused to appear out of character on *The Muppet Show*, but Sellers acknowledged it, telling Kermit that, "There is no me.... There used to be a me, but I had it surgically removed." On *The Jim Henson Hour*, however, no such concession is made because the show isn't interested in defining the difference between fiction and reality. It never acknowledges Poindexter's fictional status because he's just as real as any of the characters with whom he shares the screen.

Three non–MuppeTelevision segments prominently feature stories coming to life and interacting with their creators. The most literal of these is the recurring *The Storyteller*. Here, it isn't just characters who gain sentience, it's the tales themselves. That was an intentional decision on the part of the filmmakers. Producer Duncan Kenworthy noted, "The reason that these fairy tales lasted for centuries wasn't just because of their storylines. It was more to do with the meaning behind words. Our idea was to try to convey the power of these oral narratives through television" (Bacon 44). They put that idea into action by giving the stories themselves personalities. Screenwriter Anthony Minghella originally wanted to take this a step further, going so far as to suggest "making each story a puppet" (Bacon 45). That didn't happen, but the stories are unquestionably alive. For example, in "The Heartless Giant," the title character says, "My heart is there — in the cupboard." The Storyteller, startled at this revelation, excitedly repeats, "In the cupboard!" He might be the one telling the tale, but he seems genuinely surprised by the twist.

Further, the stories assert themselves with a physical presence in the 'real' world of the Storyteller. Sometimes the blending is only a gentle push, as elements from the stories invade the Storyteller's environment. His den is regularly filled with objects such as handkerchiefs and rings, and the stories' weather phenomena often carry over to his home as well. When a story is being told, it takes over completely. Consequently, the barriers between the two worlds often cease to exist entirely. In "The Three Ravens," the camera pans out through the Storyteller's window directly onto a courtyard where the story's lead character, a king, is mourning over his wife's casket. In "Sapsorrow," a close-up of the Storyteller's Dog pulls back to reveal that the room is full of Sapsorrow's animal friends. Later in that same story, when Sapsorrow's sisters accuse her of playing with the Queen's ring, the Dog insists, "She wasn't!" This causes one of the sisters to bend down, look him in the eye and say, "Quiet, you!" These and many other examples offer evidence of what Kenworthy was saying. These stories have an inherent power, and that power is stronger than anything offered by the real world. The stories enrich the lives of the Storyteller and his Dog — and by extension, the audience at home — because they offer a glimpse into a completely new and alien world. The real world simply can't compare, and the show underscores that the stories actually overpower it.

Another Dog comes to life in *Living with Dinosaurs*, a one-hour episode focusing on the inner life of a 9-year-old British boy named Dom. Dom is nervous, asthmatic, and completely unable to make friends at school. His only companion is a stuffed dinosaur toy named Dog. The two joke around, write out lists, and go on adventures under the pterodactyl-filled covers. As far as Dom is concerned, Dog truly is alive, and the show never definitively says otherwise. Director Anthony Minghella expressed his belief that, "the fantasy element of real life is very high" (Bacon 68), and the show always views the world through Dom's eyes, which means that Dog is always active. His primary role is to help Dom deal with various frustrations in his life — most notably an intense dislike of his father. By the story's end, Dom warms up to his father, but he'd never have allowed himself to make that connection if he hadn't first created a fictional best friend who helped him work through his problems. The act of telling stories — of immersing himself in a fictional world — gives Dom a way to deal with the real people who are most important in his life.

Matt Banting, the 14-year-old lead character in the hour-long episode *Monster Maker*, is several years older than Dom, but he also spends a lot of time creating stories in his head. Matt gets an after-school job working for special effects wizard Chauncey Bellows, who is impressed by Matt's innovative "walking" animatronic legs. Matt learns about realistic movie creatures when he sees Chauncey's masterpiece, a gigantic metallic dragon named the Ultragorgon, moving and thinking for itself. The Ultragorgon's apparent consciousness is simply part of an elaborate lesson that Chauncey teaches Matt. To Matt, though, the dragon seems to be as alive as he is. This is an extension of how filmmakers like Chauncey bring creatures to life on the screen. They create special effects that are absolutely alive, but that's only half of the job. The other half is done by the viewer, who must buy into the illusion for it to be a success. The Ultragorgon makes that clear when he snarls at Matt, "Chauncey didn't create me! You did! In your dreams!" Like all movie monsters, he's only alive because the audience (in this case Matt) says he is.

Another story comes to life in *Monster Maker* — the story of Jim Henson himself. The special isn't strictly autobiographical (it's based on a novel by Nicholas Fisk), but in the show's opening, Henson himself points out the eerie similarities between it and his own life. Like Henson, Chauncey is an American filmmaker with a creature shop in London. Chauncey is an obvious stand-in for Henson — the Ultragorgon could just as well be one of the fantasy creatures from his 80s fantasy films *The Dark Crystal* or *Labyrinth*. What Henson doesn't mention is that Matt represents other aspects of his background. As I mentioned, the teenaged Matt creates a new visual effects trick. Likewise, while still in college, Henson developed a new way to film puppets for television. In *Jim Henson: The Works*, Christopher Finch notes that, "Jim soon learned that he could employ [lenses of different focal lengths] to create a variety of illusions involving spatial perceptions" (18). It's not a stretch to say that both main characters represent Henson at different points in his life.

In *The Storyteller* and *Living With Dinosaurs* (and even in the case of the

Ultragorgon), stories come to life and interact with the world inhabited by their creators. Here, though, the entire history of Jim Henson himself informs the reality of *Monster Maker*. Those stories, reflected through Matt and Chauncey, allow us to guess about the past and future of those characters, expanding the scope of the story far beyond its official beginning and ending.

"Give my best to your folks": Storytellers as Characters

Thus far, we've looked at interactions between various levels of fiction. But *The Jim Henson Hour* was frequently invaded by inhabitants of our "real" world. The show's writers and Muppeteers (performers behind the Muppets and other puppet characters) appeared on-screen in a diverse range of capacities. Muppeteers had done cameos as humans before — *The Great Muppet Caper*, for example, contains appearances from four of *The Muppet Show*'s key performers — but no production had ever featured so many in such a short span. These appearances are fun for avid Muppet fans to spot, but on *The Jim Henson Hour* they signify something deeper. Just as fictional characters can come to life within the show's world, so could real-life people step into imaginary worlds and interact with the inhabitants. All levels of reality are given equal importance, and that includes the one the home audience lives in.

For most of that audience, the most easily noticed behind-the-scenes personality is Jim Henson himself. As previously mentioned, Henson is the program's host. This means not only that he's serving the same function Kermit did on *The Muppet Show*, but he's also serving the same function Kermit does on the MuppeTelevision segments of this program. Jim introduces Kermit at the start of each MuppeTelevision. Although he doesn't make the change on camera, slipping from one persona into the other becomes part of his performance. Since the two are sharing a job, they frequently interact directly (via monitors). This keeps the audience from thinking of them as the same person, and it also allows Henson to play around with his relationship to Kermit. At the beginning of one episode, Kermit announces an aquatic theme, saying, "It's going to be kind of a 'Friends and Relations' show for me." Henson responds, "Great. Give my best to your folks!" The unspoken joke is that as Kermit's creator, Henson is the closest thing he has to a father. Henson addressed that aspect of performance in a 1981 interview with *Cinefantastique* magazine, noting, "Performance is where the humanity is. The characters are each a little part of my soul, or someone else's. Like anything any artist puts forth, there is always a chunk of the man involved" (Harris 31). When he appears on screen with his most famous creation, Henson is simply reconnecting with that part of himself.

MuppeTelevision sketches often call for human beings other than the guest stars to appear on screen, and they are almost always played by behind-the-scenes personalities. Most often called upon were puppeteer Dan Redican and writer Chris Langham. Between the two of them, they play everything from farmers to salesmen and from beauty pageant hosts to human pests infesting the home of aliens. Watching the show, one gets the impression that the only humans on every channel in the galaxy are ones who look exactly like the show's production team. Perhaps that's intentional. After all, the Muppets see those people every day, even if they don't know why.

It's not just the people in sketches who look like puppeteers. Twice, members of the show's cast are presented as members of its audience. When Vicki devotes one entire viewing demographic to Mr. Harry Stapleton, he is played by veteran Muppeteer Jerry Nelson. Likewise, Mrs. Vivian Eggloff, the housewife who is kidnapped by the crew from Gorilla Television, is played by Muppet performer Camille Bonora. Perhaps the use of Nelson and Bonora was simply a matter of convenience. The sketches called for people, and they were on the set anyway, but maybe their presence means more than that. This was a show that was always very worried about who was going to watch it, as evidenced by all the talk of ratings and demographics. By using their own cast members as stand-ins for the audience, the show's creative team was making a statement that they were going to make a show to please themselves. They knew that if they made a show that they wanted to watch, chances were high that others would like it as well. Nelson again appears on screen in *Song of the Cloud Forest*, this time joined by fellow Muppeteer Fran Brill. In that story, the animals of the rainforest worry constantly about the threat posed by the Uprights, who they believe are trying to destroy the rainforest and kill them all. In reality, the characters played by Nelson and Brill are ecologists hoping to preserve the forest's endangered species. They aren't a threat at all. They have the same goals as the animals, which is why they're played by some of the same people.

The segment *Miss Piggy's Hollywood* features a brief cameo from another core Muppet performer, Dave Goelz. The show introduces him in a novel way. Gonzo announces that Fozzie is at the famous Comedy Store comedy club, and then we cut directly to Goelz—Gonzo's performer—as a comedian who is completely dying onstage. "So the duck says, 'If I had a match, I'd have offered you a light,'" he intones, but he gets no laughs. This might be a reflection of Goelz's own early insecurities as a performer. In *Of Muppets &*

Men, he said of puppeteering for television, "It takes maybe five years to begin to do everything without thinking about it. I still find it difficult" (84). Goelz had grown even stronger as a performer in the eight years between that statement and *The Jim Henson Hour*, but he channels that awkwardness to great effect for this appearance.

Nelson, Bonora, Brill, and Goelz all return, along with the rest of the show's core performers, in the final segment of *Secrets of the Muppets*. Here, Henson and Kermit introduce each puppeteer, and they say a little bit about themselves and their characters in turn. It's here that the show demonstrates how the various puppeteers express themselves through their work. Nelson, for example, seems very similar to his laid-back guitarist character Beard. Steve Whitmire, on the other hand, comments that Bean is a lot more comfortable on camera than he is. Immediately we see the truth in that statement, as Bean quips, "Yeah, and I'm a lot cuter, too!" With these glimpses, we see how the men and women responsible for the characters inform how they behave. They keep invading this reality because they can't help it. Even when off-camera, they influence everything that happens.

Conclusion

Even though *The Jim Henson Hour* ran for only twelve episodes, these are far from the only instances of the show exploring relationships between various levels of reality. What I've offered here are only examples, and even most of these work better in context. *The Jim Henson Hour* is a truly remarkable entry in Jim Henson's filmography, and one that has been hard to find ever since it left the air. The Henson Company's 2004 sale of the Muppets to Disney hasn't helped in that regard, as ownership is now split between the two companies. Some segments are available to own or stream, but others remained locked in company vaults. In the case that a reader does get a chance to view the program, he or she would do well to embrace it. The show really thrives on its relationship to the audience, and it deserves an audience as large and varied as the stories it presented in its too-brief run.

WORKS CITED

Bacon, Matt. *No Strings Attached: The Inside Story of Jim Henson's Creature Shop*. New York: Macmillan, 1997. Print.

Barron, Steve. "The Storyteller: Sapsorrow." *The Jim Henson Hour*. NBC, 30 July 1989. Television.

Blanchard, John. "MuppeTelevision: Monster Telethon." *The Jim Henson Hour*. NBC, 28 Apr. 1989. Television.

Davis, Michael. *Street Gang: The Complete History of Sesame Street.* New York: Viking, 2008. Print.

Finch, Christopher. *Jim Henson: The Works.* New York: Random House, 1993. Print.

_____. *Of Muppets & Men: The Making of the Muppet Show.* 1st ed. New York: Knopf, 1981. Print.

Foster, Giles. "Monster Maker." *The Jim Henson Hour.* NBC, 9 July 1989. Television.

Gikow, Louise. *Sesame Street: A Celebration: 40 Years of Life on the Street.* New York NY: Black Dog & Leventhal Publishers, 2009. Print.

Harris, Peter. "Miss Piggy's Hollywood." *The Jim Henson Hour.* NBC, 14 May 1989. Television.

_____. "MuppeTelevision: Aquatic Life." *The Jim Henson Hour.* NBC, 21 Apr. 1989. Television.

_____. "MuppeTelevision: Food." *The Jim Henson Hour.* 1990. Television.

_____. "MuppeTelevision: Garbage." *The Jim Henson Hour.* NBC, 30 July 1989. Television.

_____. "MuppeTelevision: Health and Fitness." *The Jim Henson Hour.* NBC, 16 July 1989. Television.

_____. "MuppeTelevision: Musicians." *The Jim Henson Hour.* NBC, 23 July 1989. Television.

_____. "MuppeTelevision: The Ratings Game." *The Jim Henson Hour.* NBC, 14 May 1989. Television.

_____. "Secrets of the Muppets." *The Jim Henson Hour.* Nickelodeon, 1992. Television.

Henson, Jim. "Dog City." *The Jim Henson Hour.* NBC, 5 May 1989. Television.

_____. "The Song of the Cloud Forest." *The Jim Henson Hour.* NBC, 16 July 1989. Television.

_____. "The Storyteller: The Heartless Giant." *The Jim Henson Hour.* NBC, 14 Apr. 1989. Television.

_____. "The Storyteller: The Soldier and Death." *The Jim Henson Hour.* NBC, 28 Apr. 1989. Television.

Minghella, Anthony. "Living with Dinosaurs." *The Jim Henson Hour.* Nickelodeon, 1993. Television.

Moss, Wayne. "MuppeTelevison: Science Fiction." *The Jim Henson Hour.* NBC, 14 Apr. 1989. Television.

Smith, Peter. "The Storyteller: The True Bride." *The Jim Henson Hour.* NBC, 23 July 1989. Television.

Weiland, Paul. "The Storyteller: The Three Ravens." *The Jim Henson Hour.* 1990. Television.

There Is No One Story
Nathaniel Long

The brief opening speech is always the same, delivered in John Hurt's trademark rasp, building to the autumnal, nigh sinister, but deeply tuneful string lilt: "When people told their past with stories, explained their present with stories, foretold the future with stories..." At their most basic level, this is what all tales are intended to do, and almost by definition, a tale that had no acquaintance with human nature would be unrecognizably alien. Yet the Storyteller's words could apply most strongly to a specific subset of tales: what we would call myths. However, *The Storyteller*'s spin-off series, *Greek Myths*, eschews the germane phrase above. Its opening consists of a statue of Icarus, falling through blackness to shatter on the earth. This vision is much starker, much less stylish than the original series, but this is in keeping with a show that is unapologetic in its bleakness and primal melodrama.

The first germ of *The Storyteller* was suggested by Jim Henson's daughter, who had studied myth and folklore at Harvard and felt that the stories she was covering would be perfectly suited to her father's production style, and that such stories would be fascinating when returned to their folk roots and spared any sugarcoating (Finch 191). The fact that such a return to basics was even needed demonstrates how shriveled some of these stories had become, and while it is tempting to write this off as a general 'Disneyfication' it should be acknowledged that this sort of bowdlerization goes back at least as far as Charles Perrault's day, and that even Grimm's grimmest sprang from still darker antecedents. That Jim Henson and the Creature Shop would excel at crafting the beastly menagerie of these old stories almost goes without saying, but the idea that such material should prove a natural fit with Henson's artistic style is more insightful.

Prior to *The Storyteller*, Henson and company's main forays into overt fantasy consisted of feature films, namely *The Dark Crystal* and *Labyrinth*. The first is a deeply strange film whose bizarre setting and style demonstrate a refusal to make easy concessions to its audience, which is artistically admirable but may explain why it failed to act as much of a box office draw. *Labyrinth* is a more accessible film, but one laced with fully grotesque creatures, a Pythonesque streak of black humor, and a central villain whose predatory charm provides a very mature peril in opposition to its young heroine. Both films owe as much to the visionary work of Brian Froud as to Henson himself, but they reflect an air of melancholy and discomfort that is surprisingly endemic to much of his more adult work. By all personal accounts Jim Henson was one of the most affable creators one could hope to meet, but by the time he had firmly established himself in the mid–'80s he was not afraid to indulge in thematic darkness. Though *The Storyteller* would meet with the same undeserved apathy as the two Froud collaborations, at least in the U.S., it marks the true apotheosis of Henson's fantasy output and the zenith of his artistic career. The nine installments that make up the original *Storyteller* cycle are very likely the best things that Henson ever produced.

If *The Storyteller* was something of a noble failure in terms of wide reception, the *Greek Myths* follow up is relegated to almost total obscurity. Though brilliant in its own right, it is not the unalloyed masterpiece that its counterpart is, and at a meager four episodes, it is nearly too brief to register. At worst, one might call it a footnote to a footnote. However, just as *The Storyteller* easily outclasses lighter fairy tale fare, *Greek Myths* is superlative when it comes to relating its quartet of very somber stories. The show is a far cry from, say, Kevin Sorbo's *Hercules* in terms of fidelity to its roots. It is worth comparing *The Storyteller* and *Greek Myths*, not only to pinpoint the aesthetic dissimilarities, but to consider what this dissonance says of the respective source material. Myth and folklore are kindred but very different entities, with discrete origins and applications. The contrasting elements within the two Jim Henson series reflect these differences precisely.

At the most basic level, myth differs from folklore in that it is necessarily primal. While the application of myth continues into the present day for many cultures, its first order of business is to provide explanation for the world and its beginnings and gradually cohere into a full narrative (often charmingly inconsistent and contradictory). By contrast, folklore is allowed greater freedom to mutate and to become contemporary, while setting its sights considerably lower than the mysteries of the universe. In myth, there is essentially one story, with the earth or perhaps the entire cosmos as the central character. Folklore is myth's laidback cousin, more shiftless, less reliable, but often a good deal more companionable. While myth tends to begin with gods and titans, folklore only really cares about people — and it's no accident that monsters in folktales can be as humane as many of its humans are monstrous. Last but not least, folklore is essentially free-use. While Joseph Campbell acolytes are quick to observe recurrent mythotropes — firebringers, antediluvian serpents, tricksters, and indeed, crucifixions — myth-sets are reliably segregated. There is little danger of Loki wandering into the middle of the *Ramayana*. Folklore, meanwhile, is limited solely by time and trade routes, and one should not be surprised when even the strangest or most culturally characteristic of Ukrainian yarns winds up having an equivalent number somewhere in Appalachia.

Folktales get around, which may help to explain one of the key advantages of *The Storyteller* over *Greek Myths*: its stories feel more universal, and while the title card for each episode helpfully mentions the country of origin, these are slightly redundant. *The Storyteller* is very good about employing regional flavor (the two Russian stories look genuinely Russian), but the tales themselves come from all around. "The Luck Child," for instance, is a very basic story with variants throughout Europe and beyond, while the nominally German story of "The Heartless Giant" is if anything more reminiscent of the famous Russian tale of Koschei the Deathless — the 'separable soul' motif is frequent enough to have a marker on the Aarne-Thompson index, the encyclopedic concordance of folk stories (AaTh 302: the devil's heart in the egg). The series might as well have been subtitled 'German Tales,' as these make up a full two-thirds of the total, and for that matter there are half again as many German stories as *Greek Myths* has Greek myths. Add to this the Russian duet and the rather hodge-podge Celtic tale of "A Story Short," and the series claims a mere three regions. This pool should feel intensely limited but instead reflects something expansive and timeless.

Tremendous credit for this must go to Anthony Minghella, as full a collaborator here as Froud was in Jim Henson's film fantasies. Minghella's mellifluous phrasings never put a foot wrong and ensure that the actual storytelling in *The Storyteller* is just as great an asset as the creature work from the production staff. Minghella knows the "rules" of folktales, those elements that are so obvious as to be intrinsic — and therefore surprising when directly acknowledged. Consider, for instance, the Rule of Threes, wherein every task, every curse, every set of siblings, and every pair of iron shoes must always come in triplicate. Besides being innately pleasing to most people, the Rule of Threes has real narrative purpose. *We fail, we fail, and then we succeed*, is what it seems to say, a message both optimistic (we get there in the end) and realistic (we do not get there right at the start).

More subtle, perhaps, is the Storyteller's art of insinuating himself into his tales, which will be discussed in more detail shortly. While some might consider this a "meta" or postmodern approach to the tales, it could also be read as the precise opposite effect, as a seemingly omniscient narrator would frequently appear in his own stories (for whatever reason, the Germans appear especially fond of this touch). A storyteller is very seldom a player, and his presence tends to be a comical sting when a story needs one: he will be a guest at some happy couple's wedding, and often as not, wind up in a spot, perhaps baked into a pie or even fired from a cannon. This insinuation serves a curious dual purpose: it is meant to suggest veracity, the idea that if it happened to a personal acquaintance, the story must have some truth to it, but the general silliness of such codas has the inverse effect, winking at the audience as if to say that of course this is all nonsense while offering a friendly challenge to anyone bold enough to actually call the teller's bluff.

The interaction of an audience is crucial, and *The Storyteller*'s cast manages this effect with only two characters: the title character and his dog. Just as the scripting, direction, and design of the series are practically flawless, the casting could not have been better. John Hurt is excellent as the host, trundling around his room giving us twenty-minute chunks of poetry in a voice which is simultaneously wasted and incantatory. It is never exactly clear where the room is located, only that it is tucked away in a castle-like structure that is somehow homey despite being vast and almost totally unfurnished. Hurt could do these shows as radio plays, and they would still be spellbinding, but his presence within the series proper adds a fascinating dimension, as does his cohort, the Dog, the only true unifying element between all thirteen episodes. The puppetry on the Dog is as good as anything Henson and company ever created, attaining that highest of compliments in that it is sometimes impossible to tell how they are operating it. Brian Henson likewise does never-better work, using a gentler twist of his Hoggle voice to ensure that the Dog gets all the best lines. Though the Dog is not above questioning his "master," the critical element here should not be overstated. These questions serve a purpose, cuing exposition that might otherwise feel superfluous or heavy-handed even in Minghella's neat prose. Also, the Dog does not complain *that much*. On the contrary, he serves as audience surrogate by becoming fully mesmerized by the story, his frequent and earnest exclamations of "That poor boy!" or "Oh, I hate that witch!" demonstrating how invested he is in the narrative. He also appears genuinely devastated by the series' more somber conclusions in "The Soldier and Death" and "The Heartless Giant."

The Storyteller's participation appears in clever ways. He stars in the episode "A Story Short," and while it is a very pleasing novelty to have him take center stage, and the episode is worth it solely for the Hurt-Hare creature, this may in fact be the weakest tale from a purely narrative standpoint, a collection of hurried incidents that never quite add up to more than the sum of their parts (though the least of the best is still quite good). Its greatest contribution to this discussion might be Hurt's final and rather flippant view of his own trials, explaining how by this point his original tale has probably mutated completely from where it began, because "you know how it is with stories." The Storyteller and the Dog also have a surprisingly large background role in "Hans My Hedgehog," the earliest of the episodes produced — recognizable if nothing else for the much stiffer makeup on our narrator, who looks to be overcoming a stroke at certain points — and this small fluke of style may be a result of an early approach that was promptly scrapped. Perhaps the intention was to have Hurt wandering in and out of all the stories before it was decided he could be just as effective from his armchair. Interestingly, an unproduced teleplay entitled "The Witch Baby" was later adapted into a comic book by Archaia Entertainment, and it takes a similar approach to "Hans," explicitly inserting a more youthful Storyteller as a confidant of the tale's young hero. One should also consider the various tidbits that the series employs: Hurt appears to be in possession of some of the more fantastic items from the series, such as the statue of the Thought Lion, though these may just as well be mundane visual cues for the fantasies he is narrating. In "Fearnot," he mentions that the title character is a distant relation of his, and he heard the story from their mutual friend, the tinker-thief McKay. In "Sapsorrow," he says that he went to the heroine's wedding, and in one of the series' sillier epilogues, he realizes that the bride and groom have danced themselves to exhaustion "and if I don't wake them soon they'll never get married!"

The most complex of these connections comes in "The Soldier and Death," probably the best episode of the series; Jim Henson implied that it was his favorite of the batch, the one he was most proud of, and it is not hard to see why (Finch 194). Besides the incredible Devils and the genuinely eerie Death that the Creature Shop produced, this tale is by turns the funniest and saddest of the lot. The Storyteller explains that it happened to a very old friend of his, the titular Soldier, yet it may be that the Storyteller *is* the Soldier, or a near stand in. He bears the mark of the Soldier's regiment upon his patchwork coat (admittedly not the only souvenir he has from his various stories), on two occasions the scene segues between close-ups of the men, and there is something enigmatic about the ending. When the Dog laments the Wandering Jew-like fate of the Soldier, Hurt suggests that it is no great tragedy: "He's a rare boy, my friend the soldier, he's somewhere about his business." When the Dog asks, "Are you sure?" Hurt simply offers him a biscuit in order to change the subject.

There is obviously no real evidence that the old men may be one and the same, and no particular reason it should be so, but there are small touches like these that make for a sly conspiracy theory. More to the point, all of the examples cited above show how the Storyteller interacts with his stories as much as with his audience. The layers between what is happening, what is being suggested, what we hear and what we see, and what is fiction and what is personal history all coagulate into the show's wonderfully unsteady aesthetic, in which everything is at least somewhat mutable and events proceed by their own fairy tale logic. Of course, fairy tale logic is still very much logic, and these insane stories operate by highly codified rules, compared to which the real world is treacherous and capricious.

The Greek Storyteller, played by Michael Gambon, is cast in a very different light, and the way in which his presentation differs from Hurt's is a key feature of the distinction between folktale and myth. Gambon is another tremendous actor (and another tremendous voice), but he is never really imbued with the same degree of personality as Hurt's avuncular host. Indeed, what personality there is could be said to come from the actor as much as the character, for despite his leonine bearing and stentorian voice, Gambon is known to be rather caustic and even mischievous behind the scenes. This unusual combination — a man who is equal parts trickster and Shakespearean monarch — makes him a canny choice for the role. One guide to Henson's works describes the Greek Storyteller as "rogueish" and that is as apt a summation as any (Finch 193). He is not particularly affable, and it is difficult to imagine him ever taking center stage in one of the tales. Even his interactions with the Dog feel somewhat limited. While Hurt's Storyteller is a storyteller to his core, letting the tales act as his *raison d'être*, this does not seem to be the case with Gambon. His extremely brief introduction suggests he is a thief or grifter who just happens to know all of the old myths, as he wanders through the Labyrinth of Knossos and finds random items that initiate each of his stories.

While continuity is more or less meaningless, *Greek Myths* has an established first episode: "Theseus & The Minotuar," in which the scruffy duo literally stumble into the Labyrinth in which they will spend the rest of their time — "Daedalus & Icarus" acts as something of a loose prequel/sequel, even offering a brief return appearance from the Cretan beast. The Greek Storyteller and his Dog are apparently Athenian, as the Dog comments that Daedalus and Icarus come from their home city. Gambon never participates directly in any of the stories (unlike the folktales, these myths have a clearly defined cast of characters), and there is less actual narration overall, serving more as bridging material between scenes that are longer and more fully established than in the original *Storyteller*, whose structure constantly ebbs and flows between the tale and the teller. This is not to say that the series is free of its oral influence. On the contrary, there are many fine moments of tell-don't-show, as when Gambon narrates in aching detail Daedalus's failed struggle to rescue his nephew, or when the audience is entreated to feel "the drag, the lurch... the forever fall, the plunge" when Perseus and his mother are placed in a trunk and heaved into the sea.

The words themselves may also be notably different, as Minghella is here credited in a creative capacity, while Nigel Williams handles the actual scripting. Like everything else in *Greek Myths*, Williams' contribution is laudable work that suffers only by comparison to its predecessor. The actors generally have a fine time hamming it up (which is no real difference from in Hurt's stories), and Williams provides some beautiful speeches that evoke the very real heartbreak of the Greek tragedies. This writing style is not as lyrical as Minghella's teleplays, but neither is it trying to be. If the original *Storyteller* avoids sugarcoating its material, *Greek Myths* goes a step further and gives us frankly dark and disturbing episodes that are entirely in keeping with their origins. There are small concessions to clemency, as when the apparent ghosts of Orpheus or Icarus visit the wanderers, but these do nothing to offset such drama as Daedalus boiling Minos alive, then withdrawing into his chamber to carve endless replicas of his dead son. The ending to the Theseus tale is the darkest and most unsparing of all, as it blurs the line between the hero and the monster he has slain, eschewing any frills or even closure in favor of harsh psychological drama. This is ancient and powerful stuff, and Williams handles it deftly.

If the Greek Storyteller and his narration play a reduced part, the Dog seems to enjoy a proportionately greater role by contrast. His promptings and interjections are more common (which is interesting, since he seems much more reluctant to hear the tragic Greek tales than the European stories). The Dog also seems a bit more childlike and less sarcastic than he is with Hurt, though he once again gets to exclaim, "I don't like her, she's a witch," this time in reference to Medea. Though the *Greek Myths* are very somber, there are some moments of levity, as when Gambon ambles down a corridor, bone in hand, holding it out and then withdrawing it from the eager Dog without ever turning to look at him. At another point, Zeus' golden shower ravishment of Perseus's mother is handled very tastefully, leaving much of the action unsaid even as it leads to her pregnancy, which in turn sees the Dog exclaiming, "Oh! So that's how it's done!" Confusion over sex and procreation has always been a popular means of poking gentle fun at certain characters, and repeated here, it once again shows the relative innocence of the Dog — at least in contrast to the European episodes, where he always has a bit of Hoggle in his soul. When Gambon describes the capric satyrs as being "hairy and unpredictable," the Dog, wiggling his back on the floor, proudly declares, "Like me!" which prompts a rare smile from this Storyteller. This exchange is nearly the funniest of the Dog's antics, save only for the sublime sight gag in "The Three Ravens" when Hurt is knitting, using the Dog's upturned ears to spool his thread.

Thread is one of the surprise connections between the two series, as a magic ball of the stuff in "The Three Ravens" leads unerringly through a forest maze, in very obvious homage to the gift of same that Ariadne provides Theseus in the Labyrinth; the motif is echoed promptly but obliquely by Daedalus, when he ties a string to an ant and lets it wander through an impossibly byzantine conch shell. Other connections arise in "The Luck Child," whose opening prophecy of inescapable regicide is drawn from the exact same motif in Perseus' legend (and for that matter the tale of Oedipus, which the Greek series wisely chose to forego) and whose denouement with the damned ferryman recalls Charon in spirit if not in solution. Small touches like this send echoes and adumbrations between many different stories, underlining the fact that many folktales have their roots in ancient myth. Also, despite differences in style and tone, *Greek Myths* reuses some of the first series' best visual shortcuts. Silhouettes appear frequently in *The Storyteller*, with figures either wandering past the fireplace or along the painted frieze above Hurt's mantelpiece. In the Labyrinth, Gambon dusts off old vases whose figures come to life and proceed through their life's tale. The fact that real Greek pottery was often so adorned, spinning silent and Keatsian tales in pictographic, almost comic-strip fashion, makes this a detail even more appropriate to the Greek Myths than the original series.

Both series are willing to offer their own divergent perspectives on the nature of stories. Many of those in the original series have already been mentioned, such as Hurt's starring in his own story and then insisting it has probably transmogrified beyond recognition. While the series thankfully never veers into full meta-commentary, it is savvy enough to know itself and its audience. The Dog wishes explicitly for a happy ending to "The Heartless Giant" and gets quite the opposite; later, he scoffs at the silver slipper in the Cinderella-like "Sapsorrow," showing that even he is a little tired of this oft-revisited story. In the series' most overt bait-and-switch, Hurt nearly ends "The Three Ravens" with "So they lived happily…" only to have the Dog interrupt and remind him that one of the boys has a lingering mark from his curse.

This disdain for pat endings is stretched to the breaking point in *Greek*

Myths, notably in "Orpheus & Eurydice." As Gambon says, "Sometimes a story doesn't end with two people falling in love, it starts there." Later, following the unbearable tension of Orpheus's final steps, the Dog — as distraught as he has ever been at a story — cowers and pleadingly predicts, "And they walked out into the sunlight and were happy ever after." "They didn't," says Gambon, thrice, with grim finality. The European stories are folktales, not fairy tales, but the Greek myths are even further away from sweetness. In fact, the Orpheus episode could be read as a meditation on artistry (as the myth itself surely is). Orpheus is the avatar for all failed and troubled artists, one whose gifts can evoke miracles or horrors. None of this matters to the sepulchral and truly sinister Hades who appears in the episode. He alone ignores Orpheus' show of skill, leaning forward and growling, "Fear me. I am the bored audience at the theatre." For the space of a single scene, the walls start to thin, not between this tale and its teller, but between all tales and tellers. To raconteurs like Gambon or Hurt, the brutal apathy of Hades is the supreme nightmare.

Elsewhere, Gambon makes two brief but telling comments. "Stories are true," he says in "Perseus & the Gorgon." This is a simple, frequently espoused sentiment, but with added meaning here: to the people who once told them, myths were true, and even when their plausibility began to strain at increasingly cultivated minds, their metaphorical use was amaranthine, so much so that a person may still comment on a Midas Touch or a Herculean Task even in the 21st century. In this same episode, Gambon offers what is essentially a thesis statement for the series. When the Dog questions him about the presence of two additional, unexplained gorgons, Gambon replies, "If I told you the whole story your head would burst. There is no one story. There are branches, rooms, like this place. Rooms, corridors, dead ends." Anyone who has picked up Ovid recently knows that this is so: in myths, there is no one story. Conversely, all stories are one, and until Ragnarok arrives or the Seventh Seal is broken, that story is not yet finished. This marks a key difference between folktales and myths. At best, the former might have stock characters, fan favorites, and a parade of interchangeable Jacks and Hanses and Ivans. Myth, for all of its vagaries and internal contortions, does have continuity. It must have, as its primary purpose is to illuminate. That means not only explaining how the Aegean Sea got its name, but why a poor and grieving father plunged into its welcoming oblivion in the first place, and why his son should be so cursed that they should both come to this sad end. Like Ariadne's thread, we can spool myth back further and further until all stories start to merge and reach a primordial source. There is a reason many myths begin with Chaos and Darkness. Anything further would require another story.

Excepting those tales featured in the Bible, the legends of the Greeks are the premiere myth-set of the Western World — and even when the most determinedly Christian authors like John Milton and Edmund Spenser set down their contemporary epics, they had to turn to these Pagan sources. Greco-Roman mythology was the only universally recognizable poetic and iconic language available. Given their preeminence, it is easy to forget that just as the Grecian civilization did not simply end millennia ago, so the stories continued to develop. Greek folklore is entirely different from Greek myth; in fact, while the stories themselves are excellent, a novice might be disappointed to find little connection between the legends of the classical world and a more modern myth-set that functions as most others do. Greek folklore has the same concerns as one would see in other Mediterranean and Eastern European cultures, the same quests, the same witches and warlocks, and the same shapes and patterns, including the Rule of Threes.

The same view can be applied in reverse to the German folktales that make up the bulk of the John Hurt sequence. Similar in many regards to the rest of Western Europe, they can be traced back to fairly brutal roots in Nordic myth. The violence and fatalism (and the resulting gallows humor) of the Norse myths may still arise in the tone of the German tales, even if the setting is an agrarian and Christianized world. For instance, the defining feature that sets German tales apart from even their most vicious neighbors is the penchant for insanely sadistic justice. It is exceedingly rare for the villain or betrayer in a German tale not to end up drawn and quartered, or made to dance in iron shoes upon flaming coals, or placed in a barrel of nails and rolled down a steep hill. At the end of "Sapsorrow," it is mentioned that the Bad Sisters (played with wicked relish by comedy duo Dawn French and Jennifer Saunders) are hastily pardoned in time for their sister's nuptials. In any German telling, they would be lucky not to be burned on a pyre or have their eyes pecked out by ravens. For that matter, in the German (as well as the French) version of the old Aschenputtel story, the sisters' attempts to wear the mysterious slipper are amplified when they lop off their own heels and toes to get them into shape. Still, it is unfair to say that this episode lacks spine, as it treats the audience to a MacGuffin that hinges on royal incest and sees its happy ending tied to a Prince who has been blatantly unlikable throughout the proceedings. The tales that the Storyteller recites are 'canon' in so much as one exists, but it is the nature of folktales that they are labile and have as many variants as tellers. The result is that even if one should opt for the dark version, there will always be a darker one lurking somewhere further back.

The fatalism of Norse myth has dwindled a bit to the (thankfully) more capricious narratives in the Germanic Storyteller. A number of stories hinge on prophecy, as in "The Luck Child," and providence, the latter featuring heavily in "The True Bride." However, the charm of "The True Bride" is not in its somewhat excessive *dei ex machina*, but in its lovably rough title character. Anja is a punkish farm girl, played by Jane Horrocks using her natural Lancashire accent; she actually looks and sounds like someone one might meet on a farm. This is one of the unspoken strengths of *The Storyteller*, in that even when the characters are princes and damsels, they enjoy an earthy and authentic quality that never devolves into 'fairy tale' stylings in the pejorative sense. These are real individuals from streets and fields and taverns. *The Greek Myths*, somewhat by necessity, have to focus on scenery-chewing tyrants and strapping young men making proclamations in togas. This is not to deride the often fine acting (and Derek Jacobi's Daedalus alone could justify the entire enterprise), but to admit that it is at times as stylized as the Greek theatre tragedies themselves, melodrama rather than drama.

Gambon remarks at one point, "The Gods play with us," another bromide given concise and thoughtful life in Nigel Williams' script. In fact, it may be a conscious homage to *King Lear*'s "As flies to wanton boys are we to the gods. / They kill us for their sport" (4.1.42–43) — a connection given further layers by the fact that Gambon played Lear in 1982. Save for Hades and Persephone (and Zeus embodied as sunlight), no Gods ever actually appear in these *Greek Myths*, but they are eternally present. It is axiomatic that everything that transpires in these legends is permitted if not fully orchestrated by Divine Power, the real *deus ex machina*. The original *Storyteller* series is not as beholden to this framework, just as folktales themselves rarely are. Hans the Hedgehog is betrayed, only to have his curse finally broken (by no established logic) when his bride tracks him down and loves him back to humanity. The Soldier uses a mixture of kindness and cunning to break every rule of mortality and morality; even if he finally suffers as a result, he has succeeded in running riot over the natural world and those worlds above and below.

This may be the largest different between folktale and myth, which the series illustrates admirably. Folklore blossomed in the wake of myth; it is wrong to say that it is more mature or developed, for it is often much less complicated than myth from any narrative standpoint. However, as myths set out primarily to tell us how the world came to be what it is, folklore, the lore of the folk, seems to have arisen once the earth was fully settled. People knew where they came from and what happened when they died; myth took care of the former, and religion — its close cousin — took care of the latter. In between, people had to live their lives; they had to get up and work the fields in the morning. The job of actually being a person — without the benefit of a grandly poetic death or transformation — was hard, and it was this that people needed to figure out from day to day. *The Storyteller*'s opening incantation is in some ways better suited to the world-shaping of myth, except for that single line in its heart, when people "explained their present with stories." This, more than anything else, is what folklore does for us. Myth is wonderful, but it always predates the people who tell it, lost to austerity and antiquity. The future hasn't come around yet. The only thing that is real to the average person is the present moment, and amidst its griffins and grotesques, this is what *The Storyteller* means to explain.

To this end, the presence of the Dog is no accident. Dogs may be the one animal equally likely to be found resting at the feet of kings and beggars, and as there is a little bit of both in the series' two narrators, it is hard to imagine a better companion. The question of whether it is the same dog is almost immaterial. Then again, when Hurt is bloviating about the Soldier who captures Death, becoming famous around the world, he pronounces the phrase, "Death a prisoner!" in any number of languages, only to come up dry on the Greek. The Dog pipes up: "Ekhmalotisame ton thanato!" Maybe he is Athenian after all, and maybe he's been around for a while.

WORKS CITED

Finch, Christopher. *Jim Henson: The Works*. New York: Random House, 1993. Print.
Hamilton, Edith. *Mythology*. New York: Mentor Books, 1940. Print.
Henson, Jim, dir. *Labyrinth*. TriStar Pictures, 1986. Film.
Henson, Jim and Frank Oz, dir. *The Dark Crystal*. Universal Studios and ITC Entertainment, 1982. Film.
Jim Henson's The Storyteller—The Definitive Collection. Writ. Anthony Minghella and Nigel Williams. Dir. Jim Henson, et al. Sony Pictures Home Entertainment, 2006. DVD.
Megas, Georgios A. *Folktales of Greece*. Ed. Richard M. Dorson. Trans. Helen Colaclides. Chicago, IL: University of Chicago Press, 1970. Print.
Minghella, Anthony. *Jim Henson's The Storyteller*. New York: Alfred A. Knopf, 1991. Print.
_____, et al. "The Witch Baby." *Jim Henson's The Storyteller, Volume One*. Ed. Nate Cosby. Los Angeles, CA: Archaia Entertainment, 2011. Print.
Ranke, Kurt. *Folktales of Germany*. Ed. Richard M. Dorson. Trans. Lotte Baumann. Chicago, IL: University of Chicago Press, 1966. Print.
Shakespeare, William. *Shakespeare: The Complete Dramatic and Poetic Works of William Shakespeare*. Ed. Frederick D. Losey. Philadelphia, PA: The John C. Winston Company, 1952. Print.

Emmet Otter's Jug-Band Christmas: The Gift of the Muppets
Catherine Edwards

Jim Henson's Muppets have a positive talent for telling positive stories with positive values, but they rarely follow the traditional path to "happily ever after." Conventional Hollywood wisdom says the protagonist always wins. Muppet wisdom says, "Winning isn't the only thing," and this philosophy has produced unexpected endings to more than one Muppet story. One such Muppet tale, *Emmet Otter's Jug-Band Christmas*, involves Emmet Otter, his mother and his friends, whose endeavors to win a talent contest go unpredictably awry.

Based on the book written by Russell Hoban, it is essentially a re-telling of O. Henry's "The Gift of the Magi." In O. Henry's version we are told by the narrator that a young man named Jim and his wife, Della are preparing to spend Christmas together. Although they are deeply in love and happy, they have fallen on hard times and are now quite poor. Their meager household has only two very fine things in it — a timepiece that had belonged to Jim's father and grandfather before him and Della's beautiful knee-length hair. Despite their hopes, neither has scrimped or saved enough money during the previous year to afford a nice present for the other. Della sells her hair to a wigmaker for $20, the same amount Jim earns for a week of work. She uses the money to buy Jim a silver watch chain. Jim has sold the watch to buy Della a set of beautiful carved combs to wear in her hair, which is now too short to hold them. Instead of being devastated by disappointment over these mismatched gifts, Jim and Della find themselves humbled by the great love they share. The narrator of the story concludes with the observation that the magi, the wise men who brought gifts to the Baby Jesus and invented the art of giving Christmas gifts, were indeed wise, and that he (the narrator) has only related "the uneventful chronicle of two foolish children in a flat who most unwisely sacrificed for each other the greatest treasures of their house" (Henry 17). Nevertheless, he pronounces these two reckless gift-givers possessed of a particular type of wisdom: "Of all who give and receive gifts, such as they are wisest. Everywhere they are wisest. They are the magi" (Henry 17).

Russell Hoban wrote *Emmet Otter's Jug-Band Christmas* in 1969, and it was illustrated by Lillian Hoban, his wife. The book was published by Parents' Magazine Press in 1971. The book tells the story of Emmet Otter and his mother Alice, of Frogtown Hollow, who are struggling to make ends meet as Christmas approaches. Like the characters in O. Henry's story, Emmet and his mother both want to give the other a glorious, fine, and fancy gift for Christmas, but times have always been lean, leaner since Emmet's father died and leaner still with the local economy depressed and many animals out of work. Alice Otter takes in laundry that she washes by hand in their metal washtub. Emmet fishes, cuts firewood, and does odd jobs with his father's tool box. Between them, they eke out a living with nothing to spare for impractical gifts. When Emmet and his mother both hear of a talent contest with a cash prize, they decide to take a chance on winning, sacrificing their scant security *not* for fame, but for the hope of giving a wonderful Christmas gift. The book is charming but unsentimental. It tells the struggle of Emmet and his mother in plain terms and does not attempt to diminish the tragedy that could fall on their house because of their unconstrained generosity.

The idea for adapting Hoban's story into a Christmas special came at a pivotal time in the life of the Muppets. When the Children's Television Workshop approached Henson about doing a show for preschoolers, Henson had initially been resistant to the idea (Borgenicht 183). He believed that puppetry was a medium for all ages and feared being pigeon-holed as a children's entertainer because he believed the perception would limit the audience he would be able to reach. He wanted his creations to be accessible to a variety of ages, and while the success of *Sesame Street,* which began in 1969, had made the word "Muppet" familiar to the world, Henson felt the time had come to pitch the idea of a puppet show for grown-ups. ABC was cautiously interested, and Henson and the Muppets did two 30-minute pilots for a television show: *The Muppets Valentine Show* in 1974 and *The Muppet Show: Sex and Violence* in 1975. ABC ultimately passed on the opportunity to produce Henson's vision, but Henson remained hopeful for a show of his own. Still, in 1975, he collaborated with Lorne Michaels, the executive producer of *Saturday Night Live,* to produce a series of skits with Muppets that dealt with more mature content. These sketches were set in a swampy alien planet and became known as the Land of Gorch skits. Creatively, it was a bad fit for Henson and his creations

(Sexton), and the skits ended after the first year. Had the skits been a success, Henson might not have chosen to pursue a show of his own, but luckily for Muppet fans everywhere the skits were a flop. *The Muppet Show* was finally brought to the air in 1976 through the help of Lord Lew Grade, who provided funding and support for the show to be filmed in England, where it quickly became an international hit. With the success of the television show, Henson felt the time was ripe to produce full-length features with the Muppets, but there were still some obstacles to overcome.

In 1976, Jerry Juhl, the head writer for *The Muppet Show*, wrote a draft of a Christmas special that was very different from the things Henson and his company had done before. Most of the things that the Muppets had brought to the television screen were either original material from the fertile minds of Henson and his amazingly creative team of writers and muppeteers or were essentially re-tellings of fairy tales or other stories that were part of the public consciousness. The script, based on Hoban's popular children's story with ties back to the O. Henry story, which was widely known and loved by generations of readers, seemed like a natural first (3/1–2/1977). *Emmet Otter's Jug-Band Christmas* was essentially a test run by Henson and his company to discover if they could produce an hour-long television special that lived up to their own high quality expectations and was well-received by the public. Up until this time, the variety-show format of *The Muppet Show* meant that the parts of the show could be filmed piecemeal and assembled to reach the appropriate amount of viewing time, but filming for a 30-minute show was still quite different from the rigors of a full-length movie. Henson planned to produce a one-hour adaptation of Hoban's story for HBO in 1977.

If there are Muppets, there's bound to be music, and Henson set about finding a songwriter. While Hoban's original story referenced several songs, many of which were just song *titles*, Henson planned to breathe life into those ideas and make the story a musical. He also wanted a songwriter whose style was compatible with his own. Songwriter/musician Paul Williams had recently been a first-year guest star on *The Muppet Show*, and Henson approached him about writing the songs to go along with the script by Jerry Juhl. Williams signed on to do the songs. It was the beginning of a long and satisfying collaborative relationship between Williams and the Muppets, a relationship that became important to both as the Muppets began making theatrical release films. Williams would go on to write "Rainbow Connection" and "I'm Going to Go Back There Some Day" for *The Muppet Movie*, two songs that would become integrally linked to the Muppets in the public consciousness.

The new original music that was added to the story helped make *Emmet Otter's Jug-Band Christmas* the right length for airing, but the songs also enriched the story by Hoban. Though songwriter/musician Paul Williams wrote the musical numbers specifically for this show, the songs have a familiar *feeling* to them and that is not accidental. The songs are referenced within the show as "that old song" and "a traditional song" and "an old favorite," lending a sense of history to the songs and to the story being told.

The story opens with shots of the countryside of Frogtown Hollow and the river leading up to the little town of Waterville. The cinematography faithfully recreates the life of the little village on the river as depicted in Lillian Hoban's original colorful artwork. The river is believable, and the technology that allowed Emmet to row the Otter's little green boat up and down this river was pioneered specifically for this television special by Faz Fazakas (Imdb). It was important to Henson and those who worked on the special that the world of Emmet Otter was believable, and was *real* to the viewer, so that the story could flow unimpeded. Muppeteer Dave Goelz, who performed the character of Wendell Porcupine, said this about the intricate setting,

> "I love the feeling of that Emmet Otter world. We built a 55-foot-long river that was about 10 feet wide and went all the way across the stage, and they built a radio-control rowboat for Emmet. It was so lovely and lyrical to see Emmet rowing his mom down the river. The idea that there was life along the river and that it was all interconnected was a great metaphor for people" [qtd. in Stanek 52].

The interconnectedness of all life on earth was a theme that was dear to Henson and would be explored in greater depth with later works like the series *Fraggle Rock* and short work *The Song of the Cloud Forest*.

Enter Kermit the Frog, Henson's familiar doppelganger. Although the story itself was new to many viewers, the familiar face and voice of Henson's most enduring Muppet welcomes the viewer to the story. For the first time, viewers see Kermit riding a bike, a new trick that would show up later in *The Muppet Movie*. In this introduction to the story, in addition to Kermit we also get our first glimpse of the Riverbottom Gang, a group of ruffians whose souped-up jalopy scrapes to a dusty halt in front of our amphibian host. One of the gang steals Kermit's scarf, and Kermit acknowledges that the Riverbottom Gang will show up again in the story because they, too, are a part of life along the river.

Before we even meet Emmet and his mother, they are singing. The song they sing, "The One Bathing Suit That Your Grandma Otter Wore," is a humorous homage to the legacy left to them by a relative with a heroically endowed figure. Although we may assume the story relayed in the song is fictional, the affectionate rendering of the tale sets the tone for how Emmet and his Ma respond to life—with gratitude and humor for the unexpected blessings life can offer. Emmet, a young otter, is rowing the boat, helping his mother deliver the laundry that she does in order to bring in money to support them.

Although they are cheerful and matter-of-fact, it is obvious that they face severe financial burdens and are struggling to make ends meet on a daily basis. Finances have been in short supply since Emmet's Pa died. Although it is plain from their fond reminiscences that Mr. Otter was not financially successful, times were better when he was alive. Since he died, Emmet and his mother have cobbled together a long collection of jobs in order to stay afloat financially. Emmet teases his mother for trading a pair of socks she knitted for some pumpkins that she can bake into pies, only to use the pie money to buy more wool to knit more socks, and so on. Instead of being offended by his teasing, Alice Otter laughs along with him.

There is humor and goodwill in this exchange. Emmet shows no bitterness at being expected to contribute to the family's income — instead, he shows pride and willingness to do his part. Neither Emmet nor his mother express anger about the situation that Mr. Otter's death left them in, nor do they suggest that he was not a good husband and father despite not being prosperous. We gather from their fond reminiscing that Emmet's father was kind, humorous, expansive in his optimism and not especially successful in business as a traveling snake oil salesman. An example of the wry whimsy of the story is that "selling snake oil"— a euphemism for a worthless or fraudulent medicine or treatment — is meant literally here. Hoban's droll plot point was played up by Henson, who made a habit out of taking euphemisms or wordplay to humorous heights. In a Muppet production, it is fitting that a character who "sells snake oil" would *literally* sell oil for snakes. While Pa Otter did not leave them in strong financial circumstances, Emmet and his mother remember him with great affection and try to provide for each other as well as they can. Gratefulness and industriousness help to make them happy despite the meanness of their circumstances.

Although times have been lean since Emmet's father died, they have gotten leaner in the last year. While the Henson special does not allude to the fact, the book documents a town-wide recession. Women who used to hire Alice to do their washing are now doing their own washing at home, and grown men (animals) are now competing with Emmet for the odd jobs that he used to do for money. Money has grown tighter and tighter, and there is less and less to make do with. The script illustrates this by the following exchange between Alice and Emmet as they do their shopping in Waterville.

"Is that the end of our chores?"

"No, but it's the end of the money we have to do them with. Wait now — didn't you make some money from Sam Turtle for fixing his steps?"

"No, Ma — I'm the one that broke 'em."

"Oh Emmet — you with your odd jobs and me with my socks and pumpkins — no wonder we're so rich!" Alice says with a chuckle.

Although happy, their lives are not without wants. It is obvious that they once had more than they do now, and Alice's subsequent reference to having "nothing left to pawn" underscores their financial decline. A brief look inside the music store in town touches longings in both Emmet and his mother that cannot be so easily ignored. Emmet sees a second-hand guitar in the music store window, a lovely instrument with mother-of-pearl inlay, and teasingly suggests that his mother can get him that for Christmas. Playing along, Alice is blasé about the $40 price. While they are both light-hearted in this exchange, it is obvious that Emmet longs for the guitar and that his mother desperately wishes she could buy it for him. Later in the story we learn that the Otters once owned a piano, which Alice used to play, but the instrument had to be sold to meet the financial demands of the household. For both of them, the guitar Emmet wants represents more than just a plaything or a casual want — it is a connection to their past and their past happiness when their family was intact and their home was full of music. Sadly, even this second-hand item is out of their financial reach, but that realization does not engender bitterness, only determination to improve their lot.

The Muppets' body of work suggests that it is not always your circumstances that determine your happiness, but your attitude. In *The Muppet Movie*, Kermit is happy with his life in the swamp, but the thought of making *others* happy arrives to shatter his solitary peacefulness. This goal, while apparently simplistic, was actually a fairly comprehensive statement of Jim Henson's life philosophy. Henson is often quoted as saying, "When I was young, my ambition was to be one of the people who made a difference in this world. My hope is still to leave the world a little bit better for my having been here" (*It's Not Easy* 103). The statement is profound but not pretentious. Kermit deems the goal of spreading happiness to others worth enduring some hardships along the way. The hope of fulfilling this goal alongside his friends makes him happy even as he suffers setbacks on the way to uncertain success. In *The Muppets Take Manhattan*, Kermit and his friends try to be happy and positive while they work jobs far less exciting than their ultimate dream of performing on Broadway. A certain amount of duplicity is required to carry this off, but it shows their determination to be content and show confidence in their mutual dream while circumstances work against them. In the later, post–Henson Muppet work, *It's a Very Merry Muppet Christmas Movie*, Kermit has the opportunity (albeit unintentional) to see what the world would be like without him. Miserable and lonely, separated from his friends, Kermit realizes that he can be happy regardless of his circumstances as long as he appreciates what he does have. Emmet and his mother know that although their Christmas will be meager, they will be together.

As if to contrast Emmet's well-bred restraint, Henson again presents the Riverbottom Gang in all their unruly glory. They come to town in their loud car, knock down a fruit and vegetable stand with no remorse, spit water at the fruit-stand owner and go on to terrorize the local music store. In case the viewer harbored any confusion about who the bad guys of the story were going to be, Juhl's script makes it patently obvious. In Hoban's book, the band members are not characterized as hooligans, and only appear near the end, as rivals in the talent contest, but Henson obviously felt the need to draw the lines more plainly for the viewers, with comedic effect.

On the way home from their disappointing trip to town, Emmet again brings up the upcoming holiday. Although Christmas has obviously been much on both their minds, Alice chides Emmet gently to stop thinking so much about it, fearing it will lead to disappointment. She bemoans the fact that they don't have what they need for regular days, and worries that Christmas, with its promise of bounty, will be disappointing if they expect a change in their circumstances. Emmet takes the gentle scold in the spirit it was delivered and apologizes, but he refuses to be cowed in his happy remembrance of Christmases past. He talks about the last Christmas they shared before his father died, how they decorated the Christmas branch and how Pa Otter sang while his mother played their old piano. Once again, music is a reminder of their time together as a family and the happiness they shared.

Emmet's good cheer also brings a reminder of sad times. When Alice admits that selling the old piano was one of the saddest things she ever had to do, Emmet observes that they have sold almost everything the last couple of years, perhaps attempting to soften this singular loss among the others. Emmet's good nature in the face of this decline and Alice's naturally sunny disposition prevent her from being maudlin for long. "About all I've got left is a sense of humor and the washtub," she says philosophically. Following her example, Emmet is equally philosophic: "Well, at least there ain't no hole in the washtub."

While literally true, this is also the lead in to one of the pivotal songs of the story, "Ain't No Hole in the Washtub," a song that celebrates the pleasures of industriousness. The lyrics say, in essence, that there is pleasure in their work and in making their own way. This, too, was one of Henson's deeply held beliefs. "I don't resent working long hours. I shouldn't — I'm the one who set up my life this way. I love to work. It's the thing I get the most satisfaction out of — and probably what I do best," Henson said. "But I think much of the world has the wrong idea of working. It's one of the good things in life" (*It's Not Easy* 58). Emmet and his mother obviously agree and enjoy singing the old songs to remind them of this, cheering themselves as well as all the neighbors they pass on the way home.

Hope and trouble arrive in the same package. From their separate friends, Emmet and his mother learn about a local talent contest set on Christmas Eve, with a first-place prize of $50. Christmas Eve might seem like an unlikely time for a contest, but a chance to gather and enjoy the fellowship of the other townsfolk during the holiday season would be welcome by almost anyone who lived in the small town on the river, and the talent show is likely to be well-attended. Although $50 does not sound like much in this age of technology and expensive toys, that amount of money would do a lot to stabilize the Otters' precarious financial situation.

Alice's friend Hetty Muskrat brings the news to the door. Hetty has come to use her own spinning wheel, which Alice uses so much that it seems to permanently reside at the Otters' home. At the same time, Emmet hears the news of the contest from a friend. One of the funniest exchanges in the book that is not in the Henson version is the initial exchange between Emmet and his friend.

"Do you got any talent, Emmet?"

"I don't know," said Emmet. "Do you?" (Hoban 14).

Both the Otters are slightly stunned by the thought of that much money. Hetty praises her friend's "mighty fine" singing voice and urges her to think about entering the contest. Although she blusters a bit, it is clear that Alice is considering it because of the prize money. Alice's clothes are simple, workaday clothes that show signs of wear, and she insists she has nothing to wear to perform in, using that excuse to put off her friend's suggestion. Like the impossible hope of owning the second-hand guitar, which is out of the Otters' financial reach, poverty again interposes a barrier to performing.

Emmet's friend Wendell Porcupine has delivered the same news to Emmet and suggests he enter the contest, but Emmet protests at the thought of performing by himself. Emmet's excuse is immediately shot down by the arrival of his friends Harvey Muskrat and Charlie Beaver, who propose the idea of a jug band and seem keen for Wendell and Emmet to join them. Wendell can blow a jug — a necessity for a jug band — but Emmet is more skeptical about why they want *him* to be in the band. Although talented, he is modest about his abilities. When Harvey explains that Emmet can be their bass man, playing the washtub bass, because his mother has a washtub, Emmet is adamant that he will not participate. His mother *needs* the washtub to make a living and to make a bass out of it you have to put a hole in it. Although clearly tempted by the money, he is not willing to risk their livelihood on a chance at fame and, more importantly, fortune.

The thought of the money and what it could buy consumes both of the Otters. Emmet is desperate to give his mother something fine and store-bought to counter the paucity of their day-to-day lives, and Alice longs to give Emmet the beautiful guitar he wants. Perhaps unconsciously, both of their dreams center on bringing music back into their home. It is a very beautiful moment in the story when we realize that — despite the many things they both do without — they think of the prize money primarily as a means to do something for the other. Emmet does not think, "Wow, I could put a down payment on that guitar I wanted," but longs instead to put a down payment on a used piano for his mother. Alice doesn't think about the grocery money or the many things they probably *need* for the pantry; she thinks of Emmet and his pleasure in owning the second-hand guitar.

In O. Henry's "The Gift of the Magi," the two main characters give up the one fine thing that is theirs in order to buy a special Christmas gift for the other, but each gift is tied to the thing that the other sacrificed. In much the same way, Alice is offered the potential to earn the prize money and buy Emmet a truly outstanding gift, but she must hock her husband's old tool chest in order to buy material for a costume to sing in. Emmet must decide if it is worth the risk of destroying his mother's washtub to put a down payment on a piano so their house can be full of music again. In a departure from the original theme, Alice doesn't have to decide to give up the thing *she* values the most; she has to sacrifice something that Emmet values, instead. Emmet's dilemma is similar, since he must decide whether to sacrifice his mother's washtub, her means for keeping the wolf at their door from actually coming inside the house. Each risk would threaten the livelihood of the Otter family, for Alice makes the majority of what they earn with the washtub, and Emmet supplements their income with odd jobs by using his Pa's old tools. Both of the Otters have reasonable confidence in their talent but question whether it is enough to risk everything on. Like Kermit's decision in *The Muppet Movie*, they must decide if they are willing to trade one hope for another.

Once again, it is the loving remembrance of Pa Otter that turns the tide of decision and spurs them to act. After a hard day of working, Emmet comes home with the Christmas branch, insisting that, presents or no presents, they can still have a Christmas branch to liven up their house. This time, it is Mrs. Otter who turns a sad moment into a good memory, and she begins the tale of Mr. Otter's yearly declaration that he would bring home "a real whole Christmas tree." This is obviously a reference to Mr. Otter's sincere intention to bring excess and bounty into their little home, and they laugh, remembering his exuberant and generous nature. Fond reminiscing leads Emmet to ask if his mother thinks the ice slide that his father built would be safe to use now.

Alice comes to life immediately, suddenly reminded of this simple pleasure that had been momentarily forgotten in the wake of day-to-day burdens. Assuring Emmet that the slide would undoubtedly be frozen by now, she whips a blanket over her shoulders and races her son outside. Laughing and remembering, they take turns sliding down the ice slide that Mr. Otter had made many years before. They share a fond remembrance of times past and of Pa Otter's thoughtfulness, during which Emmet is determinedly grateful. Although touched by Emmet's show of appreciation, Alice is more thoughtful: "Pa used to say, a person's got to take some chances or life'll never come to nothing!" The recollection stirs both characters to action, as each decides that Pa would have taken the chance on success in the Christmas Eve contest.

Full of determination and hopefulness, though blind to each other's secret intentions, Alice and Emmet are moved to sing Pa's favorite song, a beautiful ballad called "When the River Meets the Sea." It is a song about the acceptance of the trials and tribulations of life and the understanding that comes from being part of something larger than oneself. While the audience listens to the song, we get to watch the Otters take themselves home and see Alice tuck her son lovingly into his warm bed. This scene reminds the viewer that, while Emmet has voluntarily shouldered many of the responsibilities of an adult, he is still a child, still in need of reassurance and care. Alice's worry for her son's welfare and Emmet's obstinate cheerfulness in the face of the obstacles they face seem even more heroic.

In their eagerness to get on with the task of winning that prize money, both Emmet and his mother race out of the house in the morning, leaving notes for each other that are not read. Emmet has a particularly bad moment when he makes the irrevocable hole in the washtub, but now that he is past the point of return, he is an otter committed. At this point, Emmet's giving in is really Emmet taking charge. He becomes the driving force behind the jug band and relentlessly urges them to practice. While delighted with his agreement to join them, his friends are obviously less driven than Emmet and tease him a little about his dictatorial nature. Emmet is not the only Henson character to go from mild-mannered musician to tyrannical leader when there is much at stake. On *The Muppet Show*, Kermit is well-known for erupting into arm-waving hysteria when things backstage cross the line from *unruly* into *chaos*, and in *The Muppets*, Miss Piggy transforms almost instantly from a docile follower of Kermit's mild-mannered lead into a ferocious ninja team coordinator when their telethon and their theater are threatened. Emmet's unaccustomed bossiness is tolerated good-naturedly by his friends in pursuit of the cause.

The band plans to perform "Bar B Que," another tribute to small-town pleasures that is well-suited to the instruments and voices that they have. Despite the relative crudity of their instruments, they have a good-sounding band. All the boys sing and each one plays an instrument; Harvey even doubles on the kazoo during the musical bridge. The song is referred to as "an old favorite," and the boys believe it will play effectively to the townsfolk. Although practice goes well, they are interrupted once by the noise and rude behavior of the Riverbottom Gang riding snowmobiles outside the building where they practice. This interruption of their practice is really an excuse to remind the viewer that not everyone's intentions and behaviors are as honorable as those shown by Emmet and his mother. While Emmet practices, Alice sews her dress, and her friend Hetty, who had initially encouraged her to enter, now expresses doubt about the outcome of the contest, further fueling Alice's already rattled nerves. In most feel-good, formulaic shows, this encounter with the Riverbottom Gang would simply be to prepare the audience for the smug satisfaction of seeing the Otters triumph over doubts and boorish behavior through the power of goodness, selflessness and unprecedented talent, but this isn't most shows. This is a Henson-ized version of happily-ever-after and all bets are off.

On the evening of Christmas Eve, while the talent gathers backstage and the townspeople fill up the auditorium, Emmet and his mother still manage to remain ignorant of each other's presence and intentions. Harrison Fox, the mayor of Waterville, is the emcee of the show and when Alice arrives they have a comically edgy and malaprop-filled conversation before he directs her to the ladies' dressing room. Alice and Emmet both wait nervously for their chance to perform while a bevy of acts goes on ahead of them. The talent portrayed is very reminiscent of the vaudeville era, with creatures singing, bunnies dancing, and squirrels doing acrobatics. Kermit would probably have signed any and all of these acts to perform on *The Muppet Show*, and it is a time for the Muppeteers' skill to shine.

In this sequence, perhaps more than any other, the audience may find it difficult to remember that everything they are watching is the result of advanced and highly-skilled puppetry. In a typically Muppet-style stunt, one of the contestants in the talent contest is a dancing horse operated by two muskrats. The viewer sees two hand puppets portraying a marionette horse, which is itself portraying a third kind of large-scale puppetry. The almost magical skill with which the puppeteers work momentarily camouflages the joke-within-the-joke portrayed by the puppets-within-a-puppet. On *The*

Muppet Show, Kermit once drank milk through a straw, then broke the fourth wall to say, "Think about it, friends" (*The Muppet Show*, Episode 1.01). This stunt smacks of the same sort of cleverness, although the fourth wall remains intact in this case.

If this were a typical feel-good, root-for-the-underdog (or under-otter) story, the viewer could feel reasonably assured that either Emmet or his mother will win. The guitar can be purchased, the washtub replaced, the tool box un-hocked and all will be right with the world. Shortly before the boys are scheduled to go on, however, disaster strikes. Another performer is singing their song! Although Charlie Beaver blusters that the other contestant's lackluster performance won't count against them, the boys are concerned that they will look like copycats if they do the song they practiced. Emmet insists they go out into the alley to prepare another song, and they tromp worriedly behind the theater. Shortly thereafter, Mr. Fox finds them out there and scolds them for not waiting backstage. He is worried that they might miss their cue and make the show, and presumably himself, look unprofessional. Obediently, the boys come back inside about the time that Emmet's mother is being introduced to sing "one of the traditional songs of the river."

Alice sings, "Our World," another haunting song penned by Williams, which reinforces the messages of love and acceptance that permeate this story. While Alice Otter sings, the boys backstage listen and acknowledge her talent without any sense of disappointment or envy. "She's better than us," says Wendell honestly. When Alice leaves the stage, she sees the boys, but they are being called up, and there is little time to talk or explain. Some movies would have had Emmet and his mother each jockeying to disqualify himself or herself in order to let the other one win, but there is none of that false modesty here. Emmet and his friends go out there and do the best performance they can of the new song they have chosen, a song aptly entitled, "Brothers." The song talks about finding kindred spirits and the bonds of family that we can extend to those with whom we have things in common. This song, like "Our World," echoes themes that have been noted in previous and subsequent Henson works — the unity of all creature-kind and the ability that all individuals have to extend the hand (or paw) of friendship and expand our family tree until it encompasses all who wish to join.

Like Alice's song, the boys' performance is well-received by the crowd. At this point, the viewer has not been shown *anything* to rival either of their acts, but the show is not over. A late entry to the talent contest, the Riverbottom Nightmare Band, takes the stage. The television audience is already familiar with these boys, who are none other than the ruffians usually known as the Riverbottom Gang. In Hoban's book, both of the Otters perform after the Riverbottom Gang band, with their more humble, less technologically assisted songs being swallowed up by the river of sound from the Nightmare Band, but the Muppet special wisely saves that unpleasant surprise for the viewer until the very end of the contest. Victory seems certain for our hopeful otters, but it is not to be.

What the television audience is *supposed* to think of the Nightmare Band and their song is unclear. Although the lyrics are rude, i.e., "We don't wish to learn/But we hate what we don't understand," one must grudgingly admit that the song is well-played and, for the type of music that it is, well-sung. Whatever the *television* audience thinks of the song and the performance, the *Waterville* audience obviously likes it, and, sadly, the contest judges prefer it to the sweet, traditional, and familiar songs that Emmet and Alice sing instead. The Riverbottom Gang walks off with $50 and Emmet finds himself on the snowy road in front of the theater where the contest was held with his bandmates, his mother, and a broken washtub.

The Otters don't waste any time on recriminations before confessing the banditry which led them to the contest. While they are talking, one of the judges, Doc Bullfrog, comes out of the building and compliments both entrants on their performances, telling them that both acts favorably impressed the judges but just didn't have that "little something extra" that the judges were looking for in order to award the prize. This news is met with graciousness and thanks for his comments, another sign of the good breeding and behavior Emmet and his friends display.

While Alice and Emmet were both undeniably talented, talent alone is not enough to ensure either of them winning the contest and the longed-for prize money. The love of performing is itself a calling, and this idea is something that many later Muppet projects echoed. In *The Muppet Movie*, we first hear and then see Kermit singing and playing to himself (and perhaps Arnie the Alligator) in the swamp. Lack of an audience never seems to deter Muppet performers, with Gonzo the Great perhaps being most proof against audience reaction, or the lack thereof. Although Kermit and his friends are offered the tongue-in-cheek "Rich and Famous" contract near the end of *The Muppet Movie*, they appear financially challenged throughout their long careers. Even the most recent Muppet theatrical release, *The Muppets*, shows the theater and the performers struggling with money issues. Financial security is apparently not an automatic part of the package, even when there is obvious talent. There is no suggestion until the very end of Emmet's tale that talent alone might provide food for the table or other necessities.

The quintet of performers trudges quietly up the frozen river. Mrs. Otter walks beside Emmet and tells him she would have gotten him the guitar with the mother-of-pearl inlay if she had won the contest. Instead of being dismayed by this information, Emmet marvels at this revelation, but he has a revelation of his own. When he tells his mother he was going to get her a piano with his share of the prize money, Alice stops walking and looks at her son in amazement, awed by the thought.

"A piano — were you really?"

"Yes'm."

"Oh Emmet," Alice says, hugging him. "That's about the nicest present anybody ever *tried* to give me."

As in "The Gift of the Magi," full credit is given to the *intentions* of the gift-giver, with very little thought about the gift or its loss. It is obvious that having been deemed worthy of such tremendous risk is worth more than any material thing they could receive. Although there have been deep disappointments, bracketed by uncertainty, the predominant feeling between Emmet and his mother is a feeling of peacefulness.

Alice admits that she *ought* to feel bad about hocking the tool chest, but she *doesn't*. Instead, she feels good about entering the contest and taking a chance. Emmet confesses that he feels the same way but cannot explain his feelings, even to himself. After a thoughtful moment, Alice suggests, "I guess it's 'cause we did just what Pa would have done." Emmet and his mother both agree that taking a chance in order to give each other a wonderful gift made them feel closer to each other and closer to Pa Otter. Again, the ability of Mr. Otter to shape their daily lives even after his death is a testament to the power of love and the ties of family, another theme that would become familiar to Muppet fans in subsequent Muppet projects. At the end of *The Muppet Movie*, the newly constructed sets lie in shambles on the floor and the ceiling of their soundstage has a gaping hole in it. In the midst of that uncertainty, Kermit and his fellow Muppets sing, "Life's like a movie, write your own ending. Keep believing, keep pretending. We've done just what we set out to do." In *It's a Very Merry Muppet Christmas Movie*, the Muppets lose their theater, and it is up to Kermit to reshape how they view that loss. "It's *okay* that we lost the theater," he says, and goes on to say that what matters is their relationship to each other. In the most recent Muppet movie, *The Muppets*, once again the bad guys seem to win, leaving our heroes to declare that being together as a family is more important than what they have lost. Clearly, nobody in the Muppet universe promises a pot of gold at the end of the rainbow connection as the solution to all of life's problems.

As the Otters and their friends make their way home, the night is cold and beautiful, the river as real to us, the viewers, as it is to the creatures that walk down it. Harvey begins to play "Brothers" on his kazoo, and Mrs. Otter compliments him on it. Wendell complains a little morosely that they should have won with a great-sounding song like that, and Mrs. Otter comforts him while reminding him that things don't always work out as hoped. As they pass the lighted windows of the Riverside Rest, Emmet remarks that his mother's song was also nice. In the quiet, snowy night, something magical clicks into place.

Excitedly, Alice tells the boys that their two songs can fit together, and she coaches the boys through singing their song interwoven with hers. The merged melody combines the two like-minded lyrics into something new and different and wonderful. The Otters and their friends sing, uniting their voices and their spirits in harmony on this cold Christmas Eve, unaware that Doc Bullfrog and his patrons have all gathered at the door of his restaurant, the Riverside Rest, to listen. Their song is so alluring that the patrons leave the comfort of the restaurant and their food to stand on the frozen river and hear them harmonize.

When they finish, they are surprised to find they have an audience, and Doc Bullfrog approaches them warmly, saying, "That's fine music, folks. I thought you needed a little something extra, but what it appears to me that you needed was each other." The human condition of needing others is one of the predominant themes of the Muppets' body of work, whether those humans are frogs or bears or pigs or otters. At the end of *It's a Very Merry Muppet Christmas Movie,* the angel Danny L's question, "What did Kermit really need?" is answered the following way: "People just really need to know what matters in life, and you opened Kermit's eyes and showed him what he already had." The theme of needing each other and being needed to be successful and happy appears again as one of the key plot points of *The Muppets,* and though Kermit struggles to get the words out, he even eventually confesses his need for Miss Piggy, both as a performer and a partner: "I guess I'm not that good at saying this kind of stuff. Over the last week I realize that I —*I* miss you. And I *need* you. And maybe you don't need the whole world to love you — maybe you just need one person." Knowing that they are totally and completely loved makes Alice and Emmet feel similarly content.

The Otters and the boys are gratified by the enjoyment of their friends and by the feeling that they have brought pleasure to their community. They are both startled and thrilled when the opportunity turns lucrative and Doc Bullfrog offers them a job singing at the restaurant. Eminently practical, Alice confirms the pay and terms before they strike a deal. The boys are especially thrilled that meals are included, another unexpected source of abundance in these lean times. To the delight of the diners and the equal satisfaction of the musicians, the Otters and the band join their neighbors in the warmth of the restaurant and earn a decent night's wage and a good dinner on Christmas Eve.

Afterwards, walking home up the frozen river, they contemplate their unexpected luck. Far from being tired of singing, they are still full of joyfulness and song, and Alice asks if they can do a song — right then on the river — for Pa Otter. It is obvious that she and Emmet attribute their turn of fortune to the example of Mr. Otter, who was willing to take a risk. In the end, Alice and Emmet both take a risk and, quite literally, go for broke to wager their talent against their livelihood, and, although it does not turn out as expected, it turns out well. At the end of *The Muppet Movie*, *It's a Very Merry Muppet Christmas Movie* and *The Muppets*, the traditional happily ever after ending does not appear, but it all works out okay. In the Muppet universe, the willingness to bet everything on an unlikely dream isn't much of a long-shot. Happily-ever-after might not ever happen, but happy-no-matter-what is a pretty sure bet.

WORKS CITED

Borgenicht, David. *Sesame Street Unpaved*. New York: Hyperion, 1998. Print.
Emmet Otter's Jug-Band Christmas. Dir. Jim Henson. Perf. Jerry Nelson, Marilyn Sokol, Frank Oz, Jim Henson, Dave Goelz. HBO. 1977. Film.
"Emmet Otter's Jug-Band Christmas." *Internet Movie Database*. Web. 4 April 2012.
Finch, Christopher. *Jim Henson: The Works*. New York: Random House, 1993. Print.
Henry, O. *The Selected Stories of O. Henry*. Lawrence, Kansas: Digireads.com Publishing, 2009. Print.
Henson, Jim. *It's Not Easy Being Green and Other Things to Consider*. New York: Hyperion, 2005. Print.
Hoban, Russell. *Emmet Otter's Jug-Band Christmas*. New York: Parent's Magazine Press, 1971. Print.
It's a Very Merry Muppet Christmas Movie. Dir. Jim Henson. Perf. Jim Henson, Frank Oz, Jerry Nelson, Dave Goelz. NBC, 2002. DVD.
"Jim Henson." *Muppet Wiki*. Web. 4 April 2012.
The Muppet Movie. Dir. Jim Henson. Perf. Jim Henson, Frank Oz, Jerry Nelson, Dave Goelz. Henson Associates and ITC Entertainment, 1979. DVD.
The Muppet Show. Dir. Jim Henson. Perf. Jim Henson, Frank Oz, Jerry Nelson, Dave Goelz. ATV. 1977. Television Show.
"The Muppet Show: Sex and Violence." *Muppet Wiki*. Web. 4 April 2012.
The Muppets. Dir. Jim Henson. Perf. Jim Henson, Frank Oz, Jerry Nelson, Dave Goelz. Walt Disney Studios. 2011. Film.
"The Muppets Valentine Show." *Muppet Wiki*. Web. 4 April 2012.
"Recording Emmet Otter. Music in LA with Paul Williams." *Jim Henson's Red Book*. 3/1-2/1977 Web. 4 April 2012.
Sexton, Timothy. "Forgotten Muppets: The Land of Gorch and 'Saturday Night Live.'" *Yahoo! Movies*. Web. 4 April 2012.
Stanek, Billy. "23 Questions With ... Dave Goelz" *Disney Twenty-Three*. 3.4 (2011): 49-52. Print.

Telling Toy Stories in *The Christmas Toy*

Jennifer C. Garlen and *Anissa M. Graham*

The Henson Company has a long history of producing holiday television specials, including programs starring the familiar Muppet characters and other productions featuring original puppets and adaptations of children's stories. *Emmet Otter's Jug-Band Christmas* appeared in 1977, *John Denver and the Muppets: A Christmas Together* aired in 1979, *A Muppet Family Christmas* ran in 1987, and, more recently, *A Muppets Christmas: Letters to Santa* was broadcast in 2008. Although it is not as well known today as *Emmet Otter's Jug-Band Christmas*, *The Christmas Toy*, originally presented on ABC in 1986, represents a significant entry in the line of Henson holiday programs. Its characters proved enduring enough to inspire a television series, *The Secret Life of Toys*, in 1994, although the show suffered the same premature cancellation of many other Henson productions. The special is also noteworthy for its many provocative parallels to the later Pixar blockbuster *Toy Story*, which appeared in 1995, nearly a decade after the original Henson production. Finally, *The Christmas Toy* merits attention for its engagement of many of Henson's favorite themes, even as it delves into the darker territory that marked 1980s Henson projects like *The Dark Crystal* and *Labyrinth*. All of these elements combine to make *The Christmas Toy* worth talking about, especially now that the special is available on DVD and therefore accessible to a new and wider audience.

Directed by Eric Till, who also helmed numerous episodes of *Fraggle Rock* as well as *A Muppet Family Christmas*, *The Christmas Toy* featured collaboration with illustrator Larry DiFiori to create a world with the look and feel of a children's storybook. According to Christopher Finch, the special was intended to be "part of an extended series of twelve 'picture-book specials' that would have seasonal or holiday themes, but this project was eventually abandoned" (207–208). Laura Phillips, a writer for *Fraggle Rock*, penned the original screenplay, while Jeff Moss, best known for *Sesame Street* songs like "Rubber Ducky" and "I Love Trash," wrote the musical numbers. Puppeteers for the special included Dave Goelz, Steve Whitmire, Kathryn Mullen, Jerry Nelson, Richard Hunt, and Camille Bonora. The production was taped in Toronto and originally aired on ABC on December 6, 1986. The special opened a primetime line-up of holiday programming that also included a revisionist treatment of *A Christmas Carol* starring Robert Guillaume and a musical variety show hosted by Perry Como. The initial broadcast version of *The Christmas Toy* also featured bookend appearances by Kermit the Frog, although later releases have removed those scenes due to legal issues.

Initial response to the special was muted. Lee Margulies, a reviewer for the *Los Angeles Times*, was not particularly kind to *The Christmas Toy* or ABC's other seasonal offerings. According to Margulies, "The characters are bland, the story meanders and the ending is unusually tidy and unconvincing, the culmination of a saccharine quality that infuses the whole enterprise." Later reviewers have taken a more positive tone, especially as Henson fan bloggers have shared their nostalgic appreciation for the program in the wake of its 2008 DVD release. Overall, however, the special remains much more obscure than other Henson productions from this era, and relatively little has been written about it.

Despite the lukewarm reception, *The Christmas Toy* eventually enjoyed a brief comeback of sorts in 1994, when the Disney Channel aired *The Secret Life of Toys*, a series based on the characters and situations created for the original special. The half-hour program only ran from March to May, and the characters from *The Christmas Toy* underwent numerous revisions for the new production. Once again, the *Los Angeles Times* had little praise for the project. Reviewer Lynne Heffley panned the series as "short on the kind of wit and artistry that have infused other Muppet endeavors." After only thirteen episodes, the series was canceled, although in 2011 Disney released the entire show for streaming on Amazon Instant Video.

The failure of the special and the subsequent series to garner critical praise helps to explain their comparative obscurity, placing them in the ranks of other lesser known Henson productions like *The Muppet Musicians of Bremen* (1972), *The Tale of the Bunny Picnic* (1986), and *The Ghost of Faffner Hall* (1989). The reviewers, however, underestimate the charm that has continued to attract viewers throughout the quarter century since *The Christmas Toy* first appeared. The Jim Henson Company's website even describes the special as "a fan favorite and a holiday classic," a claim that appears to be supported by enthusiastic praise for the program, if not the bare bones DVD release, on Amazon.com. While it's admittedly a more understated, intimate production than the major feature films and ongoing series, *The Christmas Toy* still connects with both adult and child audiences, using a seemingly simple story to engage a number of complex themes.

As the title of the program implies, the original special is a Christmas story, set in the Jones family home on Christmas Eve. The family's younger children, a boy and girl, are excited about the arrival of Santa Claus and their new presents, but the holiday is a more difficult time for their toys, who come to life in the playroom when the children aren't there. The veteran toys, led by a tattered old teddy bear named Balthazar, realize that new toys often mean changing fortunes for older ones, but they have trouble explaining the situation to Rugby, a stuffed tiger who was last year's special Christmas toy. Rugby believes that Christmas will bring a repeat of his previous moment of triumph as the little girl's favorite plaything, even though Apple, a sweet-faced doll, reveals to him that she was the Christmas toy the year before him and was ousted from favor upon his arrival. Determined to reclaim his glory, Rugby sneaks down to the Christmas tree and releases the newest Christmas toy from her box in order to replace her. The other toys are stunned by the newcomer, a space action figure named Meteora who doesn't seem to realize that she's a toy. The toys struggle to return Meteora to her box before the children wake up, which is especially crucial because any toy found out of place by a human will instantly be frozen forever. By the time Christmas morning dawns, Rugby and the other toys have learned some valuable lessons about their relationships with each other and their places in their own community.

Any viewer coming to the special today will instantly be struck by the ways in which *The Christmas Toy* prefigures the characters and plots of Pixar's *Toy Story* films. There are, however, some crucial differences even in elements that at first appear very similar. The premise, in which toys become alive in the absence of human observers, is consistent in both works, although it's also an old conceit that goes at least as far back as Hans Christian Andersen's story, "The Steadfast Tin Soldier." In both *The Christmas Toy* and the first *Toy Story* movie, an older toy is threatened with the loss of status when a new favorite appears, although in the 1995 Pixar story it is Andy's birthday that occasions the new influx of playthings. The central characters, Rugby and Woody, are quite different in appearance, but both have become somewhat spoiled by their high status, although Rugby is the far more egotistical of the two. Both characters face a crisis of identity brought on by the appearance of a rival, and Rugby and Woody share their initial disbelief that any newcomer could deprive them of their exalted positions in the hearts of their owners. For Rugby, however, the emotional journey is more marked because of his more obvious character flaws. Woody is essentially a likeable cowboy, even if he has gotten a little too big for his own boots, while Rugby is so vain and conceited that only the simplest toys in the playroom, like Ditz and Mew, really admire him. Rugby has to become a sympathetic character over the course of the story, winning the audience over after his early bouts of boasting and pretension.

In both stories, the reigning favorites are confronted by unwanted replacements who are fancy, space-themed action figures: Meteora, Queen of the Asteroids, and Buzz Lightyear of Star Command. The elaborate space toys share an erroneous assumption about their own existence; they believe their own back stories about actually being the characters they represent. As a result, they both respond to their new homes as extraterrestrial environments rather than familiar domestic confines, and their initial encounters with the other toys vacillate between confusion and outright hostility. Liberated from her package, Meteora exclaims, "What planet is this?" while the newly arrived Buzz treats Andy's room like the surface of an alien world. In *Toy Story* this confusion is primarily played for laughs, but in *The Christmas Toy* Meteora's mistake presents a real danger to the other toys because her noisy violence threatens to wake the human family and result in everyone being frozen forever.

Each narrative also emphasizes the need for the toys to forge friendships and band together as a community in order to overcome the obstacles that they face. While *Toy Story* focuses on the emerging friendship between Woody and the newcomer Buzz, *The Christmas Toy* emphasizes Rugby's relationship with his predecessor, Apple, and the much-maligned cat toy, Mew. In both *The Christmas Toy* and all three of the *Toy Story* movies, the toys mount rescue missions to save their imperiled comrades, although the expeditions are fraught with hazards of different kinds. Rugby's friends need only to reach the living room downstairs, but they face a toy's version of death if they get caught. Woody, Buzz, and Andy's other toys roam all over town in their three films, from Sid's house next door to Al's Toy Barn and Sunnyside Daycare.

Secondary characters in *The Christmas Toy* also parallel supporting figures in *Toy Story*, filling out the toy community and bringing their own talents and quirks to the mix. Belmont, the nervous rocking horse, has a disposition quite similar to that of Rex the dinosaur, and Ditz the clown plays an affable but simple-minded sidekick rather like Slinky Dog. Apple, like Bo Peep, functions as a feminine voice of reason, urging the troubled protagonist to see things a different way. Other characters in *The Christmas Toy* presage those seen in the *Toy Story* sequels. The Barbie clone who can never decide what to wear in *The Christmas Toy* anticipates the roles of both Barbie and Ken in the later *Toy Story* pictures. Balthazar, the elderly teddy bear, has much in common with Lots-O-Huggin' Bear in *Toy Story 3*, including a bedraggled appearance and the use of a cane, although Balthazar functions as a benevolent mentor while Lotso proves to be a bitter antagonist.

Like *Toy Story*, *The Christmas Toy* creates a particularly nostalgic vision of the playroom world. All of the toys and furnishings of the playroom represent a call back to an earlier era; from the jack-in-the-box and the stuffed Humpty Dumpty to the traditional dollhouse and the pull-along toy telephone, the toys chosen for the two younger Jones children probably look a lot like the childhood playthings of their parents. This interest in older, perhaps simpler toys is in contrast to the world of the child viewer of the special both then and now. In 1986, children were wishing for talking toys like Teddy Ruxpin or action figures like He-Man and She-Ra. The playroom toys would have been familiar, but they would not represent the sort of toys the child audience would have routinely played with. The gap gets wider in the 21st century when children are just as likely to have a room full of digital equipment as they are toys of felt, fur, and fluff. The sense of the playroom as a nostalgic space is enhanced by the influence of illustrator Larry DiFiori, the conceptual designer for the production. The playroom intentionally resembles a storybook picture, creating what Christopher Finch calls a "children's book come to life" (208).

Within the confines of the playroom, cooperation and harmony (both emotional and musical) permeate the interactions between the toys. Those images of a happy community reflect the ways many adults wish to see their own childhoods. Moving out of the playroom as Rugby does means confronting danger because a toy might get caught out of place. If the playroom is about the past, the living room represents change and the future, as it is the setting for the emergence of the new Christmas toy; this is especially true when the new Christmas toy is Meteora, Queen of the Asteroids, an interesting blend of Flash Gordon, Buck Rogers, and She-Ra, Princess of Power. While the other toys resemble the playthings of an earlier era, Meteora is an action figure whose costume and accessories highlight her importance as the latest thing. Meteora, unlike the playroom toys, is not interested in old-fashioned ideas like cooperation or harmony; she is out to conquer and destroy. The child audience will immediately see the appeal of Meteora as she is literally shiny and new; the adult audience, however, knows that she represents a shift in the stages of childhood where the sort of play that nourishes community becomes the play of competition. The other toys, after all, finally get Meteora to return to her box by appealing to her vanity, not her sense of cooperation.

Between them, the playroom and the living room function as spaces in which *The Christmas Toy* works out its most important themes, which parallel those found in most of Henson's creations. Friendship is one of the foremost, a theme that appears in nearly every Jim Henson project from *The Muppet Movie* forward. In *The Christmas Toy*, Rugby, Apple, and Mew must work beyond their own feelings of egotism, resentment, and self-doubt to build their friendships with one another. Their relationships prove to be hard work, especially because Rugby is so convinced of his own importance and resists the other toys' efforts to help and support him. As Mew says of Rugby at an especially trying moment, "We're friends, but it's not a perfect relationship." Rugby's dawning appreciation for his friends, especially the lower caste Mew, serves as one of the special's most pivotal narrative drives, with the climactic scene featuring the song, "Old Friend, Dear Friend," Rugby's heartfelt tribute to his seemingly fallen companion. The importance of friendship in the special strongly resembles its centrality in *Fraggle Rock*, particularly in the problems created by the very different personalities and failings of each character.

Beyond individual relationships is the significance of the community as a whole. The toys form a de facto family, just like the Muppets in the Muppet movies and the Fraggles in *Fraggle Rock*. The preservation of the family unit motivates the actions of most of the characters. Throughout the story, different toys can be seen standing guard at the playroom door to protect the group from being caught by the humans, indicating a strong sense of the need to preserve the community from danger. We see this most clearly in the rescue mission mounted by Apple; while Belmont is a reluctant volunteer, Cruiser, a taxi complete with driver, and Bleep the robot, who offers to stand guard, willingly endanger themselves in order to return the prodigal tiger. Mew's participation in the rescue proves most valuable as it is his quick thinking that saves the group of would be rescuers from being found by the human father. In addition to maintaining a cohesive community, the toys of the playroom also work to create an inclusive environment that welcomes the newcomers, even the previously hostile Meteora. By the closing scene, all of the toys are united as members of a single, mutually supportive group, bound together by their shared relationship to the little girl, who tells the new toy, "I love you, Meteora, forever and ever, just like I love all my toys." The fears of the older toys are thus put to rest, and the community can move forward, confident in each member's equal claim to love and importance.

Although the more positive themes of friendship and community in *The Christmas Toy* align it with the larger body of Henson productions, the special's darker elements highlight its particular affinity with other projects of the same period. *The Dark Crystal* had arrived in theaters in 1982, followed by *Labyrinth* in 1986, and both of these original stories delved into darker and more threatening territory than the popular Muppets material. In *The Dark Crystal* in particular, mortality, war, and genocide feature as important, if difficult, themes, while *Labyrinth* presents a plot in which nightmarish creatures kidnap a child and propel the heroine on a surreal, dangerous journey fraught with sexual undertones. For a children's holiday special, *The Christmas Toy* has some surprisingly somber content, especially in its treatment of themes like death and prejudice. These serious topics might even make the special too traumatic for the youngest viewers, but they also serve a purpose in the narrative and give the story additional depth.

In *Toy Story*, the toys can confront human beings like Sid if the situation demands, but in *The Christmas Toy* there are dire consequences for being caught out of position by a living creature. Rugby and the other toys must even remain still in front of the family cat, Luigi, or else they risk being frozen forever. The story makes it clear that being frozen is the toy version of death. Early on, Ditz the clown accidentally gets caught in the doorway by the human mother. He slumps to the floor at her approach, but he does not get up after she leaves. The other toys mourn his death and carry him to a pile of similarly frozen playthings, all victims of former accidents. It's a strikingly gruesome scene, as the heap of toy corpses is regarded with horror by the playroom's surviving residents. Ditz's fate provides viewers with a strong sense of the peril faced by the other toys as they venture beyond the playroom. Their lives literally hang in the balance, giving the rescue expedition as much urgency as a war mission or a prison break.

This sense of the humans as a threatening presence also affects the way in which puppets and people occupy the screen. The mother and father are the primary causes for alarm, and we generally see them only in part or in shadow. They roam the house like unconscious angels of death for the toys, always menacing in their ability to show up unexpectedly and find a toy out of place, especially outside the relatively safe confines of the playroom. Gone is the jovial interaction between puppets and humans that characterizes *The Muppet Show* and the Muppet movies. Even more so than in *Fraggle Rock*, the puppet characters and the human beings exist in completely separate spheres while occupying the same physical space, and the adult people are the closest thing *The Christmas Toy* has to real antagonists. Like an accidental gorgon or basilisk, the mother literally kills Ditz with her gaze, rendering him an empty shell devoid of life.

As traumatic as Ditz's early death might be, it merely sets the stage for a later and even more emotionally wrenching scene, when the heroic little Mew also gets caught out of place by a human being. Logically, it seems strange that this rule would apply to a cat toy, since Luigi presumably drags Mew all over the house without the humans knowing where he ought to be, but our sense of the rule's unfairness ultimately only heightens our grief for the character. Mew has striven valiantly on Rugby's behalf throughout the adventure of the story, and he has even saved the whole group from being frozen with a timely impersonation of the family cat. Rugby finally becomes aware of Mew's friendship and importance but doesn't get the opportunity to express his altered feelings before Mew is frozen. Although Mew is eventually resurrected, either by Rugby's touching song of love or some Christmas miracle, his death is presented as exactly that, a real, emotionally painful loss for both the characters and the viewer. Small children and sentimental adults are likely to burst into tears at this point in the story, and it's certainly not a scene for those who have recently experienced a death in the family. While Mew's sudden resurrection takes the story back into the realm of comforting fantasy, it also emphasizes that being frozen is the toy version of death, and for toys there appears to be no hope of a heavenly afterlife. Mew describes his experience of death as "very dark and cold," a place of non-being without agency or companionship. Even if Mew and the other playroom toys escape this fate for the present time, it lingers as a disturbing reminder of what might happen to each of them.

Mew also serves as a lynchpin for another serious, darker theme, that of racial or class prejudice. Frequently derided by Rugby as a mere "cat toy," Mew occupies a lower position in the playroom hierarchy than any other resident. The other toys also complain about the way Mew smells, since his tiny body is stuffed with catnip. For Rugby in particular, Mew's identity as a cat toy rather than a child's toy marks him as inferior, unimportant, and unworthy of consideration or respect. The tone that Rugby uses whenever he says "cat toy" makes it function as a racial or ethnic slur, although the removal of the context from real life minorities renders the intention more subtle, and young children watching the program are likely to miss the point entirely. For adult viewers, however, the deployment of this kind of verbal oppression ought to be perfectly clear. The narrative arc of the special focuses on Rugby's initial intolerance and prejudice where Mew is concerned giving way to respect, appreciation, and even love. Mew's death thus borders on the problematic by making him an example of the token minority figure who is martyred for the benefit of the majority character's survival or psychological development, but his resurrection rescues him from that fate and returns him to the community with newfound status. Mew is further rewarded at the end of the story with the arrival of a female companion, an event that seems to promise a brighter future for the courageous little character. This aspect of the story is not as dark as the full-scale genocide waged in *The Dark Crystal*, but it does strike a very different note from the strictly sweet tones one might expect in a children's Christmas special about talking toys.

All of the various toy stories in *The Christmas Toy* are telling, especially when one considers the special as part of the larger body of Henson productions. While it's true that *The Christmas Toy* is overshadowed today by the endearing sweetness of *Emmet Otter's Jug-Band Christmas* and the blockbuster success of the *Toy Story* movies, the special still has a lot to offer to viewers who want a more complete understanding of Henson history, a thoughtful example of story-telling, or just a moving holiday entertainment. It is not a perfect production, and like Balthazar the teddy bear, it does show its age around the seams, but it warrants consideration, nonetheless, and hopefully more viewers will find it and appreciate its quirky charm in the coming years.

WORKS CITED

The Christmas Toy. Dir. Eric Till. Perf. Dave Goelz, Steve Whitmire, Kathryn Mullen, Jerry Nelson. 1986. The Jim Henson Company. DVD. 2009.

Finch, Christopher. *Jim Henson: The Works*. New York: Random House, 1993. Print.

Heffley, Lynne. "Muppets Come to Life in 'Toys.'" Rev. of *The Secret Life of Toys*. *Los Angeles Times*. 5 Mar 1994. Web. 23 May 2012.

Henson: The Jim Henson Company. The Jim Henson Company. n.d. Web. 23 May 2012.

Margulies, Lee. "A Sleighful of Christmas Specials." Rev. of *The Christmas Toy*. Dir. Eric Till. *Los Angeles Times*. 6 Dec 1986. Web. 23 May 2012.

Toy Story. Dir. John Lasseter. Perf. Tom Hanks, Tim Allen, Don Rickles, Jim Varney. Pixar. 1995. Disney/Pixar. DVD. 2010.

Toy Story 2. Dir. John Lasseter, Ash Brannon, Lee Unkrich. Perf. Tom Hanks, Tim Allen, Joan Cusack, Kelsey Grammer. Pixar. 1999. Disney/Pixar. DVD. 2010.

Toy Story 3. Dir. Lee Unrich. Perf. Tom Hanks, Tim Allen, Joan Cusack, Ned Beatty. Pixar, 2010. Disney/Pixar. DVD. 2010.

PART FOUR: JOURNEYS FORWARD AND BACK

The Muppetry of Nightmares: Figures of Fear, Danger and Terror in *The Cosby Show*, *Chappelle's Show* and *Saturday Night Live*

Michael J. Berntsen

> Man stands amazed to see his deformity
> In any other creature but himself.
> — Webster, *The Duchess of Malfi*

Part I. Don't Talk to the Hand

Playing pretend is a wonderfully strange practice that entertains and inspires children and adults alike. We regularly engage in or enjoy pretending whether we call it acting, creative writing, or office role-playing exercises. Through the art of puppetry, performers transform the habit of playing pretend to a level of timeless comedy by granting inarticulate animals and creatures speech, mannerisms, and personalities. Kelly Burkholder's *Puppets*, a children's book that introduces the history of puppetry, is a good example of how people romanticize the craft. She states, "[T]he puppeteer brings a puppet to life. He or she makes the audience believe in the puppet character.... In a puppet show you can pretend to be somebody else" (4). On the surface, Burkholder's sentiments seem absurd with their romantic notions that we breathe life into fabric. A puppeteer can only simulate life, and the reason for a puppeteer desiring to be someone else is never explicitly apparent. What Burkholder underscores, however, is the uncanny subtext that lies deep within the art of puppetry. As an art form that attracts people of all ages, it contradicts concepts of maturity and adulthood. This equalizing effect subverts conservative and traditional notions of acting grown-up. Most adults recognize that conversing with fabric would probably be reserved for children, yet the appeal puppets possess, in turn, suspends not merely disbelief but normal social practices that would typically prevent adults from playing pretend. This moment is when feelings of the uncanny emerge, and those feelings become more exaggerated in regards to Jim Henson's Muppets.

The Muppets, given their franchise status, occupy more than a fictional variety show theater. They are tangible beings that test the boundaries of playing pretend. Due to their cultural capital, they inhabit a real place in American and global cultures, which marks their uncanny presence in the world's consciousness. They have advertised Purina Dog Chow, Polaroid cameras, and Pizza Hut pizzas. Since 1976, famous celebrities and entertainers have interacted with them as if no hand controlled their mouths, ignoring the more obvious person below who is manipulating such a funny looking object. Muppets have even taken up such causes as the fight against illiteracy, an end to air pollution, and the proper ways to sneeze.

Sigmund Freud's exploration into the uncanny explains how such lifelike, ubiquitous objects can contain slight hints of horror regardless of their positive associations. Defining the uncanny as "that class of the frightening which leads back to what is known," Freud reveals the duality of any human creation that is intended to act human (224). In mimicking human behaviors and attitudes, Muppets, and identifiable puppets in general, such as Servo and Crow from *Mystery Science Theater 3000* or Triumph the Insult Comic Dog, become active participates in daily life. They demand attention by becoming legitimate forces in various sectors of society, whether it be advertising a product, acting in movies, or hosting their own variety show. This spectacle contains clear instances of narcissism because it represents the human compulsion to make everything human.

Although puppets, especially Henson's Muppets, typically exude positive images and represent childlike innocence, or in the very least a sense of safe delight, Bill Cosby, Dave Chappelle, and, not surprisingly, Jim Henson himself have explored the negative aspects of treating puppets as interlopers that assume human qualities. These instances demonstrate how the art of puppetry is inherently bizarre and whimsically enjoyable, exemplifying to what extent people will expand the boundaries of pretending. Even in more terrifying roles, including a sadistic surgeon or the embodiment of gonorrhea, Muppets and

Muppet parodies remain instruments of comedy because they pose no real threat. The base natures of the more wicked and vile Muppets or parodies are mere shadows of human failing. Our flaws, in fact, are the real threats that are punctuated whenever humanity encounters an uncanny reflection of itself.

Part II. Don't Feed Cliff After Midnight

The Cosby Show episode, "Cliff's Nightmare," contains several moments when the uncanny appears in specific relation to the Muppets. Featuring a score of fan favorite monsters, this episode demonstrates how a blend of humor and light horror produces uncanny impulses within a narrative that audiences can enjoy despite the general displeasure and discomfort of Cliff (Bill Cosby). Writers John Markus, Carmen Finestra, and Gary Kott transport the Muppets to a domain in which the uncanny always already lurks, namely Freud's favorite landscape, the territory of dreams. By having Cliff encounter the Muppets in his nightmare, Markus, Finestra, and Kott highlight how these commonly comedic figures can exhibit monstrous behavior and induce feelings of the uncanny. They also set most of the interactions at a hospital, which not only corresponds to Cliff's job but also presents a place that both children and adult audiences may equally fear. With these factors in consideration, the uncanny demands confrontation from the audience via Cliff, given how these Muppets should normally appear on a stage for entertainment purposes rather than in an institution of pain.

After a barrage of Freudian nightmarish situations, including Vanessa outplaying him on the saxophone, Theo outranking in him in the Navy, and Olivia outperforming him in the field of medicine, Cliff soon confronts the first two Muppets, The Hypocritic Oaf and the Sausage Sandwich, in his living room, which establishes the uncanny elements as devices for characterization and theme. Markus, Finestra, and Kott first focus on how Muppets often act as human doppelgängers, which is an important component to notions of the uncanny. Doubling, in particular when it appears in fiction, epitomizes how a reflection of the familiar reveals deformity or defectiveness within the original character (Vardoulakis 100). In the case of The Hypocritic Oaf, this Muppet encapsulates Cliff's natural propensity to help people while simultaneously twisting a doctor's pledge to care. Adhering to the Hippocratic Oath defines Cliff as a character, yet in this nightmare state the manifestation of it as a gray-haired, green monster attacks Cliff's ego by reducing his sacred vow to a pun. Its name, too, represents how Cliff, as a doctor, hypocritically neglects his own health by eating junk food so late at night. In this dreamscape, his conscience uses his subconscious to teach himself, as well as the audience, an important lesson in following the reliable cliché, practice what you preach.

The Sausage Sandwich, too, has a dual function, acting as a moral compass within the fantasy realm and an instrument of the uncanny. As a symbol for the actual sandwich that fuels the episode's events, it acts as a stand in for Cliff's wife, Claire. Although it is more disparaging and nagging than Claire, it helps explain to Cliff why he is caught in an uncanny domain. However, the Sausage Sandwich entraps him with an uncanny exchange instead of revealing how he can escape. After hearing the words of his wife via the Sausage Sandwich, Cliff argues with it in an attempt to regain some sort of agency or control within the dream. Once the Sausage Sandwich remarks to The Hippocratic Oath that Cliff "never listens to anyone," Cliff's tone and reactions become increasingly abrasive in a feeble attempt to dominate the debate. The Sausage Sandwich lures Cliff into a pun-drenched dispute since it verbally disagrees with Cliff as the actual sandwich is disagreeing with his stomach (and head). Trying to convince Cliff that his choice to eat the real sandwich was poor, the Sausage Sandwich ensnares Cliff to engage in an uncanny and unproductive quarrel.

The dialogue also parallels the previous exchange between Cliff and Claire, signifying that the Sausage Sandwich is a manifestation of his wife, his unconscious acknowledgement that his wife is right, and the actual sandwich that is poisoning his mind with bizarre images. The complex web of mirroring in this scene prompts Cliff to lash out since he does not want to admit that his wife and the uncanny representation of her know better. Cliff finally ceases the banter by shouting, "Why am I here arguing with a sandwich?" This moment presents a dual condition for the uncanny within the episode. Firstly, in the context of the narrative, Cliff acknowledges how strange it is to be conversing with a piece of meat stuck between two pieces of bread. Secondly, this interaction asks the audience to consider how odd it is for any person to interact with a puppet. The blending of these two aspects adds to the comedic horror that Cliff endures and we witness.

The uncanny nature to his nightmare further unravels as Sweetums and Doglion drag Cliff to the hospital and then later to Operating Theater. The obvious inclusion of these two Muppets, given their usual monstrous status in *The Muppet Show*, demonstrates how anatomically proportionate puppets are clear sources for a horrific, hoagie-induced vision. Sweetums and Doglion immediately pronounce their dominance over Cliff by their stature and their words. They intrude upon Cliff's personal space by standing too close and then begin to push and firmly squeeze him. Doglion also calls him a wimp, and Sweetums slyly remarks that they enjoy inflicting pain in order to increase Cliff's subservience to them. The fact that these brutes aggressively abduct him, taking him against his will to a place in which he typically enjoys working, establishes that their presence has demonized the familiar. Cliff is constantly portrayed as a hard-working and dedicated doctor, yet Sweetums and Doglion force him away from rescuing his wife who is hanging from a building during the nightmare to his place of work, twisting it into a realm where Cliff cannot find joy or comfort. In the nightmare, the presence of the Muppets disturbs the natural function of the hospital, given how his regular responsibility is to deliver babies. Cliff, who acts as a force of life, must confront a place now occupied by unruly Muppets.

As a space for the uncanny to perform itself, the hospital represents a reality in which Muppets become agents of carnivalesque mischief that undermine Cliff's ego. The first new player he meets is Leon, as a con-artist who dupes him out of $5,005 for two separate elevator passes and a parking permit. In the parameters of *The Cosby Show*, Cliff giving away money corresponds to the numerous jokes the show contains concerning how much parents pay for their children, yet it is not a strong enough sense of doubling. Here, Leon's success epitomizes how Cliff lacks the intelligence to acknowledge Leon's dubious mannerisms and intent. Digit, in the role of a masochistic patient, is the second major player who upsets Cliff's normally positive workplace. He demands that Cliff hit him in order to cure his ailments, but Cliff hesitantly gives Digit a gentle tap on his face. As Cliff refuses to harm him, Sweetums returns to question Cliff's authority then viciously smacks Digit across the room. Digit is cured and insults Cliff by cracking, "And you call yourself a doctor...Keep practicing." Despite the familiar surroundings, Cliff becomes the puppet of these creatures' whims and idiosyncrasies. Cliff should have automatic ethos in this setting, yet the presence of the Muppets subverts his supremacy and challenges his acumen. Even his youngest daughter, Rudy, the only other human presence in the hospital, participates in the deconstruction of Cliff. She castrates his male psyche by denying him as her father and puts him in danger by summoning Sweetums and Doglion "to show what pushing is." Her alliance with the Muppets further proves that the hospital is topsy-turvy since she has more power than her patriarch.

More terrifying for Cliff than the hospital is Gonzo's Operating Theater, where the sense of uncanny reaches its peak. The stage is an uncanny, cheap replica of *The Muppet Show* with its decorative stage and Muppet audience. Despite the similarities, this performance space offers no uplifting artistic collaborations between Muppets and humans; rather it exemplifies how the Muppets can exhibit monstrous natures when they are the masters of their domain.

The absence of Kermit as host, too, automatically creates a strange atmosphere for the viewing audience more so than for Cliff. Having Gonzo, wearing a surgical uniform, take the reigns as host signals that whatever actions occur on this stage will not be an ordinary Muppet presentation. An uncanny moment for Gonzo emerges since he assumes the role of the orchestrator of torture. Although he commonly inflicts pain upon himself during daring stunts, and he even references a time when he "preformed an appendectomy while being shot out of a cannon," Gonzo now appears to be taking revenge for the suffering by his own hands. He blatantly admits that Cliff is in danger and "will be suspended upside-down in a tank of water while playing 'Lady of Spain' on the accordion." By suggesting that Cliff will conform to Gonzo's style of injurious feats, Gonzo dons a more frightening guise and increases the presence of uncanny within the narrative.

Despite the odd venue and atypical host, the dynamic of human interaction with the Muppets is still preserved even though the alterations are hauntingly threatening. Initially, Gonzo announces that Cliff will be the first doctor to deliver a Koozebanian baby, but when the mother escapes, the Muppet audience is hungry for amusement and proceeds to chant repeatedly, "We want surgery!" Cliff, dressed in surgeon garb, too, quickly becomes the unwilling patient after Sweetums and Doglion, also crowned with large surgeon caps atop their heads, throw Cliff onto the table. Not only is he now the patient, but he transforms into an object of spectacle and dissection, a human object of entertainment for the Muppet audience to consume. Toril Moi, in "Representation of Patriarchy: Sexuality and Epistemology in Freud's 'Dora,'" articulates that castration and the uncanny have a clear link because castration fears always include "the fear of discovering that one has already been castrated" (72). Cliff's nightmare originates from his inability to control his need for junk food. The cast of Muppets at each point in this dreadful dream reinforces his lack of self-discipline by stripping him of the roles, social status, and critical thinking skills that routinely define him.

His inability to escape Digit's saw additionally confirms his (and our) worst fears — we are not autonomous beings and we are most certainly controlled by exterior forces. In Cliff's nightmare, Muppets and humans are counterparts, emphasizing the doppelgänger relationship. These creations have the uncanny potential to reflect their creators' insecurities and inadequacies. Cliff, also playing the part of Waldorf, substantiates the blurred line between human and Muppet when he barks, "He [the real or perceived real Cliff] doesn't look like he can deliver a baby!" Statler, in predictable timing and fashion, adds, "He doesn't look like he can deliver a pizza." The uncanniness of this moment overflows with its mild degradation of Cliff's abilities and the doubling of Cliff. Here, he becomes a puppet without strings, guided by his bruised ego and poisoned body. The Muppets perform Cliff's self-inflicted punishment, the product of eating the sandwich instead of heeding his wife's words. By standing in for Waldorf, he criticizes his mistake by attacking his most cherished talent, providing the best healthcare for expectant mothers.

Furthermore, his doubling reminds us that there are times when we will be puppets of chance and monsters. Freud's predecessor in the study of the uncanny, Rudolph Otto, offers an explanation as to how Cliff's metamorphosis resonates an uncanny impulse. In an attempt to pinpoint where the sense of the uncanny fits in with the human quest for God, Otto coins the phrase, "creature-feeling," describing it as the "first subjective concomitant and effect of another feeling-element, which casts it like a shadow, but which in itself indubitably has immediate and primary reference to an object outside the self" (10–11). It is the sense of recognizing one's status as a creation and feeling one's own limitations before a divine architect. Dressing and acting like Waldorf, Cliff reminds himself and the audience that we are vulnerable creations and cannot escape the threat of death or destruction even in our dreams. The Muppets, as Digit demonstrates in the hospital scene, can survive and even benefit from a major source of fear for humans, namely pain. Being creations, they occupy a sense of unnatural existence since they are inorganic, yet this unnatural nature ensures their survival and possibly secures their immortality.

Right before Cliff is about to meet his demise at the shaky hands of Digit, he wakes up to an upset stomach and a hazy head. Stumbling down the stairs, he discovers that uncanniness is difficult to escape and receives more castrating criticism from his children that he is too old to each junk food before bed. Right after they leave, Cliff opens the refrigerator to a plethora of talking food Muppets. This group proceeds to heckle Cliff, imitating the mild quips from his children, validating that the Muppets in Cliff's waking and sleeping world are meta-fictional, fictional, and nonfictional doppelgängers. The intrusion of the Muppets into Cliff's head and house dismantles his elevated position as father, doctor, and human.

At every point in the narrative, whether in dream or in reality, the Muppets act as parallel voices to their mutual human ones. The episode exhibits the many dimensions from which the uncanny emerges when Muppets collide with fantasy and reality. As a crossover episode, too, the appearance of the Muppets disrupts the narrative frame of *The Cosby Show*. Dreaming has been a previous focus of episodes, and Claire even references the time when Cliff dreamed of giving birth to a hoagie in the first act of "Cliff's Nightmare," yet the inclusion of Muppets extends the reaches of the uncanny. In "Challenging Narratives: Crossovers in Prime Time," J. Richard Kjelstrup claims that in crossovers "one set of conventions can easily be abandoned in favor of another." (43). Cliff encounters threats and castration he would normally avoid or rise above in other episodes because, as nightmarish figures, the Muppets act as uncanny, sadistic entertainers. Fans of the Muppets, of course, revel at seeing them intermingle with *Cosby Show* characters, even as slightly malevolent forces. Their presence generates undertones of horror, but more significantly, they add great surprise and humor to a show about family values and social responsibility.

Part III. Sesame Hood

While "Cliff's Nightmare" discusses the doubling of Henson's Muppets for humans and vice-versa, several parodies exist that extend the uncanny doubling shadowing the Muppets themselves. Most notably, Robert Lopez and Jeff Marx's *Avenue Q*, which humorously parodies *Sesame Street*, and Peter Jackson's *Meet the Feebles*, which perversely satires *The Muppet Show*, showcase how even the Muppets have doppelgängers. These uncanny likenesses illustrate how the Muppets are part of our cultural consciousness and that even Muppet parodies can become a part of that consciousness. Although *Meet the Feebles* will probably remain an underground cult phenomenon due to its debauched imagery, derisible mockery, and theater of cruelty methodology, *Avenue Q* is able to enjoy mainstream reception because it simultaneously cherishes and pokes fun at Henson's legacy. It playfully draws attention to the uncanny nature of the Muppets as cultural icons and *Sesame Street* as a fantasy-scape, but it does not obliterate the humor involved in doing so even when the jokes are somewhat lewd. *Meet the Feebles*, in contrast, seems to exist merely for cheap shock value, although it still attests to Muppet consciousness in popular culture.

David Chappelle continues this tradition of doubling Henson's Muppets for shocking and humorous purposes in the fan and critic favorite, "Kneehigh Park" sketch, from *Chappelle's Show*. The STD *Sesame Street* Muppet parodies, created by longtime Muppet designer, Tim Lagasse, expose the frightening consequences of adapting serious issues for puppet theater. Chappelle gives us an uncanny reflection of what *Sesame Street* would be like with foul-mouthed and disgusting puppets who represent herpes, gonorrhea, and crabs. The mixture of humor and repugnance undermines the utopian neighborhood *Sesame Street* showcases, attacking how the show is an empty nostalgic gesture to a past no community has ever truly experienced. Chappelle, by presenting such base images and bawdy songs, establishes his sketch more so as a testament to the absurd nature of *Sesame Street* than as a strict parody. Although Kneehigh Park is in no way a more real depiction of urban life, this hyperexaggerated ghetto street children's hour reveals the uncanny elements thriving on its busy, well known counterpart. In contrast to "Cliff's Nightmare," Chappelle's puppets do not function as narrative or thematic elements within the overall framework of the show; rather he intends these doppelgänger parodies as a locus of social and political commentary. This function also articulates why this sketch and *Avenue Q* invoke laughter, while *Meet the Feebles* summons disgust. The inherent messages within both parodies that encourage people to find their own way in life add dimensions of sincerity and insight, whereas *Meet the Feebles* offers an assortment of obscene puppets with no intrinsic moral values.

The didactic undercurrent of Chappelle's "Kneehigh Park" sketch begins to surface as the first resident of Kneehigh Park, Bobbo, a drug addict reminiscent at least in pigment and hair to Ernie, sings to the children that people from all different walks of life use all different types of drugs. Chappelle's political satire that Americans unjustly create a drug hierarchy reaches a comedic level even when Bobbo's over-the-top drug use crescendos with a face full of shaving cream, indicating that he is having a bad trip. What should be a horrifying spectacle, especially considering that it takes place in front of a group of children, maintains a high degree of comedy because Bobbo's moral equivocation that heroin, headache medicine, and erectile dysfunction cures are comparable drugs spoofs America's contemporary drug culture. His wailings should induce horror, but the live audience explodes with laughter even after Bobbo howls, "I'm fucking dying, man," since his existence as a Muppet parody downplays the seriousness of the situation. This dynamic calls attention to the inherent fantasy puppet theater promotes. The live audience does not feel a horrific impulse because people are playing with toys. Uncanny as it is to witness a drug addict singing to and educating children, the theatrical spectacle of puppetry molds the scenario into a comedic one.

Stinky, the next puppet to greet the kids of Kneehigh Park, is an extreme version of Oscar the Grouch. His ultimate apathy and despondent outlook, again, should instill horror since he is singing about the insignificance of life in front of children. The live audience continues to laugh because, not only does Stinky act as an instrument of parody, but he vulgarly reminds them that family should be the top priority in people's lives. Chappelle is using Stinky decisively to criticize American consumerism, which is a mature topic not often addressed by the gang at *Sesame Street*. This social commentary heightens the offensiveness and silliness of Stinky. Moreover, Chappelle shows the potential danger in letting children learn from puppets. We may trust Henson's Muppets with our children's entertainment and education, which poses a problem if the puppeteers have more sinister motives.

Once Stinky retreats into his garbage can to make himself a feces sandwich, a shirtless, human puppet named Dangle appears with Dave Chappelle. They inform the group that Dangle needs to go to the doctor because it hurts when he pees. He reveals his genitalia, causing one of the child characters to vomit and prompting the audience to shout wildly. The camera zooms in on Dangle's yellow crusted limb, which is a disturbing sight, yet the audience can quickly recover from their brief, nauseous gasps to laugh hysterically. The audience's reaction displays the uncomfortable emotions attached to STDs. Seeing even a puppet's area infected, the audience recognizes the horror and then proceeds to unleash laughter in order to alleviate the situation. We know Dangle could not contract an STD, but the thought of it still frightens us even if it we find it generally funny.

The horde of STD puppets that plagues the park after Q-Tip instructs kids how to avoid Dangle's mistakes also brings the ghost of the uncanny. These physical monuments to horrific diseases conform to standard *Sesame Street* protocol and behavior. They sing, dance, and educate. The live audience laughs through most of the musical medley until Herpes ends with, "I like it raw." At that instant, a pang of reality sets in. Under the disguise of rhyme, these threats do not seem as imposing; however, once Herpes reveals his depraved nature, the audience sours. These monsters appear harmless when they act as other *Sesame Street* characters, but they become instantly dangerous when people remember that these diseases exist in reality. The uncanny creeps in at this moment. We can laugh only so long before the image of a twisted pink growth fills us with repulsion for what we can get from each other and give to each other.

The entire sketch, even with Dave Chappelle's concluding messages that we should refrain from littering and not chase money, serves as an uncanny reminder that *Sesame Street* is a fictional haven from the decrepit side of life. As fictional places, Sesame Street and Kneehigh Park are exaggerated ends of the spectrum, but we want Sesame Street to be the street we grew up on, one that our children will grow up on. Kneehigh Park makes sense because the world is a dangerous place. Our laughter fades at such a spot when we realize that Chappelle's parody confronts issues to which the residents of Sesame Street are immune but which the residents of the real world must often face.

Part IV. So Much to Spew

Long before the many sordid parodies that have paraded on stage or screen dealt with issues of puppetry and the uncanny, Jim Henson experimented with the intrinsic uncanniness his creations harbor but failed to produce such uncanniness since the characters from the Land of Gorch are too unfamiliar. The "Land of Gorch" sketches, produced for *SNL*'s first season, epitomize how grotesque puppets can be and how the relationship between the peculiar and the uncanny is not always a given. King Ploobis, Scred, Peuta, Wisss, Vazh, and the Mighty Favog are discordant, vile, and raunchy. Certainly no other Muppets have ever come close to their degree of obscenity and hideousness, which is why they are immensely important to Muppet history. They are probably the most unlikable Muppets ever created because they lack redeemable qualities, offer no real wisdom, and are relatively not funny. This comedic staleness seems more the fault of the *SNL* writers rather than the efforts of Henson and Frank Oz (Harris "Muppet Master..."). *SNL* writer Alan Zweibel admits that "[w]hoever drew the short straw that week had to write the Muppet sketch" (Shales 69). This absence of enthusiasm certainly explains the generally unclever banter at times between these Muppets.

Ignoring many disappointing aspects to these sketches, the Land of Gorch inhabitants suggest that the feelings of the uncanny do not always lurk within puppetry performances. Besides trite one-liners, many times the comedy would fail during these sketches because the audience expects nasty looking monsters to communicate in a coarse manner. When the Mighty Favog stuffs Scred down his mouth, for example, the uncanny feelings of horror that are present when we watch Cliff's near demise cannot cultivate because the Mighty Favog is far removed from the Muppets we welcome into our homes on a weekly basis. Since the characters are completely new, this behavior does not seem as frightening, even though it is much more grotesque. Given the inaugural season's late night status, we also expect a different form of behavior from these Muppets as opposed to those on *The Muppet Show*.

An acute prick of the uncanny surfaces, however, during bit segments of the dialogue. For example, during the "Crater Head" sketch from *SNL* episode three, Peuta approaches Ploobis and shouts, "Ploobis! Ploobis! Do you *know* what your son Wisss is doing?" To which he responds, "What, has he locked himself in the bathroom with a magazine again?" Predictably, Peuta gives us a clichéd drug reference joke, "No! Your son Wisss is smoking ... craters!" Setting aside the lowest-common-denominator humor, a similar dynamic to that of the "Kneehigh Park" sketch occurs. Here, two monstrous figures mimic concerned parents with Ploobis assuming the role of the sexual minded man, while Peuta reenacts a mother worried about her son having a drug problem. This dialogue and behavior contain elements of the familiar, but the sense of uncanny remains underdeveloped due to their son's unrelatable problem. Dissimilar to Dangle, who could easily mirror one of us, Wisss' issue does not translate as well given the constructs of the Land of Gorch. The one-layered smoking references cater to an audience who likes drug rumor rather than reaching a wide audience with complex subtexts.

The array of risqué situations, from Scred showing Peuta his new sex toy, to Ploobis drinking alcohol, to the sexual innuendos between Ploobis and Vazh, never amount to a strong sense of the uncanny. What these elements demonstrate is the convention for puppeteers to make their puppets monstrous. Like Punch and Judy, Ploobis and Peuta represent man and woman at their most primitive. Guided by violent urges and sexual yearnings, the citizens of Gorch and their wisecracking totem-prophet, the Mighty Favog, are silhouettes of human depravity but without the mirror that forces us to confront those diabolical attributes. Even when the subject matter is economic corruption or endangered species, the Land of Gorch remains too detached from the everyday world to evoke meaningful connections to its small band of lascivious creatures.

Part V. The Uncanny Conclusion

In "Cliff's Nightmare," "The Kneehigh Park" sketch, and the "Land of Gorch" skits, we encounter the uncanny through puppetry at differing levels. It may leave us with a wicked chill or a dirty thought, but it generally spawns giggles and chuckles because the use of puppets as figures of terror calls attention to humanity's need to laugh at danger and death. Even when puppetry flaunts the grotesque, a small wish that all we see could be real pulsates within the section of our brains in which all our childhood dreams lay dormant or unexercised. Although each uncanny use of puppets is intended for comedic purposes in these three cases, these depictions presuppose that elements of terror innately exist within their reticulated polyfoam shells. They are not mere mirror images, but creations in our own image, revealing our dichotomous natures that fluctuate between vulgarity and valor.

As living legacies and creatures bound simply by the limit of human imagination, puppets surpass the restraints of their makers. Frank Proschan explains in "Puppet Voices and Interlocutors: Language in Folk Puppetry" that puppets can move in ways people cannot, their faces can remain unchanged, and, most importantly, they can survive a decapitation (528). The unnatural liberties that any puppet can enjoy infringes upon the rules of the physical world. In this realm, immortality is unattainable, yet even if one puppet is destroyed, an exact replica can take its place as if the incident never occurred. We need only to look to the stunts Gonzo accomplishes during his illustrious career. He's been in two places at once, his trumpet contains an array of surprises, and his arm can grow three times its size to catch a cannonball. Hence, we feel like creatures playing pretend divinity. Try as we might, we cannot ignite life within a clump of fabric, and what is really playing a trick is our uncanny compulsion for whimsical play.

In "A Political Anatomy of Monsters, Hopeful and Otherwise: Teratogeny, Transcendentalism, and Evolutionary Theorizing," Evellen Richards asserts how "monsters have always challenged the boundaries of human identity" (377). The thematic, narrative, and metaphoric uses of monsters in various art forms challenge standards of normality and aesthetics and depict conscious or unconscious fears of degeneration, disease, and deformation. Monsters are perverted mirrors that remind their beholder how frail beauty, purity, and reason are. Puppets, at times, function in a similar fashion. As physical representations of live or imagined fears and horrors, their animate and spatial existence challenges the boundaries of human emotion, activity, and thought. The distinct personality and observable mannerisms that each puppet exudes creates an uncanny resemblance to real human interaction and behavior. This uncanny nature grants comedic, anthropomorphic puppets the opportunity to become monstrous figures while retaining the human qualities we embrace. They remain our creations, yet with our whimsical natures, they retain a place among us as distant cousins with whom we enjoy sharing our material world. The Muppets are our uncanny relatives, and we celebrate that condition.

WORKS CITED

Burkholder, Kelly. *Puppets*. Vero Beach, FL: Rourke Publishing LLC, 2001. Print.
"Cliff's Nightmare." *Cosby Show: Season 6*. Writ. John Markus, Carmen Finestra, and Gary
Kott. Dir. Tony Singletary. Urban Works, 2007. DVD. "Episode 2.10." *Chappelle's Show: Season 2 Uncensored*. Writ. Neal Brennan and Dave Chappelle. Dir. Rusty Cundieff. Comedy Central, 2005. DVD.
Freud, Sigmund. "The Uncanny." In *The Standard Edition of the Complete Psychological Works of Sigmund Freud, XVII*. London: Hogarth Press, 1962. Print.
Harris, Judy. "Muppet Master: An Interview with Jim Henson." *Muppet Central*. 21 Sept. 1998. Web. 25 July 2011.
Kjelstrup, J. Richard. "Challenging Narratives: Crossovers in Prime Time." *Journal of Film and Video*. 59.1 (2007): 32–45. Print.
Moi, Toril. "Representation of Patriarchy: Sexuality and Epistemology in Freud's 'Dora.'" *Feminist Review*. 9.3 (1981): 60–74. Print.

Otto, Rudolf. *The Idea of the Holy.* Trans. John W. Harvey. New York: Oxford University Press, 1958. Print.

Proschan, Frank. "Puppet Voices and Interlocutors: Language in Folk Puppetry." *The Journal of American Folklore* 94.374 (1981): 527–555. Print.

Richards, Evellen. "A Political Anatomy of Monsters, Hopeful and Otherwise: Teratogeny, Transcendentalism, and Evolutionary Theorizing." *Isis* 85.3 (1994): 377–411. Print.

Saturday Night Live: The Complete First Season, 1975–1976. Universal Studios, 2006. DVD.

Shales, Tom and James Andrew Miller. *Live From New York An Uncensored History of Saturday Night Live.* New York: Little Brown & Co., 2002. Print.

Vardoulakis, Dimitris. "The Return of Negation: The Doppelgänger in Freud's 'The Uncanny.'" *SubStance* 35.2 (2006) 100–116. Print.

Dinosaurs and the Evolution of the Jim Henson Company

Jennifer Stoessner

Giant feet lumber across the television screen, furry animals cower in terror, and trees are pushed aside to make room for the enormous creature trudging toward its destination, all to the sound of a primal drum beat. The brute, on reaching the end of its journey, calls out, "Honey, I'm home!" The music shifts to an up-tempo shuffle, recalling the frenzy of a circus, and, in true sitcom fashion, a series of clips are shown featuring moments from the lives of the characters that inhabit the house. The sequence ends with the creature, a large green dinosaur, turning off his own television with a remote control. Thus begins the television show *Dinosaurs*, an opening that truly captures the feeling of the series. *Dinosaurs* first aired in 1991 and ran for four seasons, with a total of 65 episodes (Bacon 108). The opening displays the realistic look of the characters while showcasing the zaniness of the situation comedy legacy to which it belongs, ending with a healthy dose of self-referential zing. The show was the first television series to be produced by the Jim Henson Company after its founder's passing in 1990. It builds on the tradition of technological innovation, multi-leveled humor, and social comment that was a hallmark of Henson's career, and the show is a product of the transition from one era into the next in the Company's history.

Jim Henson originally formulated the idea and suggested to designer Kirk Thatcher that he would like to do a situation comedy starring dinosaurs. Henson had done children's programming, movies, and variety shows, but never the popular situation comedy form, a television staple. "It started with Jim and I having lunch and talking about this idea, 'Let's do a show about dinosaurs, show dinosaur thinking and let's do it as a sitcom,'" says Thatcher. This 'dinosaur thinking,' according to Thatcher, is that "there's an endless supply of natural resources and we can use them at our will and sort of, we're the biggest species on the planet and everything else can kind of ... if it's good for us, it's good for us" ("Prehysterical"). Environmentally conscious programming was certainly not new to the Jim Henson Company. *Fraggle Rock* regularly included topics involving water pollution, the importance of interspecies cooperation, and the effect one species can have on another. Brian Henson, Jim's son, *Dinosaurs* puppeteer, and executive producer of the television program, says, "He had the idea of a family of dinosaurs and that they live very irresponsibly and bigger than life and everything's reckless"(Prehysterical). *Dinosaurs* was ideally suited to utilize the characters to tell stories that reflected the nature of the creatures' dominance of the planet as well as to point at humanity's place of power and responsibility for the planet today.

The patriarch of the family is Earl Sinclair, the self-dubbed "Mighty Megalosaurus." He is a blue-collar worker in the tradition of Jackie Gleason's Ralph Kramden. He enjoys watching television, drinking beer, and being king of the castle. At work he is a mere "grunt," a tree-pusher. His job is to quite literally push trees over and uproot them to make room for real estate development. He is, however, a dinosaur on the cusp of change, one of a new generation of male dinosaurs who settle down, marry a wife, and have a house rather than wandering the planet hunting and eating smaller creatures. As co-producer Bob Young says, Earl is "caught between the pull of the wilderness which is where they were coming from and the comforts of civilization which is where they were going" (*Creatures*). He is a dinosaur everyman.

Fran Sinclair, Earl's long-suffering wife, is a homemaker for much of the series. Later in the series, she has several different jobs outside of the home, some paid, some voluntary. She is empathetic, caring, and nurturing while at the same-time being a no-nonsense counterpart for Earl. When he is challenged by any of his children, she often attempts to engage him in a conversation about changing the status quo or how to be a better parent. All the same, when Earl is challenged by the world outside his home, she takes his part to be a supportive and open spouse and mother.

The Sinclairs have three children: fifteen-year old Robbie, twelve-year old Charlene, and their newly-hatched baby, Baby (his actual name according to the second season episode, "And the Winner Is..."). Robbie is a fairly typical teenager, interested in girls and finding his way to adulthood. The oldest child, he constantly presents opposition to his father's way of life, questioning Earl about nearly every choice he makes. He is trying to figure out his place in a once dinosaur-dominated and male-dominated world that is beginning to change. Liberal to the last, Robbie adapts much more quickly to the world than his conservative father. His incessant questioning of society causes Earl no end of grief, forcing him to consider why he does the things he does rather than just plunging ahead. The relationship between conservative parent and liberal child is one often seen in situation comedies. It recalls the relationship between Mike "Meathead" Stivic and his father-in-law, the bigoted curmudgeon Archie Bunker from *All in the Family* as well as the dynamic between liberal Lisa and her father Homer on *The Simpsons*.

Middle-child Charlene Sinclair is a bit more traditional than her older brother, but at twelve years old, she is presented with a lot of change herself. Voiced by *All in the Family's* Sally Struthers, Charlene is alternately cheery and moody, facing puberty and the growth of her tail (the outward sign of female maturity) while trying to achieve popularity and to be as average as possible. She is crestfallen when she receives a C+ grade because teachers will now expect more of her. She is often allied with Earl merely because she has more prehistoric appetites than Robbie and because she is her Daddy's little girl. However, much like Struthers's Gloria on *All in the Family,* she is capable of deep thought and will question the way the world works. As the series develops, Charlene becomes concerned with more than just fashion and food, getting involved in caveperson rights and taking an interest in science. Being a young female, she is also able to spot inequity between the sexes and to call it into question immediately.

The final core family member is Baby, a pink skinned and purple-eyed bundle of joy. The first episode of the show focuses on his birth or hatching and its effect on the life of his father. He is the breakout star of the show, with a catch phrase developed by writer and series co-producer Bob Young, "I'm the Baby. Gotta love me." His other catch phrase refers to his father, whom he calls "Not the Mama," often while striking him with a blunt object like a frying pan. This youngest member of the Sinclair household really brings the opposition of present versus past into stark contrast. Unlike his siblings, Baby is seeing everything for the first time and is genuinely able to ask why and to demand an answer. His childlike innocence forces his parents to really examine why things are the way they are — sometimes leading them to the realization that they cannot explain the world to their youngster. Voiced by veteran Muppet performer Kevin Clash, puppeteer of Elmo from *Sesame Street,* Baby Sinclair especially appeals to children, partly because he is a more conventional television style puppet, manipulated from beneath by Clash, and perhaps partly because of the similarity of the characters' voices. Whichever is the case, Baby is a fully functional individual despite his age and plays the rascal to his father's buffoon, introducing chaos and mischief into the home and many plotlines.

Dinosaurs's supporting cast provides those essential supplementary situation comedy characters to flesh out the lives of the Sinclair family. Roy Hess is Earl's buddy, a Tyrannosaurus Rex version of Art Carney's Ed Norton on *The Honeymooners*. He is single, and, as such, he simultaneously reminds Earl of the freedom he left behind when he married as well as the comforts that his domesticated life brings. Earl and Roy have a malevolent boss in B.P. Richfield. Sherman Hemsley, a man who made his career in situation comedy beginning with his *All in the Family* spin-off, *The Jeffersons*, voices this heartless Triceratops. As the archetypical scoundrel, Richfield will stop at nothing to get the 'We Say So Corporation' ahead, and he is often the antagonist for Earl and his environmentally conscious oldest son. On the home front, mother-in-law Ethyl Phillips provides another type of antagonism for Earl, consistently referring to him as "Fat Boy." She is one of very few older dinosaurs as the show explains in an episode called "Hurling Day." Initially dinosaurs did not live past the age of 72 and were instead hurled bodily into a tar pit, by their loved ones or, in the case of old females, by their sons-in-law. However, during the course of the episode, Robbie finds that "throwing Grandma off a cliff" would be a "waste of a perfectly good old lady" and she becomes a semi-regular fixture in the Sinclair home. Voiced by television veteran Florence Stanley, Ethyl brings wisdom to the home while indulging her grandchildren in their challenges to the ways of the world.

In a wink at the long tradition of giving pun and descriptive names to stock characters, the names of the characters of the show add another dimension of meaning. Michael Jacobs points out, "All the character names are fossil fuel names:" Sinclair, B.P. for British Petroleum, Richfield, Hess, and Phillips ("Prehysterical"). The connection is natural — Sinclair Oil even has a dinosaur for its logo, beginning in the 1930s when Sinclair's advertising department found that the crude oils that made the best fuels were "mellowing in the ground during the Mesozoic era when dinosaurs populated the earth" (Evolution). The real Earl Sinclair was the financial manager of the firm and the brother of company founder Harry Sinclair (Success). "Earl" is also a pun name as it recalls the word "oil." The name "Ethyl" is a reference to ethyl alcohol. The dualism of the character names reinforces one of the underlying themes of the show — the danger of corporate greed and its environmental impact. One can laugh at the antics of Richfield, but one cannot forget that B.P. is the name of an oil company. After the oil catastrophe and environmental devastation of 2010, the company's name carries even more weight as a potential environmental adversary.

With the central family and the "wacky neighbors" established, the situation comedy is up and running. The show is in many senses a regular sitcom, with family struggles, heartwarming moments, and big laughs. The fact that the characters are dinosaurs only layers meaning onto the traditional family television show format. "What I wanted to do was to be able to tell contemporary stories using the dinosaurs as a frame of reference," says Michael Jacobs. Jacobs reflects, "My feeling was that we were going to be able to write for this character things that you just couldn't write out of the mouth of human beings" ("Prehysterical"). Having dinosaur characters, played by sophisticated puppets, allowed for an outsider perspective. Clearly, they are meant to be us in every sense but they are also not us — they are dinosaurs with drives and habits that define them as such. For example, in the episode, "I Never Ate for My Father," Robbie faces his own reluctance for killing and eating another creature. Earl drags him off to the swamp to catch and devour some smaller animal. In their battle of wills over the issue, they succeed in getting consumed by a larger creature. The consumption of one character by another is a staple of the Henson comedy catalog and is revisited here, bringing father and son closer together. Inside the monster's belly, they finally have a serious father-son talk. Through their earnest conversation, Earl realizes that he disagreed with his father just as often as Robbie disagrees with him. Through this conversation, father and son are brought to a new level of understanding and mutual respect. Of course, this is not *Leave It to Beaver*, and the characters are not in the patriarch's den. The saccharine sweetness of the father-son reconciliation sickens the beast that has consumed the pair. He demands that they stop being so affectionate because it turns his stomach. The Sinclair men lay it on extra thick and force their way to freedom by making the monster literally lose his lunch.

During the first season of *Dinosaurs*, the family unit and its changing dynamic are the focus with the five principal episodes introducing characters and conflicts. These episodes also allow for playfulness in the writing, particularly with regard to the television format. The presence, or perhaps omnipresence, of television in the characters' lives allows writers to indulge in a form not foreign to Muppet fans — parody. *The Muppet Show* and *Sesame Street* regularly made parodies of popular television programs with "Pigs in Space," "Veterinarians' Hospital," and "Monsterpiece Theatre" as popular examples. The *Dinosaurs* universe is able to employ this type of parody at an even faster pace because the characters themselves are watching the television and can change the channel with the click of the remote control. References to classic television fare with a dinosaur twist come in the form of "Mr. Ugh," a caveman living in the stable of a dinosaur. The caveman moves his mouth in a manner reminiscent of the infamous peanut butter treatment to produce the same effect on *Mr. Ed*.

Another program that has repeated play on the Sinclair family TV set is

"Ask Mr. Lizard," a reference to the educational science program *Mr. Wizard's World*. Education is not so much the aim on the dinosaur version of the program but rather, to put it mildly, destructive discovery. One episode of the show within a show features Mr. Lizard explaining how a rocket works to his young assistant Timmy. Mr. Lizard instructs the lad to put his head inside the rear end of the rocket. The camera sees only Mr. Lizard's reaction as the rocket ignites. He then turns off to presumably the location of his television crew and says glibly, "We're gonna need another Timmy." This catch phrase is one eagerly anticipated by both Earl and Baby when they watch the program. The destruction of the character Timmy recalls one of the early "outs" of Muppet writers where, to end a sketch, characters either consume one another, explode, or sometimes both. Another *Dinosaurs* television program that calls upon this classic Muppet destructiveness is "Totally Hidden Predator." In a format that recalls both *Candid Camera* and *TV's Bloopers and Practical Jokes*, the show's premise is to video record ordinary dinosaurs in their daily lives when they encounter the totally hidden predator. One woman encounters the predator at the Laundromat while another man chuckles when his job interview turns out to be with the predator. Both get consumed, and the home audience just laughs along with them.

Television parody runs at two levels on *Dinosaurs*. The inclusion of the Dino News Network, or DNN, with anchorman Howard Handupme, another joke name as he is a more traditional television style puppet with the performer's hand inside the character, and Dinomusic Television (DTV) with its noisy content, including Robbie's favorite band, Lyzzard Skyzzard, is merely the icing on the satirical cake. The show itself is a parody of television sitcoms with the requisite family moments and misunderstood situations. "Dinosaurs arrived at a really interesting time on television. At this point, comedy was flourishing and ABC had their TGIF evening," says Michael Jacobs ("Prehysterical"). At several points, the show even makes reference to the network with its own version, the Antediluvian Broadcasting Company. Airing on Fridays and intermingled with other family comedy fare like *Full House* and *Family Matters*, *Dinosaurs* was situated to appeal to both children and adults, with messages that spoke to both audiences.

The ability of puppet characters to appeal to audiences of every age is one that the Muppets rely upon, and this ability always allowed Jim Henson and his associates to create puppetry that spoke on many levels, perhaps in spite of the immediate identification of puppets as child's play. *Dinosaurs* was well aware of the perception that puppets are for children and should not be taken seriously and successfully skewered it throughout the series. In an episode called "How to Pick Up Girls," Baby is watching a televised children's program, with puppet characters made of socks. Earl is reading a newspaper, not watching the show. As the socks interact, he begins to pay attention. When Fran comes in, he tells her to watch the show, saying that it is actually funny. She tells him, "That's for kids." Earl replies, "Yeah, you'd think that because they're puppets so the show seems to have a children's aesthetic." He then turns his attention to a different camera, facing directly out to the television viewers, and continues, "Yet the dialogue is unquestionably sharp-edged, witty, and thematically skewed toward adults." He raises his eyebrows playfully for the home audience's benefit. Fran once again rejects the program while Earl insists, "I'm telling you it works on two levels." Fran's final response is, "They look like puppets; I'm not watching." One can only wonder how often the same dialogue played out across America during TGIF's broadcast as families watched the evening's programming.

Of course, the characters on *Dinosaurs* looked like no other puppets seen on television at the time. Technologically complex and realistically detailed, the characters drew more upon the film work of the Henson Company than its television heritage. Jim Henson had done larger than life characters on *Sesame Street* in the form of Big Bird and the monsters of *The Muppet Show*. He had been using full body puppets since the 1960s. Brian Henson says, "Early in [my father's] career, he did ads for La Choy Chinese food and he did the La Choy dragon. The La Choy dragon just wrecks everything and I think my dad always thought that was a hilarious character and I think maybe it had the roots in that" ("Prehysterical"). However, when the show was going to move forward for actual production, the design of the puppets headed in a different direction, away from the cartoonish early sketches devised by Jim Henson and Kirk Thatcher. Brian Henson reflects, "Jim would probably have wanted big, unbelievable costumes. We took the 'big' idea and made these amazing animatronic cartoon-like faces" (Bacon 78). The puppets became high-tech in keeping with the developments the Company had made during its film work on *Teenage Mutant Ninja Turtles*, a process fully explained in *No Strings Attached* by Matt Bacon. The use of radio control was key to making believable performances on the part of the lead characters. "Really we were taking what was film techniques from our Creature Shop in London and bringing it out here and trying to do a very ambitious animatronic show on a weekly basis," says Brian Henson ("Prehysterical"). Most of the principal characters were the result of the combination of three performers — one puppeteer controlling the facial expressions and mouth movements, a second performer inside the dinosaur body providing the physical performance, and a third voice actor. Allan Trautman, the puppeteer for Fran's facial expressions and mouth movements, says, "It all has to do with letting the audience know what the character is thinking and feeling at any given time" ("Prehysterical"). This multiple performer technique has been a staple of puppetry and part of the Henson toolbox for years, with puppeteers collaborating to produce a single character or performance. The Gorgs of *Fraggle Rock* were performed in a similar fashion, but were much more in keeping with the broad, animated feel of that early La Choy Dragon. The Sinclair family had a more "natural" range of emotions and movements.

The complexity of the "Performance Control System," the name given to the Creature Shop's technology for bringing the dinosaurs to life, coupled with the rigors of television made for a dynamic filming environment. The capabilities of television and puppetry were being stretched to the extreme by the grand design of the show. The tricks of the trade that were developed by the Creature Shop were being refined into an art itself. Henson says of the experience, "The performers went from playing 'chopsticks' on a piano to appearing in an orchestra" (Bacon 79). Allan Trautman explains, "The character became the lead after a while. The performers will know how to feed that character. The coordination between us wasn't so much of an issue anymore. There was this third thing we were all relating to" ("Prehysterical"). This "third thing," the creation of a believable character with a life of its own, enabled *Dinosaurs* to head off into bolder directions as the show developed.

If the first season of the show establishes the world in which the dinosaurs live and allows the performers to gain virtuosity with the puppets, the second season begins to introduce topics that had been important to Jim Henson and his colleagues for years. In "Endangered Species," Earl purchases a pair of delectable creatures called graptolites for a traditional anniversary dinner with Fran. Robbie befriends the graptolites, getting their aid with his homework assignment about why dinosaurs rule the earth. The philosophical foodstuffs guide Robbie to reconsider his initial response — "because we're big." They ask him what the value is in being the biggest and if it comes with responsibility. The creatures reveal to Robbie that they are the last of their kind. Once Earl and Fran eat them, they will be extinct. Robbie urges Earl to let the graptolites live, but his father has already sold the pair to Mr. Richfield. They are the boss's favorite food. Robbie tries an alternate tactic with the animals themselves, asking them to procreate. At first, the pair is taken aback, with the female saying, "He's never even asked me to dinner." As the time for Earl to give them to Mr. Richfield approaches, he has begun to see how important the creatures have become to his son. Though Richfield consumes the creatures, they have successfully produced offspring that get discovered by the Sinclairs. The episode concludes with Earl looking at the young graptolites and saying, "I promise." His sense of responsibility, however short-lived, is a positive step for this dominating character and provides a glimmer of hope for the dinosaurs' future.

This first environmentally themed episode of *Dinosaurs* actually recalls an earlier appearance by the Muppets on *Saturday Night Live*. The Muppets of *NBC's Saturday Night* look vastly different from the familiar fuzzy faces of *Sesame Street* and other Henson appearances. They occupy a world called "the Land of Gorch" and are scaly, bloated, and licentious. They were a definite break from the established Muppet look, and their topics are aimed solidly toward adults. When Candice Bergen hosted *Saturday Night Live*, on November 8, 1975, the Land of Gorch featured a storyline similar to the later *Dinosaurs* episode. The king of Gorch, Ploobis, and his concubine have just finished eating a delicious creature called a "glig." Ploobis craves another helping but learns that there are only two left, a male and a female. Ploobis is mystified how this could have happened as he recalls that the prairies of Gorch used to teem with herds of gligs. The species has been depleted through over hunting, either for the consumption of their delicious flesh or for the creation of garments from their pelts. Clueless about how to solve the glig population problem, Ploobis and his minion Scred turn to the Mighty Favog, a talking stone idol, for advice. The Mighty Favog asks if the problem is business, sports, or personal. Ploobis turns to Scred, who says, "Ecological, oh Grand Polluter." "It's gonna cost, ya," says the Mighty Favog. "Two chickens and a glig." Scred deposits the chickens and the female glig, who screams in terror the entire time, into the base of the idol, and they share their problem with the wise statue, ending with the query, "How do we get more gligs?" The Mighty Favog replies, "You should have said somethin' sooner," and returns the female glig to the duo, where she is released by Ploobis with the command, "Go forth, be fruitful, and multiply." There is no promise to the glig that the future will be different, but by Gorch standards, it is a step in the right direction.

Issue based programming became a staple for *Dinosaurs*, with episodes that touch on contemporary events and commented on society. "You could attack issues much better when the characters are not quite human," says Michael Jacobs (*Prehysterical*). In an episode called "What 'Sexual' Harris Meant," Fran's friend, Monica Devertebrae, an apatosaurus who is only seen as a head and neck coming through a window, is looking for a job and applies to work as a tree pusher at We Say So. She is initially rejected for the job because of being a female until Mr. Richfield realizes what an effective worker she is. Unfortunately, she gets fired from her job when she rejects her supervisor, Al "Sexual" Harris (voiced by *Seinfeld*'s Jason Alexander), and his double entendre advances. Rather than accept the termination of her job, Monica decides to go to trial to contest her dismissal and is seen on national television. Charlene and Fran are horrified as Monica is made to look like the guilty party in the situation. She is asked a series of humiliating and sexist questions before the episode ends with Monica unemployed. She wonders what she did it all for but takes heart as Charlene gets fired up at her own realization that a female will have to fight for her rights to get a great job. The young dinosaur believes that equal rights are in females' grasp and says, "How long could it possibly take?" The episode aired in December 1991, a mere two months after Anita Hill underwent similar scrutiny when she accused Judge Clarence Thomas of sexual indiscretion and harassment in the workplace.

Continuing to work on two levels, *Dinosaurs* presented an episode entitled, "A New Leaf," with Robbie discovering a plant in the forest that makes dinosaurs happy. Earl, Charlene, and even Mr. Richfield begin doing "plant" and increasingly forgetting about their cares and responsibilities. The plant is obviously a mild drug, similar to marijuana, and adults appreciate the humor of the situation and the drug references, including Mr. Richfield's rendition of "Purple Haze." The episode ends after the formerly hopped-up Sinclairs hit rock bottom and destroy what remains of the plant to save themselves. Then someone calls, "Cut! That's a wrap." The camera pulls back to reveal the Sinclair household "set" with television crew (all dinosaurs) going about their duties. Robbie turns to the camera and says, "Hi, I'm Robert Sinclair. You know me as Robbie on the adult-themed mega hit *Dinosaurs*." He walks through the shot and is congratulated for the good episode by the camera operator who says, "But it got a little preachy toward the end." Robbie agrees with him and says that drugs are a major problem in society, destroying lives, dividing families, and leading to heavy-handed preachy sitcom episodes like the one he just taped. He continues to talk to the camera about an "epidemic in television today that threatens the very fiber of the comedy we hold so dear." He is referring to the pressures to present anti-drug themed episodes because one show has already done so. He continues, "Now they're even going after the younger shows. I mean, we've only been on a year and here I am talking to the camera." He implores the viewer to say to no to drugs, to stop television endings like the one he is currently presenting. The anti-drug message is clearly broadcast to the young audience, but the tongue-in-cheek reason for the cessation of drug use is fun for the adult viewer.

Riffing on another popular television convention, the "mini-series," was a two-part episode entitled "Nuts to War," in which the two-legged dinosaurs go to battle with the "four-leggers" on the opposite side of the swamp. The cause of their conflict is as trivial as many wars even today: the unavailability and rising cost of pistachio nuts. The characters use the differences between two legged dinosaurs and four legged dinosaurs to create momentum for their cause, inventing the clever slogan, "We Are Right." Of course, the journalists covering the altercation abbreviate the slogan to the acronym, "W.A.R." Like the television framework employed in "A New Leaf," the mini-series format prevents the characters from actually going to battle, preserving their role as actors in the drama. Brian Henson reflects, "That's what the series always allowed us to do was to talk about issues that are hard to do with people. It's hard to do a good episode about prejudices within our society or bigotry. It's tough with actors. Very, very easy with dinosaurs" (*Creatures*). The convenient place of dinosaurs on the top of the food chain replicates a social hierarchy that places Western ideas and ideals at the top, with anything and anyone else subverted to a less important stature, capable of being consumed.

Another episode, "Swamp Music," introduces mammals as more than just food for the dinosaurs. Robbie learns that mammals have their own culture, music, and way of life. He goes with his wayward buddy Spike to the swamp to hear some music at a mammal club. He is entranced by the sound and wants to expose dinosaurs to the amazingly soulful singing of his new mammal acquaintances. The music, however, is stolen by "The Lizard," as the mammal characters call dinosaurs, and made into soulless bubble-gum popular music, claiming that only a dinosaur can sing about the experience of a mammal in a way that will be accepted. The ridiculous idea that a dinosaur crooner can sing a song called "I'm a Mammal" with any degree of believability should astound the viewer. The reference is to the early days of rock and roll music, when African-American artists' compositions and style were stolen and used to promote mainstream, Caucasian artists. Despite feeling betrayed by "The Lizard," the mammals realize that their music can appeal to a broader audience and decide to make their own recording label, completing the parallel to the early days of Motown. Bob Young remembers, "That was what was fun about the show is to just go all over the political map and attack everybody. Attacked right wing, attacked left wing. Attacked atheists, attacked religionists, attacked everybody and we were able to get away with it because, 'It's just a puppet show'" (*Creatures*). The same ethos fuels contemporary shows such as *Family Guy* and *South Park* where everyone's beliefs end up, by turns, looking both foolish and wise, and the controversy can be excused by the characters being cartoons. The degree of success of these programs to dismiss their opponents varies, by program and by issue, while *Dinosaurs* really only brought on true controversy as it was concluding its four-year run.

From the beginning, the writing on *Dinosaurs* possessed foreknowledge of what became of these mighty, globe-dominating creatures. As any school child knows, dinosaurs went extinct; for what reason is still a mystery. From the very first shot of the debut episode, the uncertainty of the dinosaurs' continued dominance is called into question. In the opening of the premiere, DNN newsman Howard Handupme reports, "A meteor three times the size of Earth is heading towards us in a collision course that will result in the extinction of all life on the planet." He pauses to receive a note, much in the tradition of the Newsman on *The Muppet Show*, and reports, "This just in: no, it's not." Earl, who has been watching the television broadcast, says, "Oh good." Even in the wake of catastrophic news, the dinosaurs are fairly dismissive of the possibility of their demise. Throughout the show, various hints at the outcome of the dinosaurs' reign on the planet are dropped, always humorously. Even a second season compilation episode entitled "The Clip Show" addresses the extinction of the creatures and posits a similar outcome for the planet's current dominant species. The framework for the clip show is a documentary hosted by Sir David Tushingham, a human paleontologist onsite at a dig, who hopes over the course of the documentary to explain dinosaur life and to answer the question, "Why did these immense creatures who ruled the world for millions of years end up as decorations on children's pajamas?" Various clips examining the foibles and fun of the televised dinosaurs attempt to answer the question, ultimately shedding no light. At the conclusion of the episode, Tushingham summarizes the dinosaurs' disappearance, blaming "their own failure to adapt to a changing planet" and "their tiny, embarrassingly small brains." He considers whether the same fate could befall humankind and dismisses the possibility, saying "We humans are clearly capable of learning from the past and avoiding such devastating ecological demise. Compared to the dinosaurs, we may be short but we are not short sighted." The documentary ends and two workers approach Tushingham with bags of trash and asks where they should dispose of them. He replies, "Just dump them anywhere," and the pair spills the trash all over the dig site. Even within the reflective spectrum of the scientist, humanity also seems to fall short of its own seemingly noble ideals.

If the ending of "The Clip Show" has ominous undertones, the conclusion of the series leaves no room for doubt. The final episode of *Dinosaurs* was written by Kirk Thatcher and is called "Changing Nature." It features a series of environmental catastrophes that lead to the decimation of the planet. Bob Young remembers, "We knew we wanted extinction and we proposed that to the network and we got some resistance from that. The network felt that that was going to be very hard for the younger viewers to take, especially the idea that the Baby would die" (*Creatures*). Despite the network's misgivings, the episode was produced. It begins with the Sinclair family, and all of

Pangaea, waiting for the annual return of the bunch beetles, as well as their consumption of the cider poppies that have been growing wildly. There is televised hoopla, similar to the Macy's Thanksgiving Day Parade, as the dinosaurs await the beetles in their colorful display. When one beetle finally does arrive, Charlene befriends him and leads him to the swamp where he is supposed to mate. It is the larva of the beetle that eats the poppies, so mating should not be delayed. When Charlene and the beetle, Stan, arrive at his mating ground, they are horrified to see that it has been leveled to erect a building housing "Fruit Co," makers of fine wax fruit and a division of the We Say So Corporation. Charlene meets a dinosaur groundskeeper who tries to spray poison on Stan, saying that he has been killing beetles to keep them out of the mechanisms at the factory. The episode has echoes of "The Invasion of the Toe Ticklers" from *Fraggle Rock*, in which the Gorgs' garden gets overrun by foul-smelling flowers because Ma Gorg wants to stop the fuzzy creatures, dubbed "toe ticklers" by Mokey Fraggle, from congregating on the young flowers. She orders Junior to spray poison on the flowers to kill the bugs. Mokey takes one of the creatures that she has befriended to safety in the caves of Fraggle Rock. By the end of the episode, the toe ticklers have transformed into beautiful creatures, "purple sproingers," that consume the flowers and make the Gorgs' garden lovely once more. Mokey reflects on their relief at the consumption of the smelly plants, saying, "Those Gorgs may be large but they sure don't see the big picture." The Gorgs never realize that the purple sproingers have the same appetites as the toe ticklers and do not connect their actions to the problems that have plagued them, truly prototypical *Dinosaur* thinking.

The consequences of the removal of a species for *Dinosaurs* are much more dire. Charlene turns to the television news to explain what has happened. For the first time, Earl takes notice of the situation and attempts to hush his eco-political daughter's mouth. When she complains about "progress for progress's sake," he defends it, holding up the development of "microwave toast" as a win for progress. His argument is weak but his passion is strong, and he catches the eye of Mr. Richfield, who has been getting flack for the public relations nightmare that the bunch beetle situation is causing. Richfield recruits Earl to be the spokesperson for the company, and together they launch a campaign to cease the rapid growth of the cider poppy — covering the planet with a defoliant, "botanical bye-bye juice" to kill cider poppies. Of course, it kills all the rest of the planet's plant life, so Richfield decides to create rain clouds by dropping bombs into volcanoes. He thinks that the resulting rain will cause new plants to grow and their problem will be solved. The cloud cover from the volcanoes turns out to be too thick for the sun to penetrate;

as Howard Handupme reports, it will take "tens of thousands of years before it clears up."

The world is getting colder, but We Say So is doing fine, profiting from the misery it has caused. Mr. Richfield tells Earl that people are buying "We Say So heaters, We Say So blankets, We Say So old-fashioned hot cocoa mix" and that the company is going to have the "best third quarter in history." Earl fears it will be the last third quarter in history. Mr. Richfield gives an impassioned speech, saying "Boo hoo, it's raining acid, there's a hole in the ozone, you're hurting Flipper. Bunch of tree-hugging pantywaists! They're always standing in the way of progress. And it's our job to pave right over them." The shortsightedness of Richfield's reply echoes, and it continues to be echoed by many a politician, eager to solve the problem of increasing fuel costs, for example, by introducing another problem with repercussions that will be felt by subsequent generations.

Earl returns to his family, who are huddled together around the television, wearing parkas and shivering. He apologizes to them and says, "It's so easy to take nature for granted because it's always there and technology is so bright and shiny." Baby is confused by the events of the past week and wants to know what has happened. In a beautifully sad statement, Earl tells him that he has done a bad job taking care of the world and that he does not know what will be left for Baby or his brother and sister. Baby asks his father what will happen and Earl, unable to come up with an answer, says, "I'm sure it will all work out okay. After all, dinosaurs have been on this earth for 150 million years and it's not like we're gonna just ... disappear." The camera pulls back to reveal the snow covered ground outside the Sinclair home. The show concludes as it began in the premiere episode, with Howard Handupme reporting the end of the world. He announces that it is getting colder and then says, "Good night." After a long pause, he concludes, "Goodbye."

Brian Henson says, "It's not the way you would normally end a show, but there wasn't anything that much normal about the series anyway. We were always trying to choose really big choices. You know, when we were handling an issue or problem, we would try to do it in a very, very BIG dinosaur-y way. So this was a very big dinosaur-y way to finish the series" (*Creatures*). Thatcher reflects, "We thought it would be important to kind of show the extinction, at least foreshadow it" (*Creatures*). The episode is heart wrenching, particularly Baby's failure to understand what is going to happen. Though the characters do not die on screen, the viewer knows their fate. They can also imagine that a similar fate might befall humanity, particularly in light of the present state of ecological flux. It would be interesting to show this episode now, in an era where climate change and political denial of it have become a talking point for educators, scientists, commentators, and legislators. Perhaps it would give them pause.

With such a final ending and after four seasons of production, *Dinosaurs* reached its conclusion. It won an Emmy Award in 1991 for Outstanding Art Direction for a Series and earned three Environmental Media Awards, one of which was for the final episode (Awards). More importantly, it helped to show that the Jim Henson Company could survive the loss of its founder. The company was even expanding to include a second Creature Shop in Los Angeles. "The end of *Dinosaurs* was the beginning of the L. A. shop," says Brian Henson (Bacon 108). Films such as *Babe* and *The English Patient* garnered the shop numerous awards, including the 1996 Academy Award for Best Visual Effects (Bacon 136) for *Babe* in which they produced the "most realistic animals ever built by the Creature Shop" (Bacon 185). The tradition of innovation continued as the Jim Henson Company embraced new and developing technology such as motion capture and CGI. The extinction of *Dinosaurs* was not the extinction of the artistic energy that the series had generated. This continuity and continuation must have been what Jim Henson wanted; the dedication title on the first episode of *Dinosaurs* conveys it best, "In loving memory of Jim Henson whose creative genius made this series possible." Now, twenty odd years later, the Company continues to explore those possibilities.

Works Cited

Bacon, Matt. *No Strings Attached.* New York: Macmillan, 1997.
"Creatures with a Cause: The Issues of *Dinosaurs."* DVD Bonus Feature. Interviewees Kevin Clash, Brian Henson, Kirk Thatcher, Bob Young. Buena Vista Home Entertainment, California, 2007.
Dinosaurs- The Complete First and Second Seasons. Rec. 1991–1993. DVD. Perf. Bill Baretta, Kevin Clash, Brian Henson, Allan Trautman, Steve Whitmire. Buena Vista Home Entertainment, California, 2006.
Dinosaurs-The Complete Third and Fourth Seasons. Rec. 1993–1995. DVD. Perf. Bill Barretta, Kevin Clash, Brian Henson, Allan Trautman, Steve Whitmire. Buena Vista Home Entertainment, California, 2007.
"Invasion of the Two Ticklers." The Muppets *Fraggle Rock-Complete Second Season.* Rec. 1984. DVD. Perf. Dave Goelz, Kathy Mullen, Karen Prell, Jerry Nelson, Steve Whitmire. 20th Century–Fox Home Entertainment, California, 2006.
"Prehysterical Times: The Making of *Dinosaurs."* DVD Bonus Feature. Interviewees Bill Barretta, Brian Henson, Michael Jacobs, Kirk Thatcher, Allan Trautman. Buena Vista Home Entertainment, California, 2006.
Saturday Night Live-The Complete First Season. Rec. 1975–1976. DVD. Perf. Dan Ackroyd John Belushi Chevy Chase Jane Curtain Garrett Morris Laraine Newman, Gilda Radner. NBC Studios Inc., New York, 2006.
Sinclair History. Sinclair Oil Corporation. 2011. Web. 29 Aug 2011.

Exploring the Alien Other on *Farscape*: Human, Puppet, Costume, Cosmetic

Sherry Ginn

TV Guide called *Farscape* the best science fiction show (then) on the air and ranked it #4 on its list of "The 30 Top Cult Shows Ever." During its four-year run, it won two Saturn awards, and its male and female actors garnered numerous "best" nominations. Unfortunately, that did not stop the Sci-Fi Channel from canceling the series at the end of its fourth season. Produced by Jim Henson Productions and Hallmark Entertainment, *Farscape* combined human actors with puppets, animatronics, spectacular visual effects, and superb scriptwriting in a storyline that combined action-adventure and romance and broke many of the so-called conventional rules of science fiction (Bassom; Nazzaro). These attributes ensured that it would find both male and female fan support. As stated on the Creature Shop website, "Jim Henson's Creature Shop has developed and created a breakthrough in animation with the patented Henson Digital Puppetry Studio, a powerful system that allows ... [an] exceptional base of performers and creators to work their magic with CG characters." This use of puppets and animatronics in combination with human actors on *Farscape* allowed for the exploration of a common theme in science fiction and fantasy—the Alien Other.

This theme generally examines what it means to be human by placing some type of "Alien" being in close proximity to said humans. The Alien's attempts to understand humanity serve as a stark contrast to the reality of human behavior. All versions of *Star Trek*, according to Daniel Leonard Bernardi, explored "humanness" in comparison to either a member of an alien species (the Vulcans Spock on the original series and T'Pol on *Enterprise*), an android (Data on *The Next Generation*), a changeling (Odo on *Deep Space Nine*), or a reclaimed Borg (Seven-Of-Nine on *Voyager*). *Babylon 5* had humans and aliens mix extensively, and part of the recurring plot revolved around how the human-alien hybrid Delenn learned to navigate the human as well as her original species' worlds. Adilifu Nama proposes that alien species are meant to represent African-Americans/Blacks or other marginalized people in (generally) contemporary American society. *Farscape* continued this trend but extended it further than usual: in *Farscape* John Crichton was not the only alien. John Crichton is meant to serve as "us"— the audience. That is, Crichton serves as the window through which we observe the wonders and dangers of the universe beyond Earth and even upon Earth as well. However, as Jes Battis has noted, Crichton cannot be considered a representative of the audience. The audience is not white, male, middle-class, highly educated, able-bodied, and heterosexual (24–25). Yes, Crichton is Alien to the beings that inhabit the section of the universe in which he is marooned; however, the other members of Moya's crew can also be considered Alien as well. Each member of Moya's crew as well as other important recurring characters represents and illustrates the Alien Other. Otherness is explicitly or implicitly presented through the use of costumes and cosmetics, especially for the female characters, as well as by using puppetry, animatronics, and computer-generated imagery (CGI).

Some Introductory Words on Crew and Plot

The core crew of Moya, a biomechanoid spaceship, in addition to Crichton consists of a male Luxan warrior named D'Argo, a female Delvian priest named Zhaan, a male Hynerian royal named Rygel XVI, and a female member of a space police force called the Peacekeepers, named Aeryn Sun, who is not on the ship by choice. By the end of the season they will have also acquired a female Nebari thief named Chiana (Chi for short). Moya is bonded with a Pilot who provides navigational control and other functions necessary for the ship's survival. The crew's adventures throughout the series reflect each character's desire to return to his/her home world or to find a new home in which to live in peace. New beings will join the crew at various times during its four season run, and some original members will be lost.

Crichton is truly an Alien in this universe as no one has ever encountered *Homo sapiens* before. Crichton looks like a member of a species called Sebacean; however, it is quickly established that he cannot be Sebacean because his body contains bacteria unknown in this part of the universe. The prisoners are surprised that he does not have internal translator microbes, which are injected into all beings at birth here. Crichton is an anomaly, but he does prove useful during the prisoners' attempt to keep from being re-captured ("Première" 1.1). Unfortunately for him, Crichton's exit from the wormhole results in the death of the pilot of a spaceship that crashes into his Farscape module. That pilot just happened to be the younger brother of Bialar Crais, the captain of the Peacekeeper command carrier charged with breeding the Leviathan.

Crais will be a recurring character throughout three seasons of *Farscape*. The first season finds him disobeying orders and pursuing Crichton, even into the Uncharted Territories. Crais is determined to kill Crichton and avenge his brother's death. Eventually Crais will realize that the death was accidental, and he will become an unlikely ally for Crichton as Crichton attempts to elude the Sebacean-Scarran hybrid Scorpius, who is determined to acquire Crichton's knowledge of wormholes. Crais will "bond" with the hybrid spaceship Talyn, and together they will sacrifice themselves in an unsuccessful attempt to kill Scorpius ("Into the Lion's Den Part II: Wolf in Sheep's Clothing" 3.21). As a Sebacean, Crais looks and sounds human. Other Sebaceans on the series are the loyal but ever enigmatic Lieutenant Braca (male), the ruthless and diabolical Commandant Grayza (female), and Officer Aeryn Sun, Crichton's love-interest (also female).

Female Characters Rule, in Cosmetics and Costumes

Few television programs, even those on the major networks during prime time, can boast as many strong and fascinating female characters as *Farscape*. The cast consists of seven outstanding, recurring female characters, eight if one considers that the ship is female. The three major characters are Aeryn, Zhaan, and Chiana. The others include Jool, Noranti, Sikozu, and Grayza. Grayza is ruthless, Chiana is promiscuous and amoral, Jool is very young but not so innocent as we believe, Noranti is very old and not above sacrificing everything for the greater good, Sikozu is trying to save her reputation and hide a secret, Zhaan is spiritual, and Aeryn is trying to find a place for herself in a new world, having lost everything from her old one. Moya is the ship upon which the characters live. She is alive and sentient, although her interactions with the crew are mediated by Pilot.

The costumes of the regularly-occurring female characters on *Farscape* consist of make-up rather than prosthetics or animatronics. Although by no means always true, the majority of the recurring female characters on *Farscape* are made-up to look Alien. Actually it might be more correct to state that their make-up was designed to make them look exotic and Alien, rather than human (the one exception is Aeryn). Series creator Rockne S. O'Bannon was determined that the characters would look Alien, and that their "Alienness" would not merely be the result of a prosthetic forehead, á la *Star Trek* (Simpson and Hughes). Two of the female characters for whom this is especially true are Chiana and Zhaan. Chiana's skin and hair coloring are grey with black and white over- and undertones, as is her clothing. She moves her limbs as well as her head in a stylized, jerky fashion and typically walks and stands with her arms extended from her body and bent at the elbows. Zhaan is painted blue and also wears blue clothing. Her head is shaved as well as her eyebrows, a process that apparently distressed the actor portraying the part, so much so that Virginia Hey cites it as one of the reasons she asked to be written out of the show during the third season ("Self-Inflicted Wounds Part II: Wait for the Wheel" 3.4).

Jool joins the crew during Season Three ("Self-Inflicted Wounds, Part 1: Could'a, Would'a, Should'a" 3.3). She is rescued by Moya's crew from kidnappers who plan to sell her bodily organs and, as with the others, she joins the crew hoping to return to her home one day. Jool is portrayed as very young and inexperienced. She is also the most traditionally feminine of the female crew. Jool's make-up is feminine as are her sexy costumes. Her hair, and she has a lot of it, is blonde, unless she is angry or frightened, and then it turns bright red. Her name is a play on the word "joule," a unit of energy, hence the change in hair color when she is angry or frightened.

Noranti, the Old Woman, is a refugee, rescued by Moya after the destruction of Scorpius' command carrier at the end of Season Three ("Dog with Two Bones" 3.22). She thinks in cosmic terms, beyond the personal, unlike everyone else on Moya, with the possible exception of Crichton, who walks a very fine line trying to have Aeryn while saving the galaxy from his very own wormhole knowledge. Noranti is a very spiritual being, much like Zhaan. Because she possesses a third eye, she can see things of which other people are unaware. Noranti is a doctor and becomes the ship's healer after Jool leaves. Noranti's make-up consists of very large ears and a third eye, both of which serve to make her distinctive among the other characters. In keeping with her age, her face is rather wrinkled, especially around her eyes and mouth.

Sikozu of the Kalish race happens upon Crichton at the start of Season Four literally: her ship crashes into his ("Crichton Kicks" 4.1). Sikozu is actually a member of a Kalish underground resistance group dedicated to overthrowing Scarran rule on her home world and her section of the galaxy. We are led to believe that her ability to defy gravity and to regenerate limbs is either endogenous to her species or the result of genetic engineering to help in her resistance activities. What we learn at the very end of the series is that she is actually a bioloid, created specifically for helping the resistance movement destroy the Scarrans ("We're so Screwed Parts I, II, and III" 419 — 421). Sikozu's costume is rather skimpy, and she also has long red hair.

Men Wear Make-Up, Too

Female characters are not the only ones to appear only in make-up and prosthetics on *Farscape*. One notable example of a male character is D'Argo, one of the original members of Moya's crew. The crime for which D'Argo was imprisoned on Moya was murder. His brother-in-law Macton killed his sister rather than having to face the disgrace of her marriage to a Luxan, a race inferior in all ways to the Sebaceans in Macton's belief. Macton then framed D'Argo for the murder and managed to convince D'Argo that he really might have killed Lo'Lann while in a Luxan Hyper Rage.

D'Argo's make-up evolves quite a bit over the course of Farscape's four seasons, partly because of the detail but also because of time. In the beginning it took almost three hours to apply the make-up; eventually the cosmetic department was able to reduce this to about 90 minutes. According to information presented in Simpson and Hughes' *Illustrated Companion* to Season One, D'Argo is "pure prosthetics" with no animatronics at all (130). Anthony Simcoe's size contributed to D'Argo's look: D'Argo is a member of a warrior race and thus should be imposing in stature. Slight changes to his look occurred between Seasons One and Two when the make-up department darkened his coloring and removed his contact lenses. In addition to his height, D'Argo's face is distinctly alien. He possesses a nose somewhat like a lion as well as overarching orbital bones that meet between his eyes and extend to his ears. Extending from his chin are thick but short tentacles covered with tattoos. Likewise he has long, thick snake-like tentacles extending from the top of his head; these are also covered with tattoos. D'Argo does have facial hair — mostly it extends down the sides of his face, like overgrown sideburns, with a small moustache-like section extending from his nose alongside his lips to join with the facial "sideburns." D'Argo's costumes are dark red. He wears a quilted tunic over pants and boots. These costumes are a combination of Celtic, Viking, and Samurai (Simpson and Hughes 96).

As Battis notes, Luxans are similar to Klingons, as all warrior-type characters in science fiction seem to fit into that stereotype (35–36). Nevertheless, D'Argo is much more complex than Klingons are generally depicted on the various *Star Trek* series. D'Argo introduces himself to Crichton as Ka or general. We only learn later in the series that he is not a general, only a regular soldier. Indeed, he is really a very young Luxan, basically an adolescent, with an adolescent's barely controlled rages and emotional ups-and-downs. Yet, as the series progresses, we find that D'Argo is a rather sensitive soul and is capable of great wisdom and insight. By the time we get to the unfortunate outcome of *The Peacekeeper Wars*, D'Argo has become Crichton's best friend and confidant (after Aeryn), and Crichton and Aeryn name their son in his honor.

Creating Hybrids, with Cosmetics and Costumes

The Scarrans are not necessarily the scariest species one can encounter in this part of the universe, but they are coming close to it. Their species is primarily reptilian, and there are different subspecies that look slightly different from the others. The Scarrans are bent on domination and gradually become aware of how important John Crichton is to the Peacekeepers, especially to the Scarran-Sebacean hybrid Scorpius. Scorpius is the result of the rape of a Sebacean woman by a Scarran male. The Scarrans believe that Scorpius is one of them and that, although he is rather powerful in the Peacekeeper command structure, he is actually working for their best interests. Little do they realize that Scorpius is playing a double-game and only pretending to be a Scarran spy. Scorpius wants nothing more than revenge against the Scarrans for the rape of his mother and the brutal way in which he was raised. His relentless pursuit of Crichton throughout Seasons Two through Four reflects his determination to obtain the wormhole knowledge and create a weapon that would destroy the Scarran Empire, once and for all. It is only in the sequel made-for-television miniseries that the Scarrans and Sebaceans realize that the wormhole weapon will destroy the entire universe (*The Peacekeeper Wars*).

Scorpius is not the only hybrid being in the *Farscape* universe. There is also Jothee, the son of D'Argo and his Sebacean wife, Lo'Lann. After Lo'Lann's murder and D'Argo's incarceration, Jothee is sold into slavery. Eventually D'Argo, with the crew's help, finds Jothee, who is torn between love for his father and pride that his father finally rescued him and hatred for the fact that his father did not protect him in the first place. Jothee and Chiana eventually give in to the passion they feel for one another; unfortunately, Chiana and D'Argo had been engaged in a sexual relationship for some time prior to Jothee's rescue. D'Argo forgives them for their indiscretion, and he and Chiana resume their sexual relationship by the series' end.

Thus one way in which the producers of *Farscape* create the Other or the Alien is in the hybridity of Scorpius, Jothee, and Talyn. Both Scorpius and Jothee are part Sebacean, and Talyn is bred using Sebacean/Peacekeeper technology. The Sebaceans/Peacekeepers are adamant about out-breeding and contact with other species. Although rape has always been a tactic used as a means of provoking fear, the Peacekeepers do not resort to using such a terrifying weapon. Extended contact with non–Sebacean species is anathema to them and could result in an affected commando being declared "irreversibly contaminated," for which the penalty is death. Indeed, Aeryn Sun is forced to join the escaped prisoners in "Première" because Crais suggests that contact with John Crichton has led to her contamination. Her reaction then and throughout subsequent episodes illustrates how horror-stricken she is at the thought that she can never go home again, except to die.

Scorpius is barely tolerated by many of the Sebaceans with whom he comes into contact. He is tolerated because of the knowledge that he possesses about the Scarrans and the fact that he is ruthless and merciless. His physical appearance is ghastly. *Farscape*'s costumers created a black leather suit that molded to the actor's shape. His entire body is encased; only a small part of his face is visible, and it is made to look extremely thin, with shrunken cheeks. Being part Scarran he needs heat for bodily comfort. Unfortunately, being part Sebacean means that too much heat will send him into a heat delirium and he might die. He cools himself by inserting cooling rods directly into his brain. Despite Scorpius' role as the villain in *Farscape*, he is attractive to a certain type of female, and his sexual acts with Natira and Sikozu are decidedly on the kinky side.

Puppets, Animatronics, and CGI

Another way in which the Alien Other is illustrated on *Farscape* involves the use of animatronic creatures created and constructed by Jim Henson's Creature Shop (JHCS). Best known as the creators of the Muppets, the Creature Shop also designed puppets for *Sesame Street*, as well as special digital effects and animations for other films and programs. According to their website,

> The Creature Shop was responsible for the conceptual designs of *Farscape*, including two of the show's main characters, which were animatronic and prosthetic aliens. Other main characters were enhanced with prosthetics made by the Creature Shop, and JHCS designed and created all of the aliens throughout the four seasons of the series, as well as the television mini-series ["Farscape"].

The two recurring animatronic and prosthetic aliens on *Farscape* are Pilot and the Hynerian, Dominar Rygel XVI. Partly puppet in combination with actor-provided voices, each provides an example of what the Henson Company refers to as digital puppetry. Such a technology,

> provides immediate real-time performance of 3-D generated characters by a puppeteering system, allowing an unprecedented level of spontaneity, quality and interactivity. Through a combination of proprietary hardware and software, the technology allows a puppeteer (or one primary puppeteer plus assistants) to perform live 3-dimensional computer graphics. The system consists of three major components: mechanical hand controls, a control computer, and a digital puppet workstation which renders the live on-screen image of the character. The final product allows animation to be composited into computer-generated environments in real-time. The system's animated characters are therefore also "directable," like actors, and the animation can thus be used as a pre-visualization tool as well as a final product ["Farscape"].

Use of puppets such as these allows for the human actors to more easily act with and react to the character rather than the usual blue-screen, digitally-inserted material in post-production (although *Farscape* uses this process as well, and it is a testament to the acting ability of the cast and the technological brilliance of the production crew that the graphics of the series are as brilliant and outstanding as they are).

Moya is the ship upon which the crew lives. Her species is Leviathan. They are sentient beings, who feel emotions as well as pain. Leviathans can be male or female. This fact indicates that Leviathans can breed, and probably via some form of sexual activity. However, we also know that Moya was enslaved by the Peacekeepers and impregnated in a special breeding program; we can only speculate as to how Moya was bred. Her impregnation had occurred prior to events at the start of *Farscape*, and her pregnancy was in stasis when she attempted to escape, along with D'Argo, Zhaan, and Rygel. When D'Argo removes her control collar in the episode "I, E. T. (1.4), to avoid being tracked by the Peacekeepers, the fetus is released from stasis and gestation begins. Moya's actions from that point on in Season One revolve around her pregnancy, and even though the crew is perfectly capable of engaging in horrific behavior when it suits their goals, all are unanimous in treating Moya with care, so that her offspring will not be harmed. The offspring is born at the end of Season One and it is a hybrid being, looking like a Leviathan but covered with weaponry. Aeryn is given the privilege of naming the "child," who is male, and she names him Talyn, after her father. Scenes in which Moya and Talyn are viewed in totality were created with CGI.

Leviathans are unable to communicate without the aid of a "companion/controller," and such beings are referred to as Pilots. These Pilots are physically bonded with the ship in a symbiotic fashion. Moya's Pilot is referred to as, and it is assumed that Pilot is, male. Pilot can communicate directly with the ship and then alert the crewmembers to Moya's opinions or emotions about certain aspects of a particular mission. However, sometimes Moya refuses to "discuss" her actions with the crew, especially when Talyn is in danger. Pilot is actually a very young member of his species (which is never identified), deemed by the Elders of his world to be unready for bonding with a Leviathan. His desire to see the stars up close rather than from his home world pushed Pilot to accept the Peacekeeper Velorek's proposal to bond with Moya prematurely. Pilot suffers for his impatience and his un-natural bonding with Moya, although eventually they do bond naturally.

The Pilot puppet began its genesis in the early 1990s and underwent many changes before the final design was approved. Voiced by actor Lani Tupu (who also portrays Crais), seven puppeteers control the model, which is eighteen feet long and seven-eight feet tall. Pilot looks like a crustacean, and its head was deliberately made to resemble the Sydney (Australia) Opera House (Simpson and Thomas 2001). Pilot has multiple arms that are capable of regenerating if removed, and its bottom half consists of a number of neuro-tendrils that connect with Moya in order to aid in her survival and control her many functions. Pilot's character in the early seasons of *Farscape* illustrates its youth and inexperience. Later actions serve to illustrate that Pilot is maturing, along with Moya. That does not mean that Pilot is not above banishing the crew when they become too irritating. At one time or another each crew member irritates the others; one of the most irritating and infuriating of the crew is Rygel.

Rygel was deposed by his cousin, Bishan, and incarcerated by the Peacekeepers for more than 130 cycles. That one fact means that he knows almost as much as anyone about Moya's interior spaces and is able to put that knowledge to good use when he, Zhaan, and D'Argo escape from the Peacekeepers. Having been Dominar (King) of six hundred billion subjects, Rygel is used to being waited on hand and foot. During his incarceration, he learns how to survive, and some of his tactics include lying, stealing, diplomacy, and negotiation. All of these traits come in handy as he tries to find his way home to reclaim his throne.

One early example of Rygel's cunning and duplicity occurs in the episode "The Flax" (1.12). Moya's transport pod is captured by an invisible net that floats in space; this net is monitored by Zenetan pirates who salvage the ships caught therein. While trying to find a way to free Aeryn and Crichton, who are in the transport pod with a dwindling amount of air, Rygel plays a board game with the pirate captain. Rygel allows the pirate to win the game and bears the humiliation of the loss. Yet these actions stall for time, thereby allowing D'Argo to rescue the stranded crewmembers before their oxygen supply runs out. After the pirates leave, Rygel tells the others about how hard it was to play so badly! Another example of Rygel's skill at diplomacy occurs when Crichton is accidentally marooned on a planet that was once ruled by the Hynerian Empire ("Jeremiah Crichton" 1.14). When Moya finally arrives after months of searching for Crichton, Rygel is greeted as the royalty that he is. Unfortunately, one of Rygel's ancestors left a device on the planet that drains power, meaning that it is impossible to communicate with off-worlders or for any spaceship to leave the planet once it has landed. Rygel is able to disarm the device and along the way break the power wielded by the village's High Priestess.

Rygel's incarceration for more than 130 cycles included torture at the hands of the Peacekeeper Durka. Believing Durka to be dead relieves some of Rygel's anxiety, his post-traumatic stress. However, Durka is not dead and is able to continue his torture of Rygel, albeit psychologically, in a couple of episodes early in the series ("PK Tech Girl" 1.7; "Durka Returns" 1.15). Rygel has his revenge, however, when he kills Durka and carries Durka's head around as a trophy ("Liars, Guns and Money Part II: With Friends Like These..." 2.20). Although Rygel becomes less imperious and more considerate with time, he never loses the skills that make him who he is.

Not surprisingly the people who controlled the Rygel puppet, and the man who voiced him, Jonathan Hardy, consider Rygel to be the star of the series (Simpson and Thomas (2001) 110). The puppet is about two feet tall, but it takes anywhere from three to seven people to actually control the puppet, in addition to the actor who provides his voice. Rygel is shaped somewhat like a triangle in that his bottom is bigger than his top; however, his head is flat. His mouth is rather large with wide lips, and it is generally held in a frown. His eyes are large and somewhat cat-like; his nose consists of two nostril-like slits sitting between his eyes. Each eye is adorned with a large tuft of hair over it that extends from the inner eyelid to the outer edge of his pointed ears, which extend outward from his head, contributing to its flatness. Rygel's personal habits are generally disgusting to Crichton and the rest of the crew: he eats enormous quantities of food and, when nervous, he farts helium, with the expected results on the voice of anyone in the vicinity. To facilitate his travel within the ship and on away missions, Rygel has a throne-sled that allows him to hover above the ground at eye-level with much taller species.

Conclusion

Given their roles within this universe, each of the characters on *Farscape* can be considered an "Alien Other." Zhaan is a peace-loving priest who killed her lover. She was imprisoned for that crime. Chiana is a rebellious teenager living in a society that demands conformity of its citizens. She was banished from her home world and, not only that, but infected with a sexually-transmitted disease that her species hoped she would spread throughout space. Sikozu is a bioloid, a biological android, created to be a resistance fighter, to infiltrate enemy space and effect destruction. Jool is a young woman intent on learning about other cultures and other worlds, and she is so determined to do so that she violates her ethical principles and brings dishonor upon herself. D'Argo labels himself Ka, general, even though he does not deserve the title. He mated with a Sebacean woman, whom he loved, but his love led to her death at the hands of her brother. Their hybrid son Jothee was sold into slavery and then used as a pawn in Scorpius' bid to obtain Crichton's knowledge of wormholes. Jothee is torn between love and hatred for his father; one way he gets revenge on his father is to engage in sexual relations with his father's lover. Dominar Rygel XVI was deposed by his cousin and then incarcerated to prevent any attempts to regain his throne. Physically very small, but with an ego at least 100 times larger, Rygel uses the skills he learned as a King to negotiate for goods and services for Moya and her crew. Rygel even grows beyond his earlier selfish and egotistical ways to save Crichton and Aeryn from death. Aeryn Sun is a Peacekeeper by birth and training but is forced to join Moya's crew after her irreversible contamination by contact with John Crichton. Eventually she falls in love with Crichton and chooses to remain with him rather than return to Sebacean/Peacekeeper society. The way in which she obtained her promotion to Peacekeeper pilot, by reporting her lover's sabotage, was decidedly un–Peacekeeper-like behavior and set her at odds with her comrades even before she met Crichton ("The Way We Weren't" 2.6). The fact that Aeryn participated in the murder of Moya's first Pilot also set her apart from other Peacekeepers. That Pilot's death led to the current Pilot being chosen to bond with Moya. However, Pilot was considered too young by the elders on his planet to be given a ship. He was unwilling to wait the required time they deemed necessary and jumped at the chance to Pilot a Leviathan even though that decision resulted in the murder of Moya's original Pilot. Obviously, by virtue of being human, John Crichton is an Alien Other to the beings in this part of the universe.

Crichton certainly wishes to return home after emerging from the wormhole. The fact that he looks like a Peacekeeper terrifies many beings with whom he comes into contact. They automatically assume that he is a Peacekeeper, and this fact allows him to masquerade occasionally. However, his lack of knowledge about life in this part of the universe generally advertises his "otherness" very quickly. Tara Parmiter, in her essay on "The American Journey Narrative in the Muppets Movies," notes that one of the defining themes of the Muppet movies is the journey, and that theme is readily apparent in *Farscape* as well. As she states, "we will find our selves when we find our home, and that search for home is the true purpose of our travels" (139). Like Kermit, John Crichton "may leave the swamp, face difficult hardships, and triumph over evil forces, but he does not return home; he creates a home" (139). Despite the differences between Moya's crew, which not only include species differences but philosophical differences as well, these beings grow to care deeply for one another. Zhaan loves Aeryn so much that she sacrifices part of her psychic energy to bring her back from the dead ("Season of Death" 3.1), and she eventually sacrifices herself to save Moya and the others ("Wounds" Part II). Moya and the beings that reside on her become a family. Although discussing the Muppets, another Jim Henson product, Ben Underwood notes that one can join a family by sharing a dream (14). Each of the core members of Moya's crew — Crichton, Aeryn, D'Argo, Rygel, Zhaan, Pilot, and Chiana — bond with one another, finding a place that they can call home aboard a sentient spaceship. They create a family; as a matter of fact, they create a family that is much like the blended family of contemporary Western society. In their case, the family members came from a wide variety of species, yet they manage to find common links that allow them to bond with each other and reinforce the emotional ties that they create.

Crichton learns by the end of the miniseries that he can never return home, to Earth; doing so will lead to the Scarrans and/or the Peacekeepers finding a way to Earth to find him. Crichton thus bears the weight of our world on his shoulders because the knowledge he possesses about wormholes is more valuable than all the precious metals and stones in the universe. Once Crichton makes the decision to destroy the wormhole that leads to Earth, he is at peace. He has saved the planet; he gets the girl, and if O'Bannon's stories are to be believed will live (reasonably) happily ever after.

Works Cited

Bassom, D. "The Aurora Chair: Interview with David Kemper." *Farscape: The Official Magazine*, No. 2 Sept./Oct. 2001.: 20–24. Print.
Battis, Jes. *Investigating Farscape: Uncharted Territories of Sex and Science Fiction*. London: I. B. Taurus, 2007. Print.
Bernardi, Daniel Leonard. *Star Trek and History: Race-ing toward a White Future*. New Brunswick, NJ: Rutgers University Press, 1998. Print.
"Farscape." *Jim Henson's Creature Shop*. The Jim Henson Company. n.d. Web. 29 May 2012.
Garlen, Jennifer C., and Anissa M. Graham, Eds. *Kermit Culture: Critical Perspectives on Jim Henson's Muppets*. Jefferson, NC: McFarland, 2009. Print.
Ginn, Sherry. *Our Space, Our Place: Women in the Worlds of Science Fiction Television*. Lanham, MD: University Press of America, Inc., 2005. Print.

Nama, Adilifu. *Black Space: Imagining Race in Science Fiction Film.* Austin: University of Texas Press, 2008. Print.
Nazzaro, Joe. "Out on the *Farscape.*" *StarLog 285.* April 2001: 36–40. Print.
O'Bannon, Rockne S. (2003, May). "Horizons." *Farscape: The Official Magazine*, No. 12. May 2003: 21–29.
Parmiter, Tara K. "The American Journey Narrative in the Muppets Movies." Jennifer C. Garlen, and Anissa M. Graham, eds. *Kermit Culture: Critical Perspectives on Jim Henson's Muppets.* Jefferson, NC: McFarland 2009. 129–141. Print.
Simpson, Paul. *Farscape: The Illustrated Season 4 Companion.* London: Titan Books, 2003. Print.
_____. *Farscape: The Illustrated Season 3 Companion.* London: Titan Books, 2002. Print.
_____. and David Hughes. *Farscape: The Illustrated Companion.* New York: Tom Doherty Associates, 2000. Print.
Simpson, Paul, and Ruth Thomas. *Farscape: The Illustrated Season 2 Companion.* London: Titan Books, 2001. Print.
"*TV Guide* Names the Top Cult Shows Ever." *TV Guide* 29 June 2007. Web. 25 Sept. 2011.
Underwood, Ben. "How to become a Muppet; or, the Great Muppet Paper." Jennifer C. Garlen, and Anissa M. Graham, eds. *Kermit Culture: Critical Perspectives on Jim Henson's Muppets.* Jefferson, NC: McFarland 2009. 9–24. Print.
"Who's Jool?" *Farscape: The Official Magazine.* 3 (2001) 46.
Yeffeth, Glenn. *Farscape Forever! Sex, Drugs and Killer Muppets.* Dallas, TX: BenBella Books, 2005. Print.

VIDEOGRAPHY

The Dark Crystal. Dir. Jim Henson, Frank Oz. Jim Henson Productions. 1982. DVD.
Farscape: The Complete Season One. The Jim Henson Company, 1999–2009. Episodes cited from Season One include: "Première;" "I, E. T., PK Tech Girl;" "The Flax;" "Jeremiah Crichton;" "Durka Returns." DVD.
Farscape: The Complete Season Two. The Jim Henson Company, 2003. Episodes cited from Season Two include: "The Way We Weren't;" "Look at the Princess Part I: A Kiss is But a Kiss;" "Look at the Princess Part II: I Do, I Think;" "Look at the Princess Part III: The Maltese Crichton;" "Liars, Guns and Money Part I: A Not So Simple Plan;" "Liars, Guns and Money Part II: With Friends Like These...;" "Liars, Guns and Money Part III: Plan B." DVD.
Farscape: The Complete Third Season. The Jim Henson Company, 2004. Episodes cited from Season Three include: "Season of Death;" "Self-Inflicted Wounds Part I: Could'a, Would'a, Should'a;" "Self-Inflicted Wounds Part II: Wait for the Wheel;" "Dog with Two Bones;" "Into the Lion's Den Part II: Wolf in Sheep's Clothing." DVD.
Farscape: The Complete Fourth Season. The Jim Henson Company, 2004. Episodes cited from Season Four include: "Crichton Kicks;" "We're So Screwed Part I: Fetal Attraction;" "We're So Screwed Part II: Hot to Katratzi;" "We're So Screwed Part III : 'La Bomba.'" DVD.
Farscape: The Peacekeeper Wars. Dir. Brian Henson. Perf. Ben Browder, Claudia Black. Hallmark Entertainment and the Jim Henson Company, 2004. DVD.

Muppet Memes, or Beaker Conquers YouTube

Anissa M. Graham

The story of Jim Henson's entrée into television is a staple of discussions regarding his influence on the medium. *Sam and Friends* (1955–61) ran for about five minutes, but it brought Henson and his innovations in puppetry to an audience not only of children but of their parents. Today, *Sam and Friends* can be seen as the cornerstone of many later Muppet projects, especially *The Muppet Show* and most recently the Muppets' adventures on the internet. A typical *Sam and Friends* segment might parody television shows from news broadcasts to Westerns, or the segment might feature an off-beat rendition, usually lip synched, of popular tunes like "C'est Ci Bon" or "I've Got You Under My Skin." This combination of parody and musical remix would become a part of the *Muppet Show* formula as well. Notable television parodies, like "Veterinarian's Hospital" and "Pigs in Space," helped to make Miss Piggy the star she is today. Musical remixes offered audiences the opportunity to rethink the meaning behind protest songs as in Season Two's rendition of Buffalo Springfield's "For What It's Worth." This number featured woodland creatures attempting to hide from a group of less than savvy hunters; what was once a Vietnam War protest song was now a send up of the image of hunters as gun happy nuts. Other song remixes were simply for the fun of it, as in the Season Three number, "Lullaby of Broadway," featuring a pig chorus in the Arctic complete with singing walrus. The Muppets continued to use parody/homage as they moved to the big screen; *The Muppet Movie, The Great Muppet Caper,* and *The Muppets Take Manhattan* each adopt generic formulas to explore common Muppet themes of family and community.

As the Muppets moved into the 21st century, they adapted those tried and true *Sam and Friends* elements and brought them to the internet. Beginning in 2008, the Muppets—in this case Muppets refers primarily to members of the original *Muppet Show* cast with some select additions from later productions—have been posting videos to YouTube that both participate in and respond to the rapidly evolving digital world. Their participation in various forms of social media, including Twitter, Facebook, and especially YouTube, on the surface seems quite new but is really a return to ideas and styles put in place by Henson more than 50 years ago.

When Jim Henson began playing around with puppets and television in the late 1950s, television was still quite new, and the creators of television programming were making up the rules as they went along. Today a show featuring puppets on a major commercial network, like ABC, CBS, NBC, or Fox, would probably never get a pilot, but in those early years puppets were all over television screens, particularly on local stations. For modern viewers, local programming in many markets has been reduced to news broadcasts with the occasional exception made for real estate and cooking shows, but in the 1950s and 1960s, local television stations provided much of their own content. Some of that content was directed at children, and nearly every children's show had puppets. Puppets were so common on television at the time that longtime children's show host, Chuck McCann, would claim "Puppets really launched television" ("Local Kids' TV").

Henson's work on television altered the way people thought about using puppets; his decisions to remove the puppet theater and use the television screen itself as the arch of his stage, to create puppets out of softer materials for greater expressive potential, and to use rods instead of strings for arm movements lead to programming that highlighted the fact that puppets really didn't need the human element to be entertaining. Puppet faces filled television screens in much the same way as human faces. As Jane Henson explained in a discussion of Jim's way of using puppets "Because it [the puppet face] was an abstracted face, the puppet was really able to do super human things or beyond human or get away with anything" ("Henson's Place"). With the coming of the digital age, the possibilities for puppet faces and human ones expanded thanks to advances in cameras and editing technology. Just as the television screen altered and expanded the possibilities of the movie screen to be "a magic window you could open onto any world you chose," the computer screen would allow the creation of fantastical worlds not only by professional entertainers but by the average consumer as well (Finch 18).

YouTube, perhaps the internet's most popular site for video sharing, began "broadcasting" in May of 2005 ("Timeline"). Designed to allow users to post original content, the platform quickly blossomed into a loose social network where users responded to other users and where traditional media outlets began to reach audiences on a one to one basis. YouTube has channels that highlight the work of diverse users; examples of this diversity can be seen in The Vatican Channel launched in June of 2005 ("The Vatican") and the channel Raw Radiant Health launched in June of 2009 by Natasha St. Michael, a proponent of raw food and natural health ("Raw Radiant Health"). Amazingly, according to data collected by YouTube administrators, users post one hour of video every second ("Statistics"). This wealth of content could mean that particularly entertaining content gets lost in the data flood, but thanks to YouTube's connections to multiple social networks viewers can share their impressions of videos via Facebook, Twitter, Google, or email. They can also like or dislike a video, post comments about a video, and load video responses.

All this internet chatter can lead to a video becoming viral or even memetic. In her essay on YouTube memes, Limor Shifman makes clear the difference between a viral video and a memetic one. Viral videos spread "to the masses via digital word-of-mouth mechanisms *without significant change*" while memetic videos are popular and lure "*creative user engagement* in the form of parody, pastiche, mash-ups and other derivative works" (author's emphasis, Shifman 190). In addition Shifman points out that viral videos are often used for marketing purposes and therefore are products of professional media outlets; memetic videos, on the other hand, are products of an "amateur" participatory culture (190). The Muppets' presence on YouTube presents an interesting problem for scholars like Shifman as these videos engage viewers on both levels with the Muppets as both commercial and creative participants.

YouTube would seem like an ideal place for the Muppets as it promotes memetic videos, but the Muppets entered the mix three years into YouTube's run. Part of this delay has to do with the ownership of the Muppet characters themselves. In 2004 the Walt Disney Company purchased the rights to *The Muppet Show* cast and to the cast of the children's television series *Bear and the Big Blue House* from the Henson family and the Jim Henson Company (Susman). The Muppets are managed through a Disney subsidiary, The Muppets Studios. Eager but not entirely sure what to do with their new product, in 2005 the new owners tested the marketability of their acquisition with a made for TV adaptation of *The Wizard of Oz* entitled *The Muppets' Wizard of Oz.*

That same year at least a portion of the Muppet cast made their appearance on the internet: resident critics and curdmugeons, Statler and Waldorf, began appearing in a series of film review webisodes for Movies.com (also owned by Disney). *From the Balcony* was designed to "reconnect these characters with twenty- and thirty-somethings who grew up with them and are now heavily online, as well as introduce them to new fans" according to David Spingarn, then Director of Creative Business Development (qtd. in Fritz).

The segments featured Statler and Waldorf examining new film releases in a manner meant to put viewers in mind of Gene Siskel and Roger Ebert's long-running *At The Movies*. Posted biweekly, the webisodes ran from June 2005 to September 2006; other Muppet characters appeared as reviewers, including Johnny Fiama and Pepe the King Prawn ("From the Balcony"). Currently the *From the Balcony* webisodes are unavailable, and a web search using the keywords "from the balcony" pulls up a movie review site, www.fromthebalcony.com, *not* hosted by Muppets.

Statler and Waldorf's appearances aside, the Muppet presence on the internet was muted at best. The launch also in 2005 of www.muppets.com provided a platform for new content, which included a backstage tour of the Muppet studio. Clicking on the doors in the studio brought fans into Muppet dressing rooms and gave them access to character biographies, downloadable images, and a series of short videos, the "Muppet Elevator Tapes." These "tapes" followed various cast members as they moved in and out of the studio elevator. The site has been revamped in the light of the 2011 film *The Muppets*. While the site's earlier incarnation shared some of the basic elements of the revamp, the new Muppets.com aggressively promotes the new film and its accompanying products. The web presence of the Muppets then seems to fall into a fairly standard niche for professionally generated web content, and that niche is promotional either of themselves as in the Muppets.com website or of sister organizations as in the Movies.com webisodes.

The year 2008 marked a shift in Muppet content as new Muppet material began appearing on YouTube; without a particular show, film, or DVD to promote, these short videos allowed the Muppets to return to their *Sam and Friends* roots exploring music and pop culture through the medium of internet video. Interestingly, the Muppets featured most prominently in these new videos were not Miss Piggy or even Kermit, but Fozzie, Sam the Eagle, Beaker, Animal, and the Swedish Chef. These early postings differed from those by Statler and Waldorf because they were posted by the Muppets themselves. With these videos the Muppets became part of the user-generated content community as opposed to the professional one.

The early videos posted by Fozzie, Gonzo, and Beaker were memetic in nature. Fozzie posted under the name wockawockabear; his video is one of many following the exploits of Tyson, the skateboarding dog. While the video is ostensibly about the astonishing feat of a skateboarding dog, it also offers the Muppets an opportunity to comment on this new world of online video that they've joined. Rowlf observes "Isn't there more to life than just *online* videos?," a comment voiced by many a parent whose child became obsessed with uploading videos to YouTube (wockawockabear). Like a good memetic video, Fozzie's post led to another post, this time by Rizzo the Rat. Posting as rizzratz, Rizzo's video belongs to the class of YouTube videos that focus on "those who made a colossal mistake that to their misfortune was videoed" (Shifman). In it, Rowlf attempts to duplicate Tyson's skateboarding feats with less than positive consequences; Rizzo ends up calling for a veterinarian after Rowlf wipes out. Together these videos had only about 500,000 views after being online for nearly three years, hardly an impressive showing. Still the Muppets kept producing content, creating more popular videos featuring Beaker and Gonzo.

Gonzo's video harkens back to earlier musical remixes. As Jennifer C. Garlen points out in "Gonzo, (the Great) Cultural Critic," Gonzo's function among the Muppets is as purveyor of both high and low culture. His video offering, "Classical Chicken," is more subdued than his typical *Muppet Show* performances, but it does blend elements of high culture ("The Blue Danube-Waltz") with lowbrow humor; Camilla lays an egg literally in the midst of the performance. Again the Muppets participate in memetic video sharing by responding to another YouTube video, "[Original—FULL VERSION] Dominoes Techno Chicken—FUNNY." The performance begins with Gonzo addressing the audience: "Greetings, culture lovers and citizens of the World Wide Web" (weirdowhatever). Here we see Gonzo's firm belief in the high culture aspect of his performance. He then introduces his "orchestra"—eight chickens with Camilla as the lead performer. Gonzo directs the chickens, called Pitch Perfect Poultry, in a lively rendition of Johann Strauss' "The Blue Danube Waltz" or "Free Range Strauss." The performance screen is divided into nine boxes familiar to fans of *The Brady Bunch* and *Hollywood Squares*. Those boxes initially seem to be discrete units as Gonzo moves into each unit to turn on the camera for the chickens. Once the song begins, however, the viewer discovers it's not only the fourth wall that Gonzo breaks. In her excitement, Camilla lays an egg that drops onto Gonzo's head and bounces out of range of the cameras (weirdowhatever). After that the feathers fly, as the chickens sing ever more quickly, and the bottom row of chickens begin invading one another's space. More popular than Fozzie or Rizzo's postings with nearly five million views by May of 2012, "Classical Chicken" proves Henson's ideas regarding the entertainment power of a puppet face on a small screen.

Often Gonzo's sharpest critic on *The Muppet Show*, Sam the Eagle (patrioticeagle) posted a tribute to America in late June of 2008, "Stars and Stripes FOREVER!" As was typical of his *Muppet Show* appearances, this video has Sam attempting to create a performance he deems of cultural value only to have it go awry. The video begins with a common Sam theme—hyperpatriotism. Sam walks into view of the camera decked out in a red, white, and blue sash and stops in front of a large American flag. Speaking to an unseen Muppet collaborator offstage, he complains that he would like to post the video only to the American portion of the internet. Upon realizing he's now on camera, Sam shifts to his introduction, claiming this video offers "something never before seen on the internet. Culture. Morality. And patriotism" (patrioticeagle). This intro is familiar to Muppet fans as it follows a pattern similar to the one adopted by Sam on *The Muppet Show* in his introductions of the wholesome singing duo, Wayne and Wanda. Sam's patriotic display turns out to be a musical performance much like Gonzo's "Classical Chicken." The chorus, featuring Beaker, Bobo, Animal, the Swedish Chef, and an unnamed Muppet penguin, sing "Stars and Stripes Forever" in front of a shifting background of images meant to evoke Americana. The images include a waving American flag, a soaring bald eagle, a running herd of bison, and a hot dog. Further emphasizing the patriotic theme are the costumes worn by Beaker, Animal, Bobo, and the penguin; the only one not in patriotic garb is the Swedish Chef. Beaker's costume evokes the painting *The Spirit of '76*; he even sports a bandage around his head just as the fife player in the painting does. Animal's costume is also reminiscent of the figures in the painting in particular and of the 18th century in general. Bobo sports a tri-corn hat and scarf, and the penguin wears a powdered wig.

While zany on its own, the video takes a turn for the weird midway through when Sam returns to recite the Preamble to the U.S. Constitution as the chorus continues to sing, now joined by two chickens. His recitation goes smoothly until he reaches the portion of the Preamble that mentions the establishment of justice, and he forgets what comes next; he quickly recovers by inventing his own ending. The people apparently have joined together to "keep the world safe from *weirdos*" (patrioticeagle). At this point Animal has a solo, and Sam gives up in disgust, realizing perhaps that the weirdos have already won. The video ends with Crazy Harry entering the scene with a dynamite plunger that when depressed triggers a series of explosions. Sam's patriotic tribute has succumbed to Muppet madness. Linked as it is to the 4th of July holiday, this video with nearly two million views has proved more popular than the skateboarding dog videos but not as popular as Gonzo's.

In 2010, Sam returned with another tribute to America with a rendition of "American Woman" by Canadian rockers the Guess Who. Instead of relying on others for this tribute, Sam will sing himself. Sam's other attempts at singing have not gone well; of note is his performance of "Tit Willow" from Gilbert and Sullivan's *The Mikado* in Season One of *The Muppet Show*. The video begins with Sam deriding the content of YouTube as a "steady stream of ninjas, sleeping puppies, and pirated music videos" before offering his own musical tribute with the aid of a karaoke machine (MuppetsStudio). It's clear that Sam, unlike other participants in karaoke, is unfamiliar with the song he is about to perform as he is shocked to discover that the lyrics encourage the American woman to stay away. By emphasizing pop culture influences from outside the boundaries of the continental U.S., the video skews Sam's vision of a unified American identity and touches on another type of humorous video common to YouTube, the social comment video. Views for this video were also close to the two million mark.

More popular videos come from characters the audience can barely understand, namely Beaker and the Swedish Chef. Beaker's posting is a response to another video entitled "Bach Bach Bach" and features an enthusiastic interpretation of "Ode to Joy" from Beethoven's Ninth Symphony. Utilizing a six box screen similar to the one employed by Gonzo in "Classical Chicken," Beaker sings and plays the timpani and violin. All goes well until his singing breaks a water glass and the metronome that has been helping him keep time speeds up, causing Beaker to play the violin so quickly that it catches on fire. The video ends as many a Muppet Lab sketch ended with Beaker the victim of a series of painful injuries, from smoke inhalation from the burning violin to concussion from a falling lamp and finally to electrical shock from overloading a plug. This video also went viral, and its popularity lead to a nomination and People's Voice Webby win for best music entry in online film and video in 2008. The Webbys are presented by The International Academy of Digital Arts and Sciences; nominees are eligible to win two kinds of awards — one based on the assessment of the International Academy, the other based on votes from the internet community at large (*The Webby Awards*).

Beaker joined forces with the Swedish Chef in 2009 for "Habanera." Pulling as it does from Georges Bizet's *Carmen*, this video, apparently shot in a warehouse, could easily be a performance art piece by Gonzo. The camera is set at an angle giving the video an off-kilter feel. Beaker lovingly meeps to a rose in the background while the Chef borkborks in the foreground. Animal wanders through with some la, la, las. High culture isn't necessarily brought low here as much as it is rendered surreal. The video culminates with the Chef seemingly devouring Beaker, apparently having confused the lovesong with the pepper. Muppets devouring Muppets in the course of song dates back to early renditions of "I've Grown Accustomed to Your Face" in which Kermit is eaten by Yorick and "I've Got You Under My Skin" in which a larger Muppet monster eats a smaller one. What makes this consumption different from other instances of Muppet cannibalism is that the Swedish Chef only appears to devour Beaker through a trick of the camera.

In contrast to the roughly three million views of "Habanera" are the nearly twenty-seven million hits for the Muppets' take on Queen's 1975 "Bohemian Rhapsody." This video is perhaps the group's most memetic. It begins as a recreation of Queen's video only with Gonzo and his chickens filling in for Freddie Mercury and company. The video's breakout performance, though, is Animal's plaintive singing of "Mama." While in the original lyrics the speaker explains to his mother that he has killed someone, here the hard rocking Animal searches for his mommy — a family-friendly altering of the lyrics no doubt inspired by the Muppets' home with Disney. The lyrics continue to stray from the original as the Muppets make this song their own. Dr. Teeth even complains about not getting paid for their performance, and Fozzie begs to be allowed to joke instead of asking to be let go. This video celebrates the variety of the Muppet cast members from the Electric Mayhem to the singing fruit to Doctor Strangepork. The song's final lines are wholly Muppet as sung by Miss Piggy, who is reclining on top of Rowlf's piano in a nod to *The Fabulous Baker Boys:* "Nothing really matters but moi!" (MuppetsStudio, "Bohemian"). This short won both a Webby and a People's Voice Webby in the Viral category in 2010, prompting Animal to call his mother in the response video "Good News for Mama" and for Kermit to do a behind-the-scenes commentary video "Bohemian Rhapsody [Kermit's Commentary]." These self-referential responses allow the Muppets to acknowledge and mock their own success.

The Muppets, unlike other users of YouTube, don't have to wait for someone to post a comment to know how their performances went. Just as in *The Muppet Show*, Muppets give Muppets immediate feedback. In most cases, the critics are Statler and Waldorf. The conceit here is that the two old men are watching the same video we the viewers of YouTube are. Gonzo's chickens cause them to wonder just how many hits such a video would receive, prompting Waldorf to comment, "Unfortunately, not enough to kill it" (weirdowhatever). Of Sam's attempts at patriotism, the pair are "offended" and "appalled" and will, of course, be sending the video to everyone they know (patrioticeagle). Beaker's misadventures in "Ode to Joy" elicit a hope to "never see anything like it again" from Waldorf, who, after chuckling with Statler for a bit, asks him to play the video again (meepmeepmeepow). "Habanera" causes Statler to wonder what system they're running; Waldorf's response is a typical Muppet pun: "After that, I'm running away!" (MuppetsStudio, "Habanera"). These sting note comments encourage Muppet viewers to engage in their own dialogues about the videos. Comments posted by YouTube users for these videos respond to both the main video content and to Statler and Waldorf as in a posted comment to "Stars and Stripes Forever!":

"lol that almost wanted me to email this to everyone i know! O.o ROFL" (patrioticeagle). YouTube, as a component of the larger participatory culture embodied by the internet, allows the Muppets to cater to their audiences in more immediate ways than ever before.

With the release of *The Muppets* in 2011, Muppet video content on YouTube expanded to include promotional materials that crossed platforms. As Jin Kim pointed out in an article for *Media, Culture & Society* in 2012, YouTube content has shifted from user-generated to professionally generated, and cross platform videos are increasingly becoming the norm. Cross platforming involves the use of video content in more than one medium. For instance, *The Muppets* trailers were aired on television and posted on YouTube. Several trailers posted online enhance the Muppets' status as memetic masters. From "Being Green," designed to accompany *Green Lantern*, to "The Pig with the Froggy Tattoo" riffing on *The Girl with Dragon Tattoo*, these parody trailers focus on the connections this nearly 40 year old franchise has with popular culture. The trailer "Green with Envy" doesn't parody a specific film; instead, it creates an entirely new film out of *The Muppets*, a romantic comedy complete with close-ups and soft focus. The final *The Muppets* parody trailer, though, completes a cycle of memetic video production. In it, the "Green with Envy" trailer is inverted; instead of focusing on human romance, the trailer looks at the relationship between Kermit and Miss Piggy. Like the original trailer, "The Final *Muppets* Parody Trailer" breaks the fourth wall by acknowledging that it is indeed a film set in a fantasy world, not a real one. It goes a step further and recognizes that this trailer is a spoof of an earlier spoof. The metacommentary is rounded out by a string of mini-trailer spoofs involving *Paranormal Activity 3, Puss in Boots, Happy Feet 2,* and *Twilight: Breaking Dawn.* The parody trailers inspired Game Room Films to create their own dark trailer based on *Saw.* For the DVD release, a *Hunger Games* parody trailer was uploaded presenting *The Muppets* Wocka! Wocka! Valuepack as an action film.

The success of *The Muppets*—trailers, film, and DVD—means Muppet fans will be able to see more Muppet content than ever. Through their creative participation in the YouTube community, the Muppets have revitalized themselves as an international brand. Functioning as both amateur users and professional generators of internet video, the Muppets and their postings foster the sort of idealized community posited by early proponents of both the internet and YouTube itself. When asked about the longevity of his Muppets, Jim Henson said, "It's hard to say how much, how long they'll live. I think this is something we're waiting to see from the audience" (*Henson's Place*). Based on the millions of views the Muppet videos have earned, it seems likely that the

Muppets will continue for quite some time. While the means of transmission has changed from those early days on *Sam and Friends*, the laughter generated by Muppet antics has remained the same. Using the memetic model for videos, the Muppets can bring social commentary, musical remixes, and film and television parodies to a new generation of tech savvy viewers who then can continue the process of reinvention in their own video responses and original content.

WORKS CITED

Finch, Christopher. *Jim Henson: The Works*. New York: Random House, 1993. Print.
Fritz, Ben. "Guess Who's Pulling the Strings." *Variety*. 11–17 July 2005: 7. *MasterFILE Premier*. Web. 22 May 2012.
"From the Balcony." *MuppetWiki*. Wikia, n.d.Web. 24 May 2012.
Garlen, Jennifer C. "Gonzo, (the Great) Cultural Critic." In *Kermit Culture: Critical Perspectives on Jim Henson's Muppets*. Ed. Jennifer C. Garlen and Anissa M. Graham. Jefferson, NC: McFarland, 2009. 116–26. Print.
Henson's Place: The Man Behind the Muppets. Dir. David A. Goldsmith. Perf. Jim Henson, Jane Henson, Michael Frith, Frank Oz. Platypus Productions, 1984. DVD.
Kim, Jin. "The Institutionalization of YouTube: From User-Generated Content to Professionally Generated Content." *Media, Culture & Society*. 34.1 (2012): 53–67. Web. 23 May 2012.
"Local Kids' TV." *Pioneers of Television*. PBS. WBIQ, Birmingham, AL. 8 Feb. 2011. Television.
meepmeepmeepow. "Ode to Joy." *YouTube*. YouTube. 16 July 2008. Web. 25 May 2012.
The Muppet Show: Season One–Three. Dir. Peter Harris and Paul Casson. Perf. Jim Henson, Franz Oz, Dave Goelz, Richard Hunt. 1976–79. Buena Vista Home Entertainment, 2005. DVD.
The Muppets. "The Muppets 2011." *YouTube*. YouTube. n.d. Web. 25 May 2012.
MuppetsStudio. "The Muppets: American Woman." *YouTube*. YouTube. 27 May 2010. Web. 25 May 2012.
_____. "The Muppets: Bohemian Rhapsody." *YouTube*. YouTube. 23 Nov. 2009. Web. 25 May 2012.
_____. "The Muppets: Habanera." *YouTube*. YouTube. 23 November 2009. Web. 25 May 2012.
patrioticeagle. "Stars and Stripes FOREVER!." *YouTube*. YouTube. 27 June 2008. Web. 24 May 2012.
RawRadiantHealth. "Raw Radiant Health." *YouTube*. YouTube. 30 Dec. 2011. Web. 24 May 2012.
rizzratz. "Skateboarding Dog Gets Served." *YouTube*. YouTube. n.d. Web. 24 May 2012.
Shifman, Limor. "An Anatomy of a YouTube Meme." *New Media and Society*. 14.2 (2011): 187–203. Web. 22 May 2012.
Susman, Gary. "Fozzy Math." *Entertainment Weekly*. EW.com. 18 Feb. 2004.Web. 24 May 2012.
"Statistics." *YouTube*. YouTube. n.d. Web. 24 May 2012.
"Timeline." *YouTube*. YouTube. n.d. Web. 24 May 2012.
Vatican. "The Vatican." YouTube. 24 May 2012. Web. 24 May 2012.
The Webby Awards. The Webby Awards, 2012. Web. 25 May 2012.
weirdowhatever. "Classical Chicken." *YouTube*. YouTube.16 July 2008. Web. 24 May 2012.
wockawockabear. "Rolling with the Skateboarding Dog." *YouTube*. YouTube. n.d. Web. 24 May 2012.

Fandom and Nostalgia in Disney's *The Muppets*

Jennifer C. Garlen

"I'm going to go back there someday."— Gonzo the Great

Of all of Jim Henson's imaginative worlds, the most enduring and beloved is that inhabited by the central characters of the original *Muppet Show*. It is a realm populated by humans and Muppets alike, a place where normal, everyday events are juxtaposed against the antics of talking food, performing penguins, and strange creatures of every size and stripe. This bizarre but compelling world first took shape on *The Muppet Show* television series (1976 – 1981) and was further developed and revised in a trio of early Muppet films: *The Muppet Movie* (1979), *The Great Muppet Caper* (1981), and *The Muppets Take Manhattan* (1984). After Jim Henson's death in 1990, later films and television specials attempted to return audiences to the Muppets' world, but none of them enjoyed the success of the older productions, and years of ownership changes and rights wrangling kept the Muppets more or less out of the limelight. After 1999's *Muppets from Space* flopped at the box office, there would be no new motion pictures starring the Muppets for more than a decade. In 2011, audiences finally got a long-desired opportunity to return to the Muppets' world with the release of Disney's *The Muppets*. The critical and financial success of the film made it one of 2011's most popular pictures, and the movie even earned the Muppets their first Oscar with its Best Song win for "Man or Muppet."

Several factors contributed to the success of *The Muppets*, including the presence of Jason Segel as a driving force and human star and the full power of the Disney marketing machine to promote the film. Ultimately, however, *The Muppets* works because it recognizes and remains faithful to the world that Jim Henson created. It offers longtime fans, mostly members of Generation X and their well-indoctrinated offspring, a chance to return to the Muppets' world and reclaim the feelings that the original show inspired. It pointedly recognizes Muppet fandom as an essential part of its plot, and it takes full advantage of the nostalgic feelings that the Muppets arouse in adult viewers who loved the characters and films when they were young. Through its persistent references, tributes, and jokes about *The Muppet Show* and the original movies, *The Muppets* reinforces fan devotion to the Muppet world while telling its nostalgic back story in a way that makes sense to a new generation of viewers.

Fandom and nostalgia were crucial elements of the production of *The Muppets* from the start. Jason Segel, the actor and screenwriter who also served as one of the movie's executive producers, is a serious puppetry aficionado whose ongoing passion for puppets can be seen in the puppet *Dracula* musical in *Forgetting Sarah Marshall* (2008). Segel's devotion set the tone for the whole production and helped shape the contributions of co-writer Nicholas Stoller and director James Bobin. In a 2011 *Wired* article about Segel's involvement with the film, Andrew Goldman writes,

> Fixing the Muppets, for Segel, is a restorative act, bringing back the creative purity that was the hallmark of *The Muppet Show*'s five seasons on television and the three Muppet movies Jim Henson had a hand in between 1979 and 1984: *The Muppet Movie, The Great Muppet Caper,* and *The Muppets Take Manhattan*. Segel calls them "the pantheon"; he hadn't even been born when the first one was released, but he wore out the VHS copies of the films in his Pacific Palisades childhood home [178].

Other 2011 interviews with *The New Yorker, The Huffington Post,* and NPR tell the same story of Segel's self-identification as a nostalgic fan, albeit one with the unusual opportunity to make his desire for a new Muppet film become a reality.

Given Segel's perspective, it's no surprise that fandom and a nostalgic love for the original Muppet productions permeate *The Muppets*. The film's central character, a new Muppet named Walter, personifies both of these elements, and Segel has even described Walter as "an analogue" for himself ("The Muppet Fans..."). Performed by puppeteer Peter Linz, Walter is presented throughout the film as the ultimate Muppet fan. Like many of the Muppets' original fans, Walter discovers *The Muppet Show* as a child and grows up with the characters and their films. Walter collects Muppet merchandise and memorabilia, obsessively watches Muppet programs, and longs to become part of the Muppets' world. His longing is especially poignant because Walter feels out of place in his own world, and the Muppets represent an alternative space in which a square peg like Walter might finally find a home. Because Walter is also a puppet, he does not physically alter over time, a fact demonstrated by his unchanging height on the growth chart kept in the doorway of his family's home. Like his body, his love for the Muppets remains perpetually childlike and innocent. Early in the film Walter describes himself as the Muppets' "number one fan" and states that "as long as there are Muppets, for me, there's still ... hope." His faith in the Muppets is critical to the plot because it inspires Kermit and the rest of the characters to try to save the old theater and get the gang back together. Ultimately, of course, they recognize Walter as one of their own, and he lives out every fan's dream of becoming a part of the world he adores.

In opposition to Walter and Segel's character, Gary, who is Walter's human brother, stand the characters in the film who reject nostalgic love for the Muppets, particularly Tex Richman (Chris Cooper), the wealthy oil baron who intends to tear down the Muppet's old theater. Tex, cast as a villain in the Doc Hopper mold, cares only about money and "progress," and it must be noted that he also bears a strong similarity to Joan Cusack's villainess, Rachel Bitterman, in the 2002 television special, *It's a Very Merry Muppet Christmas Movie*. Like all rank capitalists in the Muppets' world, Tex is consumed by getting and spending. The film's depiction of him as a villain even made news by offending the conservative sensibilities of Fox Business Network's "Follow the Money" host Eric Bolling and Dan Gainor of the Media Research Center. The commentators derided *The Muppets* as communist and "anti-corporate" because of the character's role in the film ("The Muppets Are Communist..."). While Tex's corporate greed is certainly an important part of his personality, other elements of his makeup are equally if not more important when it comes to the movie's major themes. Tex's function as the anti-fan is symbolized by his physical inability to laugh; in other words, he is literally unable to provide the one response that Muppets exist to inspire, and therefore he cannot understand or appreciate their importance to the world. He has to hire underlings to laugh for him, a situation as tragic as it is ridiculous. Tex has no interest in nostalgia, either. To him, the Muppet studios are worth nothing compared to the oil underneath, and the Muppets are only valuable to the extent that their names can be sold for profit. When Kermit and his friends ask Tex to return the theater, he replies, "You're relics, Muppets! The world has moved on." Like Doc Hopper before him, Tex proves a difficult antagonist to convert to the Muppets' values, and it's only during the end credits that we see Tex regain his ability to laugh and subsequently return the theater and the Muppet names to their rightful owners.

Ironically, the film's other anti-fans are not human beings but other puppets, a crass coterie of opportunistic imposters called the Moopets. With Fozzie as a token member of the band to provide some semblance of legitimacy, the Moopets take advantage of nostalgic fan feeling in order to cash in for their own benefit. They have no love for the original characters they imitate, and they mistreat the vulnerable Fozzie by berating him and taking advantage of his trusting nature. Their cover of "Rainbow Connection" remade as a casino jingle is both funny and appalling, a perfect example of the commercial hijacking of fans' most cherished memories. The Moopets are debauched parodies of familiar Muppets: Miss Poogy, Animool, Roowlf, Kermoot, Janooce, and eventually Foozie. Like the Muppets, they are all puppets, except, oddly enough, for Animool, played by Foo Fighters front man and former Nirvana drummer Dave Grohl. Grungy, irritable, and foul-tempered, the Moopets recall the puppet characters of Peter Jackson's cult film *Meet the Feebles* (1989), as well as the 2002 television series *Greg the Bunny*. Much like the puppets discussed in Michael J. Berntsen's essay, "The Muppetry of Nightmares," the Moopets represent the flip side of the nostalgia and laughter normally associated with the Muppets. As Fozzie says early in the film, "They terrify me." The Moopets are everything fans don't want to see the Muppets become, and it's telling that the Moopets join forces with Tex Richman because they want to usurp the Muppets' names and replace them as "updated" version of the originals. Tex describes them as "a hard, cynical act for a hard, cynical world," suggesting that the Muppets' optimism and humor have no place in the 21st century.

The plot of the film is thus structured as a struggle between true fandom and mere commercial opportunism, with the Muppets representing an honest desire to regain their fame and success by actually deserving them. The theme of the plot translates into the larger aim of the film as a whole. *The Muppets* attempts to be a commercial success by earning the approval of the characters' most devoted fans, the real life counterparts of Walter. It works at this goal by incorporating elements that only hardcore Muppet devotees can appreciate, while at the same time providing introductions to the major characters and ongoing situations for the benefit of novices.

The Muppets themselves represent the most important territory for this two-fold approach. The core characters—particularly Kermit, Piggy, Fozzie, and Gonzo—get more exposition because newcomers need to know them to understand the basic dynamics of the group. At the same time, fans who regard them as old friends want new information about the characters, so the film provides introductions that also offer glimpses of what the gang has been up to in the years since the Muppet heyday. Kermit has become something of a Hollywood hermit, hiding in his mansion like an amphibian Howard Hughes. Piggy is the plus-sized editor of *French Vogue*, a perfect career for the porcine fashionista. Fozzie, always a sad clown, is reduced to a cover band gig in a low-rent casino, while Gonzo presides over a plumbing empire, having traded his daredevil ways for capitalist success in order to please his beloved Camilla. All of the other regulars also get their moments to shine; the film showcases The Electric Mayhem (particularly Animal), Statler and Waldorf, Rowlf, Scooter, Dr. Bunsen Honeydew, Beaker, and the Swedish Chef.

The baedeker of Muppet characters goes far beyond the usual roster, however, for the gratification of lifelong Muppet fans, and this tactic emphasizes the 2011 film as a serious, deeply conscious tribute to *The Muppet Show*. The most striking inclusion of an obscure Muppet is the casting of Uncle Deadly as one of Tex Richman's henchmen, along with the somewhat more familiar Bobo the Bear from *Muppets Tonight*. Bobo had been featured prominently in the ill-fated *Muppets from Space*, but Uncle Deadly is a true *Muppet Show* curiosity, a character who only appears in a handful of episodes of the original television series. A blue, reptilian creature with a deep voice and a penchant for the theatrical, Uncle Deadly is beloved by Muppet fans for his appearance with Vincent Price and his performance as The Phantom of The Muppet Show. Because of his sinister features, Uncle Deadly is a perfect choice for the villain's sidekick, but hardcore fan enthusiasm for the character is amply repaid when Uncle Deadly changes his allegiance in the picture's climax and aligns himself with his fellow Muppets, declaring to Richman, "Just because I have a terrifying name and an evil English accent does not preclude the fact that, in my heart, I am a Muppet, not a Moopet!" For fans, it's one of the best moments in the entire film.

In addition to Uncle Deadly, *The Muppets* also takes time to feature less familiar fan favorites like Lew Zealand, Wayne and Wanda, Sweetums, Crazy Harry, Link Hogthrob, Beauregard, Marvin Suggs, and even a quick glimpse of Bobby Benson and his Baby Band. One particularly funny bit reveals Wayne and Wanda, regaled on the original show by Sam the Eagle as "church people," locked in a passionate embrace after the theater's lights go out. It's a moment sure to delight fans who remember the straight-laced couple from the early seasons of *The Muppet Show*, even though most of the new movie's audience will have no idea who they are. Despite the unfamiliarity of such characters to casual viewers and newcomers, their presence has tremendous significance for hardcore fans. It's just not *The Muppet Show* without them, and the film's inclusion of them underscores its effort to recreate the world that fans remember and still love.

Featuring a diverse group of *Muppet Show* characters is only one of the ways in which *The Muppets* highlights its relationship to the original series. The opening of the movie explicitly evokes the television show as Gary and Walter watch it together for the first time as kids; like Jason Segel in real life, the brothers are too young to have seen the series in 1976, but they watch it on VHS. The clips and background images introduce *The Muppet Show* to viewers who have never seen it, but they also play as a nostalgic greeting to fans who can identify every sketch shown, from Peter Sellers doing his Queen Victoria impersonation to the musical number, "Mahna Mahna." Later, photographs in Kermit's office continue the roll call of memorable *Muppet Show* guest stars and sketches. For Kermit himself, nostalgic longing for the show's early days is represented during the musical number, "Pictures in My Head," during which Kermit sings to and with portraits of his old costars, all depicted in scenes and postures that recall their appearances on *The Muppet Show*.

The centrality of the Muppet Theater to the plot also highlights the movie's nostalgic emphasis on the original show. The theater, which is unique to the series and not seen at all in the films (although it does play an important role in *It's a Very Merry Muppet Christmas Movie*), is presented as the heart and home of the Muppets, a place to which they must return in order to regain their identity and coherence as a family. The Muppets' arrival at the dilapidated, neglected theater represents an important moment of homecoming, an answer to the persistent call of nostalgic desire. During the montage sequence set to Starship's "We Built This City," the Muppets reform as a family by restoring the theater to its former glory. The telethon program then functions as a de facto episode of the show, with a variety of acts performed in the Muppet Theater in front of a live audience and typical pandemonium and chaos backstage. At the beginning of the telethon segment, viewers are treated to a complete recreation of the opening of *The Muppet Show*, which for a large number of Gen Xers carries the same nostalgic valence as the theme songs of *Star Wars* and *Indiana Jones*. For fans, too, the moment is a long-awaited homecoming. The acts reproduce the format typical of the original show, although the barber shop version of "Smells Like Teen Spirit" also ties into the more recent viral videos released online. Fozzie tells his awful jokes, Statler and Waldorf heckle from the balcony, and Gonzo attempts another insane stunt that goes awry, just as fans would expect them to do. Even Jack Black's appearance as a kidnapped guest star harkens back to episodes of *The Muppet Show*, in which guests like John Cleese were sometimes extremely reluctant to be associated with the Muppets and their weird program.

The film's relationship with the first three Muppet films is no less intricate than its evocation of the original show. Numerous scenes create connections between *The Muppets* and *The Muppet Movie*, *The Great Muppet Caper*, and

The Muppets Take Manhattan. Together, those films established certain elements as staples of a Muppet movie, including musical numbers, celebrity cameos, and a particular comedic style of dialogue and delivery that often breaks the fourth wall. All of these duly appear in *The Muppets*. Musical numbers in the film offer a mix of original songs, parodic takes on popular tunes, and nostalgic renditions of classic Muppet songs, most notably "Rainbow Connection" and "Mahna Mahna." The cameo appearances include Alan Arkin, Zach Galifianakis, Whoopi Goldberg, Neil Patrick Harris, Mickey Rooney, Jim Parsons, Emily Blunt, and Judd Hirsch, just to name a few. *The Muppets* also milks classic Muppet style gags like the idea of "traveling by map," the self-conscious references to montage sequences, and the movie's general awareness of itself as a film. The tradition of breaking the fourth wall goes back to the first Muppet movie, where Fozzie and Kermit use the script for their film to catch The Electric Mayhem up on the action and later are found by the band thanks to the information about subsequent scenes. In *The Muppets*, Fozzie reacts to an explosion by saying, "Wow, that was such an expensive looking explosion! I can't believe we had that in the budget." Other similar gags abound, emphasizing the use of the same kind of humor that had been a hallmark of both *The Muppet Show* and the early films.

Of the three original films, *The Muppet Movie* is the most significant, and *The Muppets* repeatedly evokes its images and themes. We see a banjo collection on the wall in Kermit's office, reminding us of his performance of "Rainbow Connection" at the beginning of *The Muppet Movie*. Statler and Waldorf introduce the "standard rich and famous contract" given to Kermit by Lew Lord (Orson Welles) after the Muppets first arrive in Hollywood to realize their dream. When Gary and Walter wonder how Kermit will get the gang back together, Kermit replies, "Didn't you see our first movie? We drive." The subsequent road trip then mimics the collecting of characters first seen in *The Muppet Movie*, although a montage condenses the action to a few minutes. Fozzie's pathetic existence at the Pechoolo Casino resembles his first appearance in *The Muppet Movie* as a failing comedian in a seedy bar; the bear has sunk to the level of his lowly origins, it seems, without the support of his friends to keep him afloat. Gonzo's introduction as a plumbing company magnate also recalls his initial appearance in *The Muppet Movie* as a traveling plumber, a "prince of plungers" already romantically connected with Camilla the Chicken. In one of the funniest snippets, the newer film recreates a favorite *Muppet Movie* moment in which the gang leaves an eager Sweetums behind at a used car lot. The original movie features Milton Berle as Mad Man Mooney, who sells the Muppets a car and employs Sweetums as a "Jack." In the tribute scene, the audience can see that Mad Man Mooney and Sons is still in business, and once again Sweetums must chase the Muppets in hopes of joining their quest.

The most important homage to *The Muppet Movie* occurs near the film's climax, when Kermit and Piggy perform a duet of "Rainbow Connection." Along with "Bein' Green," the song has become a signature piece for the Muppets, an expression of all the emotions that the characters inspire in their fans. Although the recreation of the number takes place on the Muppet Theater's stage, the setting clearly recalls the swamp where Kermit first sings the song in the 1979 film. In the original version, Kermit's solo ends with the arrival of Dom DeLuise in a boat, but this time Piggy appears and joins the song. Over the course of the number, all of the Muppets join hands and begin singing. Their performance mixes fan nostalgia for this particular song with a sense of the Muppets being reborn in the moment. By returning to their roots, symbolized by the theater and the iconic song, they have returned to our hearts, and hopefully to public notice, as well.

Also important in terms of the earlier films is the status of Kermit and Piggy's relationship, symbolized by the torn half of a wedding photograph that each character keeps. Fans will recognize the picture from *The Muppets Take Manhattan*, which ends with the staged wedding of Kermit and Piggy as the finale of their Broadway show, *Manhattan Melodies*. Part of the publicity for the 1984 movie included rampant speculation about whether the marriage was "real" or not, with Piggy insisting in interviews that she and Kermit were actually married, and Kermit just as vehemently denying the claim. In *The Muppets*, the characters' complicated romance recognizes the failures of their shared history more explicitly than any other Muppet film to date, although each film treats their relationship as a difficult, often stormy affair. For Kermit and Piggy, their past is another source of nostalgic longing; the film subtly suggests that they are holding on to a memory that is a quarter century old. The later Muppet films are elided in this record, but the connection still creates a sense of the Muppets' own awareness of their personal histories. Fans remember Kermit and Piggy being happy together at the end of *The Muppets Take Manhattan*, and apparently Kermit and Piggy remember it, too. The collapse of their relationship has happened somewhere in between *The Muppets Take Manhattan* and *The Muppets*, and restoring that relationship is as critical to the coherent identity of the Muppets as repairing the theater and reviving the show. Of course, *The Muppets* is too cagey to imagine a happily ever after ending for the pair; the closing credits show them wrangling over Piggy's desire to make their relationship a media event, but that's just what fans would expect from them. The balance between frog and pig has been restored.

Few if any of these elements will be appreciated by children and adults for whom the 2011 film represents a first foray into the Muppets' world, but their presence in the movie matters a great deal. The picture relies upon the earlier productions for inspiration and guidance, but it also makes a conscious effort to be part of the ongoing history of that world, to function as a natural extension of the television series and original films rather than as a "reboot" or departure from them. For fans, *The Muppets* succeeds because it brings the Muppets back to us more or less the way we remember them, even if the puppets themselves have literally changed hands in the intervening years. The end of the movie reveals a nostalgic outpouring of love from fans as the Muppets step out of the theater and into a street filled with throngs of sign-waving Muppet supporters. "Your fans!" Walter shouts, "They love you guys!" It's the awareness of that sentiment demonstrated throughout *The Muppets* that makes it a welcome return to one of the best and brightest places that Jim Henson created.

WORKS CITED

Berntsen, Michael J. "The Muppetry of Nightmares: Figures of Fear, Danger, and Terror in *The Cosby Show*, *Chappelle's Show*, and *Saturday Night Live*." *From Fraggle Rock to Farscape: Essays on the Worlds of Jim Henson*. Ed. Jennifer C. Garlen and Anissa M. Graham. Jefferson, NC: McFarland, 2012. PAGE #s. Print.
Goldman, Andrew. "Master of Puppets." *Wired* Nov. 2011: 176–179, 210–212. Print.
The Muppet Movie. Dir. James Frawley. Perf. Jim Henson, Frank Oz, Jerry Nelson. Sony Pictures, 1979. DVD.
The Muppets. Dir. James Bobin. Perf. Jason Segel, Amy Adams, Chris Cooper. Walt Disney Pictures, 2011. DVD.
"The Muppets Are Communist, Fox Business Network Says." *The Huffington Post*. 5 Dec. 2011. Web. 9 May 2012.
'The Muppets Fans Who Made 'The Muppets' Movie." *Fresh Air*. NPR. WHYY. Philadelphia. 23 Nov. 2011. Radio.
The Muppets Take Manhattan. Dir. Frank Oz. Perf. Jim Henson, Dave Goelz. Sony Pictures, 1984. DVD.

About the Contributors

Michael J. **Berntsen** teaches literature, composition, and creative writing at the University of Louisiana at Lafayette. His works can be found in various publications, including *Untoward Magazine*, *St. Sebastian Review*, and *Canyon Voices*.

David R. **Burns** is an associate professor with an M.F.A. in design and technology from Parsons School of Design. After practicing digital media art in New York City and teaching at Parsons School of Design and Pratt Institute in Manhattan, he joined the faculty of Southern Illinois University and developed the university's first 3D computer animation courses and its first 3D computer modeling and animation lab.

Deborah **Burns** is a doctoral candidate in the education department at Southern Illinois University Carbondale, where she teaches education courses and is an academic advisor. She holds an M.A. in higher education administration from New York University and an M.A. in English literature from Columbia University. Her research interests include film studies, media, and higher education.

Aaron **Calbreath-Frasieur** is a doctoral candidate in the University of Nottingham's Department of Culture, Film and Media. His research examines and categorizes media franchises in relation to industrial practices, using the Muppets franchise and the Jim Henson Company as the primary case study. He has also served as articles editor for *Scope: an Online Journal of Film and Television Studies*.

Catherine **Edwards** is a teacher, poet and life-long Muppet fan. She has experience in public relations, advertising, editing, and teaching. She currently teaches children in public school and has taught adults for the past six years at a local trade school.

Maryanne L. **Fisher** is an associate professor in the Department of Psychology at Saint Mary's University and a member of the interuniversity Women and Gender Studies Program. Her primary research area is the evolutionary foundation of human interpersonal relationships, specifically women's competition for mates, and the intersection of biological, cultural, and social explanations for behavior.

Jennifer C. **Garlen** is an independent scholar and writer with an interest in literature, film, and popular culture. A graduate of Agnes Scott College and Georgia Southern University, she holds a Ph.D. in English from Auburn and is the co-editor of *Kermit Culture: Critical Perspectives on Jim Henson's Muppets*, with Anissa M. Graham.

About the Contributors

Sherry **Ginn** earned a Ph.D. in general-experimental psychology from the University of South Carolina. She currently teaches at Rowan-Cabarrus Community College. She has published numerous articles in the fields of neuroscience and psychology, but also focuses on popular culture, as demonstrated by her books, *Our Space, Our Place: Women in the Worlds of Science Fiction Television* and *Power and Control in the Whedonverses*.

Anissa M. **Graham** teaches composition and literature as an instructor of English at the University of North Alabama. After receiving degrees from Georgia Southern University and Auburn University, she has gone on to study 18th and 19th century British fiction as well as popular culture topics. She is the co-editor of *Kermit Culture: Critical Perspectives on Jim Henson's Muppets*, with Jennifer C. Garlen.

Gideon **Haberkorn** holds degrees in English and philosophy from Gutenberg Universität Mainz, Germany. He splits his time between teaching English, ethics and philosophy in Germany's secondary education system and publishing scholarly articles. In 2010, he co-edited *Comics as a Nexus of Cultures*; he is a member of the International Association for the Fantastic in the Arts.

Roxanne **Harde** is an associate professor of English and a McCalla University Professor at the University of Alberta, Augustana Faculty. She studies and teaches American literature and culture. She has recently published *Reading the Boss: Interdisciplinary Approaches to the Works of Bruce Springsteen*, and has written essays for several journals. She is the editor of *Bookbird: A Journal of International Children's Literature*.

Tom **Holste** is a freelance writer who has contributed submissions for SGN Scoops and PurplePens.com. He runs a website offering script analysis services and lives in the south suburbs of Chicago.

Andrew **Leal** received an M.A. in English literature from the University of Syracuse. Specializing in animation, his book contributions include essays in *Animation Art*, *The Animated Movie Guide*, and *Kermit Culture*. Since 2006, he has been an administrator and key contributor to Muppet Wiki.

Nathaniel **Long** is a graduate student at the University of Texas at El Paso and serves as actor and dramaturge for the area's Shakespeare on the Rocks theatre company. Beyond the Bard, his primary interests focus on Romanticism and myth and folklore studies, ranging from Edith Hamilton and Robert Graves to Katharine Briggs and Richard M. Dorson.

Catriona **McAra** submitted her doctoral dissertation on the history of art at the University of Glasgow, and is a research assistant in cultural theory at the University of Huddersfield. She has published essays on the art of Joseph Cornell, the literature of Dorothea Tanning, and Lewis Carroll, and is writing a book about conceptual design and fantasy films of the 1980s.

Tami **Meredith** has a Ph.D. in computer science, and is a sessional instructor and research assistant at Saint Mary's University in Halifax, Canada. She has published on evolutionary psychology, human-computer interaction, software engineering, and education, often with a focus on sex or gender issues.

Jennifer **Stoessner** has a doctoral degree in theatre history from Ohio State University. Her research focuses on contemporary performance and American puppetry. She was a contributor to *Kermit Culture: Critical Perspectives on Jim Henson's Muppets*. She was a Vail Artist-in-Residence at Denison University in 2010, designing puppets and puppetry effects for *Shipwrecked! An Entertainment* by Donald Marguiles.

Anthony F. **Strand** received an M.S. in library and information science from the University of Missouri in 2010 and is currently a librarian fellow at Reeves Library, Westminster College in Fulton, Missouri. He contributed to the *Encyclopedia of Comic Books and Graphic Novels* and *Comics Through Time*.

Justin **Werfel** is a research scientist at Harvard University's Wyss Institute for Biologically Inspired Engineering. He received his Ph.D. from MIT in 2006, followed by postdoctoral work at Harvard and the New England Complex Systems Institute. His interests include swarm robotics, DNA self-assembly, evolutionary theory, and collective intelligence.

Index

Alien Other 228–239
All in the Family 215
Anderson, Louie 148
Apple (character) 191, 192
"Ask Mr. Lizard" 218
Aughra 85, 88–91, 97–100, 106–107

Baker, Martin G. 27
Balthazar 191, 192–193
Banting, Matt 156–157
Beaker (character) 247
Bean Bunny 3, 144–145, 150–151, 159
Bellows, Chauncey 156–157
Bildungsroman 131
Bobbo 207
Bobo the Bear 255
"Bohemian Rhapsody" 248
Bonora, Camille 158, 159
Boober (Fraggle) 44, 46, 49, 50, 53, 57–58
Bootsie and Brad 146–147
Bowie, David 121, 126–127
Brill, Fran 158, 159

Cantus (Fraggle) 19
The Captain (character) 31–33
Cave Fraggles 69–70
Chappelle, David 206–208
Chappelle's Show 206
Chiana 231, 237–238
A Christmas Carol 129
The Christmas Toy 3, 5, 189–197
Clash, Kevin 215
Clifford 147
community connections 135–139
Conan (stories) 81–82
The Cosby Show 201–206
Crais, Bialar 230
Crichton, John 229–20, 238–239
Croquette (character) 30
The Crystal 112–113

Crystal Bats 111–112
The Cube 122

Dangle (character) 208
Danson, Ted 147
D'Argo 232–233, 238
The Dark Crystal 2, 4, 73, 85–86, 88–100, 101–116, 118, 162, 194–195, 196
Devertebrae, Monica 221–222
Dickow, Hans-Helmut 29
Diegesis 9, 14–16
DiFiori, Larry 193
Digit (character) 148–149, 152, 203
Dinosaurs 3, 5, 213–227
Ditz (character) 195
Ditzies 63, 67
Doc 22, 26, 28–32
Dog (character) 153–154, 155, 164–165, 166, 167–168, 172
Dog City 153
Doglion 202–204
Dom 155–156
Doozers 13–14, 54–55, 59, 63, 64, 66, 67, 78–79, 84

eco-criticism 74–75
Emmet Otter's Jug Band Christmas (book) 174
Emmet Otter's Jug Band Christmas (special) 1–2, 5, 173–188
Encyclopedia Fragglia 10
Ewoks 105
extinction 224–226

family relationships 132–135
Farscape 3, 5, 228–239
Fierys 120
Fizzgig 111
Fozzie Bear 244, 255, 257
Fraggle Rock 2, 4, 7–22, 24–39, 41–59, 62–72, 73, 77–80, 84–85, 194, 195, 225

Freud, Sigmund 200
Frith, Michael 8, 12, 21–22
Froud, Brian 2, 90, 92, 101–115, 118, 162
Froud, Wendy 108

Gambon, Michael 166–169, 171
Garthim 110–111
Gelflings 75–76, 89–92, 107–108
genre criticism 80–83
"The Gift of the Magi" 173–174, 186
Gobo (Fraggle) 7, 13, 15–16, 22, 25, 36, 44, 45, 48, 58–59
Goelz, Dave 158–159, 176
Gonzo 124, 144, 148–149, 158, 203–204, 211, 245, 255, 257
Gorg King 56,
Gorg Queen 55–56, 225
Gorgs 41, 54–56, 79, 225
Graphic, Waldo C. 150
The Great Muppet Caper 2, 123–124
Gulliver's Travels 77

Haakskeekah Stone 113
Henry, O. 173–174, 181
Henson, Brian 164, 219
Henson, Jim 1–3, 24–25, 37–38, 89, 102–104, 117–130, 131, 133, 140–141, 143, 150, 156–157, 157–158, 159, 161–162, 174–175, 178, 179–180, 213–214, 219, 241, 242
"The Hero's Journey" 128–129
Hess, Roy 216
Hoban, Russell 173–174
Horrocks, Jane 171
Howard, Robert E. 81–82
Hurt, John 164–165
Huxtable, Cliff 201–206
Hypocritic Oaf (character) 201

It's a Very Merry Muppet Christmas Movie 178–179, 186, 187, 188

Jareth 126–127
Jen 75, 91–92, 107–108
The Jim Henson Company 189, 219–220, 227
The Jim Henson Hour 3, 5, 143–159
Jim Henson's Creature Shop 103–104, 219–220, 228, 234
Johansen, David 154
Jool 231, 238
Jothee 233, 238
Juhl, Jerry 24, 37–38, 119, 175
Junior (Gorg) 56
The Junk Lady 137–139
junk world 139–140

Kenworthy, Duncan 27, 32, 34, 35, 155
Kermit the Frog 119, 123–124, 144–145, 148–149, 150, 152–153, 176, 178–179, 183–184, 185, 186, 187, 254–255, 256, 257–258
Kira 75, 91–92, 107–108
Klingons 232–233
"Kneehigh Park" 207–208
Kurtz, Gary 105

Labyrinth 2, 4, 117–130, 131–141, 162, 194–195
Land of Gorch 102, 174–175, 209–210, 221
Landstriders 110–111
Langham, Chris 158
Lee, Alan 104
Leviathan 235–236
Lightyear, Buzz 192
Living with Dinosaurs 155–156
Long, Geoffrey 17
The Lord of the Rings 82, 104–105

MacKay, Fulton 31
magic 16, 22
Marjorie the Trash Heap 57
Marxist criticism 77–80
Meet the Feebles 206, 254
Merggles 20, 70–71
metafiction 83
Meteora 191, 192, 193, 194
Mew (character) 194, 195–196
The Mighty Favog (character) 209–210, 221
mimetic video 243
Minghella, Anthony 163, 167
Miss Piggy 57, 145–146, 182, 254–255, 258
Mr. Bertwhistle 32
Mokey (Fraggle) 44, 45, 47, 51–52, 58, 79, 225
Monster Maker 156
Moopets 254
Moore, Dudley 146
Moya 235, 239
Muppet Babies 2
The Muppet Movie 2, 123, 178, 185, 186, 188, 257–258
The Muppet Show 26, 27, 120, 150, 153, 175, 182, 183–184, 217, 251, 255–256
Muppet Theater 256
MuppeTelevision 144–154, 157-8
The Muppets 5, 182, 185, 186, 187, 188, 249, 251–259
The Muppets Take Manhattan 2, 178, 258
MuppetWiki 11
music 121

negative capability 9, 17–18, 21
Nelson, Jerry 158, 159

noble savage 76
Noranti 231

Old Gypsy Lady (Fraggle) 19–20
Otter, Alice 174, 176–188
Otter, Emmet 174, 176–188
Otto, Rudolph 205
Outer Space 25, 41
Oz, Frank 107

Peuta (character) 209–210, 221
Phillips, Ethyl 216
Pilot (character) 235–236, 239
Ploobis (character) 209–210, 221
Pod People (Podlings) 76, 92–93, 111
Poindexter, Buster 154
Poison Cacklers 16–17
post-colonial criticism 75–77
Prell, Karen 10
puppetry 199–200, 210–211, 218–220, 234–235, 242

Red (Fraggle) 13, 20, 44, 45, 47–48, 58
Redican, Dan 158
Richfield, B.P. 216, 225–226
Richman, Tex 253
Riverbottom Gang 176, 179, 184–185
Rizzo the Rat 245
Robin, Ralph 146
Rock Hockey Hannah 19–20
Rowlf 153, 244–245
Rugby (character) 191–192, 193, 194, 195, 196
Rygel XVI 236–237, 238

Sam and Friends 119, 121, 241
Sam the Eagle 245–247
Sarah 122–130, 131–141
Saturday Night Live 174–175
Sausage Sandwich (character) 201–202
Scarrans 233
Scorpius 233–234
Scred (character) 221
Sebacean 229–230
The Secret Life of Toys 190
Segel, Jason 252
Sellers, Peter 154
Sesame Street 27, 28, 206–208
SideBottom (Fraggle) 49, 57–58
Sikozu 231, 238
Sinclair, Baby 215
Sinclair, Charlene 215, 221–222, 225
Sinclair, Earl 214, 220–221, 225–223
Sinclair, Fran 214, 221–222

Sinclair, Robbie 214–215, 220, 222–223
Skeksis 76, 85, 93–95, 108–110
Song of the Cloud Forest 158
Sprocket 22, 28, 29, 30, 31–32
Stapleton, Harry 151
Star Trek 228–229, 232–233
Star Wars trilogy 105
Statler 243–244, 248–249
Stinky (character) 207–208
Storyteller (character) 155, 163–166
The Storyteller 5, 153–154, 155, 161–172
Storyteller, Greek (character) 166–9
The Storyteller: Greek Myths 5, 161, 161–172
Struthers, Sally 215
Sun, Aeryn 238
Swedish Chef 247
Sweetums 202–204

Timepiece 121
toe ticklers 225
Tolkien, J.R.R. 81
Toy Story 191–193, 195
Trautman, Allan 214–215
Traveling Matt (Fraggle) 7–8, 25, 33–37

Ultragorgon 156
uncanny 200–206, 209–211
Uncle Deadly 255
urRu 76, 85, 95–96, 108–110
urSkeks 96–97

Vicki 149, 150
viral video 243

Waldorf 243–244, 248–249
Walt Disney Company 243
Walter 252–253
war 21
Wayne and Wanda 255
Wembley (Fraggle) 44, 45, 49, 50, 53, 58
Whitmire, Steve 29, 159
Williams, Nigel 167
Williams, Paul 175–176
Wisss (character) 209–210
Wizard (Fraggle) 18–19
The Wizard of Oz 123
Woody (character) 191–192
world building 8, 14
"The World of *The Dark Crystal*" 89

YouTube 242–250

Zhaan 230, 237
Zondra 151–152

www.ingramcontent.com/pod-product-compliance
Ingram Content Group UK Ltd.
Pitfield, Milton Keynes, MK11 3LW, UK
UKHW041916140426
5217IPUK00013B/186